ANIMAL RIGHTS

ISSN 1546-6736

ANIMAL RIGHTS

Kim Masters Evans

INFORMATION PLUS® REFERENCE SERIES
Formerly Published by Information Plus, Wylie, Texas

GALE
CENGAGE Learning·

Detroit • New York • San Francisco • New Haven, Conn • Waterville, Maine • London

Animal Rights

Kim Masters Evans

Kepos Media, Inc.: Steven Long and Janice Jorgensen, Series Editors

Project Editors: Elizabeth Manar, Kathleen J. Edgar, Kimberley McGrath

Rights Acquisition and Management: Sheila Spencer

Composition: Evi Abou-El-Seoud, Mary Beth Trimper

Manufacturing: Rita Wimberley

For product information and technology assistance, contact us at
Gale Customer Support, 1-800-877-4253.
For permission to use material from this text or product,
submit all requests online at **www.cengage.com/permissions.**
Further permissions questions can be e-mailed to
permissionrequest@cengage.com

Cover photograph: © Ragne Kabanova/Shutterstock.com.

Gale
27500 Drake Rd.
Farmington Hills, MI 48331-3535

ISBN-13: 978-0-7876-5103-9 (set)   ISBN-10: 0-7876-5103-6 (set)
ISBN-13: 978-1-56995-787-5   ISBN-10: 1-56995-787-8

ISSN 1546-6736

This title is also available as an e-book.
ISBN-978-1-56995-838-4 (set)
ISBN-10: 1-56995-838-6 (set)
Contact your Gale sales representative for ordering information.

Printed in the United States of America
1 2 3 4 5   17 16 15 14 13

TABLE OF CONTENTS

PREFACE

Animal Rights is part of the *Information Plus Reference Series*. The purpose of each volume of the series is to present the latest facts on a topic of pressing concern in modern American life. These topics include the most controversial and studied social issues of the 21st century: abortion, capital punishment, care of senior citizens, education, the environment, health care, immigration, minorities, national security, social welfare, water, women, youth, and many more. Even though this series is written especially for high school and undergraduate students, it is an excellent resource for anyone in need of factual information on current affairs.

By presenting the facts, it is the intention of Gale, Cengage Learning to provide its readers with everything they need to reach an informed opinion on current issues. To that end, there is a particular emphasis in this series on the presentation of scientific studies, surveys, and statistics. These data are generally presented in the form of tables, charts, and other graphics placed within the text of each book. Every graphic is directly referred to and carefully explained in the text. The source of each graphic is presented within the graphic itself. The data used in these graphics are drawn from the most reputable and reliable sources, such as from the various branches of the U.S. government and from private organizations and associations. Every effort has been made to secure the most recent information available. Readers should bear in mind that many major studies take years to conduct and that additional years often pass before the data from these studies are made available to the public. Therefore, in many cases the most recent information available in 2013 is dated from 2010 or 2011. Older statistics are sometimes presented as well, if they are landmark studies or of particular interest and no more-recent information exists.

Although statistics are a major focus of the *Information Plus Reference Series*, they are by no means its only content. Each book also presents the widely held positions and important ideas that shape how the book's subject is discussed in the United States. These positions are explained in detail and, where possible, in the words of their proponents. Some of the other material to be found in these books includes historical background, descriptions of major events related to the subject, relevant laws and court cases, and examples of how these issues play out in American life. Some books also feature primary documents or have pro and con debate sections that provide the words and opinions of prominent Americans on both sides of a controversial topic. All material is presented in an evenhanded and unbiased manner; readers will never be encouraged to accept one view of an issue over another.

HOW TO USE THIS BOOK

Animals have been important to humans for around 2 million years as sources of food and other natural products, objects of worship and sport, and beasts of burden. Nevertheless, it was not until the 17th century that animal welfare began to concern Western society. What legal and moral rights do animals currently possess in the United States and how does society balance such rights with animals' enormous economic value? How do "abolitionists" and "welfarists" differ on these and other issues? In what ways should governments protect, regulate, and control wildlife? Under what conditions are farm animals raised and slaughtered? Should research animals be used in medical and veterinary investigations, product testing, and science classes? Do horse racing, greyhound racing, sled dog racing, and rodeos cause unwarranted harm to animal participants? How should entertainment animals, service animals, and pets be treated? These and other basic questions are discussed in this volume.

Animal Rights consists of nine chapters and three appendixes. Each chapter is devoted to a particular aspect of animal rights in the United States. For a summary of the information covered in each chapter, please see the synopses provided in the Table of Contents. Chapters generally begin with an overview of the basic facts and background information on the chapter's topic, then proceed to examine subtopics of particular interest. For example, Chapter 8, Service Animals, describes how working animals are used to benefit humans during hunting, by guarding territory and people, and performing manual labor. In addition, the chapter explores how animals are used in law enforcement and search, rescue, and recovery tasks. Perhaps the most admired service animals are the ones that enhance the physical and mental well-being of humans by providing services, such as guiding the blind or assisting in therapy sessions. This chapter ends with the most controversial use of working animals, which is military service. Readers can find their way through a chapter by looking for the section and subsection headings, which are clearly set off from the text. They can also refer to the book's extensive Index, if they already know what they are looking for.

Statistical Information

The tables and figures featured throughout *Animal Rights* will be of particular use to readers in learning about this topic. These tables and figures represent an extensive collection of the most recent and valuable statistics on animal rights, as well as related issues—for example, graphics cover what species are on the federal list of endangered and threatened animals, the number of people who participate in recreational/sport fishing (or angling), what percentage of people believe that buying and wearing clothing made of animal fur is morally acceptable, and what type of animals are pursued by the vast majority of hunters. Gale, Cengage Learning believes that making this information available to readers is the most important way to fulfill the goal of this book: to help readers understand the issues and controversies surrounding animal rights in the United States and reach their own conclusions.

Each table or figure has a unique identifier appearing above it for ease of identification and reference. Titles for the tables and figures explain their purpose. At the end of each table or figure, the original source of the data is provided.

To help readers understand these often complicated statistics, all tables and figures are explained in the text. References in the text direct readers to the relevant statistics. Furthermore, the contents of all tables and figures are fully indexed. Please see the opening section of the Index at the back of this volume for a description of how to find tables and figures within it.

Appendixes

Besides the main body text and images, *Animal Rights* has three appendixes. The first is the Important Names and Addresses directory. Here, readers will find contact information for a number of government and private organizations that can provide further information on aspects of animal rights in the United States. The second appendix is the Resources section, which can also assist readers in conducting their own research. In this section, the author and editors of *Animal Rights* describe some of the sources that were most useful during the compilation of this book. The final appendix is the Index. It has been greatly expanded from previous editions and should make it even easier to find specific topics in this book.

ADVISORY BOARD CONTRIBUTIONS

The staff of Information Plus would like to extend its heartfelt appreciation to the Information Plus Advisory Board. This dedicated group of media professionals provides feedback on the series on an ongoing basis. Their comments allow the editorial staff who work on the project to make the series better and more user-friendly. The staff's top priority is to produce the highest-quality and most useful books possible, and the Information Plus Advisory Board's contributions to this process are invaluable.

The members of the Information Plus Advisory Board are:

- Kathleen R. Bonn, Librarian, Newbury Park High School, Newbury Park, California

- Madelyn Garner, Librarian, San Jacinto College, North Campus, Houston, Texas

- Anne Oxenrider, Media Specialist, Dundee High School, Dundee, Michigan

- Charles R. Rodgers, Director of Libraries, Pasco-Hernando Community College, Dade City, Florida

- James N. Zitzelsberger, Library Media Department Chairman, Oshkosh West High School, Oshkosh, Wisconsin

COMMENTS AND SUGGESTIONS

The editors of the *Information Plus Reference Series* welcome your feedback on *Animal Rights*. Please direct all correspondence to:

Editors
Information Plus Reference Series
27500 Drake Rd.
Farmington Hills, MI 48331-3535

CHAPTER 1
THE HISTORY OF HUMAN-ANIMAL INTERACTION

At the heart of the animal rights debate is the issue of how humans and animals should interact with each other. Are animals a natural resource for humans to use as they choose? Or are animals free beings with the right to live their lives without human interference? Is there an acceptable compromise somewhere in between? People answer these questions differently depending on their cultural practices, religious and ethical beliefs, and everyday experiences with animals. To understand how the debate has evolved over the centuries, it is necessary to examine history and see how the human-animal relationship developed and changed over time.

PREHISTORIC TIMES

Evolutionary science holds that humans are animals that have changed and adapted over millions of years to take on their current form. Biologists classify the human animal as a member of the order Primate, along with chimpanzees and gorillas. Scientists believe that humans and other primates shared a common ancestor millions of years ago and that at some point human animals split off to form their own evolutionary path. About 2 million years ago human primates began using stone tools and weapons. This was the beginning of the Stone Age. The use of stone-tipped spears allowed humans to hunt large game, such as wooly mammoths. Humans at that time survived by hunting and fishing and by foraging for edible vegetation, nuts, and seeds; hence, they are called hunter-gatherers. Most lived as nomads, traveling in small groups from place to place. When they exhausted all the animals and plants in an area, they moved to a new location.

The earliest known cave drawings date back approximately 30,000 years. Many cave drawings depict buffalo, horses, lions, mammoths, and rhinoceroses. Figure 1.1 shows a cave painting of a horse.

The vast majority of prehistoric cave drawings depict animals, not people. Some scientists believe that humans were in awe of the wild and fierce animals that they hunted. The hunters may have believed that they could exert some kind of magical power over animals by drawing pictures of them. Even though little is known for certain about the religious beliefs of the time, it is thought that prehistoric humans believed in a hidden world that was inhabited by the spirits of their dead ancestors, animals, and birds. People may have offered sacrifices of animals or other food to keep the spirits happy.

A belief system called animism has been traced back to the Paleolithic Age (the earliest period of the Stone Age). Animism is the belief that every object, living or not, contains a soul. Thus, animals, trees, and even rocks had spiritual meaning to prehistoric peoples. Some wild animals may have been worshipped as gods by early humans.

Changing Climate

Around 15,000 to 13,000 BC the massive glaciers that had covered much of the Northern Hemisphere during the Great Ice Age began to subside. The habitats and food supplies for both humans and animals began to change. The hunter-gatherers had increasing difficulty finding the big game they had hunted before. Scientists believe that mammoths and many other large animals were driven to extinction around 10,000 BC because of climate changes, overhunting by humans, or both. Humans turned to hunting smaller animals and began gathering and cultivating plants in centralized locations. This major shift from nomadic life to settled existence had a tremendous effect on the human-animal relationship.

ANIMAL DOMESTICATION

Between 13,000 and 2,500 BC humans actively worked to domesticate dogs, cats, cattle, goats, horses, and sheep from their wild counterparts. In "From Wild Animals to Domestic Pets, an Evolutionary View of Domestication" (*Proceedings of the National Academy*

FIGURE 1.1

Cave painting of a horse, c. 13,000 BC, Lascaux, France. (© *Pierre Andrieu/AP Images.*)

of Sciences, vol. 106, no. 1, June 16, 2009), Carlos A. Driscoll, David W. Macdonald, and Stephen J. O'Brien explain that domestication is not the same as taming. Individual wild animals can be tamed to behave in a docile manner around humans. By contrast, domestication is a process that takes place across a population of animals over many generations. According to Driscoll, Macdonald, and O'Brien, domestication occurs via a combination of natural and artificial (human-induced) mechanisms. Humans capitalized on the fact that some wild animal populations were naturally predisposed to tolerating people and adapted well to captivity (or at least to living in close contact with people). Humans further drove the domestication process by selectively breeding animals with desirable characteristics in terms of size, disposition, utility, and appearance.

Characteristics of Domesticated Animals

Driscoll, Macdonald, and O'Brien note, "When is an animal truly domesticated? Hard definitions are elusive because domestication is a continuous transition, attributes differ by species, and genes and environment interact to produce selectable characters that may vary with circumstance." Domesticated animals are not just tamer than their wild ancestors (or their relatives still existing in the wild); domesticated animals are different genetically from their wild counterparts. Driscoll, Macdonald, and O'Brien explain that these differences are commonly evident when comparing the physiology (internal biological processes, such as metabolism and reproduction) and morphology (form and shape) between domestic and wild populations. Thus, there are some physical differences between the two. For example, most domesticated populations are smaller and fatter and have smaller teeth and brains than their wild counterparts.

Domestication of Dogs and Cats

The dog is thought to have been the first animal to be domesticated, sometime around 13,000 to 10,000 BC, from its wolflike ancestor *Canis lupus*. Scientists believe that humans either adopted cubs and raised them or just began to accept into their groups some of the less fierce wolves that hung around their camps scrounging for leftovers. In either event, humans soon found dogs to be a welcome addition. The arrangement benefited both sides, as domesticated wolves helped humans with hunting and guarding duties and shared the food that was obtained.

The ancient Egyptians are usually credited with domesticating wild cats (*Felis silvestris libyca*, originating in Africa and southwestern Asia) around 4,000 BC. The Egyptians most likely raised cats to protect their grain stores from rats and mice. Cat domestication is strongly associated with the establishment of permanent settlements and the growing and storage of grains. Cats became important to agricultural societies, just as dogs had been important to hunting cultures.

Domestication of Livestock

The domestication of livestock—chiefly pigs, cows, sheep, horses, and goats—is thought to have occurred between 9,000 and 5,000 BC as agriculture became more of a factor in human societies that were scattered across Asia and Europe.

History shows that the most suitable animals for domestication (and use by humans) are those that naturally live in groups with a hierarchical social structure. This allows humans to assume a dominant role in the hierarchy and exert control over the animals' behavior. The ability to keep and control groups of meat-supplying animals allowed humans to give up their previously nomadic lives and produce excess food. This freed people to build cities and roads, invent new things, and cultivate the arts.

ANCIENT CULTURES AND RELIGIONS

The peoples of most ancient civilizations were polytheistic (believed in more than one god). Many ancient peoples worshipped animals as gods, used animals to represent their gods, or thought that their gods could assume animal form when they wished.

Some early civilizations also worshipped heavenly bodies, such as the sun and moon. These cultures believed that the stars and planets had magical influences over earthly events. They tracked the positions and aspects of the heavenly bodies closely and believed that such information could be used to foresee the future. Astrology and the zodiac evolved from these beliefs and were adopted by people in many different cultures, including the Babylonians, Egyptians, Hindus, and early Chinese, who used 12 different animals to represent different years in a 12-year cycle. (See Table 1.1.) Most ancient zodiacs used animals to represent some or all the constellations. In fact, the word *zodiac* comes from the Greek term *zodion kuklos*, meaning "circle of little animals."

Even though ancient Indians had varied spiritual beliefs, many of these beliefs were blended together into the practice of Hinduism around 3,000 BC. In general, Hindus believe that animals and people experience rebirth after they die. In other words, a human can be reincarnated as an animal, or vice versa. This means that all life-forms are to be respected. Because Hindus consider virtually everything to be divine, they worship many animal gods and believe that their gods can take many forms, including human-animal forms.

Buddhism was founded during the sixth century BC by Siddhartha Gautama (c. 563–c. 483 BC), an Indian philosopher who came to be called Buddha. Buddha believed that animals were important spiritually and were evolving toward a higher consciousness, just as humans were. Therefore, Buddhists consider it wrong to cause any harm to an animal or any other living being.

Jainism also originated in India and is similar in many respects to Buddhism, although it is perhaps much older. The Jains are so adamantly opposed to killing any life-form that they allow themselves to be bitten by gnats and mosquitoes rather than swatting them. They often carry brooms so they can brush insects out of their path to avoid stepping on them. The Jains strongly condemn the eating of any meat. They became well known in later centuries for their animal hospitals.

Archaeological evidence indicates that livestock raising was practiced in ancient China and that horse-drawn chariots were in use. A Chinese emperor of the first century BC established the Garden of Intelligence, one of the largest zoos in the world. Confucianism is based on the teachings of Confucius (551–479 BC), a Chinese philosopher who became famous for his sayings about how to live a happy and responsible life. In general, Confucius encouraged respect for animals, but not reverence. In other words, animals were not to be treated as deities.

Taoism is a spiritual philosophy that developed in China during the fifth and fourth centuries BC. Taoists believe that there is a power that envelops and flows through all living and nonliving things and that all life should be respected.

Hebrew Tribes and Judaism

The origins of Judaism lie with Hebrew tribes that populated the Mesopotamian region of the Middle East. Even though the Hebrews followed various worship practices, including animism, they eventually developed a central religion known as Judaism. The followers of Judaism came to be called Jews. Judaism was unique among the many religions of the time because it was monotheistic. The Jews worship only one god instead of many gods, and the Hebrew God is anthropomorphic, or humanlike.

According to the first book (Genesis) of the Hebrew Bible, God created the earth and populated it with all kinds of creatures. God granted humans "dominion over the fish of the sea, and over the birds of the air, and over all the wild animals of the earth, and over every creeping thing that creeps upon the earth." This idea of dominion can be interpreted in many ways and was to have a profound effect on Western civilization for centuries to

TABLE 1.1

Chinese zodiac

Rat	Ox	Tiger	Rabbit	Dragon	Snake	Horse	Sheep	Monkey	Rooster	Dog	Boar
1912	1913	1914	1915	1916	1917	1918	1919	1920	1921	1922	1923
1924	1925	1926	1927	1928	1929	1930	1931	1932	1933	1934	1935
1936	1937	1938	1939	1940	1941	1942	1943	1944	1945	1946	1947
1948	1949	1950	1951	1952	1953	1954	1955	1956	1957	1958	1959
1960	1961	1962	1963	1964	1965	1966	1967	1968	1969	1970	1971
1972	1973	1974	1975	1976	1977	1978	1979	1980	1981	1982	1983
1984	1985	1986	1987	1988	1989	1990	1991	1992	1993	1994	1995
1996	1997	1998	1999	2000	2001	2002	2003	2004	2005	2006	2007
2008	2009	2010	2011	2012	2013	2014	2015	2016	2017	2018	2019

SOURCE: Created by Kim Masters Evans for Gale, 2011

come. However, the Old Testament states that "a righteous man regards the life of his animals."

Arabic Cultures and Islam

The first kingdom appeared in the Arabian desert around 1,000 BC. Before that time the region was inhabited by scattered families and clans, many of whom were nomads, called Bedouins, who raised camels. The Bedouins were animists who believed that spirits lived within all natural things. They also worshipped their ancestors and heavenly bodies.

Over the next few centuries society became more centralized, and the worship of many gods became common in temples and cults throughout the Arabian Peninsula. Islam was founded by the prophet Muhammad (c. AD 570–632), who believed in only one god. The Koran is the Islamic sacred text and includes many references to animals, particularly camels. Falcons, pigeons, cats, and horses were also considered important in early Islamic cultures. Legend has it that Muhammad was so fond of cats that he once cut a hole in his robe to keep from disturbing a cat that had fallen asleep on his sleeve. Muhammad also spoke highly of horses and considered their breeding to be an honorable task. The Arabs bred fast horses that were used in warfare, transportation, and sporting events.

The Koran does not specifically mention animal souls, but it does teach respect for all living creatures.

Classical Greece

Even though Greece was associated with a variety of cultures, the classical Greek period from 500 to 323 BC was the most influential for future ideas about animals. The classical Greeks did not have one central philosophy but followed the teachings of various schools that were established by wise men and philosophers. Some of the most famous were Socrates (470?–399? BC), Plato (428–348 BC), and Aristotle (384–322 BC).

In general, animals were widely used for food, clothing, and work in Greek society. These uses were not questioned on moral or philosophical grounds because the people believed that everything in nature had a purpose. In other words, plants existed for animals and both plants and animals existed for the welfare and enjoyment of humans. However, the philosopher and mathematician Pythagoras (c. 570–c. 490 BC) and his followers did not eat meat because they believed that animals had souls. Many other Greeks, including Plato, recommended a vegetarian diet for ethical or practical reasons.

Plato's student Aristotle is considered the father of zoology in Western history. He wrote extensively about animal anatomy, behavior, and reproduction in *History of Animals* and *On the Parts of Animals*. Aristotle believed that there was a natural hierarchy in which humans, animals, plants, and inanimate objects were arranged by their level of perfection. This arrangement came to be called the *scala naturae* or "ladder of nature." Later philosophers called it the "Great Chain of Being."

The top rungs of Aristotle's ladder were occupied by humans, because Aristotle believed that they alone had rational souls that were capable of belief, reason, and thought. Below the humans were animals; Aristotle believed that animals had limited souls that allowed them to feel, but not to reason. Plants had the lowest forms of souls and ranked the lowest on the ladder. Among humans, Aristotle believed that there was a natural hierarchy, with free men ranked above slaves, women, and children. Aristotle's ideas about the rank of humans and animals in society would influence thinking in Western cultures for centuries.

Christianity

Christianity began as a sect of Judaism during the first century AD. Its followers believe that God had come among them in the form of a human named Jesus Christ (4? BC–AD 29?). They set down their beliefs in scriptures that came to be known as the New Testament of the Bible.

Jesus's followers considered his death to be a human sacrifice, similar to the animal sacrifices that were common in Jewish religious practice. This symbolism played an important role in the new religion. The New Testament mentions many animals, but mostly in the context of everyday life and as food sources. Christians did maintain the belief from the Hebrew Bible that humans had dominion over animals. The importance of the human soul was central to Christian theology. Many Christian philosophers of later centuries, such as Saint Augustine of Hippo (354–430), argued that only humans (not animals) had rational minds and souls.

Roman Empire

The Roman Empire actually began as a single city, the city of Rome, which became a republic in 510 BC. The Romans had a warrior mentality and built their empire by conquering other peoples and cultures. The rulers of the Roman Empire delighted in brutal competitions and sports and invented many "games" to entertain their citizens. The Coliseum of Rome was a massive arena that featured events in which wild animals fought to the death with each other or with humans. Ancient texts describe the deaths of bulls, elephants, lions, tigers, and other animals. Often, the animals were chained together or tormented with burning irons and darts to make the fighting more fierce.

Historical evidence shows that the Romans were fond of horses. Their economy, troops, and postal service were dependent on the work done by horses. The Romans also raised livestock and kept cats and dogs as pets or working animals. Christianity became the official religion of the Roman Empire in AD 325. This put an end to the killing of humans in the Coliseum, because the human soul is sacred to Christianity. There is no evidence that animal games ceased, however, until the empire became too poor to acquire exotic and wild animals for them.

MEDIEVAL PERIOD

In general, Europe's medieval period, also called the Middle Ages, is considered the era from the fall of the Roman Empire in the late fifth century through the 16th century. The early centuries of the period are called the Dark Ages, because few known scientific and cultural achievements were made by Western societies during this time. Once the Roman emperors were gone, the authorities of the Christian church began to hold great power over the peoples of Europe.

Saint Francis of Assisi (1182–1226) is arguably the most famous animal lover of the medieval period in Europe. The Franciscan friar was said to preach to birds and animals and release captured animals from traps. There are many legends about the saint, the most famous being that he once convinced a wolf to stop terrorizing a town and eating the livestock. Saint Francis was said to have "the gift of sympathy" for animals and in modern Catholicism is the patron saint of animals and ecology.

One of the most influential philosophers of the Middle Ages was Saint Thomas Aquinas (c. 1225–1274). In 1264 he published *Of God and His Creatures*, in which he included a section titled "That the Souls of Dumb Animals Are Not Immortal." Thomas argued that animals can neither understand nor reason and that their actions are driven entirely by natural instincts rather than by "art" or self-consciousness. Because animals can comprehend only the present and not the future, Thomas believed that their souls are not immortal like human souls.

Crusades

During the medieval period the Christian church worked to stamp out paganism, cults, animal worship, and all other non-Christian beliefs. Many Crusades, or holy wars, were launched between 1095 and 1291 to try to conquer the Muslims, who had taken over Jerusalem. Thousands of people (and horses) on both sides were killed during these wars.

Domestic crusades were also launched against groups and individuals throughout Europe who were considered dangerous to the church or its teachings. Medieval people became obsessed with the devil and believed that he and his servants assumed human and animal forms. Even though different animals were suspected of being agents of the devil at different times and places, the cat was by far the most closely associated with evil. During the Middle Ages cats were burned at the stake, along with

their owners, on suspicion of being witches. By the beginning of the 14th century Europe's cat population had been severely depleted.

In 1347 the bubonic plague began to sweep across Europe. Called the Black Death, it killed 25 million people (nearly a third of Europe's population) in only three years. The disease was spread to humans by fleas on infected rodents. Centuries of cat slaughter had allowed the rodent population to surge out of control. The persecution of cats during the Middle Ages seems to have been unique to Europe. In Asia and the Middle East during the same period, cats retained their prestige as protectors of grains and other food supplies.

AGE OF ENLIGHTENMENT AND THE USE OF VIVISECTION

The centuries immediately following the Middle Ages are called the Age of Enlightenment because waves of intellectual and scientific advancement spread throughout Europe. Many superstitions and customs disappeared as societies became more urban and less rural. Church authorities began to lose much of their power over people's lives. Medical researchers gained permission to perform autopsies (mostly on executed prisoners) to learn about human anatomy. Autopsies had been forbidden by the church for centuries, and little medical progress had been made in the field of anatomy. Animal experimentation was to become a major research tool of modern medicine.

In 1543 the Belgian physician Andreas Vesalius (1514–1564) published "Some Observations on the Dissection of Living Animals" in *On the Structure of the Human Body*. Vesalius hoped to convince other physicians that the study of anatomy was essential to improving medical care. He advocated cutting open living animals to teach students about blood circulation.

During the 1600s the French philosopher and mathematician René Descartes (1596–1650) published some influential essays in which he argued that animals could not think at all. Descartes said that only humans had eternal souls; thus, only humans could reason. He described the human gift of language as proof that humans were philosophically different from animals. Descartes was fascinated with the field of mechanics and extended its ideas to nonhuman animals. He wrote that animals were mechanical things like clocks and therefore could not feel pain. This helped make it socially acceptable to cut open animals while they were still alive for medical and scientific purposes. The process became known as vivisection and was widespread in Europe during the 17th and 18th centuries.

Literature from this period describes live dogs being nailed to tables in classrooms and dissected to learn about their anatomy. Writers dismissed the cries of the dogs as being similar to the screeching sounds that a piece of machinery makes when it is forcibly taken apart.

BLOOD SPORTS

As the Middle Ages drew to a close, sports in which animals were pitted against each other became popular in England. These so-called blood sports included bull- and bear-baiting with dogs, cockfighting, and dogfighting.

Baiting began as more of a practical matter than a sport. Medieval people believed that an animal that was whipped immediately before slaughter would provide more tender meat. Whippings administered by butchers eventually evolved into events where teams of dogs were allowed to set upon bulls and bite and tear at their flesh. Such baitings soon became popular entertainment and were expanded to include other animals, such as bears. Baiting events were generally held in a ring or arena or in a field near a town's shops.

Most church authorities considered animal blood sports to be harmless pastimes, but this was not true of the Puritans. The Puritans were a Christian group that wanted to change the Church of England. In 1583 the Puritan social reformer Philip Stubbes (c. 1555–c. 1610) published *The Anatomie of Abuses*, in which he asked, "What Christian heart can take pleasure to see one poor beast rend, tear, and kill another?" The Puritans took power over the British Parliament during the mid-1600s and outlawed baiting and other blood sports for a short time. However, when the Puritans were thrown out of power, blood sports returned and became even more popular.

MOVE TO NORTH AMERICA

During the 17th century many Puritans fled England for North America. The Puritans brought their unique perspective on animals with them. In 1641 the Massachusetts Bay Colony enacted a Body of Liberties that set out the fundamental rights of the colonists. Included in these rights was Article 92, which stated, "No man shall exercise any Tirranny or Crueltie towards any Bruite creature which are usuallie kept for man's use." This is generally considered to be the first modern law against animal cruelty; however, it did not have a major effect on American laws or customs regarding animals.

Livestock was vitally important to the new colonies because of its economic value. Thus, laws were passed making it a capital crime to kill a farm animal without the owner's permission.

EUROPEAN PHILOSOPHERS ARGUE AGAINST CRUELTY TO ANIMALS

Meanwhile, new social and philosophical movements in Europe were to have far-reaching effects on the welfare of animals. During the 17th and 18th centuries several notable philosophers and writers spoke out against the mistreatment of animals. The British philosopher and political theorist John Locke (1632–1704) wrote that children should be taught from an early age that torturing and killing any living thing was despicable. In 1713 the British poet Alexander Pope (1688–1744) wrote the article "Against Barbarity to Animals" for London's *Guardian* newspaper.

The Scottish philosopher David Hume (1711–1776) advocated "gentle usage" of animals for the sake of humanity. The German philosopher Immanuel Kant (1724–1804) argued that cruelty to animals easily escalated to cruelty to humans and should therefore be stopped. Stopping animal cruelty for the sake of humans became a popular idea and was embraced more easily than the idea of preventing cruelty just for animals' sake.

In 1751 the British engraver William Hogarth (1697–1764) released a series of etchings called *The Four Stages of Cruelty*. The graphic images depicted the life of a fictional boy named Tom Nero who graduates from harming animals as a child to harming people as an adult. In the first scene the boy tortures a dog with an arrow. Even though one boy tries to stop him, the boys are surrounded by other children who also torturing animals. In the second scene Tom Nero is shown as a young man beating a horse on the street, while other acts of animal cruelty take place around him. The third scene shows fully grown Tom Nero immediately after he has murdered his girlfriend. In the fourth scene Tom Nero has been hanged for his crime, and his body is being dissected at a medical school.

Hogarth's intention was to illustrate some of the horrors of animal cruelty, but the connection between cruelty to animals and cruelty to humans was what captured people's attention. Even those who did not care about animal issues could see the dangers to civilized society of ignoring animal cruelty.

In 1764 the mechanical animal theory that was advocated by Descartes during the previous century was attacked by the French philosopher Voltaire (1694–1778) in *Dictionnaire philosophique portatif*. Voltaire argued that the scientists who dissected live animals found "organs of feeling" within them similar to those of humans, thus proving that animals could indeed feel pain.

In 1776 the Anglican clergyman Humphrey Primatt (1736–1779) published *A Dissertation on the Duty of Mercy and Sin of Cruelty to Brute Animals*. Primatt wrote, "Pain is pain, whether it be inflicted on man or on beast." He equated cruelty to animals with sin and even atheism and complained that legal authorities were doing little to stop it. Primatt argued that eliminating barbaric practices against animals might cut down on the number of "shocking murders" that were occurring.

One of the most poignant pleas for animals was made by the British philosopher and political scientist Jeremy Bentham (1748–1832). In 1789 he published *An Introduction to the Principles of Morals and Legislation*, in which he advocated making cruelty to animals punishable by law. Bentham wrote, "The question is not, Can they reason? nor, Can they talk? but, Can they suffer?" Toward the end of the 18th century a few court cases were successfully tried against people who had abused animals, but only because the animals did not belong to the guilty parties.

BRITISH LAW TAKES HOLD

Modern legal protections for animals date back to 19th-century England. In 1822 Richard Martin (1754–1834), a member of the Parliament, sponsored a bill that prohibited cruelty to cattle, horses, and sheep. It became the first anticruelty law of its kind.

"Humanity Martin," as he came to be called, soon learned that having a law in effect and getting it enforced were two different things. The authorities were not interested in spending time gathering evidence and prosecuting animal abuse cases. Martin conducted his own investigations and was helped by a group of people who were led by the Reverend Arthur Broome. In 1824 this group became the Society for the Prevention of Cruelty to Animals (SPCA).

In 1835 Martin's original act was expanded to protect dogs and bulls. In addition, cockfighting and the practice of baiting were outlawed. In 1840 the SPCA was recognized by Queen Victoria (1819–1901) and became the Royal Society for the Prevention of Cruelty to Animals (RSPCA). The RSPCA appointed inspectors to patrol the markets and slaughterhouses of London and other large cities. The group continued to push for new and tougher legislation against animal cruelty.

Many people involved in furthering animal welfare in England were also involved in other humanitarian movements of the time, including child welfare and anti-slavery causes. They believed that these issues were all related by common problems: abuse of power and the domination of the strong over the weak using cruel measures. There was also a growing moral belief that permitting cruelty to animals would lead to violence against humans and weaken society in general. It was also during the mid-1800s that the keeping of pets became popular among the middle classes.

EARLY U.S. LAWS

Early U.S. law was patterned after British common law, which viewed animals as pieces of property. However, the reform movements that swept England during the 19th century also reached the United States. The Animal Legal and Historical Center notes in "Statutes/Laws" (2013, http://www.animallaw.info/historical/statutes/sthusny1829.htm) that in 1829 New York passed the first law against animal cruelty, which read: "Every person who shall maliciously kill, maim or wound any horse, ox or other cattle, or any sheep, belonging to another, or shall maliciously and cruelly beat or torture any such animal, whether belonging to himself or another, shall, upon conviction, be adjudged guilty of a misdemeanor."

Within the next decade similar laws were passed in states throughout the Northeast and Midwest. Some state laws covered only livestock, whereas others included all domestic animals. Some laws applied only if the animal belonged to someone other than the abuser.

In 1866 Henry Bergh (1811–1888) founded the American Society for the Prevention of Cruelty to Animals (ASPCA; 2013, http://www.aspca.org/about-us/history.html). Fashioned after the RSPCA, the ASPCA received permission from the New York legislature to enforce anticruelty laws in the state. This meant that ASPCA officers could arrest and seek convictions of animal abusers. Bergh was elected the first ASPCA president and held that post for 22 years. Similar societies soon formed in other major cities, including Philadelphia, Pennsylvania, and Boston, Massachusetts.

Vivisection, which had been practiced in European medical schools for some time, had also been incorporated into U.S. medical training. According to the New England Anti-Vivisection Society, in "A Brief History of NEAVS" (2013, http://www.neavs.org/about/history/brief), in 1871 Harvard University established one of the first vivisection laboratories in the country. Even though various antivivisection societies were started in the United States, their attempts to outlaw the practice failed.

The first federal law in the United States that dealt with animal cruelty was the 28-Hour Law of 1873. This law required that livestock being transported across state lines be rested and watered at least once every 28 hours during the journey.

CHANGING ATTITUDES TOWARD ANIMALS

The late 1800s and early 1900s witnessed many developments that would profoundly affect the future of the animal rights debate in the United States. The roles for which humans used animals began to change dramatically as American society became increasingly urban, industrial, and prosperous. Working animals, such as horses, were gradually replaced with machinery on farms and city streets. A vast railroad network allowed ranchers and farmers west of the Mississippi River to ship their goods to the fast-growing populations in the East. Live cattle by the thousands were transported via railcars to massive stockyards and slaughterhouses in Chicago,

Illinois, which was the hub of the nation's meatpacking industry. The invention of refrigerated railcars during the late 1800s revolutionized the animal agriculture business by allowing meat, butter, and eggs to be transported over long distances. Easier availability spurred much greater demand for these products.

Meanwhile, the growing middle class had more time and money for leisure activities, many of which involved animals—hunting, fishing, keeping pets, and visiting wildlife refuges, circuses, zoos, and animal parks. Conservation of some of the undeveloped lands in the United States became a national priority. In 1872 Yellowstone National Park became the first U.S. national park. It would be joined by dozens more over the subsequent decades. The management of wild animals, such as buffalo and wolves, on federal government lands would eventually become an issue of keen controversy. In 1900 Congress passed the Lacey Act, the first major federal law that impacted wildlife. Numerous state laws already prohibited poaching (illegal hunting). These laws were designed to prevent the depletion of certain species, not for the benefit of the animals themselves, but so that future hunters would also have prey. The Lacey Act outlawed the interstate commerce of poached game. In "Nation Marks Lacey Act Centennial, 100 Years of Federal Wildlife Law Enforcement" (May 30, 2000, http://www.fws.gov/pacific/news/2000/2000-98.htm), the U.S. Fish and Wildlife Service (USFWS) notes that the goal of the law was "safeguarding wildlife resources."

Exotic wild animals (wild animals from foreign lands) have long been items of curiosity for many Americans. During the early 1800s animal exhibitors brought tigers and elephants to the United States and created menageries that featured various exotic animals. In 1871 the entrepreneur Phineas Taylor Barnum (1810–1891) founded P.T. Barnum's Grand Traveling Museum, Menagerie, Caravan, and Circus, which was billed as the country's largest traveling circus. In 1874 the first U.S. zoo opened to the public in Philadelphia. The word *zoo* was derived from the term *zoological park*, which was commonly used in England to describe permanent (rather than traveling) exhibits of captive wild animals. Zoos served both recreational and educational functions by entertaining the public and providing information about wild species and their habitats.

During the early 20th century businesses that commercialized the natural athletic prowess of certain animals were founded. Horse racing and greyhound racing both became popular sports during the 1930s as many states legalized this type of gambling. The treatment and fate of sports animals would become a major theme of animal protection advocates. In 1938 the Food, Drug, and Cosmetic Act was passed. This legislation required animal testing of certain chemicals and drugs to ensure their safety for human use. It was to have a

profound effect on the human-animal relationship and later debates on the topic of animal rights. Following World War II (1939–1945) the use of animals in medical and scientific research skyrocketed. The demand for dogs and cats in the laboratory led to animal procurement laws in many states, allowing scientists to obtain test subjects from dog pounds and animal shelters.

By this time the country's animal protection organizations had largely turned their attention from farm animals to pets. Some people within these groups were deeply opposed to the use of animals in research, whereas others saw it as a regrettable necessity. Differences in opinion led to splintering and the formation of new organizations. The Animal Welfare Institute and the Humane Society of the United States (HSUS) were both founded during the early 1950s.

Animal protection groups began developing separate identities and missions. Some retained a local focus, whereas others focused on national issues. They gained an ally in Senator Hubert Humphrey (1911–1978; D-MN), who championed animal causes as well as civil rights and other social movements. Humphrey was instrumental in the passage of the Humane Methods of Slaughter Act of 1958, which required the use of humane slaughter methods at slaughterhouses that were subject to federal inspection. Table 1.2 provides a list of major pieces of federal legislation related to animal protection that were enacted beginning in 1958.

The Animal Welfare Act

During the 1960s another animal issue, this time pet related, achieved national prominence due to the efforts of a handful of people. Pepper was a family pet that disappeared from her backyard in Pennsylvania in 1965

TABLE 1.2

Major federal animal-related legislation enacted, selected years 1958–2011

Year	Federal legislation
1958	Humane Methods of Slaughter Act
1959	Wild Horses Act
1962	Bald and Golden Eagle Act
1966	Endangered Species Preservation Act
	Laboratory Animal Welfare Act
	Fur Seal Act
1969	Endangered Species Conservation Act
1970	Animal Welfare Act
	Horse Protection Act
1972	Marine Mammal Protection Act
1973	Endangered Species Act
1985	Health Research Extension Act
1992	Animal Enterprise Protection Act
2000	Chimpanzee Health Improvement, Maintenance, and Protection Act
	Shark Finning Prohibition Act
2006	Pets Evacuation and Transportation Standards Act
	Animal Enterprise Terrorism Act
2010	Animal Crush Video Prohibition Act
2011	Shark Conservation Act

SOURCE: Created by Kim Masters Evans for Gale, 2013

TABLE 1.3

The Animal Welfare Act and its amendments

Laboratory Animal Welfare Act
Public Law 89-544 (August 24, 1966)

Authorizes the Secretary of Agriculture to regulate transport, sale, and handling of dogs, cats, nonhuman primates, guinea pigs, hamsters, and rabbits intended to be used in research or "for other purposes."
Requires licensing and inspection of dog and cat dealers and humane handling at auction sales.

Animal Welfare Act of 1970
Public Law 91-579 (December 24, 1970)

Expands the list of animals covered by the Act.
Incorporates exhibitors into the act and defines research facilities.
Exempts retail pet stores, state and county fairs, rodeos, purebred dog and cat shows, and agricultural exhibition.
Directs development of regulations regarding recordkeeping and humane care and treatment of animals in or during commerce, exhibition, experimentation, and transport.
Establishes inspections, and appropriate anesthetics, analgesics, and tranquilizers.
Includes regulations on dog and cat commerce.

Animal Welfare Act Amendments of 1976
Public Law 94-279 (April 22, 1976)

Primarily refines previous regulations on animal transport and commerce.
Licenses, method of payment, and penalties for violations are discussed.
Introduces and defines "animal fighting ventures."
Exempts animals used in hunting waterfowl, foxes, etc.
Makes it illegal to exhibit or transport via interstate or foreign commerce animals used in fighting ventures such as dogs or roosters.

Food Security Act of 1985, Subtitle F–Animal Welfare
Also called "The Improved Standards for Laboratory Animals Act"
Public Law 99-198 (December 23, 1985)

Clarifies and specifies "humane care" specifics such as sanitation, housing, and ventilation.
Directs development of regulations to provide exercise for dogs and an adequate physical environment to promote the psychological well-being of nonhuman primates.
Specifies that pain and distress must be minimized in experimental procedures and that alternatives to such procedures be considered by the principal investigator.
Defines practices that are considered to be painful.
Stipulates that no animal can be used in more than one major operative experiment with recovery (exceptions are listed).
Establishes the Institutional Animal Care and Use Committee (IACUC).
Forms an information service at the National Agricultural Library to assist those regulated by the act.
Explains the penalties for release of trade secrets by regulators and the regulated community.

Food, Agriculture, Conservation, and Trade Act of 1990, Section 2503–Protection of Pets
Public Law 101-624 (November 28, 1990)

Establishes a holding period for dogs and cats at shelters and other holding facilities before sale to dealers.
Requires dealers to provide written certification regarding each animal's background to the recipient.

Farm Security and Rural Investment Act of 2002, Title X–Miscellaneous, Subtitle D–Animal Welfare
Public Law 107-171 (January 23, 2002)

Changed the definition of "animal" in the Animal Welfare Act, specifically excluding birds, rats of the genus Rattus, and mice of the genus Mus, bred for use in research.
Also addressed animal fighting ventures by making it a misdemeanor to ship a bird in interstate commerce for fighting purposes, or to sponsor or exhibit a bird in a fight that had been shipped for such purposes.

Animal Fighting Prohibition Enforcement Act of 2007
Public Law 110-22 (May 3, 2007)

Makes it illegal to knowingly sell, buy, transport, or deliver in interstate or foreign commerce a knife, a gaff, or any other sharp instrument attached, or designed or intended to be attached, to the leg of a bird for use in animal fighting.

Food, Conservation, and Energy Act of 2008 Public Law 110–246 (June 18, 2008)

Strengthens penalties related to animal fighting by adding prohibitions on possession, training, and advertising animals or sharp instruments for use in animal fighting.
Increases criminal penalty from 3 to 5 years imprisonment for animal fighting.
Prohibits imports for resale of dogs except under certain conditions.
Increases fines for violations of the Animal Welfare Act from $2,500 to $10,000 per violation, per animal, per day.
Addresses the use of cats and dogs in federal research by asking for an independent review of the use of Class B dogs and cats by the National Institutes of Health.

SOURCE: Adapted from "Amendments," in *Government and Professional Resources: Animal Welfare Act*, U.S. Department of Agriculture, National Agricultural Library, Animal Welfare Information Center, 2013, http://awic.nal.usda.gov/government-and-professional-resources/federal-laws/animal-welfare-act (accessed March 26, 2013)

and wound up dead in a New York City laboratory. Pepper's family diligently tracked down what had happened to her and helped expose a network of shady animal dealers and pet thieves who sold animals by the pound to research laboratories. The public demanded action. In 1966 Congress passed the Laboratory Animal Welfare Act, which required the licensing of animal dealers and the regulation of laboratory animals. Later renamed the Animal Welfare Act (AWA), it is still the primary federal law that covers the welfare of animals used in research and public exhibitions and that regulates aspects of the handling, transport, care, and commerce related to covered animals. The major provisions of the act and its four amendments are shown in Table 1.3.

The Animal and Plant Health Inspection Service

The major federal agency responsible for carrying out the AWA is the Animal and Plant Health Inspection Service (APHIS) within the U.S. Department of Agriculture (USDA). In *A 40-Year Retrospective of APHIS, 1972–2012*

TABLE 1.4

Selected milestones in the history of the Animal and Plant Health Inspection Service (APHIS), 1960s and 1970s

1966	Congress enacts the Laboratory Animal Welfare Act, regulating dealers who handle dogs and cats, as well as laboratories that use dogs, cats, hamsters, guinea pigs, rabbits, or nonhuman primates in research.
1970	The Laboratory Animal Welfare Act is renamed the Animal Welfare Act (AWA) and amended to include the regulation of other warm-blooded animals when used in research, exhibition, or the wholesale pet trade.
1970	Congress passes the Horse Protection Act (HPA), prohibiting the showing, sale, auction, exhibition, or transport of sored horses. Congress declares the soring of horses cruel and inhumane, and that sored horses, when shown or exhibited, compete unfairly with horses that are not sore.
1976	The AWA is amended to prohibit most animal fighting ventures and regulate the commercial transportation of certain animals.
1976	The HPA is amended by Congress to expand the inspection program, directing the Secretary of Agriculture to prescribe, by regulation, requirements for appointing "persons qualified to conduct inspections" for the purpose of enforcing the Act. The Designated Qualified Person (DQP) program is established in 1979.

SOURCE: Adapted from "Timeline of APHIS History," in *A 40-Year Retrospective of APHIS, 1972–2012*, U.S. Department of Agriculture, Animal and Plant Health Inspection Service, 2012, http://www.aphis.usda.gov/about_aphis/downloads/40_Year_Retrospective.pdf (accessed March 15, 2013)

(2012, http://www.aphis.usda.gov/about_aphis/downloads/40_Year_Retrospective.pdf), APHIS notes that it evolved as a specialized agency within the USDA during the early 1970s. The USDA was created in 1862 and had long been responsible for ensuring livestock health by investigating common animal diseases and developing vaccines against them. In this role the USDA helped farmers and ranchers protect their valuable commodities (i.e., their livestock) for the good of the agricultural industry. The USDA also enforced the Meat Inspection Act, which was passed in 1890 and amended several times. It covered the inspection, certification, and slaughter of certain livestock and was overseen by various offices within the USDA. In 1972 the USDA combined multiple inspection functions under APHIS and gave the agency primary responsibility for the health of plant and animal commodities in the United States. APHIS also took over regulation of laboratory animals under the Laboratory Animal Welfare Act, which was passed in 1966. Table 1.4 shows the major milestones in APHIS history from 1966 through the 1970s. Passage of the Horse Protection Act (HPA) in 1970 gave APHIS additional responsibilities for protecting the well-being of show horses. The chief goal of the act was to prevent soring, which is a practice in which some show horse owners purposely use painful techniques on the animals to elicit popular gaits, particularly high-stepping gaits. As shown in Table 1.4, the AWA was amended in 1976 to outlaw animal fighting ventures and regulate the commercial transportation of some animals.

Wild Animals

Following passage of the Lacey Act in 1900 numerous federal laws were passed over subsequent decades devoted to wild animals, particularly game species (wild animals that are killed for consumption or for recreational or sporting purposes). As a result, many of the laws were related to hunting and fishing. One of their primary purposes was to raise money for the conservation of game species to ensure that sufficient numbers of these species would exist for future human use. However, certain wild species were granted protection under federal law for sentimental reasons.

For example, the bald eagle—which had been the national bird of the United States since 1782—received protection under the Bald Eagle Protection Act of 1940, when the species appeared to be on the brink of extinction. In 1959 Congress passed the Wild Horses Act to outlaw the use of motorized vehicles and the poisoning of watering holes "for the purpose of trapping, killing, wounding, or maiming" wild horses on federal lands.

INJURIOUS AND NUISANCE WILD ANIMALS. The USFWS reports in "Animal Damage Control Act" (2013, http://www.fws.gov/laws/lawsdigest/ANDAMAG.HTML) that when Congress enacted the Animal Damage Control Act in 1931, it gave the U.S. Department of the Interior "broad authority for investigation, demonstrations and control of mammalian predators, rodents and birds." Mammalian predators include species such as wolves and coyotes that prey on livestock, particularly sheep, lambs, and chickens. Rodents and birds subject to the law are broadly known as nuisance animals or pests, because they do things that displease humans. Under the law the authority to "control" injurious and nuisance species includes the use of lethal force. In other words, wild species that damage or threaten things of value to humans (e.g., livestock, crops, wild game, and trees) can be exterminated. The government's role in killing injurious and nuisance species to protect "things" has become a very contentious issue. Less controversial are the control measures that are expended to protect human health and safety, for example, by controlling bird populations at airports to prevent airplane strikes and by controlling species that carry certain diseases, particularly zoonotic diseases (diseases that can be spread from animals to humans).

ENDANGERED WILD ANIMALS. In 1966 the Endangered Species Preservation Act was passed. This landmark federal law was driven by growing concern that some species were in danger of extinction and needed human protection. It was followed in 1969 by the Endangered Species Conservation Act and in 1973 by the Endangered Species Act (ESA). The ESA has been substantially amended since its original passage, and there is a complex legal process by which animal and plant species can be listed under the act as endangered or threatened. In "Endangered Species Act: Overview" (February 11, 2013, http://www.fws.gov/endangered/laws-policies/), the USFWS defines "endangered" as meaning "a species is in danger of extinction throughout all or a significant portion of its range." By contrast, the agency defines "threatened" as meaning "a species is likely to become endangered within the foreseeable future."

The ESA is administered by the USFWS and the National Marine Fisheries Service (NMFS), which is an agency with the U.S. Department of Commerce. The USFWS has responsibility for terrestrial (land-based) and freshwater species, while the NMFS is responsible for mostly marine wildlife. In "ESA Basics: 40 Years of Conserving Endangered Species" (January 2013, http://www.fws.gov/endangered/esa-library/pdf/ESA_basics.pdf), the USFWS notes that "the law's ultimate goal is to 'recover' species so they no longer need protection under the ESA." Recovery is facilitated by prohibiting taking, which means "to harass, harm, pursue, hunt, shoot, wound, kill, trap, capture, or collect [protected species] or attempt to engage in any such conduct." The law also forbids the importation, exportation, and interstate or foreign sales of protected species without a special permit. In addition, federal agencies must take specific actions so as to conserve any listed species that could be affected by actions they "authorize, fund, or carry out."

The ESA has become probably the most controversial wildlife law ever passed in the United States, because it raises conflicts between ecological priorities and property rights concerns. Many imperiled species inhabit ecosystems that are valued by humans for economic reasons. For example, the northern spotted owl has its primary habitat in the old-growth forests of the Pacific Northwest. Decades of heavy logging depleted the ecosystem and imperiled the species' chances for survival. In 1990 it was listed as threatened under the ESA, hampering further logging of the forests. As a result, a contentious legal and political battle has raged into the 21st century over the conflicting interests of northern spotted owls and humans.

Beloved Marine Mammals

During the 1960s and 1970s many wild animal protection issues were intertwined with causes that were devoted to conservation, ecology, and the environment, particularly in regards to the world's oceans. "Save the Whales" became a popular slogan. However, at the same time the business of using marine mammals for entertainment purposes began to boom. In 1963 the movie *Flipper*, about a boy befriending a wild dolphin, was released. It spawned a hit television show that greatly popularized the idea of using captive marine mammals to entertain humans. In 1964 the first of several SeaWorld marine parks opened in San Diego, California. Although performing animals, such as trained tigers, bears, and elephants, had long been a staple of menageries and circuses, the newly emerging theme parks staged elaborate choreographed shows that used marine animals such as dolphins, seals, and whales. The novelty of these species and general public affection for them made the new ventures highly popular and profitable. Eventually, they incited controversy as activists began criticizing the concept of keeping any wild animals in captivity, particularly ocean-dwelling species. However, like zoos and circuses, these businesses defended their use of animals as a means for raising public awareness about wild animals and for promoting conservation efforts.

ANIMAL RIGHTS BECOMES AN ISSUE

In 1975 a new twist developed in an old movement. The Australian philosopher Peter Singer (1946–) published the book *Animal Liberation: A New Ethics for Our Treatment of Animals*, which called for a fundamental change in the human-animal relationship. Singer argued that animals are victimized by humans on a massive scale because of a social evil called speciesism, a term coined by the British psychologist Richard D. Ryder (1940–) that Singer used for the widespread belief that the human species is superior to all others. Singer equated humans' mistreatment of animals throughout history with racism and sexism and blamed speciesism for the systematic abuse of animals in agriculture, research, and other human activities. The year after Singer's book was published, Animal Rights International was founded by the social reformer Henry Spira (1927–1998).

Some people working for animal causes embraced the idea that animals are not resources to be protected by benevolent humans but are individual beings with their own interests and rights. This meant that humans could not use animals for any purpose (food, clothing, sport, entertainment, and so on) because it was morally and ethically wrong to do so. This opened a new agenda in the animal welfare movement that went beyond calls for kind treatment and humane methods of slaughter. Adherence to the most radical animal rights theory meant that eating meat and killing all types of animals were wrong. So were zoos and circuses, hunting and fishing, and experimenting on animals to find cures for human diseases—no matter how humanely any of these activities were carried out.

This philosophical leap was too much for many people, and the idea that animals had rights like humans was not generally embraced. The public supported anticruelty laws and animal protection measures up to a point, but did not go so far as to say that animals have a moral standing in society that makes it inherently wrong to eat or use them. Opponents of animal rights argued that to do so would go against centuries of tradition and beliefs, disrupt many accepted systems for feeding and entertaining people, have crippling economic consequences, hurt millions of people who earned their living through animals, and impede scientific progress. Because of such arguments, most Americans of the 1970s rejected the idea of animal rights. So did most of the traditional animal protection organizations, though they continued their work to educate and reform.

However, this idea did not go away. More books examining this issue were published, and new organizations were formed, including People for the Ethical Treatment of Animals in 1980. Many others followed. These animal rights groups were much bolder than traditional animal welfare organizations. They held protest marches and publicly condemned companies and research institutions that used animals for various purposes. The radical group Animal Liberation Front raided laboratories and farms to "free" animals and destroy property.

Some animal rights groups worked through the legal system to achieve change by filing lawsuits and working with prosecutors to strengthen animal protection laws. The more traditional animal protection groups supported these efforts. Legal reform was one area in which the entire animal movement found some common ground. The traditional groups increased their political power during the 1980s through swelling membership rolls, and animal issues gained momentum in society, particularly among pet owners.

DEVELOPMENTS SINCE THE 1980S

In *The State of the Animals III: 2005* (2005), the HSUS notes that the animal movement rose "from political oblivion in the first half of the twentieth century to a position where lawmakers would listen if the context and the proposal were timely and supported by the societal and political mood." Table 1.5 lists the major milestones in APHIS history for the 1980s. Because APHIS is the chief overseer of the AWA, reviewing the agency's history provides an overview of many of the key developments in animal protection legislation.

In 1985 the AWA was amended by the Improved Standards for Laboratory Animals Act. (See Table 1.5.) The law introduced new standards for relieving the pain and distress of laboratory animals and for limiting their deaths during procedures. It also required that laboratory dogs be provided exercise opportunities and mandated measures to benefit the "psychological well-being" of nonhuman primates, such as apes and chimpanzees, in laboratory settings. Also in 1985 APHIS was given responsibility for the federal Animal Damage Control Program, which had been operated by the USFWS since passage of the Animal Damage Control Act of 1931. During the 1990s APHIS gained broader enforcement powers under the AWA and the HPA. (See Table 1.6.) The agency's Wildlife Services division conducted a massive national campaign to combat rabies among dogs and wild animals, mainly coyotes, gray foxes, and raccoons.

As shown in Table 1.7, during the first decade of the 21st century APHIS worked to develop a plan for managing bison populations at Yellowstone National Park. Bison, which are also known as American buffalo, were nearly driven to extinction during the 1800s by overhunting. Conservation efforts, particularly at Yellowstone, helped their numbers to rebound. However, bison can carry a disease called brucellosis that is transmittable to cattle. APHIS notes in "Brucellosis and Yellowstone Bison" (January 2007, http://www.aphis.usda.gov/animal_health/animal_dis_spec/cattle/downloads/cattle-bison.pdf) that the disease has been largely eradicated from the nation's cattle population but is still found among bison and elk at Yellowstone. Keeping a free-ranging bison herd at the park has proved controversial, because of fears from ranchers that the bison will transmit the disease to cattle. It is one example of the conflicting demands that often characterize animal protection efforts.

In 2003 APHIS dealt with an outbreak of monkeypox, a disease that was carried into the United States from Africa by infected rodents imported as pets. (See Table 1.7.) The popularity of exotic pets and their inherent threats to public health and safety have become major

TABLE 1.5

Selected milestones in the history of the Animal and Plant Health Inspection Service (APHIS), 1980s

1984	APHIS starts using beagles trained to sniff out food in luggage at international airports—the "Beagle Brigade" program.
1984	The Brucellosis Information System—APHIS' first national computer system—is implemented.
1985	The Secretary of Agriculture officially designates APHIS as responsible for regulating biotechnology-derived products that affect animal and plant health.
1985	The Animal Damage Control (ADC) program is transferred to APHIS from the U.S. Fish and Wildlife Service.
1985	The Improved Standards for Laboratory Animals Act amends the AWA to create additional standards for the use of animals in research.
1987	Congress gives USDA the authority to conduct—and enter into agreements to conduct—control activities for nuisance mammals and birds.
1988	The Centers for Epidemiology and Animal Health (CEAH) is formed.
1989	In response to the Improved Standards for Laboratory Animals Act, USDA amends regulations to establish standards for the exercise of dogs, the psychological well-being of nonhuman primates, minimization of animal pain and distress, proper use of anesthetics, analgesics, and tranquilizers, and to require researchers to consider alternatives to potentially painful or distressful procedures. The amendments also require each research facility to establish an Institutional Animal Care and Use Committee to approve and monitor all research conducted at the institution.
1989	The National Animal Health Monitoring System is established.

SOURCE: Adapted from "Timeline of APHIS History," in *A 40-Year Retrospective of APHIS, 1972–2012*, U.S. Department of Agriculture, Animal and Plant Health Inspection Service, 2012, http://www.aphis.usda.gov/about_aphis/downloads/40_Year_Retrospective.pdf (accessed March 15, 2013)

TABLE 1.6

Selected milestones in the history of the Animal and Plant Health Inspection Service (APHIS), 1990s

1990	The Food, Agriculture, Conservation and Trade Act of 1990 strengthens the AWA; USDA can now prevent licensed entities from continuing to violate the AWA while charges are pending.
1990	USDA begins regulating horses used for biomedical or other nonagricultural research and other farm animals used for biomedical or other nonagricultural research or for nonagricultural exhibition.
1992	APHIS begins work on the development and testing of wildlife contraceptives.
1993	APHIS establishes holding periods for animals in pounds and shelters and certification requirements to ensure that animals have been held for the duration of these periods.
1997	Wildlife Services (WS)—the newly renamed Animal Damage Control program—implements a nationally coordinated wildlife rabies management program among more than 20 States to control and eliminate rabies virus variants adapted to coyotes, gray foxes, and raccoons.
1997	WS collaborates with States, the Centers for Disease Control and Prevention (CDC), and others in coordinated oral rabies vaccination campaigns leading to the elimination of canine rabies in the United States, no reported cases of a unique variant of gray fox rabies in Texas for nearly 3 years, and no appreciable spread of raccoon rabies to new areas of the United States.
1999	APHIS dedicates the $14 million, state-of-the-art Wildlife Sciences Building, the principle administrative and laboratory facility for the National Wildlife Research Center (NWRC) in Fort Collins, CO.
1999	AC program successfully negotiates a Cooperative Enforcement Agreement with the horse industry for Horse Industry Organizations (HIOs) to partner with Animal Care (AC) officials in enforcement of the HPA.
1999	AC publishes a final rule on perimeter fencing requirements for animals covered under the AWA, with emphasis on wild and exotic animals.

SOURCE: Adapted from "Timeline of APHIS History," in *A 40-Year Retrospective of APHIS, 1972–2012*, U.S. Department of Agriculture, Animal and Plant Health Inspection Service, 2012, http://www.aphis.usda.gov/about_aphis/downloads/40_Year_Retrospective.pdf (accessed March 15, 2013)

TABLE 1.7

Selected milestones in the history of the Animal and Plant Health Inspection Service (APHIS), first decade of the 21st century

2000	The Record of Decision for Final Environmental Impact Statement (EIS) and Bison Management Plan for the State of Montana and Yellowstone National Park (YNP) is signed with the goal of maintaining a wild, free-ranging bison population while minimizing the risk of transmitting brucellosis from bison to domestic cattle on public and private lands adjacent to YNP.
2000	The Electronic Guard, a nonlethal tool to protect sheep from coyote predation developed by NWRC, becomes available.
2001	APHIS publishes a final rule to address several AWA issues related to marine mammal exhibitors.
2002	The Animal Health Protection Act is passed as part of the 2002 Farm Bill, consolidating USDA's animal authorities into one law that replaced and updated dozens of statutes, some dating back to 1884.
2002	USDA distributes $20.6 million in homeland security funding to States to help establish national animal and plant diagnostic laboratory networks. The National Animal Health Laboratory Network is established.
2003	The first cases of monkeypox occur in the United States. Infected African rodents, imported as pets, transmit the disease to prairie dogs, also sold as pets, which then transmit monkeypox to their owners. APHIS AC, VS, and WS work with CDC and the Food and Drug Administration to successfully contain the outbreak and continue surveillance for the disease.
2003	The first case of bovine spongiform encephalopathy (BSE) in the United States is detected in a cow in Washington State.
2004	AC begins to apply AWA regulations and standards for the humane transportation of animals in commerce to all foreign air carriers operating to or from any point within the United States, its territories, possessions, or the District of Columbia.
2005	Following back-to-back hurricanes Katrina and Rita in the Gulf region, APHIS veterinarians, wildlife specialists, and other experts work with States, veterinary medical assistance teams, the HSUS, and other animal rescue groups to rescue, shelter, and feed displaced and vulnerable livestock, companion animals, and research animals in Louisiana and Mississippi. APHIS helps rescue and shelter more than 11,000 small animals and nearly 3,000 large animals from storm-ravaged areas.
2006	APHIS' Center for Veterinary Biologics licenses three vaccines to protect horses from West Nile virus (WNV); APHIS continues to work with the CDC and the U.S. Geological Survey's National Wildlife Health Center to survey for WNV in a wide range of wild birds and to determine distribution in U.S. bird and mosquito populations.
2008	WS predation damage management efforts at the Hobe Sound National Wildlife Refuge in Florida increase by 128,000 the number of sea turtles that emerge from nests. The loggerhead, as well as the endangered leatherback, green and Kemp's ridley sea turtles return to nest at the refuge, where previously up to 95 percent of turtle nests were destroyed by predators.
2009	The EPA registers GonaCon®, the first single-shot, multiyear wildlife contraceptive for mammals, developed by NWRC, for use in free-ranging female white-tailed deer.
2009	The "forced landing" of US Airways Flight 1549 in the Hudson River on January 15 after Canada geese were ingested in both engines on the Airbus 320 demonstrates to the public at large that bird strikes are a grave concern to aviation safety and focuses attention on WS efforts.

SOURCE: Adapted from "Timeline of APHIS History," in *A 40-Year Retrospective of APHIS, 1972–2012*, U.S. Department of Agriculture, Animal and Plant Health Inspection Service, 2012, http://www.aphis.usda.gov/about_aphis/downloads/40_Year_Retrospective.pdf (accessed March 15, 2013)

issues in the animal rights debate. The first U.S. case of bovine spongiform encephalopathy (BSE; mad cow disease) was also detected in 2003. BSE is a zoonotic disease that is lethal to humans who consume beef from infected animals. The discovery focused keen scrutiny on the practices of the nation's cattle slaughterhouses and the safety of the U.S. meat supply. During the first decade of the 21st century APHIS's Wildlife Services division continued its work under the Animal Damage Control Program. As noted in Table 1.7, that program attracted renewed attention in 2009 after a commercial airliner sucked Canada geese into its engines and had to make a forced landing on the Hudson River in New York City. Fortunately, all the passengers and crew survived.

Some of the major actions of APHIS during the second decade of the 21st century are listed in Table 1.8. The agency was involved in a variety of functions including controlling damaging wildlife, fighting rabies, ensuring that traveling elephant exhibits comply with AWA requirements, training dogs to sniff out illegally transported plants, and rescuing wildlife impacted by a major

TABLE 1.8

Selected milestones in the history of the Animal and Plant Health Inspection Service (APHIS), second decade of the 21st century

2010	For more than 5 consecutive months, WS' emergency response to the Deepwater Horizon Oil Spill protects wildlife; program staff collect over 20 percent of all rehabilitated wildlife throughout the Gulf of Mexico. WS deploys 82 employees and maintains wildlife response teams throughout the Gulf between May and September.
2010	As a result of WS-Wisconsin trapping of parasitic nesting cowbirds, a successful Kirtland Warbler nesting/fledgling occurs—for the first time in decades—outside the state of Michigan.
2010	AC creates a traveling elephant exhibitors team, comprised of veterinary medical officers, to inspect USDA-licensed, traveling elephant exhibitors across the country.
2010	Plant Protection and Quarantine (PPQ) dedicates a new National Detector Dog Training Center in Newnan, GA.
2011	For the first time in nearly 20 years, WS conducts a field trial aimed at licensing an additional oral rabies vaccine to facilitate more aggressive rabies control efforts.
2011	APHIS launches the Center for Animal Welfare in Kansas City, MO, to serve as a national resource for policy development and analysis, education and outreach, and science and technology related to improving the welfare of animals.

SOURCE: Adapted from "Timeline of APHIS History," in *A 40-Year Retrospective of APHIS, 1972–2012*, U.S. Department of Agriculture, Animal and Plant Health Inspection Service, 2012, http://www.aphis.usda.gov/about_aphis/downloads/40_Year_Retrospective.pdf (accessed March 15, 2013)

TABLE 1.9

Proposed fiscal year 2013 budget for the Animal and Plant Health Inspection Service (APHIS)

Budget authority (Dollars in millions)

Program	2011 Enacted	2012 Estimate	2013 Budget
Discretionary:			
Safeguarding and emergency preparedness/response:			
Animal health:			
Animal health technical services	$30	$33	$38
Aquatic animal health	5	2	3
Avian health	50	52	50
Cattle health	112	99	90
Equine & cervid health	19	5	4
Sheep & goat health	19	17	14
Swine health	26	23	20
Veterinary diagnostics	29	32	31
All other animal health	31	28	28
Total, animal health	321	291	279
Plant health:			
Agricultural Quarantine Inspection (AQI)	26	28	25
Cotton pests	21	18	9
Field crop & rangeland ecosystems pests	11	9	9
Specialty crop pests	150	154	151
Tree & wood pests	76	56	44
All other plant health	48	47	45
Total, plant health	332	312	283
Wildlife services:			
Wildlife Damage Management	76	73	68
Wildlife services methods development	18	18	17
Total, wildlife services	94	91	84
Regulatory services:			
Animal & Plant Health Regulatory Enforcement	14	16	16
Biotechnology Regulatory Services	14	18	17
Total, regulatory services	28	34	33
Emergency management:			
Contingency fund	2	1	2
Emergency preparedness & response	20	17	17
Total, emergency management	22	18	19
Total, safeguarding and emergency preparedness	798	746	698

TABLE 1.9

Proposed fiscal year 2013 budget for the Animal and Plant Health Inspection Service (APHIS) [CONTINUED]

Budget authority (Dollars in millions)

Program	2011 Enacted	2012 Estimate	2013 Budget
Discretionary:			
Safe trade and international assistance:			
Animal agriculture import/export	$13	$13	$13
Overseas technical & trade operations	20	20	18
Total, safe trade and international assistance	33	33	31
Animal welfare	23	28	25
Agency management	10	10	9
Total, salaries and expenses	864	817	762
Buildings and facilities	4	3	3
Total, ongoing activities	867	820	765
Emergency funding (Commodity Credit Corporation)	11	0	0
Total, APHIS discretionary programs	878	820	765
Mandatory:			
AQI fees[a]	216	215	216
Trust funds and user fees	9	12	12
Farm bill:			
National Clean Plant Network	5	5	[b]
Plant Pest and Disease Management			
Total, farm bill programs	55	55	50
Total, mandatory programs	280	282	278
Total, APHIS programs	$1,158	$1,102	$1,043

[a]Total estimated collections are $535 million in 2011, $540 million in 2012 and $545 million in 2013. Of the total, $319 million, $325 million and $329 million are transferred to the Department of Homeland Security in 2011, 2012 and 2013, respectively.
[b]Subject to reauthorization.

SOURCE: "Animal and Plant Health Inspection Service (APHIS) Budget Authority (Dollars in Millions)," in *USDA FY 2013 Budget Summary and Annual Performance Plan*, U.S. Department of Agriculture, February 2012, http://www.obpa.usda.gov/budsum/FY13budsum.pdf (accessed March 15, 2013)

oil spill in the Gulf of Mexico. The list illustrates the diversity of the responsibilities borne by the agency, which many critics say is underfunded.

Table 1.9 shows the APHIS budgets enacted in fiscal year (FY) 2011, estimated for FY 2012, and requested for FY 2013. (The federal government's fiscal year runs from October 1 through September 30.) In FY 2011 the agency had a budget of nearly $1.2 billion. Of this total, $23 million (or less than 2%) was devoted to animal welfare programs. For FY 2012, the agency had a total budget estimated at $1.1 billion, which was 5% less than the amount enacted for FY 2011. APHIS requested just over $1 billion for its operations in FY 2013. This amount was down by 5% compared with the previous year. For FY 2013, the agency anticipated needing $25 million for its animal welfare programs. This amount accounted for 2.4% of the total budget for that fiscal year.

Political Clout of the Animal Movement

By the 1990s the major animal welfare organizations were starting to achieve sufficient financial support and political clout to successfully pursue their efforts for change in two main areas: the courts and the ballot box. For example, in "Litigation" (2013, http://www.humanesociety.org/about/departments/litigation/), the HSUS's Animal Protection Litigation Section reports that in May 2013 it employed 13 lawyers and was engaged in dozens of lawsuits that pertained to animal issues around the country. In many of the cases the HSUS partnered with one or more other animal welfare or conservation organizations, such as the ASPCA or the Defenders of Wildlife. Targets of the litigation included various corporate entities involved in animal-related businesses and government agencies in charge of implementing laws and regulations that pertain to animals.

The HSUS also has an arm called the Humane Society Legislative Fund (HSLF). In "About Us" (2013, http://www.hslf.org/about_us/), the HSLF states that it "works to pass animal protection laws at the state and federal level, to educate the public about animal protection issues, and to support humane candidates for office." One of the goals of the HSLF is to persuade people to vote for candidates it considers supporters of animal protection. It does this through targeted media campaigns and mass mailings to potential voters and by compiling and publishing Humane Scorecards for members of Congress (and some state legislatures) that rate their performance on animal-related issues.

New Federal Laws

The Animal Crush Video Prohibition Act was enacted in 2010. In *Humane Scorecard: The 111th Congress in Review* (February 1, 2011, http://www.hslf.org/humanescorecard/Humane-Scorecard-2010-Final.pdf), the HSLF notes that the law bans "the creation, sale, and distribution of obscene videos that show the intentional crushing, burning, drowning, suffocating, or impaling of live animals—often by women in stiletto heels—for the sexual gratification of viewers." As noted in Table 1.2, Congress first attempted such a ban in 1999; however, that law was found unconstitutional by the U.S. Supreme Court. The 2010 law was recrafted in hopes of avoiding further constitutionality challenges.

In January 2011 Congress passed the Shark Conservation Act. The law bans the finning of sharks in U.S. waters. Finning is a practice in which people capture sharks, cut off their fins, and then toss the mortally wounded animals back into the water to die. Shark fins are considered a delicacy in some Asian cuisines.

State Laws

Many animal protection groups have actively pursued stricter state laws that deal with animal cruelty and neglect. Table 1.10 is a listing compiled by the HSUS of state animal anticruelty laws as of 2013.

One of the ways in which animal organizations achieve change at the state level is through initiative petitions. In many states, citizens can have initiatives put directly on the ballot for the general population to vote on, bypassing state legislatures, if the backers of the initiative can gather enough signatures in support of their petition. According to the HSUS, in *State of the Animals III*, initiative petition drives coordinated by animal protection groups were largely unsuccessful until 1990, when a new approach was undertaken. The HSUS and the Fund for Animals began selectively targeting specific animal issues in states where research indicated there was a good chance to put particular measures on the ballot and win support for them on election day.

For example, during the summer of 2008 the HSUS and other animal groups waged a petition drive in California that resulted in inclusion of a measure called Proposition 2 on the state's ballot in November of that year. Proposition 2 was passed by California voters. Beginning in 2015 it will impose a ban on the use of certain confinement techniques for farm animals. Its passage was heralded by animal welfare proponents as a major victory and criticized by opponents as an economic blow to the farming industry.

Link between Animal Abuse and Violence against People

As illustrated in Hogarth's *The Four Stages of Cruelty*, there has long been a belief that cruelty toward animals and cruelty toward humans are related. In more recent times this belief has been reinforced by scientific and anecdotal evidence, for example, in the HSUS's *First Strike: The Violence Connection* (2008, http://www.humanesociety.org/assets/pdfs/abuse/first_strike.pdf), which reviews studies that link animal cruelty to criminal acts against humans.

Many animal welfare activists, sociologists, psychologists, and law enforcement officials agree that a person who has abused animals will likely become involved in further antisocial and/or criminal behavior at some point. As a result, animal abuse is increasingly recognized as a serious crime in itself, with more states bringing felony charges against offenders. Additionally, successful programs have been created across the United States that join animal welfare organizations, law enforcement agencies, animal control departments, and child protective services so that all parties can be trained to look for signs of both animal abuse and domestic violence.

TABLE 1.10

State animal anticruelty laws, 2013

[Forty-eight states, the District of Columbia, Puerto Rico and the Virgin Islands have laws making certain types of animal cruelty a felony offense]

State	Max penalty	Applies to	Max fine[a]	Max jail time[a]	Neglect penalty	Bonding or reimbursement of costs	Counseling	Future ownership	Year felony enacted
AL	Class C felony (1st offense)	Felony: dog or cat / Misd: all animals	$15,000	10 years	Class B misdemeanor	May reimburse (dogs/cats only)			2000
AK	Class C felony (1st offense)	Felony: vertebrates, except fish / Misd: vertebrates, except fish	$50,000	5 years	Class A misdemeanor / Class C felony (subsequent offense within 10 years)	May reimburse		May ban ownership for up to 10 years	2008
AZ	Class 6 felony (1st offense)	Felony: all animals except fish / Misd: all animals except fish	$150,000	1½ years	Class 1 misdemeanor / Class 6 felony (intentionally/knowingly and results in serious physical injury to animal)	Shall reimburse			1999
AR	Class D felony (1st offense) / Class C felony (subsequent offense)	Felony: dogs, cats, horses / Misd: all animals	$10,000	10 years	Unclassified misdemeanor / Class D felony (4th or more within 5 years of previous offense)	Shall bond	Mandatory evaluation, may order treatment		2009
CA	Felony (1st offense)	Felony: all animals / Misd: all animals	$20,000	3 years	Felony or misdemeanor	Shall reimburse	Mandatory	May ban ownership as a condition of probation	1988
CO	Class 6 felony (1st offense) / Class 5 felony (subsequent offense)	Felony: all animals / Misd: all animals	$500,000	3 years	Class 1 misdemeanor / Class 6 felony (subsequent offense)	Shall bond	1st offense: may order / 2nd offense: mandatory		2002
CT	Class D felony (1st offense)	Felony: all animals / Misd: all animals	$5,000	5 years	Unclassified misdemeanor	Shall bond	May order		1996
DE	Class F felony (1st offense)	Felony: all animals, except fish, crustaceans and mollusks / Misd: all animals, except fish, crustaceans and mollusks	Court determined	3 years	Class A misdemeanor	Shall reimburse		Shall ban future ownership for 5 years for misdemeanor; 15 years for felony	1994
FL	3rd degree felony (1st offense)	Felony: all animals / Misd: all animals	$10,000	5 years	Misd of 1st degree	May reimburse	Mandatory for torture	May ban future ownership	1989
GA	Felony (1st offense)	Felony: all animals, except fish and "pests" / Misd: all animals, except fish and "pests"	$100,000	5 years	Misdemeanor / Misd of a high and aggravated nature (subsequent offense that results in death of animal)	Lien on animal for costs	May order evaluation		2000
HI	Class C felony (1st offense)	Felony: pet animals and horses / Misd: all animals	$10,000	5 years	Misdemeanor	May bond			2007
ID	Felony (3rd offense)	Any animal	$10,000	1 year	Misdemeanor (3rd or subsequent violation within 15 years of the 1st conviction)	Shall bond		May ban future ownership	N/A
IL	Class 3 felony (1st offense)	Felony torture: all animals / Felony aggravated cruelty: companion animals / Misd: all animals	$25,000	5 years	Class A misdemeanor / Class 4 felony (subsequent offense)	May bond (companion animals only)	Mandatory for juveniles, torture and hoarders; may order for other crimes	May ban future ownership	1999
IN	Class D felony (1st offense)	Felony: vertebrate animal / Misd: vertebrate animals	$10,000	3 years	Class A misdemeanor / Class D felony (with prior unrelated conviction under chapter that is not for the harboring of a non-immunized dog)	May bond	May order		1998

TABLE 1.10

State animal anticruelty laws, 2013 [CONTINUED]

[Forty-eight states, the District of Columbia, Puerto Rico and the Virgin Islands have laws making certain types of animal cruelty a felony offense]

State	Max penalty	Applies to	Max fine[a]	Max jail time[a]	Neglect penalty	Bonding or reimbursement of costs	Counseling	Future ownership	Year felony enacted
IA	Class D felony (2nd offense)	Felony: vertebrates other than livestock, game, furbearer, fish, reptile, amphibian or nuisance wildlife Misd: vertebrates other than livestock, game, furbearer, fish, reptile, amphibian or nuisance wildlife	$7,500	5 years	Simple misdemeanor Serious misdemeanor (intentionally and results in serious injury of death of animal)	Shall bond	Mandatory for torture		2000
KS	Non-person felony (1st offense)	Felony: all vertebrates Misd: all vertebrates	$5,000	1 year	Class A non-person misdemeanor Non-person felony (subsequent offense)	Shall bond Shall reimburse	Mandatory evaluation	Illegal to possess animals for 5 years after cruelty conviction	2006
KY	Class D felony (1st offense)	Felony: dog and cat Misd: any animal	$10,000	5 years	Class A misdemeanor				2003
LA	Felony (1st offense)	Felony: all animals Misd: all animals	$25,000	10 years	Misdemeanor felony (subsequent offense; or 1st offense intentionally/with criminal negligence)	Shall bond	May order evaluation for cruelty; mandatory for felony cruelty		1995
ME	Class C crime (1st offense)	Felony: all animals Misd: all animals	$10,000	5 years	Class D crime Class C crime (3rd offense)	May bond	May order	May ban future ownership	2001
MD	Felony (1st offense)	Felony: all animals Misd: all animals	$5,000	3 years	Misdemeanor		May order	May ban future ownership	2001
MA	Felony level[b] (1st offense)	Felony: all animals	$2,500	5 years	Felony	May bond			1804
MI	Felony (1st offense)	Felony: all vertebrates Misd: all vertebrates	$20,000	4 years	Misdemeanor Felony (4 or more animals; or subsequent offense)	May bond May reimburse	May order	May ban for probationary period; permanently on second offense	1931
MN	Felony (1st offense)	Felony: pets or companion animals Misd: all animals	$10,000	4 years	Misdemeanor Gross misdemeanor (subsequent offense within 5 years of previous violation)	May bond	May order	May ban future ownership	2001
MS	Felony (2nd offense)	Felony: dogs and cats	$5,000	5 years	Misdemeanor (dogs and cats)	Shall bond		May ban future ownership	2011
MO	Class D felony (1st offense)	Felony: all vertebrates Misd: all vertebrates	$5,000	4 years	Class A misdemeanor Class D felony (subsequent offense)	May bond			1994
MT	Felony (1st offense)	Felony: all animals Misd: all animals	$2,500	2 years	Misdemeanor Felony (subsequent offense)	Shall reimburse May bond		May ban future ownership for term of sentence	1993
NE	Class IV felony (1st offense)	Felony: all vertebrates except uncaptured wild animals Misd: all vertebrates except uncaptured wild animals	$10,000	5 years	Class I misdemeanor Class IV felony (result in serious injury or illness or death of animal)	May reimburse Lien on animal for costs		For felonies, shall ban future ownership for 5–15 years; for misdemeanors, may ban future ownership for up to 5 years	2002
NV	Category D felony (1st offense) Category C felony (3rd offense)	Felony: animals belonging to another Misd (3rd offense felony): all animals	$10,000	5 years	Misdemeanor (1st or 2nd offense in preceding 7 years) Category C felony (3rd or more within the immediately preceding 7 years)	Shall reimburse Lien on animal for costs	Mandatory for juveniles		1999

TABLE 1.10

State animal anticruelty laws, 2013 (CONTINUED)

[Forty-eight states, the District of Columbia, Puerto Rico and the Virgin Islands have laws making certain types of animal cruelty a felony offense]

State	Max penalty	Applies to	Max fine[a]	Max jail time[a]	Neglect penalty	Bonding or reimbursement of costs	Counseling	Future ownership	Year felony enacted
NH	Class B felony (1st offense)	Felony: domestic animals, household pets or wild animals in captivity; Misd: domestic animals, household pets or wild animals in captivity	$4,000	7 years	Misdemeanor (1st offense); Class B felony (subsequent offense)	Shall reimburse; May bond on appeal		May ban future ownership	1994
NJ	Crime of the 3rd degree[b] (1st offense)	Felony: all animals; Misd: all animals	$15,000	5 years	Disorderly persons offense	May reimburse	Mandatory for juveniles		2001
NM	4th degree felony (1st offense)	Felony: all animals except reptiles; Misd: all animals except reptiles	$5,000	18 months	Misdemeanor; 4th degree felony (4th offense)	May bond; Shall reimburse	Mandatory for juveniles; May order for adults		1999
NY	Class E felony (1st offense)	Felony: companion animals; Misd: all animals	$5,000	2 years	Class A misdemeanor	May bond		May ban future ownership	1999
NC	Class I felony (1st offense)	Felony: all vertebrates; Misd: all vertebrates	Court determined	1 year	Class 1 misdemeanor; Class H felony (intentional deprivation leading to death of animal; or maliciously and results in death of animal)				1998
ND	Class F felony	All animals	$5,000	5 years	Class A misdemeanor	May bond (companion animals only)	May order	May ban future ownership	2013
OH	5th degree felony (2nd offense)	Felony: companion animals; Misd: all animals	$2,000	1 year	Misd of the 2nd degree (non-companion animal); Misd of the 2nd degree (1st offense to companion animal); Misd of the 1st degree (subsequent offense to companion animal)	May reimburse			2002
OK	Felony (1st offense)	Felony: all animals	$5,000	5 years	Felony	May bond		Illegal to possess domestic animals for 5 years for misdemeanor; 15 years for felony	1887
OR	Class C felony (1st offense)	Felony: all animals; Misd: all animals	$125,000	5 years	Class B misd; Class A misd (results in serious physical injury or death of animal)	May bond; May reimburse	May order		1995
PA	3rd degree felony (2nd offense)	Felony: dogs and cats; Misd: domestic animal or domestic fowl; Summary offense: all animals	$15,000	7 years	Summary offense; Misd of 3rd degree (subsequent offense and offenses were towards dog/cat and dog/cat was seriously injured, suffered severe physical distress or was placed at imminent risk of serious physical harm)	Shall reimburse; Lien on animals for cost	May order evaluation	May ban for term of the sentence	1995
RI	Felony (1st offense)	Felony: all animals; Misd: all animals	$1,000	2 years	Misdemeanor	Shall reimburse; Lien on animals for cost	May order		1896
SC	Felony (1st offense)	Felony: vertebrates, except fowl; Misd: vertebrates, except fowl	$5,000	5 years	Misdemeanor	Shall reimburse; Lien on animals for cost			2000
SD	Class 1 misdemeanor	Misd: all animals	$2,000	1 year	Class 1 misdemeanor	Lien on animal for costs			N/A
TN	Class E felony (1st offense)	Felony: companion animal; Misd: domestic animal or wild animal in captivity	$3,000	6 years	Class A misdemeanor; Class E felony (subsequent conviction)	May bond	May order	May ban future ownership	2001

TABLE 1.10

State animal anticruelty laws, 2013 [CONTINUED]

[Forty-eight states, the District of Columbia, Puerto Rico and the Virgin Islands have laws making certain types of animal cruelty a felony offense]

State	Max penalty	Applies to	Max fine[a]	Max jail time[a]	Neglect penalty	Bonding or reimbursement of costs	Counseling	Future ownership	Year felony enacted
TX	State jail felony (1st & 2nd offense) 3rd degree felony (3rd offense)	Felony: domesticated animal, stray/feral dogs or cats, wild animals in captivity Misd: domesticated animal, stray/feral dogs or cats, wild animals in captivity	$10,000	10 years	Class A misdemeanor State jail felony (3rd offense)	Shall reimburse	Mandatory for juveniles		1997
UT	3rd degree felony (1st offense)	Felony: dog or cat Misd: all vertebrates, except zoo animals, animals kept to train hunting dogs or raptors, and animals temporarily in the state with a USDA licensed exhibitor	$5,000	5 years	Class B misd (if intentionally/knowingly; on subsequent offense becomes Class A misd) Class C misd (if recklessly/with criminal negligence; on subsequent offense becomes Class B misd)	May reimburse	May order	May ban future ownership	2008
VT	Felony (1st offense)	Felony: all animals Misd: all animals	$7,500	5 years	Civil citation (if not previously adjudicated in violation of chapter) Misd (otherwise)	Shall reimburse Lien on animal for costs	May order	May ban future ownership	1998
VA	Felony (1st offense)	1st offense felony: dog or cat 2nd offense felony: all vertebrates except fish Misd: all vertebrates except fish	$2,500	5 years	Class 1 misdemeanor Class 6 felony (maliciously and has been convicted for cruelty to animals within 5 years if any current or previous violation resulted in death or necessary euthanasia of animal)	May bond Shall reimburse	May order	May ban future ownership	1999
WA	Class C felony (1st offense)	Felony: all animals Misd: all animals	$10,000	5 years	Class C felony (with criminal negligence and resultantly causes substantial and unjustifiable physical pain that extends for a period sufficient to cause considerable suffering or death to animal) Gross misd (under circumstances not amounting to above first degree animal cruelty and the animal suffers unnecessary or unjustifiable physical pain as a result)	Shall reimburse	May order	Shall ban future ownership if animal dies or on 2nd offense; may ban for others. If ban is ordered, court shall ban for 2 years for misdemeanor and permanently for felonies or subsequent misdemeanors	1994
WV	Felony (1st offense)	Felony: all animals Misd: all animals	$5,000	5 years	Misdemeanor	Shall bond Shall reimburse	Shall order evaluation (prior to probation)	Shall ban future ownership for 5 years for misdemeanor; 15 years for felony	2003

The History of Human-Animal Interaction

TABLE 1.10

State animal anticruelty laws, 2013 [CONTINUED]

[Forty-eight states, the District of Columbia, Puerto Rico and the Virgin Islands have laws making certain types of animal cruelty a felony offense]

State	Max penalty	Applies to	Max fine[a]	Max jail time[a]	Neglect penalty	Bonding or reimbursement of costs	Counseling	Future ownership	Year felony enacted
WI	Class I felony (1st offense)	Felony: mammals, reptiles and amphibians Misd: mammals, reptiles and amphibians	$10,000	3½ years	Class C forfeiture Class A forfeiture (violation within 3 years after a humane officer issues abatement order) Class A misdemeanor (intentionally or negligently)	May bond Shall reimburse		May ban future ownership for up to 5 years	1986
WY	Felony (1st offense)	Felony: all animals Misd: all animals	$5,000	2 years	Misdemeanor High misd (subsequent offense)	Shall bond May reimburse		May ban future ownership	2003
DC	Felony (1st offense)	Felony: all animals Misd: all animals	$25,000	5 years	Petty misdemeanor	May reimburse Lien on animal for costs	May order	May ban future ownership	2001
Guam	Petty misdemeanor	Misd: all animals	$500	60 days	Misdemeanor 3rd degree felony (if result in serious physical injury or death to animal)		May order		N/A
Puerto Rico	2nd degree felony (1st offense)	Felony: domestic animals, birds or other animals kept in captivity Misd: domestic animals, birds or other animals kept in captivity	$10,000	15 years	Misdemeanor (with negligence) 4th degree felony (if serious disregard for the life and safety of animal and with intention of causing serious bodily harm)				2004
Virgin Islands	Felony	Felony: mammals, birds, reptiles and amphibians, but not pests	$5,000	2 years	Misdemeanor	Shall reimburse	Shall order (prior to probation)	Shall ban future ownership for 5–20 years	2005

[a]In some states, these maximum penalties apply only on a second or subsequent offense. Penalties for a first offense may be lower.
[b]These states do not classify offenses as felonies, but have felony level penalties.
Note: Misd = Misdemeanor. USDA = United States Department of Agriculture.

SOURCE: Adapted from "State Animal Cruelty Chart," in *State Animal Protection Laws*, Humane Society of the United States, 2013, http://www.humanesociety.org/assets/pdfs/abuse/state_animal_cruelty_laws_13.pdf (accessed March 15, 2013)

CHAPTER 2
THE ANIMAL RIGHTS DEBATE

According to *Merriam-Webster's Collegiate Dictionary* (2003), a right is a "power or privilege to which one is justly entitled." In *The Animal Rights Crusade: The Growth of a Moral Protest* (1992), James M. Jasper and Dorothy Nelkin define a right as "a moral trump card that cannot be disputed." The term *human rights* came into usage during the late 1700s to refer to generally recognized privileges (or freedoms) that every person should enjoy.

RIGHTS AND SOCIETY

The United Nations has the Universal Declaration of Human Rights (1998, http://www.un.org/rights/50/decla .htm), which states, "Everyone has the right to life, liberty and security of person." The declaration specifies dozens of particular human rights, including the right to be free from slavery, torture, and cruel or degrading treatment.

The U.S. Declaration of Independence, which was written in 1776, states, "We hold these truths to be self-evident, that all men are created equal, that they are endowed by their Creator with certain unalienable Rights, that among these are Life, Liberty and the pursuit of Happiness." Even though the United States' founding fathers considered these rights to be inherent, they did note that people form governments to "secure these rights." Thus, even though rights have a moral basis, they are upheld through the law.

Since the 1970s a debate has arisen about whether animals have moral rights that should be recognized and protected by human society. This is largely a philosophical question, but the answer has many practical consequences. For example, if animals have a right to life, then it is wrong to kill them. If animals have a right to liberty, then it is wrong to hold them in captivity. If animals have a right to pursue happiness and enjoy security, then it is wrong to interfere in their natural lives.

Societies and governments make decisions about who should be granted rights and how those rights should be secured. In general, an individual's legal right to life and liberty ends if that person infringes on someone else's right to life and liberty. In some states a person who kills another person can be executed by the government. At the very least, the government can restrict the killer's liberty. People debate the moral issues involved in such affairs, but the legal issues are generally spelled out clearly in U.S. law.

Sometimes it is not considered morally or legally wrong for one person to kill another—for example, in the case of self-defense or in defense of others. The same holds true for a person killing an animal. There is general moral and legal agreement that killing an attacking tiger or rabid dog is reasonable and right behavior. In human society the moral and legal arguments that protect a person acting in self-defense begin to melt away as the threat level decreases. Killing an unarmed burglar or trespasser may or may not be perceived as justified under the law. Killing a loud, annoying neighbor crosses over the line.

This line is set much lower when it comes to killing animals. People can sometimes kill animals that burgle or trespass, make too much noise, or become a nuisance without moral or legal condemnation. The same holds true for animals that taste good, have attractive skin or pelts, or are useful laboratory subjects. Why is it acceptable to kill an animal for these reasons, but not a human?

People answer this question in different ways, depending on their belief system and moral and social influences, including religion, philosophy, and education. The following are some of the most common reasons people give for denying animals rights:

- Animals do not have souls.

- God gave humans dominion over the animals.

- Humans are intellectually superior to animals.

- Animals do not reason, think, or feel pain like humans do.

- Animals are a natural resource to be used as humans see fit.

- Animals kill each other.

Animal Rights Activists and Welfarists

Some people believe it is not acceptable to use animals for any human purpose at all. They believe animals have moral rights to life, liberty, and other privileges that should be upheld by society and the rule of law. These are the hard-core believers in animal rights, the fundamentalists of the animal rights movement. When they speak out, write, march, or otherwise publicize their beliefs, they are called animal rights activists. An activist is someone who takes direct and vigorous action to further a cause (especially a controversial cause).

Other people believe some animals have (or should have) moral and/or legal rights under certain circumstances. They may rescue abandoned pets, lobby for legislation against animal abuse, feed pigeons in the park, or do any number of other things on behalf of animals. These people are broadly categorized as animal welfarists. Their adherence to the idea of animal rights generally depends on the circumstances. For example, a welfarist might defend the rights of pet dogs and cats but still eat chicken, steak, or pork.

This is unacceptable to animal rights fundamentalists. They argue that all animals (not just the lovable or attractive ones) have rights that apply all the time (not just when it is convenient). Such fundamentalists face opposition from a variety of sources. Some of this opposition is driven by moral and philosophical differences of opinion. Some is also driven by economics.

Many animals (alive or dead) have financial value to humans. Livestock farmers, ranchers, pharmaceutical scientists, zookeepers, circus trainers, jockeys, and breeders are among the many people who have a financial interest in the animal trade. If humans were to stop using animals, these people would be out of work. Many others would be deprived of their favorite sport and leisure activities. Given such economic arguments and the moral and philosophical arguments noted previously, those opposed to the idea of animal rights feel as strongly about the topic as those who support it.

THE HISTORY OF THE ANIMAL RIGHTS DEBATE

It was not until the 1970s that the question of animal rights became a major social issue. In 1970 the British psychologist Richard D. Ryder (1940–) coined the term *speciesism* to describe prejudice and discrimination practiced by humans against animals. Ryder's ideas received little publicity, but they were embraced by the Australian philosopher Peter Singer (1946–). In 1975 Singer published the influential book *Animal Liberation: A New Ethics for Our Treatment of Animals*, which describes in vivid detail the ways in which animals are subjected to pain and suffering on farms, in slaughterhouses, and in laboratory experiments. Singer publicizes the notion of speciesism and calls for an end to it. He argues that speciesism is similar to racism and sexism, in that they all deny moral and legal rights to one group in favor of another.

Henry Spira (1927–1998) formed Animal Rights International after attending one of Singer's lectures. Spira was a social reformer who had worked in the civil rights and women's liberation movements. Barnaby J. Feder notes in the obituary "Henry Spira, 71, Animal Rights Crusader" (NYTimes.com, September 15, 1998) that Spira turned his attention to the animal rights movement after he "began to wonder why we cuddle some animals and put a fork in others." Spira was instrumental in bringing various animal groups together to work for common causes. Many people credit him with pressuring cosmetics companies to seek alternatives to animal testing for their products during the late 1980s.

By 1980 the animal rights movement had become prominent enough to attract the attention of critics. In *Interests and Rights: The Case against Animals* (1980), the philosopher Raymond G. Frey argues that animals do not have moral rights. He insists that animal lives do not have the same moral value as human lives because animals cannot and do not undergo the same emotional and intellectual experiences as humans.

In 1979 the organization Attorneys for Animal Rights was founded by Joyce Tischler (1956?–). The group held the first national conference on animal rights law in 1980. The following year it successfully sued the U.S. Navy and prevented the killing of 5,000 burros at a weapons-testing center in California. In 1984 the group adopted a new name: the Animal Legal Defense Fund (ALDF). One of the ALDF's goals is to end the belief that animals are merely property. The group's anticruelty division also works with state prosecutors and law enforcement agencies to draft felony anticruelty laws and stiffen penalties for violations.

The British philosopher Mary Midgley (1919–) joined the debate when she published *Beast and Man: The Roots of Human Nature* (1978) and *Animals and Why They Matter* (1983). Midgley argues that Charles Darwin's (1809–1882) *On the Origin of Species by Means of Natural Selection* (1859) was the catalyst for ending the moral separation that humans felt toward animals because it proved that humans were in fact animals. Midgley compares speciesism to other social problems, such as racism, sexism, and age discrimination.

It was during the 1970s and 1980s that some animal rights advocates began using high-profile tactics, such as sit-ins at buildings and protest marches on the streets, to attract public attention to their cause. These are examples of civil disobedience (refusing in a nonviolent way to obey government regulations or social standards). A radical element of the movement went even further by breaking into laboratories and fur farms to release animals and damaging buildings and equipment. Some people who used these methods referred to themselves as part of the Animal Liberation Front (ALF). ALF followers became known as the "domestic terrorists" of the animal movement.

People for the Ethical Treatment of Animals (PETA) was founded in 1980 and quickly came to prominence. One of the group's cofounders infiltrated a research laboratory and obtained photographs of the primates being held there. The incident attracted national media attention and greatly helped Spira's efforts to reduce animal use in cosmetic testing. Animal issues also became important to a larger number of Americans during the 1980s.

Many in the scientific community were disturbed by this new wave of moral and social opposition to the use of animals in research. The Foundation for Biomedical Research was founded in 1981 to defend such usage and promote greater understanding of its medical and scientific benefits among the general public. The foundation began tracking and reporting on the activities of criminal animal activists who broke into laboratories to release animals and/or destroy property.

In 1983 Tom Regan (1938–) of North Carolina State University published *The Case for Animal Rights*. He argues that animal pain and suffering are consequences of a bigger problem: The idea that animals are a resource for people. Regan presents detailed philosophical arguments that outline why he believes animals have moral rights as "subjects-of-a-life." Regan states that acknowledging the rights of animals requires people to cease using them for any purpose, not just those associated with pain and suffering.

Moral vegetarianism (adhering to a vegetarian diet due to the belief that eating meat is morally wrong) dates back centuries. The Italian artist Leonardo da Vinci (1452–1519) once wrote in his notebook, "The time will come when men such as I will look upon the murder of animals as they now look upon the murder of men." Moral vegetarianism was advocated by the Indian religious leader Mahatma Gandhi (1869–1948) during the early 1930s as a moral duty of humans toward animals. Strict vegetarians do not eat meat, and some reject other animal-derived foods, such as eggs, milk, butter, and so forth. For example, lacto-vegetarians eschew meat and eggs, but consume milk and cheese. Vegans do not consume any animal-derived foods at all. The Vegan

Society is a private organization formed in the United Kingdom in 1944 that advocates veganism. In "The Vegan News" (November 1944, http://www.vegansociety.com/uploadedFiles/About_The_Society/Publications/The_Vegan_magazine/Feature_Articles/1944-news.pdf), the founder Donald Watson (1910–2005) notes "the unquestionable cruelty associated with the production of dairy produce has made it clear that lacto-vegetarianism is but a halfway house between flesh-eating and a truly humane, civilized diet, and we think, therefore, that during our life on earth we should try to evolve sufficiently to make the 'full journey.'" Moral vegetarianism and veganism gained new life during the animal rights movement of the 1970s. Frey responded to the growing pro-vegetarian movement in 1983 with *Rights, Killing, and Suffering: Moral Vegetarianism and Applied Ethics*, in which he argues that a widespread adherence to such lifestyles would result in the collapse of animal agriculture and other animal-based industries and massive social disruption.

In 1984 Ernest Partridge of the University of California, Riverside, attacked Singer's speciesism philosophy and Regan's animal rights view in "Three Wrong Leads in a Search for an Environmental Ethic: Tom Regan on Animal Rights, Inherent Values, and 'Deep Ecology'" (*Ethics and Animals*, vol. 5, no. 3). Partridge maintains that both Singer and Regan miss a crucial point about the nature of rights: that rights have no biological basis, only a moral basis. In other words, it does not matter how humans and animals are alike or dissimilar in biology. What really matters is that no animals exhibit the capacities of "personhood," such as rationality and self-consciousness. Partridge contends that the lack of personhood effectively disqualifies animals from being rights holders.

Carl Cohen (1931–) of the University of Michigan Medical School also attacked Singer's and Regan's views in "The Case for the Use of Animals in Biomedical Research" (*New England Journal of Medicine*, vol. 315, no. 14, October 2, 1986). Cohen acknowledges that speciesism exists, but denies that it is similar to racism or sexism. He argues that racism and sexism are unacceptable because there is no moral difference between races or between sexes. However, he writes that there is a moral difference between humans and animals that denies rights to animals and allows animals to be used by humans.

Animals as Property

In 1988 researchers at Harvard University obtained a patent for the OncoMouse—a mouse that had been genetically engineered to be susceptible to cancer. This was the first patent ever issued for an animal. The ALDF challenged the issuance of the patent in court, but the case was dismissed because the court found that the

ALDF had no legal standing in the matter. Since that time, several other animals have been patented, including pigs, sheep, goats, and cattle.

In 1995 Gary L. Francione (1954–) published *Animals, Property, and the Law*, in which he argues that there is an enormous contradiction between public sentiment and legal treatment when it comes to animals. Francione notes that most of the public agrees that animals should be treated humanely and not subjected to unnecessary suffering, but he claims that the legal system does not uphold these moral principles because it regards animals as property.

Francione compares the treatment of animals in modern times to the treatment of slaves before the Civil War (1861–1865). Even though there were laws that supposedly protected slaves from being abused by slave owners, they were seldom enforced. Slaves, like animals, were considered property, and the law protects the right of people to own and use property as they see fit. Property rights date back to English common law. According to Francione, the law has always relied on the assumption that property owners will treat their property appropriately to protect its economic value. Under this reasoning, the courts of the 19th century refused to recognize that a badly beaten slave was "abused," as defined by the law.

Francione believes this same logic gives legal support to common practices in which animals are mistreated—for example, by the farming industry or by research laboratories. He explains that humans are granted "respect-based" rights by the law and that animals are only considered in terms of their utility and economic value. Francione points out that animals are treated by the legal system as "means to ends and never as ends in themselves." In other words, existing animal laws protect animals because animals have value to people, not because animals have inherent value as living beings.

Bob Torres also believes that exploitation lies at the root of human-animal interactions. In *Making a Killing: The Political Economy of Animal Rights* (2007), he states, "Animals labor to produce commodities or to be commodities, and they do this as the mere property of humans. We generally talk of this relationship in magnanimous terms, describing our 'care' of animals as 'husbandry,' or as us being guardians of their 'welfare,' yet, underneath these comfortable and bucolic notions of animal-human relations, there is a system of exploitation that yields value for the producer while denying the animal [its] right to live fully."

PHILOSOPHICAL ARGUMENTS

At the base of the animal rights debate is philosophy. Philosophical discussions involve abstract ideas and theories about questions of ethics and morality. These can be difficult subjects to comprehend and apply to real-life situations, but philosophy is important because it explains people's motivations and why people feel the way they do about a particular issue. Philosophical arguments are commonly used to either justify or condemn certain actions toward animals.

Not all people involved in the animal movement believe in animal rights. Many are motivated to work for animal causes for other reasons. Historically, the most common motivator has been concern for animal welfare, or welfarism.

Welfarism

When applied to animals, welfarism assumes that humans have the primary responsibility for the welfare of animals. Welfarists acknowledge that society uses animals for various purposes. Their goal is to reduce the amount of pain and suffering that animals endure. Welfarism centers on compassionate and humane care and treatment.

The best-known welfarist organization in the United States is the American Society for the Prevention of Cruelty to Animals (ASPCA), which was founded in 1866. In "About the ASPCA" (2013, http://www.aspca.org/about-us/about-the-aspca.aspx), the organization quotes its founder, Henry Bergh (1811–1888), in stating its mission: "To provide effective means for the prevention of cruelty to animals throughout the United States." The ASPCA defines itself not as an animal rights organization but as an animal welfare or animal protection organization. Even though the ASPCA does advocate for stronger anticruelty laws, it does not actively promote issues such as vegetarianism or banning the use of animals in medical research.

The Humane Society of the United States (HSUS) was founded in 1954. It is an animal organization that fits into the welfarist category, but its agenda is more sweeping than that of the ASPCA because it encompasses the protection of wild and marine animals as well as companion animals. Even though it defines itself as an animal protection organization, critics charge that the HSUS supports an animal rights agenda because it is openly against the use of animals in research, inhumane farming practices, and the fur industry.

Animal welfarists believe humans have a responsibility to ensure the well-being of animals and reduce their suffering. This responsibility is upheld by society in the form of anticruelty laws. However, these laws do not prevent farm animals from being slaughtered for food or laboratory animals from being experimented on, usually without anesthetic to numb their pain. In these situations, welfarists work for humane slaughtering methods and for the prevention of "unnecessary" or excessive suffering during experimentation.

Utilitarianism

Utilitarianism is a philosophy popularized by the British philosopher and political scientist Jeremy Bentham (1748–1832) in *An Introduction to the Principles of Morals and Legislation* (1789). The basic premise of utilitarianism is that right actions are those that maximize utility. Bentham defines utility as either the presence of positive consequences, "benefit, advantage, pleasure, good, or happiness," or the absence of negative consequences, "mischief, pain, evil, or unhappiness." In other words, right actions are those that maximize the best consequences or minimize the worst consequences. An important aspect of utilitarianism is that the interests of all parties involved in a particular situation must be considered. Likewise, the consequences to all parties involved must be taken into account. This is a difficult enough task when only humans are involved; it becomes much more complicated when animals are taken into consideration.

Singer uses a form of utilitarian logic in *Animal Liberation*. He argues that the suffering endured by animals on farms and during slaughtering far outweighs the pleasure and nutrition that the meat gives to humans. Likewise, he contends that the pain laboratory animals experience outweighs their usefulness to humans as test subjects. Singer concludes that the moral consequences of these practices (and other practices in which animals suffer) are so severe that they must be abolished. As a result, advocates of Singer's theory are often called liberationists or abolitionists. Even though his book is frequently called the bible of the animal rights movement, Singer does not specifically call for animal rights in the book. He has stated, however, that he believes the term is politically useful for drawing attention to animal suffering.

Many philosophers reject the notion that utilitarianism can be applied to human-animal situations because, historically, animals have not been considered to have interests at all, or their interests have not been considered equal to human interests. In 1992 the philosopher Peter Carruthers (1952–) published *The Animals Issue: Moral Theory in Practice*, in which he argues that utilitarianism is not an acceptable moral theory for examining animal issues because it equates animal lives and suffering with human lives and suffering, an idea Carruthers calls "intuitively abhorrent" and a violation of "common-sense beliefs." In *Interests and Rights*, Frey also discounts the utilitarian theory as a model of morality for dealing with animals, saying that animals do not have interests because they do not experience wants, desires, expectations, or remembrances.

Contractarianism

Contractarianism is another philosophy that is used to examine morality. According to this theory, society establishes right actions (or moral norms) through an arrangement in which individuals (called agents) voluntarily agree to abide by certain rules of morality. Following these rules is beneficial to both individuals and society in general. Even though there are many different models of contractarianism, the most common are based on the writings of the German philosopher Immanuel Kant (1724–1804) and the American philosopher John Rawls (1921–2002). Kant believes the moral code arising out of contractarianism reflects what rational agents would choose under ideal circumstances. Rawls expands this view by explaining that the right actions are those that rational agents would choose if they were unaware of their own personal ambitions or prejudices.

When contractarianism is used to discuss human society, the rational agents are assumed to have direct duties. In other words, the rational agents know they are bound by a moral contract and are responsible for acting accordingly. The rational agents also have direct rights under the contract and have duties to those who lack the rationality to enter into the contract, such as infants, small children, and the mentally challenged.

Some philosophers use the contractarian model to explain the moral relationship between humans and animals. In *Animals Issue*, Carruthers argues that contractarianism is the best moral model for describing the human-animal relationship, but he concludes that animals do not have moral standing under the contract because they do not qualify as rational agents. He notes that humans have only indirect duties toward animals, one of which is to treat them humanely out of respect for the feelings of the rational agents (other humans) who care about them. Carruthers does, however, extend direct rights to human beings who are not rational agents (such as infants), noting that this is necessary to maintain social stability.

In the contractarian model, humans are moral agents, meaning that they make decisions and take actions based on morality. Many philosophers believe animals are amoral—neither moral nor immoral. For example, a lion that kills a baby zebra to feed her cubs is acting out of instinct. The action is neither morally good nor morally bad. Some opponents of animal rights argue that because animals do not make decisions based on morality, they are not part of the moral contract and do not have moral rights. Tibor R. Machan (1939–) is an outspoken critic of the notion of animal rights. In *Putting Humans First: Why We Are Nature's Favorite* (2004), he argues that animals cannot have rights because they are not capable of making moral decisions.

In practice, the moral code of contractarianism seems to provide some protections for selected species of animals. For example, in American society there is widespread moral repugnance to the idea of eating dogs and cats or killing animals with sentimental or patriotic significance (such as bald eagles). These views might be argued to be rooted in their moral and philosophical impact on humans and could therefore be extensions of the contractarian model.

Rights View

The rights view is defined and defended by Regan in *Case for Animal Rights* and in many subsequent books. He maintains that all beings who are "subjects-of-a-life with an experiential welfare" have inherent value that qualifies them to be treated with respect and gives them a right to that treatment. In other words, living beings with conscious awareness and self-identity deserve moral rights. Regan does not define exactly which animals fall into this category, but higher species, such as vertebrates (animals with a spinal cord), fit his criteria.

This philosophy is fundamentally different from welfarism and utilitarianism. The rights view holds that animals have moral rights to certain privileges and freedoms, just as humans do. However, it does not mean that animals have exactly the same rights as humans. Most animal rights advocates believe that animals at least have the right to life and the right to freedom from bodily interference.

The philosopher best known for criticizing the animal rights view is Carl Cohen (1931–). In 2001 Cohen and Regan coauthored *The Animal Rights Debate*, which presents a point-counterpoint examination of the issue. Cohen sums up his argument against animal rights by stating that "animals cannot be the bearers of rights, because the concept of rights is *essentially human*; it is rooted in the human moral world and has force and applicability only within that world." He admits that animals are sentient (conscious of sensory impressions), feel pain, and can experience suffering, but insists that sharing these traits with humans does not make animals morally equal to humans.

Cohen writes that some people confuse rights with obligations and assume that because humans have obligations to animals, it means that animals have rights. This assumption is called symmetrical reciprocity, and he believes it is based on false logic. The difference, Cohen explains, is that an obligation is what "we ought to do," whereas a right is "what others can justly demand that we do."

Cohen states that humans are moral agents who are restrained by moral principles from treating animals inhumanely. This means that humans should not inflict "gratuitous" pain and suffering on animals. However, it does not mean that humans must stop every activity that could or does harm animals in some way. Medical research on animals is an example. He believes that scientists have moral obligations to humanity to use animals in their experiments if that is the best way for them to achieve their goals. According to Cohen, "Our duties to human subjects are of a different moral order from our duties to the rodents we use."

Cohen's overall conclusion—that rights do not apply to animals because rights are essentially human—is a point commonly made by those who oppose the animal rights movement. Many of them find it ludicrous to even debate the issue. Adrian R. Morrison (1935–) is a scientist engaged in animal research and a vocal critic of the animal rights movement. In "Understanding the Effect of Animal-Rights Activism on Biomedical Research" (*Actas de Fisiología*, vol. 8, 2002), he notes that few philosophers besides Cohen and almost no scientists bother to dispute in detail the philosophy behind the animal rights view. Morrison suggests that most scientists and philosophers "think the subject to be too far from reality to be worth the trouble."

The Moral Controversy over Great Apes

There are a handful of scientists who recognize or advocate for moral-based rights for animals. A prime example is the famed chimpanzee researcher Jane Goodall (1934–). Goodall has emphasized the high cognitive abilities of chimpanzees and other primates as a reason to grant them moral rights. In 1994 she contributed the article "Chimpanzees—Bridging the Gap" (http://www.animal-rights-library.com/texts-m/goodall01.pdf) that was published in *The Great Ape Project: Equality beyond Humanity*. Goodall asks, "In what terms should we think of these beings, nonhuman yet possessing so very many human-like characteristics? How should we treat them? Surely we should treat them with the same consideration and kindness as we show to other humans; and as we recognise human rights, so too should we recognise the rights of the great apes? Yes."

The book was edited by Singer and fellow philosopher Paola Cavalieri (1950–). Its publication accompanied their founding of a movement called the Great Ape Project (GAP). As of May 2013, the GAP Project International was headquartered at GAP Project Brazil. In "GAP Project" (2013, http://www.greatapeproject.org/), the organization states that "GAP is an international movement that aims to defend the rights of the non-human great primates—chimpanzees, gorillas, orangutans and bonobos, our closest relatives in the animal kingdom. The main rights are: the right to life, the protection of individual liberty and the prohibition of torture." Note that these are the same key rights that are guaranteed by the United Nations' Universal Declaration of Human Rights described earlier in this chapter. The GAP's sweeping call for the recognition of human-like rights for great apes had not been met by May 2013, but some progress had been made in reducing usage of certain primates in medical research. This issue is discussed in detail in Chapter 5.

Some of the GAP's original supporters later took issue with the organization, particularly Francione. In

"The Great Ape Project: Not so Great" (2006, http://www.abolitionistapproach.com/the-great-ape-project-not-so-great/#.UXamIsrUuZE), he notes that he originally supported the project and contributed to *The Great Ape Project: Equality beyond Humanity*. However, he had a change of heart, stating, "I now see that the entire GAP project was ill-conceived and I regret my participation." Francione faults GAP supporters for using the argument that great apes deserve rights because of their close similarity to humans, a position he calls "the similar minds position." By contrast, Francione asserts that "only sentience is necessary for personhood." In other words, he believes that all sentient animals—not just the ones most like humans—have rights. He notes that GAP's campaign only serves to engrain speciesism because it incorrectly "links moral significance with human characteristics."

The Moral Controversy over Dolphins

In 2001 Diana Reiss (1948–) and Lori Marino provided evidence that dolphins could recognize themselves in mirrors, a cognitive feat that was formerly believed to be possible only by humans and great apes. Their findings were reported in "Mirror Self-Recognition in the Bottlenose Dolphin: A Case of Cognitive Convergence" (*Proceedings of the National Academy of Sciences*, vol. 98, no. 10, May 8, 2001). Since that time Reiss and Marino have become vocal activists for dolphin causes. In "It's Complicated: The Lives of Dolphins & Scientists" (DiscoverMagainze.com, September 7, 2011), Erik Vance describes the professional and private consequences of their activism. It is important to understand that, in general, scientists believe they must maintain an emotional detachment from the subjects they study. For example, Vance notes that Marino's long-time mentor, the dolphin scientist Gordon Gallup, "held that any public activism tainted a scientist's reputation." Nevertheless, Reiss and Marino became vocal critics of an annual dolphin and whale hunt that is conducted in Taiji, Japan. As described in Chapter 3, the controversial hunt results in the deaths of thousands of the animals and is the subject of *The Cove*, a movie that won an Academy Award for best documentary of 2009.

Despite their shared opposition to the Taiji hunt, Reiss and Marino have undergone a very public rift over their divergent views on the morality of keeping dolphins in captivity. According to Vance, the two, who had been friends for decades, "now seem permanently estranged." He notes that Reiss has continued her work at the National Aquarium in Baltimore, Maryland, and supports studying dolphins in captivity for educational purposes. Reiss is quoted as saying, "I want to use aquariums to get the message out. I want to get as much information as I can about these animals so that we can protect them." Marino disagrees with this approach, and according to Vance has publicly criticized "the captivity industry." In fact, in Sep-

tember 2010 Marino wrote a letter to the *New York Times* (http://www.nytimes.com/2010/09/28/science/28lett-CAPTIVEDOLPH_LETTERS.html?_r=0) in response to an article in that publication describing Reiss's activism for dolphins. In her letter, Marino states, "Many of us who are scientist-advocates for dolphins and whales were surprised to find Dr. Reiss's activities defined as activism. The mirror self-recognition study with Dr. Reiss was the last I ever did with captive dolphins. Dr. Reiss, however, continues to work with captive dolphins despite her own findings that they are self-aware."

PRACTICAL IMPLICATIONS OF THE RIGHTS VIEW

Assuming that all animals have rights would have massive consequences to society. If animals have moral rights to life and freedom from bodily interference, then they cannot be purposely killed, harmed, or kept in captivity by humans. Billions of domesticated animals would be spared from slaughter and would have to be released from cages and pens.

PETA (2013, http://www.peta.org/) states its position quite bluntly: "Animals are not ours to eat, wear, experiment on, use for entertainment, or abuse in any way." Implementation of these beliefs would mean the elimination of all commercial animal operations: livestock and fur farms, animal research facilities, circuses, zoos, animal parks and aquariums, game ranches, hunting lodges, animal breeding facilities, pet stores, dog and horse racetracks, and so on. All the people working in these businesses would be put out of work. The economic consequences would be enormous. Animal rights advocates point out that dismantling the institution of slavery after the Civil War was costly as well, but it was done anyway because it was the right thing to do.

Besides an economic cost, there would also be a scientific cost. Medical and scientific research has relied on animal test subjects for centuries. Some research and development would be put on hold until alternatives could be found. Students in schools and universities would have to learn anatomy and biology without dissecting animals. Doctors, surgeons, and veterinarians in training would have to practice on something besides animals. Cloning, twinning, and other genetic manipulation of animals would have to stop. Eliminating the use of animals would disrupt the entire scientific community. Animal rights activists believe the move is overdue because it would force scientists to think about their research in new ways. For example, many school districts have already implemented alternatives to animal dissection, including computer models that accurately mimic animal bodies.

There are also implications to private individuals in terms of dining, fashion, sport, recreation, and leisure.

None of these activities could include the personal use of animals. Hunting, fishing, eating meat, wearing leather, and keeping pets would have to stop. The activity that would affect the most Americans would be the elimination of meat and animal products (milk, eggs, cheese, and so on) from their diet. Most animal rights advocates and liberationists are vegetarians or vegans. They believe a vegetarian diet would not only help animals but would also be healthier for humans and be better for the environment.

Opponents of animal rights point out that if animals had rights, keeping pets would be forbidden. Ingrid Newkirk (1949–), a PETA cofounder, has been quoted as saying that pets are a symbol of the human manipulation of animals, and the notion of pets should be phased out. This idea is controversial even within the animal rights community because it is so radical. Many people involved in both the animal rights and animal welfare movements refer to pets as "companion animals" and to owners as "animal guardians" or "animal caretakers." These terms are intended to downplay the ownership element between humans and animals.

Legally, most animals are considered property. In fact, the term *cattle* derives from a Latin word meaning "property." Carolyn B. Matlack suggests in "Sentient Property: Unleashing Legal Respect for Our Companion Animals" (*Animal Law Section*, Summer 2003) that companion animals should be given a new property classification under the law: sentient property (feeling property). She argues that courts could determine the best interests of sentient property based on the testimony of experts, as is done for young children and the mentally disabled.

Even wild animals are categorized by ownership. Private landowners assume power of ownership over wild animals on their land. As long as the animals are not protected by specific legislation, property owners may kill them as they please. Wild animals inhabiting government lands are considered public property and are treated as such. The mission of the U.S. Fish and Wildlife Service (December 29, 2006, http://www.fws.gov/help/mission.cfm) is "to conserve, protect and enhance fish, wildlife, and plants and their habitats for the continuing benefit of the American people."

Public and private landowners exhibit implied animal ownership when they grant hunters permission to hunt on lands under their control. If these animals are assumed to have moral rights, then they can no longer be considered property.

Many animal welfarists are uneasy with the animal rights movement. They worry that it draws attention away from the goals that are more easily obtainable for animals in the near future. They also worry that the radical statements and actions of some animal rights activists will turn the public against the entire animal movement. Radical animal rights activists have been known to demonstrate in the nude, splash paint on people wearing fur coats, and destroy and vandalize property. Many have spent time in prison for their actions.

Even though welfarists and liberationists/abolitionists sometimes work together to achieve change, there is a philosophical gulf between them. This was made clear by the animal rights advocate Joan Dunayer in *Speciesism* (2004). Dunayer supports the idea that humans and animals should have "absolute moral equality." She accuses animal rights groups of compromising their beliefs by campaigning for welfarist reforms in animal treatment, rather than for complete liberation. Dunayer compares the plight of animals to that of prisoners in Nazi concentration camps during World War II (1939–1945), arguing that the prisoners would have begged their supporters on the outside to work for liberation rather than for more humane living conditions or kinder slaughtering techniques.

In 2008 the philosophical fight between the two factions intensified during the passage of a ballot initiative in California. Proposition 2 (a ban on certain confinement techniques for some farm animals) was championed by the HSUS and other mainline animal welfare groups. Animal rights advocates were bitterly opposed to it. In "A Losing Proposition" (2008, http://animalrights.about.com/od/proposition2ca2008/a/FrancioneProp2.htm), Francione criticizes the measure, noting that "animals raised for food in California will still be tortured. The only difference will be that the torture will have the stamp of approval of the Humane Society of the United States." He suggests the money that is spent on so-called humane ballot measures would be better spent on promoting veganism. Other animal rights activists derisively say that welfarists endorse "happy meat," instead of working to free farm animals from slavery and exploitation.

Abolitionists ask welfarists to give up meat and leather; close down all circuses, zoos, animal parks, aquariums, and racetracks; and stop laboratories from using animals. Most welfarists are not willing to go so far; instead, they prefer to focus on finding practical solutions to problems such as pet overpopulation and cruelty to domestic animals.

At the other end of the spectrum is the radical element of the animal movement. This element does not debate philosophy but takes direct action—sometimes illegally—to free animals from farms and laboratories. The ALF is not really a group, as it has no leadership structure, but is instead a set of guidelines. "The ALF Credo and Guidelines" (2013, http://www.animalliberationfront.com/ALFront/alf_credo.htm) states that "the ALF's short-term aim is to save as many animals as possible and directly disrupt the practice of animal abuse. [The] long-term aim is to end all animal suffering by forcing animal abuse companies out of business." The ALF also states that any vegans or vegetarians who carry out actions according to ALF guidelines can regard themselves as part of the ALF. These actions include liberating animals from "places of abuse" and inflicting "economic damage" on the people involved in such abuse. ALF followers are urged to take precautions to prevent harming humans and animals. The ALF receives funding from the ALF Supporters Group, which consists of people who believe in the ALF guidelines but do not want to be involved in criminal activities.

PUBLIC OPINION

The issue of whether or not animals should have moral or legal rights does not receive a lot of attention in mainstream media sources. As of May 2013, the most recent comprehensive public opinion polls conducted on the subject date to May 2008, when the Gallup Organization gauged Americans' opinions regarding animal rights issues. The results were reported by Frank Newport in *Post-Derby Tragedy, 38% Support Banning Animal Racing* (May 15, 2008, http://www.gallup.com/poll/107293/PostDerby-Tragedy-38-Support-Banning-Animal-Racing.aspx).

According to Newport, 25% of those asked believed animals deserve the same rights as people. A large majority (72%) said animals deserve some protection but can still be used to benefit people. Only a small percentage (3%) said animals do not need much protection from harm and exploitation. These results are virtually identical to the results that were obtained by Gallup in a May 2003 poll on the same subject.

The poll participants in 2008 were also asked whether they supported or opposed four specific proposals concerning the treatment of animals. Passing strict laws regarding the treatment of farm animals was supported by 64% of participants, 39% supported a ban on all product testing performed on laboratory animals, 35% favored a similar ban on medical research testing on animals, and 21% favored a total ban on hunting.

Gallup also conducts an annual morality poll in which it surveys Americans about their opinions on some controversial moral issues. In May 2012 participants were asked to rate 16 specific issues or actions as "morally acceptable" or "morally wrong." Three of the moral issues/actions were animal related. (See Table 2.1.)

TABLE 2.1

Public opinion on the morality of various issues, May 2012

[Ranked by "Difference"]

	Morally acceptable	Morally wrong	Difference
	%	%	Pct. pts.
Birth control	89	8	81
Divorce	67	25	42
Gambling	64	31	33
Buying and wearing clothing made of animal fur	60	35	25
Medical research using stem cells obtained from human embryos	58	33	25
The death penalty	58	34	24
Sex between an unmarried man and woman	59	38	21
Medical testing on animals	55	38	17
Gay or lesbian relations	54	42	12
Having a baby outside of marriage	54	42	12
Doctor assisted suicide	45	48	−3
Abortion	38	51	−13
Cloning animals	34	60	−26
Pornography	31	64	−33
Suicide	14	80	−66
Polygamy, when a married person has more than one spouse at the same time	11	86	−75
Cloning humans	10	86	−76
Married men and women having an affair	7	89	−82

SOURCE: Frank Newport, "U.S. Perceived Moral Acceptability of Behaviors and Social Policies," in *Americans, Including Catholics, Say Birth Control Is Morally OK*, The Gallup Organization, May 22, 2012, http://www.gallup.com/poll/154799/Americans-Including-Catholics-Say-Birth-Control-Morally.aspx (accessed March 15, 2013). Copyright © 2012 Gallup, Inc. All rights reserved. The content is used with permission; however, Gallup retains all rights of republication.

Buying and wearing clothing made of animal fur was considered morally acceptable by 60% of those polled. A slightly lower percentage (55%) of respondents rated medical testing on animals as morally acceptable. Only 34% of poll participants rated the cloning of animals as morally acceptable. Gallup found some differences between people with varying political affiliations, as shown in Table 2.2. Republicans (71%) were more likely than Independents (55%) or Democrats (55%) to state that the buying and wearing of animal fur was morally acceptable. A similar split was apparent on the issue of conducting medical tests on animals, which 69% of Republicans felt was morally acceptable, compared with 50% of Independents and 48% of Democrats. All three groups found the cloning of animals to be objectionable. Only 32% of Republicans and Democrats considered this morally acceptable; 37% of Independents felt this way.

TABLE 2.2

Public opinion on the morality of various issues, by political affiliation, May 2012

% morally acceptable, sorted by "Gap"

	Republicans	Independents	Democrats	Gap, Republicans minus Democrats
	%	%	%	Pct. pts.
The death penalty	73	62	42	31
Medical testing on animals	69	50	48	21
Buying and wearing clothing made of animal fur	71	55	55	16
Cloning animals	32	37	32	0
Birth control	87	89	90	−3
Cloning humans	10	9	13	−3
Married men and women having an affair	3	10	8	−5
Polygamy, when a married person has more than one spouse at the same time	5	14	11	−6
Divorce	60	71	69	−9
Gambling	57	68	67	−10
Suicide	9	12	21	−12
Doctor-assisted suicide	33	51	49	−16
Pornography	21	32	39	−18
Sex between an unmarried man and woman	42	68	66	−24
Medical research using stem cells obtained from human embryos	44	57	72	−28
Having a baby outside of marriage	35	60	64	−29
Gay or lesbian relations	36	58	66	−30
Abortion	22	40	52	−30

SOURCE: Frank Newport, "Perceived Moral Acceptability of 2012's Most Controversial Issues—by Party ID," in *Americans, including Catholics, Say Birth Control Is Morally OK*, The Gallup Organization, May 22, 2012, http://www.gallup.com/poll/154799/Americans-Including-Catholics-Say-Birth-Control-Morally.aspx (accessed March 15, 2013). Copyright © 2012 Gallup, Inc. All rights reserved. The content is used with permission; however, Gallup retains all rights of republication.

CHAPTER 3
WILDLIFE

Wild animals are animals that have not been domesticated. As explained in Chapter 1, domestication is a gradual process that happens over multiple generations, occurs across an entire population, and results in biological changes, for example, in metabolism and reproductive traits. Carlos A. Driscoll, David W. Macdonald, and Stephen J. O'Brien point out in "From Wild Animals to Domestic Pets, an Evolutionary View of Domestication" (*Proceedings of the National Academy of Sciences*, vol. 106, no. 1, June 16, 2009) that domestication is a continuous process and as such, it is difficult to say with certainty that some animal populations are truly domesticated. To make matters more complicated, many people use the terms *domesticated* and *tamed* interchangeably and only in reference to animal temperament or docility (i.e., how animals behave toward humans). Individual wild animals can be tamed and some wild species are more amenable to taming than others. In Asia, for example, many elephants have been tamed by humans for use as beasts of burden (or working animals). Most scientists, however, do not consider Asian elephant populations to be domesticated as a whole. For instance, Driscoll, Macdonald, and O'Brien note that "Asian elephants are wild animals that with taming manifest outward signs of domestication, yet their breeding is not human controlled and thus they are not true domesticates."

Wild animals are certainly not immune from human interference. Humans control, manage, manipulate, use, and kill wildlife for various reasons. Humans tend to think of wild animals in terms of the threat they pose to people or the value the animals hold for them. Some wildlife threaten human safety, health, property, or quality of life. This is true of large carnivores (such as lions, tigers, and alligators), poisonous snakes and spiders, disease-carrying animals (such as rats), and animals that endanger moving vehicles. In addition, there are carnivores (such as coyotes and bobcats) that prey on livestock and pets, herbivores that eat crops and lawns, beavers that dam up streams, and wild animals that invade or damage human spaces. Many rodents, skunks, rabbits, deer, and birds are considered to be nuisance animals.

Nevertheless, most wild animals, even dangerous ones, have value to humans. This value might be economic, educational, or emotional in nature. Valuable wildlife fall into the following categories:

- Wild animals that produce products people want to eat, use, or wear. This category includes buffalo, deer, elk, wildfowl, fur-bearing creatures, many fish and marine mammals, and animals such as bears and tigers with bones and organs that are used in traditional medicines.

- Wild animals that humans kill for sport through hunting or fishing. In the United States people primarily hunt native game, such as bears, deer, rabbits, squirrels, and waterfowl. Exotic (foreign) animals are imported and killed at some hunting ranches. African lions, Angora goats, antelopes, Cape buffalo, Corsican sheep, gazelles, and giraffes are some of the most popular. Sport fish include a variety of fresh- and saltwater species.

- Wild animals that can be manipulated to do labor or entertain people. Elephants are used as beasts of burden and trained to perform in circuses and shows, along with bears, birds, dolphins, lions, primates, seals, tigers, whales, and other trainable animals. Some wild animals even have military uses, particularly dolphins, sea lions, and whales.

- Wild animals that humans enjoy feeding, hearing, photographing, or watching. This category is very diverse and ranges from songbirds in the backyard to whales in the open sea. (See Figure 3.1.) It includes a variety of animals that humans can encounter in the wild and at entertainment venues, parks, refuges, sanctuaries, and zoos.

FIGURE 3.1

A humpback whale. (*© Richard Fitzer/Shutterstock.com.*)

- Wild animals that are useful in scientific and medical research. These include primates and some strains of mice, rabbits, and rats.

- Wild animals that are kept as pets. This includes a wide variety of species, some of which are dangerous to humans. Keeping wild animals as pets is highly controversial and, in many states, illegal.

Animal rights advocates believe wild animals should not be used at all—not for clothing, companionship, food, entertainment, or any other purpose. They consider wild animals not as commodities but as free beings with the right to live undisturbed in their natural habitat. Animal welfarists are concerned that wild animals are exploited and mistreated because of human greed and ignorance. They work to publicize the fate of animals in captivity and to save them from mistreatment.

Most people consider wildlife a valuable natural resource, such as water or coal. They may disagree about how wild animals should be used, but they generally agree that humans have the right to use them, especially if the supply is plentiful. Wild species threatened by extinction, however, are a different matter, as many people rally to conserve them. Successful conservation ensures that the species will continue to thrive in the future.

Every aspect of human-wildlife interaction raises questions in the animal rights debate. For example:

- The American bison was nearly hunted into extinction during the 19th century. Thanks to conservationists, the species was saved and is even thriving. By 2000 bison burgers were being sold at trendy restaurants. Is it acceptable to save an endangered species and then eat it?

- The government allows people to kill deer to keep the population under control. Some animal welfare groups believe hunting aggravates population problems, as evidenced by the growth in the deer population despite years of hunting. Which position is correct?

- Many people enjoy experiencing wildlife up close for its educational and entertainment value. Should wild animals be kept in captivity to satisfy this desire?

These are just some of the major questions in the animal rights debate.

HISTORY

Problems with wildlife management plagued the first European colonists in North America. Historical records show that the colonists fought off animal predators, including bears, cougars, coyotes, mountain lions, and wolves. They also lost domesticated animals to wild predators. Livestock, particularly hogs, sometimes wandered away and lived in the wild. Their offspring were feral animals (animals born and living in the wild that are descendants of domesticated animals). The colonists killed wild and feral animals whenever they could because such animals were a threat to livestock and crops. The colonists found wolves to be particularly bothersome. Early governing bodies established wolf bounty acts that paid people for killing wolves.

By the early 1700s official hunting seasons for certain species were established in some colonies. Over the next century state governments set up fish and game departments and enacted hunting restrictions by requiring licenses and setting limits on the number of species that could be killed during each hunting season.

Colonization severely depleted the ranks of some native wild species through a combination of overhunting and disease. The introduction of livestock brought new animal diseases that were devastating to some native species. Passenger pigeons and heath hens died out altogether. Beaver, bison, and elk populations were severely diminished, although they did not become extinct.

Development of the Conservation Movement

During the latter half of the 19th century, people became more aware of the value of natural resources, such as land, water, and wildlife, and worked to conserve wilderness spaces and protect them from development. Early conservationists initiated programs that helped wild animals by preserving natural habitats, but they were not always motivated by the same concerns that drove people who were involved in the animal welfare movement. Many prominent conservationists were avid hunters, whereas many welfarists were opposed to hunting for sport. The ethical battle over hunting that began between conservationists and welfarists in the 19th century continues into the 21st century.

GOVERNMENT ENACTS LAWS. During the 20th century dozens of federal laws that regulated wildlife were enacted. Table 3.1 lists the most notable ones, as well as one from the early 21st century. The first federal wildlife law was the Lacey Act of 1900. In "Lacey Act" (2013, http://www.fws.gov/international/laws-treaties-agreements/us-conservation-laws/lacey-act.html), the U.S. Fish and Wildlife Service (USFWS) notes that "under the Lacey Act, it is unlawful to import, export, sell, acquire, or purchase fish, wildlife or plants that are taken, possessed, transported, or sold: 1) in violation of U.S. or Indian [Native American]

TABLE 3.1

Major federal laws impacting wildlife, 1900–2003

Major federal laws impacting wildlife	Year enacted
Lacey Act	1900
Game and Bird Preserves Act	1905
Weeks-McLean Act	1912
National Park Service Act	1916
Migratory Bird Treaty Act	1918
Migratory Bird Conservation Act	1920s
Tariff Act (Enhanced Lacey Act)	1930
Animal Damage Control Act	1931
Fish and Wildlife Coordination Act	1934
Migratory Bird Hunting and Conservation Stamp Act (Duck Stamp Act)	1934
Taylor Grazing Act	1934
Federal Aid in Wildlife Restoration Act (Pittman-Robertson Act)	1937
Bald Eagle Protection Act	1940
Federal Aid in Sport Fish Restoration Act (Dingell-Johnson Act)	1950
Whaling Convention Act	1950
Tuna Conventions Act	1950
Fisherman's Protective Act	1954
Fish and Wildlife Act	1956
Great Lakes Fishery Act	1956
Multiple Use Act	1960
Surplus Grain for Wildlife Act	1961
Refuge Recreation Act	1962
Wilderness Act	1964
Refuge Revenue Sharing Act	1964
Land and Water Conservation Fund Act	1965
Anadromous Fish Conservation Act	1965
National Wildlife Refuge System Administration Act	1966
Endangered Species Preservation Act	1966
Fur Seal Act	1966
National Environmental Policy Act	1969
Endangered Species Conservation Act	1969
Federal Wild and Free Roaming Horses and Burros Act	1971
Marine Mammal Protection Act	1972
Endangered Species Act	1973
Alaska National Interest Lands Conservation Act	1980
Fish and Wildlife Conservation Act	1980
National Aquaculture Act	1980
Salmon and Steelhead Conservation and Enhancement Act	1980
Atlantic Salmon Convention Act	1982
Northern Pacific Halibut Act	1982
Atlantic Striped Bass Conservation Act	1984
Pacific Salmon Treaty Act	1985
The North American Wetlands Conservation Act	1986
South Pacific Tuna Act	1988
The African Elephant Conservation Act	1988
Dolphin Protection Consumer Information Act	1990
Non-Indigenous Aquatic Nuisance Prevention and Control Act	1990
Wild Bird Conservation Act	1992
Alien Species Prevention and Enforcement Act	1992
Rhinoceros and Tiger Conservation Act	1994
National Wildlife Refuge System Improvement Act	1997
Captive Wildlife Safety Act	2003

SOURCE: Created by Kim Masters Evans for Gale, 2011

law, or 2) in interstate or foreign commerce involving any fish, wildlife, or plants taken possessed or sold in violation of State or foreign law." Many wildlife laws listed in Table 3.1 were designed to fund conservation efforts through hunting fees. For example, the Migratory Bird Hunting and Conservation Stamp Act of 1934 required people to purchase a stamp before they could hunt waterfowl. Likewise, the Federal Aid in Wildlife Restoration Act of 1937 added a special tax on guns and ammunition.

By the early 21st century wildlife in the United States was extensively regulated. The USFWS lists in "Digest of Federal Resource Laws" (January 10, 2013, http://www.fws.gov/laws/lawsdigest/Resourcelaws.html) 164 federal laws that have been passed dealing with the control, preservation, eradication, and management of wildlife. Some laws pertain directly to particular species, whereas others address the preservation of habitat and the use of federal lands.

GOVERNMENT AGENCIES THAT CONTROL WILDLIFE

Wildlife issues in the United States are overseen by various federal and state agencies. At the federal level, the USFWS is the primary agency. Originally called the U.S. Commission on Fish and Fisheries, the USFWS was formed in 1871 to examine problems with declining food-fish stocks and recommend remedies. In 1903 the agency was given oversight of the first national wildlife refuge, Pelican Island, a 3-acre (1.2-hectare [ha]) bird sanctuary in Sebastian, Florida.

The USFWS notes in the fact sheet "National Wildlife Refuge System: Overview" (http://www.fws.gov/refuges/about/pdfs/OverviewFactSheetApril2013.pdf) that as of April 2013, the National Wildlife Refuge System covered 150 million acres (60.7 million ha) and included more than 560 refuges, 38 wetland management districts, and "other protected areas" around the country. The USFWS also manages migratory bird conservation, oversees thousands of wetlands and other management areas, and operates dozens of national fish hatcheries, fishery resources offices, and ecological services field stations. The agency administers and enforces many federal wildlife laws and issues import and export permits under those laws.

The USFWS works with the U.S. Customs and Border Protection and the U.S. Department of Agriculture (USDA) to monitor wildlife trade and stop illegal shipments of protected plants and animals. The USFWS also enforces the country's participation in the Convention on International Trade in Endangered Species of Wild Fauna and Flora (CITES). This international agreement regulates the importing and exporting of thousands of species. Other federal agencies involved in controlling wild populations include the Wildlife Services (WS) within the Animal and Plant Health Inspection Service (APHIS) of the USDA, the Bureau of Reclamation, and the National Park Service. The WS is the primary federal agency in charge of controlling wildlife that can damage agriculture, property, and natural resources or threaten public health and safety. It operates the National Wildlife Research Center in Fort Collins, Colorado.

FEDERAL WILDLIFE CONTROL

Historically, wildlife control efforts in the United States have focused on protecting human interests and preserving endangered species. Human interests include health, safety, property, and resources (e.g., livestock, crops, trees, lawns, structures, water, food supplies, vehicles, and pets). Wild animals that threaten human interests are subject to removal or elimination.

Table 3.2 provides a breakdown of WS funding for fiscal year (FY) 2011 by funding source and resource. The federal FY extends from October 1 to September 30; thus, FY 2011 ran from October 1, 2010, through September 30, 2011. Note that cooperative funds are funds provided by nonfederal partners, such as state wildlife agencies. In FY 2011 WS funding totaled $110.6 million. The largest portion ($42.9 million, or 39%) was devoted to agricultural sources. This was followed by human health and safety ($36.3 million, or 33%), property resources ($17.9 million, or 16%), and natural resources ($13.4 million, or 12%).

Protecting Health and Safety

Violent confrontations between wild animals and people are relatively rare in contemporary times. Of greater concern is the danger from zoonotic diseases (diseases that can be passed from animals to people). Zoonotic diseases that are associated with wild animals include rabies, West Nile virus, Lyme disease, bovine tuberculosis (a respiratory disease associated with bison, buffalo, and deer), chlamydiosis (a respiratory disease most commonly found in tropical birds, such as parrots),

TABLE 3.2

Wildlife Services funding, by funding source and resource, fiscal year 2011

[All states in the western and eastern regions, summary]

Funding source	Agriculture	HH & S*	Property	Natural resources	Total
Cooperative	20,167,215	15,332,294	10,248,218	5,340,317	$51,088,044
Federal cooperative	2,240,497	8,563,850	4,247,061	5,555,761	$20,607,169
Federal	20,484,184	12,438,593	3,396,315	2,544,348	$38,863,441
Total	**42,891,896**	**36,334,738**	**17,891,594**	**13,440,426**	**$110,558,653**

*Human health and safety.

SOURCE: "Wildlife Services—Fiscal Year 2011, Federal and Cooperative Funding," in *Wildlife Damage Management: Wildlife Services' 2011 Program Data Reports, PDR A*, U.S. Department of Agriculture, Animal and Plant Health Inspection Service, October 31, 2012, http://www.aphis.usda.gov/wildlife_damage/prog_data/2011_prog_data/PDR_A/Basic_Tables_PDR_A/PDR_Table_A.pdf (accessed March 16, 2013)

histoplasmosis (a lung disease transmitted through bat and bird droppings), salmonellosis (an intestinal illness transmitted through contaminated feces, particularly from infected reptiles), and granulocytic ehrlichiosis (a tick-borne disease similar to Lyme disease).

One of the most feared zoonotic diseases is rabies. During the early 20th century rabies killed an average of 100 people annually, but a combination of control methods greatly reduced its threat. By the end of the century only one or two people died each year from the disease. Vaccination campaigns for domestic animals (e.g., cats and dogs) have been waged since the 1940s in an effort to stem the transmission of rabies to humans. During the 1990s federal and state wildlife officials began distributing baits that were laden with oral rabies vaccine to some at-risk populations of wild animals, such as coyotes, foxes, and raccoons.

The Centers for Disease Control and Prevention (CDC) conducts rabies epidemiology (the study of the distribution and causes of disease in populations). Jesse D. Blanton et al. of the CDC state in "Rabies Surveillance in the United States during 2011" (*Journal of the American Veterinary Medical Association*, vol. 241, no. 6, September 15, 2012) that there were 6,031 reported cases of animal rabies, as well as six cases of human rabies, in the United States in 2011. Wild animals, primarily raccoons, skunks, bats, and foxes, accounted for 92% of the animal cases.

Besides diseases acquired from animals, humans face dangers posed by collisions between moving vehicles and wild animals, including birds. According to APHIS, in *Protecting People from Predators, Wildlife Conflict and Collisions and Wildlife-Borne Disease* (2006, http://www.aphis.usda.gov/wildlife_damage/misc_pdfs/Fy%202007%20Notebook%20Sections/Protecting%20People/Protecting%20People.pdf), between 1 million and 1.5 million collisions between deer and automobiles occur each year, costing $1.1 billion in repairs to vehicles. The Insurance Institute for Highway Safety (IIHS) notes in "Losses Due to Animal Strikes" (*Highway Loss Data Institute Bulletin*, vol. 29, no. 2, April 2012) that between 2006 and 2011 an average of 6.5 insurance claims per 1,000 insured vehicle years because of animal strikes were reported. The agency suspects that deer accounted for most of strikes because claim frequency was nearly three times higher in November than in other months. (The IIHS indicates that November is a peak month in the deer mating season and is a time when "bucks are likely to be roaming.")

The USDA and the Federal Aviation Administration (FAA) state in the joint report *Wildlife Strikes to Civil Aircraft in the United States, 1990–2011* (July 2012, http://www.faa.gov/airports/airport_safety/wildlife/resources/media/bash90-11.pdf) that 119,917 animal strikes by

civilian aircraft were reported to the FAA between 1990 and 2011. Birds were responsible for 97.1% of the strikes, followed by terrestrial mammals (2.3%), bats (0.5%), and reptiles (0.1%). In January 2009 an airliner leaving New York City's LaGuardia Airport was forced to land in the Hudson River after losing power in both engines because of a reported bird strike. All 155 passengers and crew survived.

Protecting Human Resources

APHIS states in the fact sheet "Wildlife Damage Management" (2006, http://www.aphis.usda.gov/wildlife_damage/misc_pdfs/002-WSfacts.pdf) that wildlife causes an estimated $944 million worth of damage annually to agriculture. Another $71 million in livestock is lost annually to wild predators.

Federal and state wildlife agencies use a variety of direct control methods, including relocation, poisons, sharpshooters, contraceptives, and repellents, to deal with so-called nuisance wildlife. The WS issues an annual report on its wildlife dispersal and control methods. As of May 2013, the most recent report available was for FY 2011.

Figure 3.2 depicts the breakdown of the resources that were damaged by wildlife in FY 2011 according to the WS. Property resources accounted for the largest portion (39%), followed by agricultural resources (31%), human health and safety resources (26%), and natural

FIGURE 3.2

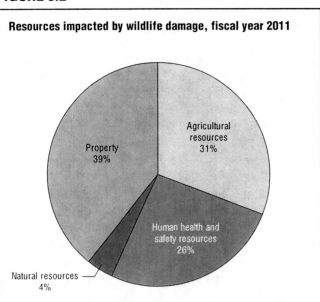

Resources impacted by wildlife damage, fiscal year 2011

SOURCE: Adapted from "Table C. Occurrence of Damage and Threats to Resources by Wildlife Reported By Wildlife Services—FY 2011," in *Wildlife Damage Management: Wildlife Services' 2011 Program Data Reports, PDR C*, U.S. Department of Agriculture, Animal and Plant Health Inspection Service, October 31, 2012, http://www.aphis.usda.gov/wildlife_damage/prog_data/2011_prog_data/PDR_C/Basic_Tables_PDR_C/Table_C_Full_Report.pdf (accessed March 16, 2013)

TABLE 3.3

Top-20 species involved in occurrences of resource damage or threats by wildlife, fiscal year 2011

Coyotes	27,522
Raccoons	21,413
Skunks, striped	19,141
Beavers	12,442
Opossums, Virginia	6,837
Swine, feral	6,596
Bears, black	5,607
Geese, Canada	4,226
Lions, mountain (cougars)	2,916
Foxes, red	2,694
Deer, white tailed	2,205
Starlings, European	1,728
Wolves, gray/timber	1,586
Marmots/woodchucks	1,563
Bobcats	1,475
Vultures, black	1,448
Cats, feral/free ranging	1,367
Pigeons, feral (rock)	1,129
Crows, American	1,105
Dogs, feral, free-ranging and hybrids	1,079

SOURCE: Adapted from "Table C-5. Species Involved and Numbers of Occurrences of Resource Damage or Threats by Wildlife Reported by Wildlife Services—FY 2011," in *Wildlife Damage Management: Wildlife Services' 2011 Program Data Reports, PDR C*, U.S. Department of Agriculture, Animal and Plant Health Inspection Service, October 31, 2012, http://www.aphis.usda.gov/wildlife_damage/prog_data/2011_prog_data/PDR_C/Basic_Tables_PDR_C/Table_C-5_%20Occurrence_by_Species.pdf (accessed March 16, 2013)

TABLE 3.4

Fate of wildlife under Wildlife Services control, fiscal year 2011

Wildlife fate	Number
Killed or euthanized	3,752,356
Dens or burrows were removed or destroyed	26,668
Freed, released, or relocated	27,233
Dispersed	29,395,000

SOURCE: Adapted from "Table G. Animals Taken by Wildlife Services—FY 2011," in *Wildlife Damage Management: Wildlife Services' 2011 Program Data Reports, PDR G*, U.S. Department of Agriculture, Animal and Plant Health Inspection Service, October 31, 2012, http://www.aphis.usda.gov/wildlife_damage/prog_data/2011_prog_data/PDR_G/Basic_Tables_PDR_G/Table%20G_ShortReport.pdf (accessed March 16, 2013)

TABLE 3.5

Top-20 species dispersed by Wildlife Services, fiscal year 2011

Starlings, European	12,417,995
Blackbirds, (mixed species)	5,760,988
Gulls, ring-billed	1,821,181
Blackbirds, red-winged	1,777,960
Crows, American	1,016,438
Gulls, herring	991,843
Geese, Canada	682,007
Gulls, glaucous-winged	360,321
Gulls, laughing	334,814
Mannikins, chestnut	302,633
Plovers, golden, Pacific	262,857
Cormorants, double-crested	242,932
Doves, mourning	220,090
Gulls, California	218,628
Gulls, black-backed, greater	176,615
Cowbirds, brown-headed	173,588
Swallows, barn	156,508
Pigeons, feral (rock)	154,487
Kittiwakes, red-legged	141,660
Mannikins, nutmeg	136,291

SOURCE: Adapted from "Table G-1. Animals Dispersed by Wildlife Services—FY 2011," in *Table G-1. Animals Dispersed by Wildlife Services—FY 2011*, U.S. Department of Agriculture, Animal and Plant Health Inspection Service, October 31, 2012, http://www.aphis.usda.gov/wildlife_damage/prog_data/2011_prog_data/PDR_G/Basic_Tables_PDR_G/Table_G-1_Dispersed.pdf (accessed March 16, 2013)

resources (4%). Table 3.3 lists the top-20 species that were involved in occurrences of resource damage or threats in FY 2011. Coyotes topped the list with 27,522 occurrences. Other mammal species and some bird species were also on the list.

As shown in Table 3.4, the WS indicates that it dispersed nearly 29.4 million animals during FY 2011; killed or euthanized approximately 3.8 million animals; freed, released, or relocated 27,233 animals; and removed or destroyed the dens or burrows of 26,668 animals. The top-20 species dispersed by the WS in FY 2011 are listed in Table 3.5. All of them were bird species. European starlings, at 12.4 million were, by far, the most dispersed species. Table 3.6 lists the 20 most-killed species in FY 2011. Overall, birds made up 13 of the 20 species that were killed the most by the WS. The seven nonbird species were coyotes, northern pikeminnows, feral swine (hogs), beavers, brown tree snakes, black-tailed prairie dogs, and raccoons. Table 3.7 shows the top-20 species that were freed or released by the WS in FY 2011. Raccoons dominated the list; 10,461 of them were freed.

CONTROVERSY OVER KILLING. In 2012 the *Sacramento (California) Bee* published a number of articles by Tom Knudson that were highly critical of the WS. In "The Killing Agency: Wildlife Services' Brutal Methods Leave a Trail of Animal Death" (April 29, 2012), Knudson recounts interviews with former WS employees and cites documents collected from the agency that highlight troubling activities. Knudson notes the investigation "found the agency's practices to be indiscriminate, at odds with science, inhumane and sometimes illegal." In particular, he asserts that since 2000 the WS has accidentally killed more than 50,000 animals that were not a problem to agricultural or ranching resources. Knudson indicates that among the nontarget animals have been "federally protected golden and bald eagles; more than 1,100 dogs, including family pets; and several species considered rare or imperiled by wildlife biologists." In "Wildlife Services' Deadly Force Opens Pandora's Box of Environmental Problems" (April 30, 2012), Knudson interviews scientists who believe that WS's focus on killing predators, such as coyotes, fails to protect livestock and wild big game and has negative ecological consequences in the West. He notes that "after several decades of intense federal hunting, there are

TABLE 3.6

Top-20 species euthanized or killed by Wildlife Services, fiscal year 2011

Starlings, European	1,500,463
Cowbirds, brown-headed	846,633
Blackbirds, red-winged	657,134
Pigeons, feral (rock)	96,734
Coyotes	83,242
Pikeminnows, northern	39,742
Grackles, common	39,431
Mannikins, chestnut	33,294
Swine, feral	32,573
Beavers	27,842
Cormorants, double-crested	24,690
Geese, Canada	23,703
Snakes, brown tree	22,976
Doves, mourning	21,898
Blackbirds, Brewer's	20,796
Doves, zebra	19,839
Mannikins, nutmeg	17,963
Doves, white-winged	17,781
Prairie Dogs, black-tailed	16,277
Raccoons	14,392

SOURCE: Adapted from "Table G-2. Animals Euthanized or Killed by Wildlife Services—FY 2011," in *Wildlife Damage Management: Wildlife Services' 2011 Program Data Reports, PDR G*, U.S. Department of Agriculture, Animal and Plant Health Inspection Service, October 31, 2012, http://www.aphis.usda.gov/wildlife_damage/prog_data/2011_prog_data/PDR_G/Basic_Tables_PDR_G/Table_G-2_Euth-Killed.pdf (accessed March 16, 2013)

TABLE 3.7

Top-20 species freed or relocated by Wildlife Services, fiscal year 2011

Raccoons	10,461
Fish (other)	3,783
Geese, Canada	2,520
Opossums, Virginia	1,586
Hawks, red-tailed	993
Cats, feral or free-ranging	806
Bears, black	598
Falcons, American Kestrels	565
Turtles, common snapping	549
Albatrosses, Layson	429
Juncos, dark-eyed	427
Skunks, striped	372
Doves, mourning	328
Starlings, European	282
Ducks, mallard	262
Dogs, feral, free-ranging and hybrids	199
Beavers	179
Owls, great-horned	138
Sparrows, house/English	131
Marmots/woodchucks	118
Turtles, other	118

SOURCE: Adapted from "Table G-3. Animals Freed or Relocated by Wildlife Services—FY 2011," in *Wildlife Damage Management: Wildlife Services' 2011 Program Data Reports, PDR G*, U.S. Department of Agriculture, Animal and Plant Health Inspection Service, October 31, 2012, http://www.aphis.usda.gov/wildlife_damage/prog_data/2011_prog_data/PDR_G/Basic_Tables_PDR_G/Table_G-3_Freed-Relocated.pdf (accessed March 16, 2013)

more coyotes in more places than ever." Some scientists point out that thinning the coyote population appears to have resulted in coyotes having larger litters because less competition means more food for the surviving coyotes, who respond by birthing more pups. In "Fed-eral Wildlife Services Makes a Killing in Animal-Control Business" (November 18, 2012), Knudson notes that private companies engaged in wildlife control strongly resent what they see as unfair competition from the WS, which is heavily funded by taxpayer dollars.

Problem Wild Horses and Burros

Wild horse and burro populations on public lands are managed by the Bureau of Land Management (BLM). The agency uses designated herd management areas in each of 10 western states and an appropriate management level (AML) per each of those states. AMLs have been established by the federal government as the maximum number of wild horses or burros that are appropriate for a particular area. At the end of FY 2012 populations in all 10 states except Oregon exceeded their AMLs. (See Table 3.8.)

The BLM states in "Factsheet on Challenges Facing the BLM in Its Management of Wild Horses and Burros" (October 20, 2009, http://www.blm.gov/wo/st/en/prog/wild_horse_and_burro/wh_b_information_center/blm_statements/new_factsheet.html) that its policy "is to manage healthy herds of wild horses and burros on healthy Western rangelands." The animals are gathered and held in holding pens. Some are adopted out to private citizens or organizations.

In December 2004 Congress passed the FY 2005 Omnibus Appropriations Bill, which included an amendment that allowed some "excess" wild horses and burros to be sold at auction "without limitation." The bill applied to animals that are more than 10 years old and those that have unsuccessfully been offered for adoption at least three times. The amendment was added by Senator Conrad Burns (1935–; R-MT), who argued that the animals damage valuable grazing land and that

TABLE 3.8

Wild horse and burro herd populations and appropriate management levels (AML), by state, fiscal year 2012

State	Horses	Burros	Total	Max. AML
Arizona	502	3,194	3,696	1,676
California	1,965	939	2,904	2,063
Colorado	967	0	967	812
Idaho	640	0	640	617
Montana	170	0	170	120
Nevada	18,425	1,456	19,881	12,778
New Mexico	108	0	108	83
Oregon	2,093	35	2,128	2,715
Utah	3,040	217	3,257	1,956
Wyoming	3,543	0	3,543	3,725
Total	**31,453**	**5,841**	**37,294**	**26,545**

SOURCE: "FY 2012 Wild Horse and Burro Herd Populations and Appropriate Management Levels (AMLs) by State," in *Wild Horse and Burro Quick Facts*, U.S. Department of the Interior, Bureau of Land Management, March 8, 2013, http://www.blm.gov/wo/st/en/prog/whbprogram/history_and_facts/quick_facts.html (accessed March 16, 2013)

maintaining them in holding pens is too expensive for the federal government. Critics complained that the phrase "without limitation" means that the animals can be slaughtered for horse meat.

In May 2005 Maryann Mott reported in "Wild Horses Sold by U.S. Agency Sent to Slaughter" (*National Geographic*) that 41 wild horses sold by the BLM had been slaughtered for meat at a slaughterhouse in Illinois. According to Mott, a BLM spokesperson stated that the agency was "very upset" to learn the horses had been slaughtered. Animal groups were furious about the news. An additional 52 wild horses that had been sold to the slaughterhouse were bought back by the Ford Motor Company.

In "Wild Horse and Burro Quick Facts" (March 8, 2013, http://www.blm.gov/wo/st/en/prog/whbprogram/history_and_facts/quick_facts.html), the BLM indicates that approximately 37,300 wild horses and burros were free-roaming on BLM-managed rangelands in February 2012. The agency points out that this number "exceeds by nearly 11,000 the number that the BLM has determined can exist in balance with other public rangeland resources and uses." As of March 2012, more than 50,000 additional animals were being held in corrals and pastures. The BLM observes that in FY 2012 holding costs accounted for nearly $43 million (59.3%) out of its total budget of $74.9 million for wild horse and burro management. The agency placed 2,598 of the animals through adoption during FY 2012. Since 1971 the BLM has adopted out more than 230,000 wild horses and burros. More than 5,400 wild horses and burros have been sold by the agency since the sale authority law was enacted in 2004. The agency insists that "the BLM, despite the unrestricted sales authority of the Burns Amendment, has not been selling any wild horses or burros to slaughterhouses or to 'killer buyers.'" The BLM notes in "Ending Wild Horse and Burro Sale Statistics for FY 09 and FY 10" (February 2011, http://www.blm.gov/) that it requires buyers to "sign a statement confirming that they are not obtaining the animal for the purpose of sending it to slaughter."

Table 3.9 shows a breakdown by state or BLM office of the wild horses and burros adopted out between FY 1971 and FY 2011.

The Endangered Species Act

As explained in Chapter 1, the Endangered Species Act (ESA) was passed in 1973. It built on protection measures that were first laid out in the Endangered Species Preservation Act of 1966. The purpose of the

TABLE 3.9

Wild horses and burros, adoptions and animals removed, by jurisdiction, fiscal years (FY) 1971–2010 and 2011

	Animals adopted				Animals removed[c]	
	FY 1971–FY 2010[a]		FY 2011		FY 2011	
Administrative state[b]	Horses	Burros	Horses	Burros	Horses	Burros
Arizona	3,621	3,090	96	30	0	102
California[b]	18,870	6,777	186	78	88	311
Colorado	7,172	864	205	13	370	0
Eastern states[b]	61,271	15,027	810	127	0	0
Idaho	4,374	315	54	9	42	0
Montana[b]	10,018	1,316	13	7	1	0
Nevada	4,285	316	82	2	3,991	0
New Mexico[b]	22,688	4,197	511	45	86	0
Oregon[b]	14,092	1,332	164	1	1,060	0
Utah	6,204	544	135	20	359	0
Wyoming[b]	16,818	1,159	111	8	2,467	0
National Program Office[b]	21,671	1,327	120	17	0	0
Total	**191,084**	**36,264**	**2,487**	**357**	**8,464**	**413**

Total adopted, FY 1971 through 2010[a]: 227,348

Total adopted, FY 2011: 2,844

Total removed, FY 2011[c]: 8,877

Note: Mules are reported as burros.

[a]Historic adoption numbers have not been adjusted downward to account for animals that have been returned or re-adopted by the Bureau of Land Management (BLM). In 2009, there were 470 returned of which 158 were re-adopted. Adjustments, which have been made from 2004 to 2009, will be reapportioned in the 2012 statistics.

[b]Prior to 1996, adoptions were reported by geographic state, including the District of Columbia. Since 1996, adoptions were reported by the BLM administrative state. Beginning in 1999, adoptions conducted in the national centers, Elm Creek, Nebraska, and Palomino Valley, Nevada, are reported under the National Program Office. California administers the wild horse and burro program in Hawaii; Eastern States Office administers the program in the 31 states east of and bordering on the Mississippi River and the District of Columbia; Montana administers the program in North and South Dakota; New Mexico administers the program in Kansas, Oklahoma, and Texas; Oregon administers the program in the State of Washington; and Wyoming administers the program in Nebraska.

[c]Removal numbers include 92 animals removed from Forest Service (FS) territories; 67 in Arizona; 4 in California; and 21 in Oregon. Jointly managed areas (BLM/FS) are not reflected in these totals.

SOURCE: "Table 5-13. Wild Free-Roaming Horse and Burro Removal and Adoption by Office, Fiscal Year 2011," in *Wild Horse and Burro Program Data*, U.S. Department of the Interior, Bureau of Land Management, undated, http://www.blm.gov/pgdata/etc/medialib/blm/wo/Planning_and_Renewable_Resources/wild_horses_and_burros/statistics_and_maps/transparency_page.Par.28130.File.dat/11pls5-13Template.doc (accessed March 16, 2013)

ESA is to conserve the ecosystems that endangered and threatened species depend on and to conserve and recover listed species. An endangered species is in danger of extinction throughout all or a significant portion of its range. A threatened species is considered likely to become endangered in the future. Some species are listed as endangered in some areas of the country and only threatened in other areas.

According to the USFWS, in *Species Reports* (http://ecos.fws.gov/tess_public/TESSBoxscore), as of March 18, 2013, there were 619 native animal species on the federal list of endangered and threatened animals and plants—448 endangered animal species and 171 threatened animal species. (See Table 3.10.) Animals are placed on the list based on their biological status and the threats to their existence. Some species are put on the list because they closely resemble endangered or threatened species. Table 3.11 shows the list of 85 native mammals that were listed under the ESA as of March 18, 2013.

The USFWS and the National Marine Fisheries Service (NMFS), an agency within the National Oceanic and Atmospheric Administration (NOAA), share responsibility for administering the ESA. They work in partnership with state agencies to enforce the act and to develop and maintain conservation programs.

PROTECTIVE MEASURES. The ESA prohibits any person from taking a listed species. Taking includes actions that "harass, harm, pursue, hunt, shoot, wound, kill, trap, capture, or collect" listed species or attempt to do so. Harm is defined as an action that kills or injures the animal and includes actions that significantly modify or degrade habitats or significantly impair essential behavior patterns such as breeding, feeding, and sheltering. These measures are designed to allow endangered and threatened species to repopulate. Under the ESA, the government must develop (when prudent) a recovery plan for each listed species that includes recovery criteria and goals, species management activities, and estimates of

TABLE 3.10

Count of endangered and threatened species as of March 18, 2013

Group	United States[a] Endangered	Threatened	Total listings	Foreign Endangered	Threatened	Total listings	Total listings (U.S. and foreign)	U.S. listings with active recovery plans[b]
Mammals	70	15	85	256	20	276	361	63
Birds	78	15	93	208	16	224	317	86
Reptiles	14	22	36	69	19	88	124	35
Amphibians	16	10	26	8	1	9	35	17
Fishes	83	70	153	11	1	12	165	102
Clams	72	11	83	2	0	2	85	70
Snails	27	13	40	1	0	1	41	29
Insects	57	10	67	4	0	4	71	40
Arachnids	12	0	12	0	0	0	12	12
Crustaceans	19	3	22	0	0	0	22	18
Corals	0	2	2	0	0	0	2	0
Animal totals	**448**	**171**	**619**	**559**	**57**	**616**	**1,235**	**472**
Flowering plants	635	147	782	1	0	1	783	640
Conifers and cycads	2	1	3	0	2	2	5	3
Ferns and allies	28	2	30	0	0	0	30	26
Lichens	2	0	2	0	0	0	2	2
Plant totals	**667**	**150**	**817**	**1**	**2**	**3**	**820**	**671**
Grand totals	**1,115**	**321**	**1,436**	**560**	**59**	**619**	**2,055**	**1,143**

Notes: 17 animal species (11 in the U.S.[a] and 6 foreign) are counted more than once in the above table, primarily because these animals have distinct population segments (each with its own individual listing status). USFWS = U.S. Fish and Wildlife Service. NMFS = National Marine Fisheries Service. CFR = Code of Federal Regulations.

The U.S. species counted more than once are:

Plover, piping (Charadriusmelodus)
Salamander, California tiger (Ambystomacaliforniense)
Salmon, chinook (Oncorhynchus (=Salmo) tshawytscha)
Salmon, chum (Oncorhynchus (=Salmo) keta)
Salmon, coho (Oncorhynchus (=Salmo) kisutch)
Salmon, sockeye (Oncorhynchus (=Salmo) nerka)
Sea-lion, Steller (Eumetopiasjubatus)
Sea turtle, green (Cheloniamydas)
Sea turtle, loggerhead (Carettacaretta)
Steelhead (Oncorhynchus (=Salmo) mykiss)
Tern, roseate (Sterna dougalliidougallii)

The foreign species counted more than once are:

Argali (Ovisammon)
Chimpanzee (Pan troglodytes)
Crocodile, saltwater (Crocodylusporosus)
Dugong (Dugong dugon)
Leopard (Pantherapardus)
Sea turtle, loggerhead (Carettacaretta)

[a]United States listings include those populations in which the United States shares jurisdiction with another nation.
[b]There are a total of 592 distinct active (draft and final) recovery plans. Some recovery plans cover more than one species, and a few species have separate plans covering different parts of their ranges. This count includes only plans generated by the USFWS (or jointly by the USFWS and NMFS), and only listed species that occur in the United States.

SOURCE: "Summary of Listed Species, Listed Populations, and Recovery Plans as of Mon, 18 Mar 2013 12:19:42 UTC," in *Species Reports*, U.S. Department of the Interior, U.S. Fish and Wildlife Service, March 18, 2013, http://ecos.fws.gov/tess_public/pub/Boxscore.do (accessed March 18, 2013)

TABLE 3.11

List of U.S. endangered and threatened mammal species as of March 18, 2013

Inverted common name	Listing status
Bat, gray	E
Bat, Hawaiian hoary	E
Bat, Indiana	E
Bat, lesser long-nosed	E
Bat, little Mariana fruit	E
Bat, Mariana fruit (=Mariana flying fox)	T
Bat, Mexican long-nosed	E
Bat, Ozark big-eared	E
Bat, Virginia big-eared	E
Bear, grizzly	T
Bear, Louisiana black	T
Bear, polar	T
Bison, wood	T
Caribou, woodland	E
Deer, Columbian white-tailed	E
Deer, key	E
Ferret, black-footed	E
Fox, San Joaquin kit	E
Fox, San Miguel Island	E
Fox, Santa Catalina Island	E
Fox, Santa Cruz Island	E
Fox, Santa Rosa Island	E
Jaguar	E
Jaguarundi, Gulf Coast	E
Jaguarundi, Sinaloan	E
Kangaroo rat, Fresno	E
Kangaroo rat, giant	E
Kangaroo rat, Morro Bay	E
Kangaroo rat, San Bernardino Merriam's	E
Kangaroo rat, Stephens'	E
Kangaroo rat, Tipton	E
Lynx, Canada	T
Manatee, West Indian	E
Mountain beaver, Point Arena	E
Mouse, Alabama beach	E
Mouse, Anastasia Island beach	E
Mouse, Choctawhatchee beach	E
Mouse, Key Largo cotton	E
Mouse, Pacific pocket	E
Mouse, Perdido Key beach	E
Mouse, Preble's meadow jumping	T
Mouse, salt marsh harvest	E
Mouse, southeastern beach	T
Mouse, St. Andrew beach	E
Ocelot	E
Otter, Northern Sea	T
Otter, southern sea	T
Panther, Florida	E
Prairie dog, Utah	T
Pronghorn, Sonoran	E
Puma (=cougar), eastern	E
Rabbit, Lower Keys marsh	E
Rabbit, pygmy	E
Rabbit, riparian brush	E
Rice rat	E
Seal, Guadalupe fur	T
Seal, Hawaiian monk	E
Sea-lion, Steller	E
Sea-lion, Steller	T
Seal, spotted	T
Sheep, Peninsular bighorn	E
Sheep, Sierra Nevada bighorn	E
Shrew, Buena Vista Lake ornate	E
Squirrel, Carolina northern flying	E
Squirrel, Delmarva Peninsula fox	E
Squirrel, Mount Graham red	E
Squirrel, northern Idaho ground	T
Squirrel, Virginia northern flying	E
Vole, Amargosa	E
Vole, Florida salt marsh	E
Vole, Hualapai Mexican	E

TABLE 3.11

List of U.S. endangered and threatened mammal species as of March 18, 2013 [CONTINUED]

Inverted common name	Listing status
Whale, Beluga	E
Whale, blue	E
Whale, bowhead	E
Whale, finback	E
Whale, humpback	E
Whale, killer	E
Whale, North Atlantic Right	E
Whale, North Pacific Right	E
Whale, Sei	E
Whale, sperm	E
Wolf, gray	E
Wolf, red	E
Woodrat, Key Largo	E
Woodrat, riparian (=San Joaquin Valley)	E

Notes: E = Endangered. T = Threatened.

SOURCE: Adapted from "Listed Animals," in *Species Reports*, U.S. Department of the Interior, U.S. Fish and Wildlife Service, March 18, 2013, http://ecos.fws.gov/tess_public/pub/listedAnimals.jsp (accessed March 18, 2013)

the amounts of time and money that will likely be needed to achieve recovery. As shown in Table 3.10, 472 native animal species had active recovery plans as of March 18, 2013.

One protective measure used for some ESA-listed species in the United States is the designation of "critical habitat." In "Listing and Critical Habitat" (May 7, 2013, http://www.fws.gov/endangered/what-we-do/critical-hab itats.html), the USFWS notes that the federal government designates areas as critical habitat if the areas are "believed to be essential to the species' conservation." The designation, however, does not mean that further human development is prohibited in the areas. The USFWS indicates "only activities that involve a Federal permit, license, or funding, and are likely to destroy or adversely modify the area of critical habitat" are subject to restriction. As shown in Table 3.12, as of March 18, 2013, the federal government had designated critical habitat for 661 of the native species listed under the ESA.

DELISTED POPULATIONS. Once a species (or a population thereof) is listed under the ESA, it remains on the list until it is officially delisted (removed from the list through a specific legal process). According to the USFWS (http://ecos.fws.gov/tess_public/DelistingReport .do), as of May 2013 partial or entire populations of 13 native animal species had been delisted because of recovery:

- Aleutian Canada goose

- American alligator

- American peregrine falcon

- Arctic peregrine falcon

TABLE 3.12

Number of U.S. endangered and threatened species with critical habitat specified, March 18, 2013

Mammals	32
Birds	27
Reptiles	14
Amphibians	13
Fish	74
Clams	35
Snails	11
Insects	35
Arachnids	8
Crustaceans	11
Corals	2
Flowering plants	383
Ferns and allies	16
Total	**661**

SOURCE: Adapted from "Listed Species with Critical Habitat," in *Species Reports*, U.S. Department of the Interior, U.S. Fish and Wildlife Service, March 18, 2013, http://ecos.fws.gov/tess_public/CriticalHabitat.do?nmfs=1 (accessed March 18, 2013)

- Bald eagle
- Columbian white-tailed deer
- Brown pelican
- Concho water snake
- Gray whale
- Gray wolf
- Lake Erie water snake
- Tinian monarch (old world flycatcher)
- Virginia northern flying squirrel

The agency notes that delisting also occurs in cases in which species go extinct. As of May 2013, 10 animal species/populations had been delisted for this reason. In addition, nine animal species/populations have been delisted for procedural reasons, for example, because new data came to light indicating that the species was not as imperiled as originally believed.

SPECIES ON HOLD. So many species have been suggested to the USFWS and NMFS as candidates for ESA listing that the agencies have not had the funding or resources to list all of them. Instead, the agencies prioritize suggested species and officially propose for listing only the ones they consider to be the most imperiled. Species that fail to be listed but are good future candidates for listing are called candidate species. The USFWS indicates in "Candidate Species Report" (http://ecos .fws.gov/tess_public/pub/candidateSpecies.jsp) that as of May 2013 it had on hold 182 candidate species for future consideration for listing. Likewise, the NMFS in "Candidate and Proposed Species under the Endangered Species Act (ESA)" (http://www.nmfs.noaa.gov/pr/species/ esa/candidate.htm) had on hold 22 candidate species.

The large number of candidate species is a source of great controversy and has spurred numerous lawsuits against the agencies by private organizations concerned about imperiled species. In "Improving ESA Implementation" (May 7, 2013, http://www.fws.gov/endangered/ improving_ESA/listing_workplan.html), the USFWS notes that several of the lawsuits were bundled together and resolved in 2011 through legal settlements. The agency agreed to make listing decisions by 2017 for more than 250 species that were candidate species as of 2010. Nevertheless, it remains to be seen if Congress will adequately fund the agency for this endeavor.

NOTABLE LISTED SPECIES. Many of the species listed under the ESA are obscure animals, but some listings make national headlines. This was the case in 2008, when the polar bear was listed as threatened. (See Table 3.11.) The listing was the first ever attributed to the effects of climate change. Scientists believe that polar bears are imperiled because of the melting and thinning of sea ice in their Arctic habitat, including parts of Alaska. Many environmental and conservation groups hoped the listing would put an end to oil and gas exploration in those regions. The USFWS, however, issued a special rule under the ESA that permits such exploration to continue. As of May 2013, the agency (http://ecos.fws.gov/species Profile/profile/speciesProfile.action?spcode=A0IJ) did not provide population data for the polar bear on its web page that profiles the polar bear. Nevertheless, in "Polar Bear: *Ursus maritimus*" (October 2009, http://www.fws.gov/ endangered/esa-library/pdf/polar_bear.pdf), the USFWS estimates that as of October 2009 there were 20,000 to 25,000 polar bears worldwide.

In December 2010 the federal government proposed a threatened listing under the ESA for four subspecies of ringed seals and two populations of bearded seals that are also believed to be imperiled because of climate change. The article "Alaska: Protection Sought for Seals" (Associated Press, December 3, 2010) notes that the seals are the "main prey of Alaska's polar bears" and are imperiled because of the "early breakup" of ice during seal pup-rearing season. In December 2012, NOAA officially listed the seals under the ESA, as recorded in the *Federal Register* (vol. 77, no. 249, December 28, 2012). The listings became effective in February 2013. In "Bearded Seal (*Erignathus barbatus*)" (December 21, 2012, http:// www.nmfs.noaa.gov/pr/species/mammals/pinnipeds/beard edseal.htm), NOAA states that one stock of bearded seals—the Alaska stock—is found in U.S. waters. The agency estimates the stock population at 250,000 to 300,000 animals, but indicates that abundance and population trends for the animal are not known. Likewise, in "Ringed Seal (*Phoca hispida*)" (December 21, 2012, http://www.nmfs.noaa.gov/pr/species/mammals/pinnipeds/ ringedseal.htm), NOAA notes that the only U.S. stock of ringed seals is the Alaska stock, which numbers about 249,000 animals. Again, population trends for the animal are unknown.

Another species making headlines because of an environmental problem is the bluefin tuna. This large fish is an extremely popular food fish, particularly in Japan. Andrew W. Lehren and Justin Gillis report in "Endangered-Species Status Is Sought for Bluefin Tuna" (NYTimes.com, June 23, 2010) that in May 2010 the Center for Biological Diversity, an environmental group, petitioned the U.S. government to list the species as endangered. The action was spurred by fears that the large oil spill that occurred in the Gulf of Mexico during the spring of 2010 (following the explosion of the Deepwater Horizon oil-drilling rig) dealt a devastating blow to the species' survival. Lehren and Gillis state that the Gulf of Mexico is "a prime spawning ground" for the bluefin tuna. In "Atlantic Bluefin Tuna (*Thunnus thynnus*)" (February 27, 2013, http://www.nmfs.noaa.gov/pr/species/fish/blue fintuna.htm), NOAA notes that in May 2011 it found the listing was not warranted and designated the species a "species of concern," which is NMFS terminology for a candidate species.

THE FIGHT OVER WOLVES. As noted earlier, a listing under the ESA makes it illegal for people to harm a species. Nevertheless, endangered species that pose a threat to humans and livestock can be killed under certain circumstances. Red wolves once ranged throughout the eastern and south-central United States, while gray wolves, which are sometimes called timber wolves (see Figure 3.3), were widely found across the country. In 1967 red and gray wolves were listed as endangered because centuries of extermination had severely depleted their numbers. During the 1990s the U.S. government began moving gray wolves from Canada and reintroducing them to certain areas of the western United States. This was highly controversial and drew strong condemnation from ranchers and other livestock owners. Some of the gray wolf populations were designated as "nonessential experimental populations." This designation allowed government agencies and private citizens flexibility in controlling the wolves. For example, they could be killed, moved, or harassed to protect domestic livestock. By the 21st century gray wolf populations in some states had reached the government's recovery goals. Attempts to delist these populations, however, have been met with court challenges by some animal conservation groups. Before the species can be delisted, the USFWS requires that state and tribal governments have approved wolf management plans in place that will protect both the wolves and human interests.

As of May 2013, the USFWS (http://ecos.fws.gov/speciesProfile/profile/speciesProfile.action?spcode=A00D) recognized five different populations of gray wolves. Three of the populations have been delisted because of

FIGURE 3.3

A timber wolf. (© *Geoffrey Kuchera/Shutterstock.com.*)

recovery. They are found in the eastern areas of North Dakota and South Dakota and eastward to Ohio. A nonessential experimental population lives in portions of Arizona, New Mexico, and Texas. Gray wolves in much of the remaining United States (excluding Alaska) were listed as endangered under the ESA.

INTERESTS OF HUMANS VERSUS THOSE OF ENDANGERED SPECIES. Protecting endangered and threatened species becomes extremely controversial when it threatens human economic interests. One example is the northern spotted owl. Its primary habitat is among old-growth trees (greater than 100 years old) in the coniferous forests of the Pacific Northwest, which were heavily logged during the 1960s. John Weier reports in "Spotting the Spotted Owl" (June 15, 1999, http://earthobservatory.nasa.gov/Study/SpottedOwls/) that in 1972 researchers at Oregon State University estimated that 85% to 90% of the owl's suitable habitat had already been eliminated. The researchers assessed the future harvest plans of major logging companies and learned that most of the remaining old-growth trees in these forests were also to be cut down. The resulting publicity caused a major showdown between environmental conservation groups and the logging industry.

Environmental activists chained themselves to trees and damaged logging equipment to protest the logging of the old-growth forests. Protest marches captured national headlines. There was tremendous political pressure to protect the owl's remaining habitat, particularly because approximately half of it was on federal lands. Since the mid-1980s the U.S. Forest Service has tried to develop plans for managing federal forests in the Pacific Northwest that balance timber harvesting with habitat protection. Neither side has been happy with the proposals. The timber industry complains that protecting owls puts loggers out of work. Environmentalists believe all old-growth forests should be saved. In 1990 the USFWS added the northern spotted owl to the federal list of threatened species. The decision followed years of study and lawsuits filed by environmental groups and representatives of the timber industry.

The legal battles continued throughout the 1990s and into the 21st century. In 1993 the administration of President Bill Clinton (1946–) formulated the Northwest Forest Plan (NWFP; November 28, 2006, http://www.reo.gov/general/aboutNWFP.htm) in a futile attempt to satisfy both sides. The plan includes measures that are designed to protect the northern spotted owl's habitat. Critics contend that this protection has caused people to lose jobs in the forest products industry. Nevertheless, the NWFP has continued to be implemented by subsequent administrations, most recently the administration of President Barack Obama (1961–).

In June 2011 the USFWS published *Revised Recovery Plan for the Northern Spotted Owl (Strix occidentalis caurina)* (http://ecos.fws.gov/docs/recovery_plan/Revised NSORecPlan2011_1.pdf). The agency notes that "loss of habitat due to timber harvest has been greatly reduced on Federal lands over the past two decades." The USFWS states, however, that "many populations of spotted owls continue to decline." Although human-caused habitat loss and degradation still pose a threat to northern spotted owls, the agency indicates that a significant threat to the species' survival is habitat competition from larger and more aggressive barred owls. The USFWS set a 30-year timetable for delisting the northern spotted owl from the ESA because of recovery.

Conflicts between conservation and economic interests have raged in the United States over the protection of other animal species. These include snail darters in the Tennessee River valley, gopher tortoises in Florida, jaguars in southern Arizona and New Mexico, and coho salmon and sucker fish in Oregon's Klamath River basin.

INTERNATIONAL EFFORTS. On the international front, endangered wild animals are protected by CITES. Under the ESA, the United States participates in CITES to prohibit trade in listed species.

CITES includes three lists:

- Appendix I—species for which no commercial trade is allowed. Noncommercial trade is permitted if it does not jeopardize species survival in the wild. Importers and exporters of Appendix I species must obtain permits.

- Appendix II—species for which commercial trade is tightly regulated and managed with permits.

- Appendix III—species that may be negatively affected by commercial trade. Permits are used to monitor trade in these species.

The listing of any species in Appendix I or II requires approval by a two-thirds majority of CITES member nations. The CITES appendixes list thousands of animals from all over the world. Animals of major international concern include Asian and African elephants and primates. These species are imperiled because of a variety of factors, including loss of habitat and poaching (illegal hunting). The latter is largely driven by consumer demand for ivory from elephant tusks and for bushmeat (meat from animals, such as primates, that are found in the wilds of tropical regions).

WILDLIFE-RELATED RECREATION

The USFWS conducts a national survey on hunting, fishing, and other wildlife-related activities every five years. As of May 2013, the most recent survey was conducted in 2011 and published in 2012. In *2011 National Survey of Fishing, Hunting, and Wildlife-Associated Recreation* (December 2012, http://digitalmedia.fws.gov/utils/getfile/collection/document/id/860/filename/861.pdf), the USFWS finds that 90.1 million U.S. residents aged 16 years and older participated in wildlife-related recreation in 2011 and spent $144.7 billion on these activities. (See Table 3.13.) The largest number (71.8 million) were wildlife watchers, meaning that they fed, observed, or photographed wildlife around their home or away from home. Wildlife watchers spent $54.9 billion on these activities in 2011. Hunting and angling (fishing) were also popular pastimes, with 37.4 million people participating in these recreational activities. This number included 33.1 million anglers and 13.7 million hunters. Note that 9.4 million of the survey respondents reported both fishing and hunting activities. Total hunting and fishing expenditures amounted to $89.8 billion.

Participation rates in hunting and fishing are of particular importance to the USFWS and to state fish and wildlife agencies because the agencies collect taxes and fees that are associated with these activities. These

TABLE 3.13

Wildlife-related recreation statistics, 2011

Participants	90.1 million
Expenditures	$144.7 billion
Sportspersons	
Total participants[a]	37.4 million
Anglers	33.1 million
Hunters	13.7 million
Total days	836 million
Fishing	554 million
Hunting	282 million
Total expenditures	$89.8 billion
Fishing	41.8 billion
Hunting	33.7 billion
Unspecified	14.3 billion
Wildlife-watchers	
Total participants[b]	71.8 million
Around the home	68.6 million
Away from home	22.5 million
Total expenditures	$54.9 billion

[a]9.4 million both fished and hunted.
[b]19.3 million wildlife watched both around the home and away from home.

SOURCE: "Total Wildlife-Related Recreation," in *2011 National Survey of Fishing, Hunting, and Wildlife-Associated Recreation*, U.S. Department of the Interior, U.S. Fish and Wildlife Service and U.S. Department of Commerce, U.S. Census Bureau, December 2012, http://digitalmedia.fws .gov/utils/getfile/collection/document/id/860/filename/861.pdf (accessed March 16, 2013)

FIGURE 3.4

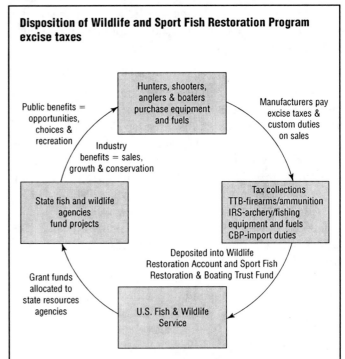

Disposition of Wildlife and Sport Fish Restoration Program excise taxes

SOURCE: "Cycle of Success," in *Wildlife and Sport Fish Restoration Program*, U.S. Department of the Interior, U.S. Fish and Wildlife Service, June 2011, http://wsfrprograms.fws.gov/Subpages/AboutUs/ WSFRProgramBrochure2011.pdf (accessed March 18, 2013)

FIGURE 3.5

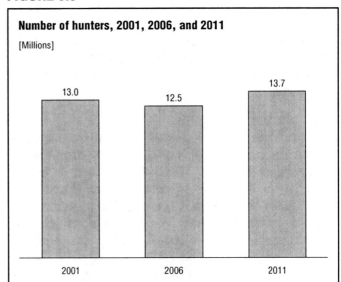

Number of hunters, 2001, 2006, and 2011

SOURCE: "Number of Hunters," in *2011 National Survey of Fishing, Hunting, and Wildlife-Associated Recreation*, U.S. Department of the Interior, U.S. Fish and Wildlife Service and U.S. Department of Commerce, U.S. Census Bureau, December 2012, http://digitalmedia .fws.gov/utils/getfile/collection/document/id/860/filename/861.pdf (accessed March 16, 2013)

moneys include fees for hunting and fishing licenses, tags, and permits and a federal excise tax on certain hunting and fishing supplies. The excise tax supports the federal Wildlife and Sport Fish Restoration Program. (See Figure 3.4.) The collected funds are allocated to state fish and wildlife agencies for them to spend on wildlife-related programs. In the press release "U.S. Fish and Wildlife Service Announces $882.4 Million in User-Generated Funding to State Wildlife Agencies" (March 21, 2013, http://www.fws.gov/midwest/news/626.html), the USFWS states that more than $882.4 million collected in 2012 would be "distributed to state and territorial fish and wildlife agencies to fund fish and wildlife conservation and recreation projects across the nation."

Hunting

The number of people participating in hunting declined from 13 million in 2001 to 12.5 million in 2006 and then increased to 13.7 million in 2011. (See Figure 3.5.) The number of days and the amount of money that was spent by hunters followed a similar trend. (See Figure 3.6 and Figure 3.7.) As shown in Figure 3.8, the vast majority of hunters surveyed in 2011 (nearly 11.6 million) pursued big game, such as deer, elk, bears, and wild turkeys. Small game, migratory birds, and other prey were far less popular. Deer were, by far, the most hunted big game animal. (See Table 3.14.) Almost 94% of big game hunters hunted deer in 2011. Nearly 5 million hunters reported hunting small game, such as squirrels, rabbits, and pheasants. Migratory birds, such as ducks, doves, and geese, were the targets for 2.6 million hunters. Note that some hunters hunt multiple types of animals.

FIGURE 3.6

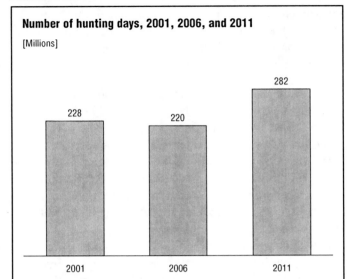

Number of hunting days, 2001, 2006, and 2011

[Millions]

SOURCE: "Days of Hunting," in *2011 National Survey of Fishing, Hunting, and Wildlife-Associated Recreation*, U.S. Department of the Interior, U.S. Fish and Wildlife Service and U.S. Department of Commerce, U.S. Census Bureau, December 2012, http://digitalmedia .fws.gov/utils/getfile/collection/document/id/860/filename/861.pdf (accessed March 16, 2013)

FIGURE 3.7

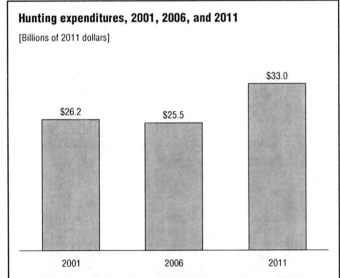

Hunting expenditures, 2001, 2006, and 2011

[Billions of 2011 dollars]

SOURCE: "Hunting Expenditures," in *2011 National Survey of Fishing, Hunting, and Wildlife-Associated Recreation*, U.S. Department of the Interior, U.S. Fish and Wildlife Service and U.S. Department of Commerce, U.S. Census Bureau, December 2012, http://digitalmedia .fws.gov/utils/getfile/collection/document/id/860/filename/861.pdf (accessed March 16, 2013)

FIGURE 3.8

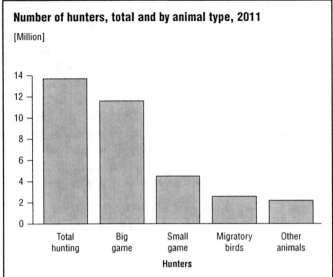

Number of hunters, total and by animal type, 2011

[Million]

SOURCE: Adapted from "Hunting," in *2011 National Survey of Fishing, Hunting, and Wildlife-Associated Recreation*, U.S. Department of the Interior, U.S. Fish and Wildlife Service and U.S. Department of Commerce, U.S. Census Bureau, December 2012, http://digitalmedia .fws.gov/utils/getfile/collection/document/id/860/filename/861.pdf (accessed March 16, 2013)

TABLE 3.14

Number of hunters and hunting days, by animal, 2011

[In millions]

Type of hunting	Hunters	Days
Big game, total	**11.6**	**212**
Deer	10.9	168
Wild turkey	3.1	33
Elk	0.9	8
Bear	0.5	5
Small game, total	**4.5**	**51**
Squirrel	1.7	21
Rabbit and hare	1.5	17
Pheasant	1.5	10
Quail	0.8	9
Grouse/prairie chicken	0.8	8
Migratory birds, total	**2.6**	**23**
Ducks	1.4	15
Doves	1.3	7
Geese	0.8	9

SOURCE: "Selected Game by Type of Hunting," in *2011 National Survey of Fishing, Hunting, and Wildlife-Associated Recreation*, U.S. Department of the Interior, U.S. Fish and Wildlife Service and U.S. Department of Commerce, U.S. Census Bureau, December 2012, http://digitalmedia.fws .gov/utils/getfile/collection/document/id/860/filename/861.pdf (accessed March 16, 2013)

OPPOSITION TO HUNTING. Hunting is bitterly opposed by some animal protection groups. They claim that hunters injure millions of animals; damage habitats; and disrupt the eating, migration, hibernation, and mating habits of animals. For example, the animal protection group In Defense of Animals complains in "Hunting— 'The Murderous Business'" (2013, http://www.idausa.org/ campaigns/wild-free2/habitats-campaign/anti-hunting/) that "wildlife management, population control and wildlife conservation are euphemisms for killing—hunting, trapping and fishing for fun. A percentage of the wild animal population is specifically mandated to be killed. Hunters want us to believe that killing animals equals population control equals conservation, when in fact hunting causes overpopulation of deer, the hunters' preferred victim species, destroys animal families, and leads to ecological disruption as well as skewed population dynamics."

HUNTING AND TRAPPING ON NATIONAL WILDLIFE REFUGES. Most people assume that national wildlife refuges are truly refuges, where animals are protected from hunting and trapping. Federal law, however, allows the government to permit secondary uses, such as hunting, on wildlife refuges if a review of the potential effects indicates that protected wildlife will not be adversely affected. Other allowed secondary uses include fishing, wildlife watching, and environmental education programs.

The USFWS notes in "Where Can I Go Hunting?" (2013, http://www.fws.gov/hunting/wherego.html) that hunting was permitted on 317 of the nation's more than 550 national wildlife refuges.

A killing method that receives much criticism from animal protection groups is the trapping of fur-bearing animals. Welfarists consider traps to be especially cruel because the panicked animals are often trapped for a long period before being discovered and killed; sometimes they chew off their own limbs to escape. Trapping is used as a control method on federal lands, including refuges. It is done by refuge staff, by trappers under contract to the refuges, and by members of the public who obtain special permits.

HUNTING AS A WILDLIFE CONTROL AND CONSERVATION METHOD. Government wildlife agencies maintain that hunting is necessary to manage wildlife populations. Some animal protection groups are openly skeptical to the idea that hunting is an effective solution to overpopulation. They note that hunters seek out not starving animals but large and healthy ones.

Deer are the animals most often associated with hunts that are designed to prevent overpopulation. The deer population exploded during the latter part of the 20th century for a variety of reasons, including a lack of natural predators. The USFWS and state wildlife agencies commonly justify hunting as a humane method of killing deer that would otherwise starve because of overpopulation. By contrast, animal welfare groups believe hunting actually aggravates population problems, claiming it upsets the natural ratio between bucks (male deer) and does (female deer) and results in higher reproduction rates. In Defense of Animals believes that sport hunting should be banned and that natural predators, such as mountain lions and wolves, should be reintroduced wherever possible to control deer populations.

Hunters defend their sport and their role in conserving wildlife just as vigorously. The U.S. Sportsmen's Alliance (USSA) and the Safari Club International (SCI) are major groups that represent the interests of hunters. The USSA operates the Sportsmen's Legal Defense Fund (SLDF). The SLDF and the SCI intervene in lawsuits that are filed by antihunting groups against government wildlife management and natural resources agencies. The SCI also operates Sportsmen against Hunger, a program that donates wild game meat to hunger-relief agencies.

Hunting proponents note that hunting fees support government conservation programs. In "Federal Duck Stamp Office: What Are Duck Stamps?" (March 8, 2013, http://www.fws.gov/duckstamps/Info/Stamps/stampinfo.htm), the USFWS indicates the duck stamp has raised over $800 million since its inception in 1934, and this money has purchased or leased more than 6 million acres (2.4 million ha) of land for the wildlife refuge system. Many private organizations raise money and team with government agencies to conserve or enhance lands that support wildlife. Nevertheless, some of these organizations, such as Ducks Unlimited and Pheasants Forever, engage in conservation primarily to ensure that there will be enough animals to hunt. Other private organizations neither condone nor advocate hunting but do focus primarily on the benefits of conservation to humans.

Likewise, critics claim the government uses money that is obtained from hunting fees to set aside more areas for hunting. They want greater focus on activities such as wildlife watching and environmental education at wildlife refuges. The USFWS indicates in *2011 National Survey of Fishing, Hunting, and Wildlife-Associated Recreation* that the number of wildlife watchers increased from 66.1 million in 2001 to 71.1 million in 2006 to 71.8 million in 2011. (See Figure 3.9.) The number of days

FIGURE 3.9

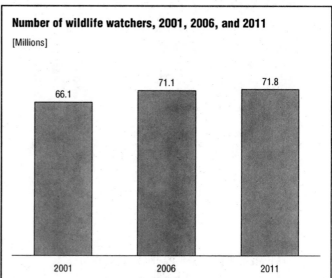

Number of wildlife watchers, 2001, 2006, and 2011

[Millions]

SOURCE: "Number of Wildlife Watchers," in *2011 National Survey of Fishing, Hunting, and Wildlife-Associated Recreation*, U.S. Department of the Interior, U.S. Fish and Wildlife Service and U.S. Department of Commerce, U.S. Census Bureau, December 2012, http://digitalmedia.fws.gov/utils/getfile/collection/document/id/860/filename/861.pdf (accessed March 16, 2013)

spent away from home watching wildlife decreased from 372 million in 2001 to 352 million in 2006 and then declined to 336 million in 2011. (See Figure 3.10.) The expenditures of wildlife watchers increased from $48.8 billion in 2001 to $51.1 billion in 2006 to $54.9 billion in 2011. (See Figure 3.11.)

FIGURE 3.10

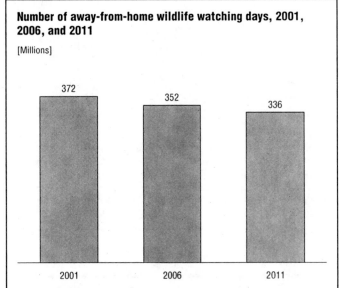

Number of away-from-home wildlife watching days, 2001, 2006, and 2011

[Millions]

SOURCE: "Days of Away-from-Home Wildlife Watching," in *2011 National Survey of Fishing, Hunting, and Wildlife-Associated Recreation*, U.S. Department of the Interior, U.S. Fish and Wildlife Service and U.S. Department of Commerce, U.S. Census Bureau, December 2012, http://digitalmedia.fws.gov/utils/getfile/collection/document/id/860/filename/861.pdf (accessed March 16, 2013)

FIGURE 3.11

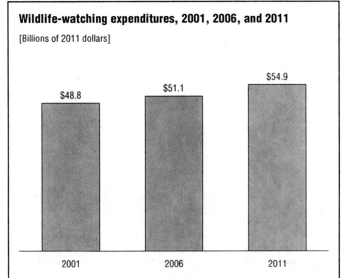

Wildlife-watching expenditures, 2001, 2006, and 2011

[Billions of 2011 dollars]

SOURCE: "Wildlife-Watching Expenditures," in *2011 National Survey of Fishing, Hunting, and Wildlife-Associated Recreation*, U.S. Department of the Interior, U.S. Fish and Wildlife Service and U.S. Department of Commerce, U.S. Census Bureau, December 2012, http://digitalmedia.fws.gov/utils/getfile/collection/document/id/860/filename/861.pdf (accessed March 16, 2013)

TROPHY HUNTING AND CANNED HUNTS. Trophy hunting is the hunting of animals, particularly exotic species, for collection of the carcasses or parts thereof (such as the head or horns) as trophies, or symbols, of the hunter's conquest over the animal. One type of trophy hunting conducted by commercial enterprises is called canned hunting. This is a type of hunting in which animals are fenced in or otherwise enclosed in a space for the enjoyment of trophy hunters.

The Humane Society of the United States (HSUS) estimates that there are hundreds of canned (or captive) hunt operators in the United States. Many offer a "no kill, no pay" policy. The most common animals involved in canned hunting are exotic species of antelope, bears, big cats, cattle, deer, goats, sheep, swine, and zebras. Hunters generally pay a set price for each exotic animal that is killed.

The HSUS and other animal welfare groups are opposed to all types of canned hunting. They consider it unsportsmanlike and cruel. Animal welfare groups believe many relatively tame animals that are dumped by circuses, exhibitors, and zoos wind up being the victims of canned hunts. These animals are not afraid of humans and make easy targets for trophy hunters. There are many surplus exotic animals in the United States because of overbreeding. The HSUS believes canned hunts provide a financial incentive that aggravates the problem. Unwanted and purposely overbred exotic animals are passed on by breeders and dealers to game and hunting preserves that specialize in canned hunts.

RECREATIONAL FISHING. According to the USFWS, in *2011 National Survey of Fishing, Hunting, and Wildlife-Associated Recreation*, the number of U.S. residents aged 16 years and older participating in recreational/sport fishing (or angling) decreased from 34.1 million in 2001 to 30 million in 2006 and then increased to 33.1 million in 2011. (See Figure 3.12.) The number of days spent fishing by the anglers in each of these years followed a similar pattern. (See Figure 3.13.) However, fishing expenditures increased from $45.3 billion in 2001 to $47 billion in 2006, and then decreased to $41.8 billion in 2011. (See Figure 3.14.) As shown in Table 3.15, 83% of the anglers surveyed said they fished for freshwater species in 2011, while 27% targeted saltwater species. Note that the values do not sum to 100% because some anglers fished for both freshwater and saltwater species.

The federal government's Sport Fish Restoration Program funnels excise tax receipts from the sale of certain fishing and boating equipment to various federal and state agencies and programs that are devoted to furthering sports fishing. In a certificate of apportionment (March 19, 2013, http://wsfrprograms.fws.gov/Subpages/GrantPrograms/SFR/SFRFinalApportionment2013.pdf),

FIGURE 3.12

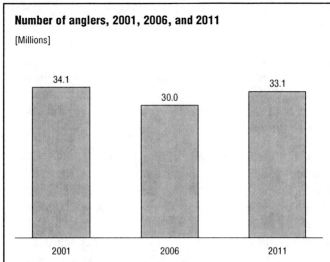

Number of anglers, 2001, 2006, and 2011

[Millions]

SOURCE: "Number of Anglers," in *2011 National Survey of Fishing, Hunting, and Wildlife-Associated Recreation*, U.S. Department of the Interior, U.S. Fish and Wildlife Service and U.S. Department of Commerce, U.S. Census Bureau, December 2012, http://digitalmedia.fws.gov/utils/getfile/collection/document/id/860/filename/861.pdf (accessed March 16, 2013)

FIGURE 3.13

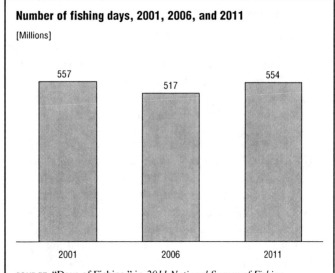

Number of fishing days, 2001, 2006, and 2011

[Millions]

SOURCE: "Days of Fishing," in *2011 National Survey of Fishing, Hunting, and Wildlife-Associated Recreation*, U.S. Department of the Interior, U.S. Fish and Wildlife Service and U.S. Department of Commerce, U.S. Census Bureau, December 2012, http://digitalmedia.fws.gov/utils/getfile/collection/document/id/860/filename/861.pdf (accessed March 16, 2013)

the USFWS announced how $359.9 million would be dispersed for FY 2013.

WILD ANIMAL COMMODITIES

Many wild animals are killed purely for their fur or parts. The most common wildlife commodities are:

- Fur from bears, beavers, foxes, minks, rabbits, and seals
- Hides from leopards, tigers, and other big cats

FIGURE 3.14

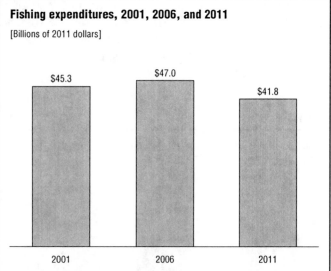

Fishing expenditures, 2001, 2006, and 2011

[Billions of 2011 dollars]

SOURCE: "Fishing Expenditures," in *2011 National Survey of Fishing, Hunting, and Wildlife-Associated Recreation*, U.S. Department of the Interior, U.S. Fish and Wildlife Service and U.S. Department of Commerce, U.S. Census Bureau, December 2012, http://digitalmedia.fws.gov/utils/getfile/collection/document/id/860/filename/861.pdf (accessed March 16, 2013)

TABLE 3.15

Breakdown of fishing participants, days, and expenditures, by category, 2011

[U.S. population 16 years old and older. Numbers in thousands.]

	2011	
	Number	Percent
Anglers, total	**33,112**	**100**
All freshwater	27,547	83
Freshwater, except Great Lakes	27,060	82
Great Lakes	1,665	5
Saltwater	8,889	27
Days, total	**553,841**	**100**
All freshwater	455,862	82
Freshwater, except Great Lakes	443,223	80
Great Lakes	19,661	4
Saltwater	99,474	18
Fishing, total (2011 dollars)	**$41,788,936**	**100**
Trip-related	21,789,465	52
Equipment, total	15,506,433	37
Fishing equipment	6,141,895	15
Auxiliary equipment	1,106,865	3
Special equipment	8,257,673	20
Other	4,493,037	11

SOURCE: Adapted from "2001–2011 Fishing Participants, Days, and Expenditures," in *2011 National Survey of Fishing, Hunting, and Wildlife-Associated Recreation*, U.S. Department of the Interior, U.S. Fish and Wildlife Service and U.S. Department of Commerce, U.S. Census Bureau, December 2012, http://digitalmedia.fws.gov/utils/getfile/collection/document/id/860/filename/861.pdf (accessed March 16, 2013)

- Reindeer antlers; rhinoceros horns; shark fins; snake blood; various organs; and the penises from rhinoceroses, seals, and tigers (these items are believed by some people to act as aphrodisiacs—supplements that enhance sexual performance)

- Bones, brains, claws, eyeballs, fangs, paws, tails, and internal organs from tigers (all are used in traditional Asian medicines)
- Bile from bears, snakes, and wild boars (used in aphrodisiacs and traditional Asian medicines)
- Elephant tusks (for ivory)
- Bear paws (considered a delicacy in some Asian countries)

Seals

Many animals used in the fur trade are bred and raised in cages on farms. Some animals, however, are still trapped or killed in the wild, particularly seals. The killing of seals for fur was a high-profile issue of the animal rights movement during the 1970s. Greenpeace activists traveled to hunting areas to splash dye on seals and draw media attention to their slaughter.

The killing of seals caught public attention because seals—usually babies only a few weeks old—on ice floes were clubbed in the head, then dragged with hooks across the ice. Animal welfarists who witnessed seal hunts claimed to have seen seals skinned while still alive and conscious. Seal hunters argued that clubbing was humane and killed the seals quickly. Seals swimming in the water were shot instead of clubbed. Critics claimed that many of these seals were injured and drowned after they sank below the surface.

In 1972 the United States banned the importation of all seal products. A decade later the European Union put strict importation limits on seal pelts. As a result, Canada's seal fur industry was nearly eliminated. However, in "New Demand Drives Canada's Baby Seal Hunt" (NYTimes.com, April 5, 2004), Clifford Krauss reports that Canada's seal fur industry survived because of high demand from eastern Europe and China. Krauss notes that baby seals are still clubbed to death on the ice, but new regulations mean that only seals older than two weeks are subject to the hunt. At this age the seals have lost their pure white fur and developed a gray spotted coat. According to Krauss, the renewed hunt has not aroused widespread public protest because "tougher hunting rules, including stiffer regulations to avert skinning the seals alive, have muted the effort to stop the hunt and eased the consciences of Canadians."

In 2004 many animal rights and welfare groups launched new campaigns against Canadian seal hunting. Dozens of groups, including the American Society for the Prevention of Cruelty to Animals, the HSUS, the Fund for Animals, and Greenpeace, joined together to form the Protect Seals Network. The network calls for a boycott of Canadian seafood to protest the seal hunt. In 2009 the European Union enacted a ban on the marketing of seal products. The ban took effect in 2010. Despite repeated court challenges from the sealing industry, as of May 2013 the ban was still in effect. According to the HSUS, in "Canada's Commercial Seal Slaughter Explained" (2013, https://secure.humanesociety.org/site/SPageServer?pagename=seals_infographic&s_src=web_ig_redirect2013), other countries that have recently banned the trade of seal products include Russia, Belarus, and Kazakhstan in 2011 and Taiwan in 2013.

The Humane Society International (HSI) notes in "Nearly 60,000 Seals Killed without Quota in Commercial Seal Hunt" (http://www.hsi.org/world/canada/news/releases/2013/04/no_seal_quota_041813.html) that as of April 18, 2013, nearly 60,000 seals had been killed during the opening weeks of the 2013 sealing season in eastern Canada. The organization blames government subsidies for funding the hunt despite the lack of markets for seal products. The HSI states that "global markets for seal products have closed, and there is little demand for seal fur as a result. However, $3.6 million in financing from the Newfoundland government is funding a Norwegian owned company to purchase seal furs this year."

Big Cats

A huge market exists for wild animal parts throughout Asia, particularly in China. Many parts are used in traditional remedies for various illnesses and diseases. In addition, animal penises are sold as aphrodisiacs. The animal most sought after is the tiger. Tiger hides are popular, and tiger bones are ground up and used in medicines for rheumatism and arthritis. Tiger penises are used in aphrodisiacs, soups, and various medicines.

Tigers are listed as endangered under the ESA. According to the USFWS, many tigers are worth more dead than alive. The animals breed easily in captivity and have been extremely overbred in the United States. Baby tigers are popular at animal parks and zoos, but they grow up quickly and are expensive to care for as adults. Unwanted and overbred tigers from game parks, refuges, and zoos can wind up in the hands of unscrupulous dealers who kill the animals for their valuable parts. Federal law allows the possession of captive-bred tigers, but only if their use enhances the propagation or survival of the species. It is illegal to kill the animals for profit or to sell their hide, meat, or parts in interstate commerce. It is not illegal to donate the animals.

Elephants

Ivory is a hard, white substance that composes the tusks of African elephants and some male Asian elephants. Demand for ivory was so high during the 20th century that hundreds of thousands of elephants were poached for it. Conservation groups estimate that more than half the population of African elephants was wiped out during the 1980s alone. In 1990 an international ban on ivory trade was established under CITES. Even though the ban helped to severely reduce elephant poaching, it did not eliminate the problem. It is believed that numerous elephants are still killed illegally each year for their ivory. Dan Levin states in "The Price of Ivory: From Elephants' Mouths, an Illicit Trail to China" (NYTimes.com, March 1, 2013) that "since the beginning of 2012, more than 32,000 elephants have been illegally killed, according to the Born Free Foundation, a wildlife organization."

WHALING, DOLPHIN HUNTING, AND COMMERCIAL FISHING

Whaling

Whaling has been an industry in northern seas for hundreds of years. The blubber, bones, and meat from whales were popular commodities in many markets. This market demand led to the introduction of more powerful ships and intense whaling methods during the 19th century. By the beginning of the 20th century whaling had taken a significant toll on whale populations. The United States banned commercial whaling in 1928. In 1946 the International Whaling Commission (IWC) was founded by 24 member countries (including the United States) as a means of self-regulating the industry and limiting the number and types of whales that could be killed. In 1986 all IWC member countries agreed to ban commercial whaling after most whale populations were placed under Appendix I of the CITES agreement. However, whaling was still allowed for so-called scientific purposes.

Conservation and animal rights groups have complained for years that some IWC member countries, particularly Japan, kill many whales under this loophole. Whalers and some scientists say that some whale species are not endangered and should be subject to controlled hunts.

In 2002 Iceland rejoined the IWC after dropping out in 1991, but with the reservation that it would not support a ban on commercial whaling. This started an internal battle within the IWC about what the commission's role should be. Some countries believe the IWC's focus should be entirely on conservation. Others want the IWC to be more industry-friendly. The IWC notes in "Membership and Contracting Governments" (http://www.iwcoffice.org/commission/members.htm) that in May 2013 it had 89 member countries.

Dolphin Hunting

In 2009 the documentary film *The Cove* brought international attention to an annual dolphin hunt that is conducted in Taiji, Japan. Japan sets an annual kill quota for various marine mammals. The article "Japan's Dolphin Hunt Sags over Mercury Fears" (Associated Press, January 31, 2008) notes that much of the hunting takes place by harpooning out at sea. The Taiji hunt, however, is accomplished by fishermen using boats to herd (or drive) dolphins into a small cove where they are slaughtered by hand. The Taiji hunt has long aroused harsh criticism from dolphin activists but is defended by the Japanese government. According to the article "Dolphin Slaughter Film a Hit at Sundance" (JapanTimes.co.jp, January 27, 2009), *The Cove* "was made secretly throughout 2007 using underwater microphones and high-definition cameras disguised as rocks, and with a camouflaged camera crew hidden on headlands." The film, which showed the bloody slaying of approximately 2,500 dolphins, won awards from the U.S. movie industry, including an Academy Award.

The film points out that some of the dolphins captured during the hunt are taken alive and sold to entertainment venues, such as aquariums and marine mammal parks. In "Dolphins Are Dying to Amuse Us" (Salon .com, August 7, 2009), Katharine Mieszkowski notes "the film argues that it's the trade in live dolphins that creates the real economic incentive for the whole cruel hunt." Although the film helped energize dolphin activists, the Taiji hunt continues to occur. One of the key people involved in the film was Ric O'Barry (1939–), the director of the Save Japan Dolphins project, which is operated by the Earth Island Institute, a nonprofit organization that is devoted to ecological causes. O'Barry was a dolphin trainer for the hit television show *Flipper*, which aired in the United States during the 1960s and greatly popularized the idea of human interaction with dolphins. O'Barry has since become a dolphin activist and outspoken critic of the captive dolphin industry. In "Taiji Slaughter Season Ends in Blood" (March 6, 2013, http://savejapandolphins.org/blog/post/taiji-slaughter-season-ends-in-blood), O'Barry notes that the most recent hunt season at Taiji lasted from September 2012 through March 2013, and it is estimated that slightly fewer than 900 dolphins were killed. In addition, an estimated 247 dolphins were captured alive for sale to entertainment venues. According to O'Barry, the number of dolphins killed in the hunt has been declining annually because of poor sales of dolphin meat, which has been shown to contain high levels of mercury.

Commercial Fishing

Demand for fish has skyrocketed since the 1980s. In the United States the NMFS tracks the commodities that are landed (brought ashore) by the commercial fishing industry. Figure 3.15 shows the number of pounds and the dollar value of commercial fish landings between 1950 and 2011. Through the mid-1970s fewer than 6 billion pounds (2.7 billion kilograms [kg]) of fish per year were landed. By 2000 this value was in excess of 8 billion pounds (3.6 billion kg) per year. After a dip between 2008 and 2010, commercial fish landings climbed

FIGURE 3.15

Pounds and dollar value of commercial fish landings, 1950–2011

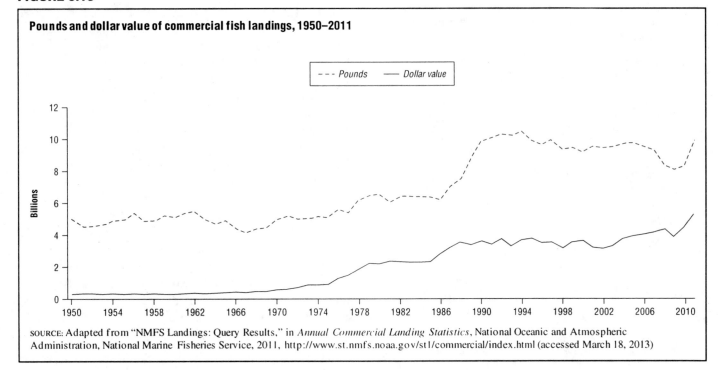

SOURCE: Adapted from "NMFS Landings: Query Results," in *Annual Commercial Landing Statistics*, National Oceanic and Atmospheric Administration, National Marine Fisheries Service, 2011, http://www.st.nmfs.noaa.gov/st1/commercial/index.html (accessed March 18, 2013)

to nearly 10 billion pounds (4.5 billion kg) in 2011. Likewise, the value of commercially fished commodities increased from less than $1 billion per year during the 1950s and 1960s to more than $3 billion per year during the first decade of the 21st century. In 2011 the value soared to more than $5.3 billion.

Table 3.16 and Table 3.17 list the top-20 fish species that were commercially landed in the United States as of March 18, 2013, by pounds and by dollars, respectively. Walleye pollock (a white fish widely used in fast-food fish sandwiches) was the number-one landed species pound-wise. Sea scallops were the highest valued species on a dollar basis.

Commercial fishing of many species is blamed for a host of environmental and conservation problems in the world's oceans. Overfishing and poor management have caused severe declines in some populations. In 2012 the Food and Agriculture Organization (FAO) of the United Nations released *The State of World Fisheries and Aquaculture, 2012* (http://www.fao.org/docrep/016/i2727e/i2727e.pdf). According to the FAO, commercial fisheries and aquaculture produced 169.8 million tons (154 million metric tons [t]) of fish in 2011, based on preliminary data. The vast majority—144.4 million tons (131 million t), or 85% of the total—was for food fish (fish for human consumption). Commercial fisheries accounted for over half (59%) of the total fish production, while aquaculture accounted for 41% of the total. The FAO divides the world's fisheries into three categories based on sustainability. More than half (57.4%) of the fisheries were considered to be fully exploited in 2009, meaning that

TABLE 3.16

Top-20 fish species commercially landed, by pounds, as of March 18, 2013

AFS species name	Pounds
Pollock, walleye	2,810,795,809
Menhaden	1,874,996,693
Cod, pacific	664,292,833
Hake, Pacific (whiting)	496,363,122
Salmon, pink	388,378,116
Sole, yellowfin	322,789,013
Squid, California market	267,983,047
Salmon, sockeye	249,532,002
Crab, blue	196,830,747
Herring, Atlantic	174,295,396
Sole, rock	130,454,657
Lobster, American	126,222,896
Shrimp, brown	125,397,040
Atka mackerel	112,595,525
Salmon, chum	102,518,542
Sardine, pacific	102,127,953
Shrimp, white	102,044,116
Herring, pacific	99,077,942
Flounder, arrowtooth	93,896,027
Rockfish, Pacific Ocean perch	80,661,902

Note: AFS = American Fisheries Society.

SOURCE: Adapted from "Annual Landings by Species for United States as of 18-MAR-13," in *Annual Commercial Landings by Group*, National Oceanic and Atmospheric Administration, National Marine Fisheries Service, March 18, 2013, http://www.st.nmfs.noaa.gov/commercial-fisheries/commercial-landings/annual-landings-with-group-subtotals/index (accessed March 18, 2013)

catches were "very close to their maximum sustainable production and have no room for further expansion and require effective management to avoid decline." Another 29.9% of fisheries in 2009 were rated as overexploited, meaning that they were "producing lower yields than

TABLE 3.17

Top-20 fish species commercially landed, by dollar value, as of March 18, 2013

AFS species name	Dollars
Scallop, sea	585,157,399
Lobster, American	422,803,014
Pollock, walleye	362,593,872
Salmon, sockeye	298,555,333
Shrimp, white	240,985,784
Shrimp, brown	215,630,447
Halibut, Pacific	213,091,697
Cod, Pacific	203,573,882
Crab, Dungeness	187,732,007
Sablefish	184,174,664
Crab, blue	175,138,202
Salmon, pink	167,484,878
Menhaden	143,679,168
Crab, snow	115,501,885
Crab, king	110,597,865
Oyster, eastern	90,519,490
Salmon, chum	80,167,341
Clam, Pacific geoduck	72,180,683
Squid, California market	66,567,098
Tuna, bigeye	59,105,917

Note: AFS = American Fisheries Society.

SOURCE: Adapted from "Annual Landings by Species for United States as of 18-MAR-13," in *Annual Commercial Landings by Group*, National Oceanic and Atmospheric Administration, National Marine Fisheries Service, March 18, 2013, http://www.st.nmfs.noaa.gov/commercial-fisheries/commercial-landings/annual-landings-with-group-subtotals/index (accessed March 18, 2013)

their biological and ecological potential and in need of strict management plans to restore their full and sustainable productivity." The remaining 12.7% of fisheries were rated by the agency as nonfully exploited.

Another criticism of commercial fishing is that it endangers marine mammals and other fish besides those the fishermen want to catch. Experts estimate that thousands of nontarget specimens (called bycatch) are killed each year after becoming entangled in fishing nets and devices. According to Earthtrust, a nonprofit wildlife conservation organization, in "Dolphin-Safe Tuna Certification Program Fact Sheet" (2013, http://www.earthtrust.org/fsa.html), approximately 7 million dolphins were killed between 1959 and 1991 because of purse seining in the eastern tropical Pacific Ocean. Purse seining is a fishing technique in which giant nets are encircled around schools of fish. It is a popular way to capture tuna. Schools of tuna are frequently accompanied by pods of dolphins. In fact, some fishermen chase and set their nets around dolphins to capture the nearby tuna. Because dolphins are mammals, they require air to breathe. The dolphins get caught and drown in the nets. Negative publicity about the problem during the 1980s led consumers to demand changes in tuna fishing and labeling.

In 1990 the Dolphin Protection Consumer Information Act was passed in the United States, establishing an official definition of "dolphin-safe" tuna. Canners must meet certain criteria before they can label their tuna dolphin safe, and U.S. fishermen have had to modify their fishing techniques to meet the criteria. Purse seining is still widely practiced by foreign fishing industries, particularly in Mexico and South America. Nevertheless, tuna products sold in the United States cannot be labeled as dolphin safe unless they meet the provisions of the 1990 law.

CHAPTER 4
FARM ANIMALS

Farm animals are animals that are kept for agricultural purposes. This includes domesticated animals such as cows and chickens, and wild animals that are raised in confinement, including mink and fish. Animals are farmed for a variety of reasons. Most are raised to be killed. Meat from cattle, hogs, and chickens provides the bulk of protein in the American diet, whereas animals with beautiful fur are killed for their pelts. However, some farm animals are more useful and profitable alive. These animals produce something of value to humans, such as milk, eggs, wool, or honey, or are farmed for their skills, such as horses, mules, and burros. Whatever the reason, the cultivation of farm animals is an enormous business.

The National Agricultural Statistics Service (NASS), a part of the U.S. Department of Agriculture (USDA), compiles and publishes data on the demographics, economic value, and health of the nation's livestock. Much of these data are released yearly, or even monthly, for the most commonly farmed animals. In addition, every five years the NASS conducts a national Census of Agriculture in which it does a comprehensive livestock count and collects detailed information on farming and ranching operations. Each census produces numerous reports on a variety of topics that are published as they become available. As of May 2013, full results for *2007 Census of Agriculture* (http://www.agcensus.usda.gov/Publications/2007/Full_Report/usv1.pdf) were available, having been published in 2009. (Participants had until May 31, 2013, to submit response forms as part of the 2012 census.)

The number of animals involved in the agricultural industry is staggering. Table 4.1 shows slaughter statistics for 2012 for a variety of farmed animals. Nearly 9 billion farm animals were slaughtered in 2012. The largest number, by far, were chickens. Nearly 8.6 billion of them were slaughtered in 2012. This was followed by 250.2 million turkeys, 113.2 million hogs, 32.6 million cattle, 24.2 million ducks, 2.2 million sheep and lambs,

731,800 goats, and 51,400 bison (American buffalo). Table 4.1 specifies the inspection status of the slaughtered animals. In "Inspection for Food Safety: The Basics" (April 24, 2012, http://www.fsis.usda.gov/Fact_Sheets/Inspection_for_Food_Safety_the_Basics/index.asp), the USDA's Food Safety and Inspection Service explains, "only federally inspected and passed products can enter interstate commerce or be exported to foreign countries." Slaughterhouses that are not federally inspected may be state-inspected slaughterhouses that process meat for in-state sales or custom slaughterhouses that process meat for personal use.

Many NASS publications focus on the number of pounds of livestock that are produced and the economic value of that production to livestock farmers. As shown in Figure 4.1, about 125 billion pounds (56.7 billion kilograms [kg]) of cattle, broilers (food chickens), hogs, and turkeys were produced in 2011, up from approximately 55 billion pounds (24.9 billion kg) in 1960. The 2011 value of production for these animals was in excess of $90 billion, up from about $16 billion in 1960. (See Figure 4.2.)

Table 4.2 shows production and consumption data for so-called red meats (i.e., meat from cattle, pigs, sheep, and lambs) and lard (pig fat) between 2003 and 2012. Approximately 48.9 billion pounds (22.2 billion kg) of these meats were produced in 2012, and 44.2 billion pounds (20 billion kg) of these meats were consumed. The estimated per capita consumption of red meat and lard in 2012 was 141 pounds (64 kg).

In 2012 more farm animals were living in the United States than there were humans on the earth. The use and well-being of these animals is of major importance to people concerned with animal rights and welfare. Animal rights activists abhor the idea that animals are commodities at all. They believe that animals should not be used for any purpose, especially to feed humans. Animal

TABLE 4.1

Slaughter statistics, selected farm animals, 2012

Data item	Number of head
Chickens, FI	8,576,194,000
Ducks, FI	24,183,000
Turkeys, FI	250,192,000
Cattle, commercial	32,646,500
Cattle, steers, commercial, FI	16,159,500
Cattle, heifers, commercial, FI	9,269,100
Cattle, cows, commercial, FI	6,445,700
Cattle, cows, (excluding milk), commercial, FI	3,344,100
Cattle, cows, milk, commercial, FI	3,101,300
Cattle, calves, commercial	772,200
Cattle, calves, commercial, FI	759,800
Cattle, calves, commercial, NFI	12,500
Goats, commercial	731,800
Goats, commercial, FI	557,900
Goats, commercial, NFI	173,800
Hogs, commercial	113,152,100
Hogs, commercial, FI	112,265,300
Hogs, barrows & gilts, commercial, FI	108,912,000
Hogs, boars, commercial, FI	344,400
Hogs, sows, commercial, FI	3,008,600
Hogs, commercial, NFI	886,800
Sheep, including lambs, commercial	2,183,000
Sheep, including lambs, commercial, FI	2,012,300
Sheep, including lambs, commercial, NFI	170,700
Bison, commercial	51,400
Bison, commercial, FI	40,900
Bison, commercial, NFI	10,300

Notes: FI = Federally inspected. NFI = Non-federally inspected.

SOURCE: Adapted from *Quick Stats*, U.S. Department of Agriculture, National Agricultural Statistics Service, 2013, http://quickstats.nass.usda.gov/ (accessed March 20, 2013)

welfarists focus their attention on the treatment of farmed animals—how they are housed, fed, transported, and slaughtered.

People in the U.S. livestock industry argue that farm animals are well treated. They point to the high productivity of the industry as proof. In other words, farm animals must be thriving because there are so many of them. The American Meat Institute (AMI; 2013, http://www.animalhandling.org/ht/d/Home/pid/25725), a trade organization that represents the U.S. meat and poultry industry, sums up this viewpoint by stating: "Optimal handling is ethically appropriate, creates positive workplaces, and ensures higher quality meat products." The link between humane animal treatment and high production of good-quality products is commonly cited by the livestock industry. Critics argue that high productivity is an indicator of the efficiency of the overall system, not the welfare of individual animals. They have a long list of complaints about how farm animals are raised and slaughtered in the United States.

Animal farming is an old and respected business. It feeds people and supplies products they want. Forcing farmers to radically change the way they treat animals might jeopardize the relatively cheap and plentiful supply of animal products that Americans enjoy. Would society tolerate this just for the sake of the animals? This is the ultimate question at the center of the farm animal debate.

FIGURE 4.1

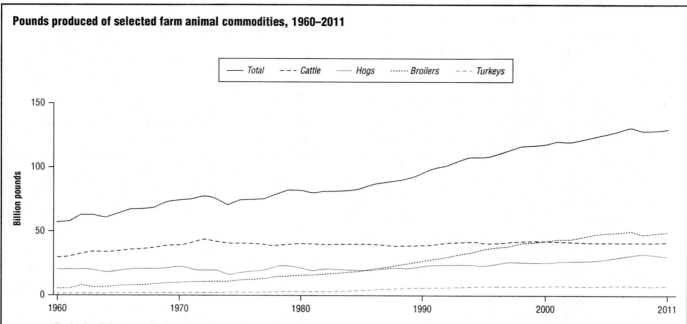

Pounds produced of selected farm animal commodities, 1960–2011

SOURCE: "Cattle, Broilers, Hogs, Turkeys Pounds Produced, 1960–2011," in *Charts and Maps: Meat Animals: Production by Year, U.S.*, U.S. Department of Agriculture, National Agricultural Statistics Service, April 26, 2012, http://www.nass.usda.gov/Charts_and_Maps/Meat_Animals_PDI/lbspr.asp (accessed March 18, 2013)

FIGURE 4.2

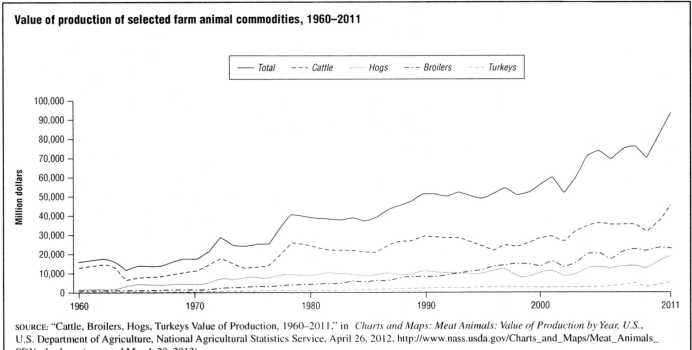

Value of production of selected farm animal commodities, 1960–2011

Legend: — Total - - - Cattle .... Hogs - · - Broilers - - - Turkeys

Y-axis: Million dollars (0 to 100,000)
X-axis: 1960 to 2011

SOURCE: "Cattle, Broilers, Hogs, Turkeys Value of Production, 1960–2011," in *Charts and Maps: Meat Animals: Value of Production by Year, U.S.,* U.S. Department of Agriculture, National Agricultural Statistics Service, April 26, 2012, http://www.nass.usda.gov/Charts_and_Maps/Meat_Animals_PDI/valprd.asp (accessed March 20, 2013)

LIVESTOCK PROTECTION LAWS

During the 1800s a number of laws were enacted in England and the United States to protect animals from abuse, neglect, and mistreatment by their owners. Some of these laws specifically included livestock, whereas others did not. Many state anticruelty laws excluded what they called "customary agricultural practices." These laws were often interpreted not to apply to animals that were raised for food.

The 28-Hour Law of 1873 was the first federal law dealing with livestock welfare. It required that livestock being transported across state lines be rested and watered at least once every 28 hours during the journey. At the time, livestock transport was done by rail, and for more than 130 years the law was only enforced on railroad transport of livestock. In 2005 the animal group Compassion over Killing conducted an undercover investigation of a pig transport operation and produced videos documenting the suffering allegedly inflicted on pigs that are forced to travel by truck for long periods. The USDA launched its own investigation after learning that more than 150 pigs transported by truck for more than 28 hours in the summer heat arrived dead at a livestock facility in Texas. Compassion over Killing and other animal welfare organizations petitioned the USDA to include truck transport under the provisions of the 28-Hour Law. In 2006 the USDA concluded that "'trucks' which operate as express carriers or common carriers" for livestock are covered under the law.

The Animal Welfare Act was enacted in 1966 to provide protection for animals that are used for certain purposes,

but the regulations enforcing the law specifically excluded livestock. The major legislation of the 20th century to affect livestock was the Humane Methods of Slaughter Act of 1958. The law required slaughter by humane methods at slaughterhouses that are subject to federal inspection. This meant that livestock had to be rendered insensitive to pain before being slaughtered. The act excluded chickens and all animals that are slaughtered using techniques associated with religious rituals. For decades, animal welfare organizations have contested the USDA policy that excludes some animals, particularly chickens and turkeys, from coverage under this law. However, repeated legal challenges to the exclusion have been rejected by the courts. In 2010 the U.S. Ninth Court of Appeals once again dismissed a case brought by the Humane Society of the United States (HSUS) to include poultry among animals protected under the act, ruling that the HSUS was unable to prove alleged injuries to poultry.

Concern Grows

Following the Humane Methods of Slaughter Act, farm animals did not receive much attention until a 1964 book by Ruth Harrison (1920–2000) was published. *Animal Machines: The New Factory Farming Industry* described the brutality that was inflicted on livestock in the United Kingdom by the modern farming industry. In 1975 Peter Singer (1946–) published *Animal Liberation: A New Ethics for Our Treatment of Animals,* which detailed similar problems on U.S. factory farms. It was also during the 1960s and 1970s that the vegetarian movement gained momentum.

TABLE 4.2

Red meat and lard production and consumption, by meat type, 2003–12

[Statistics of cattle, hogs, and sheep]

	Beef			Veal			Lamb and mutton			Pork			All meats		
		Consumption			Consumption			Consumption			Consumption			Consumption	
Year	Production	Total	Per capita	Production	Total	Per capita	Production	Total	Per capita	Production	Total	Per capita	Production	Total	Per capita
	Million pounds	Million pounds	Pounds	Million pounds	Million pounds	Pounds	Million pounds	Million pounds	Pounds	Million pounds	Million pounds	Pounds	Million pounds	Million pounds	Pounds
2003	26,339	27,000	92.9	202	204	0.7	203	367	1.3	19,966	19,443	66.9	46,710	47,013	162
2004	24,650	27,750	94.6	176	177	0.6	200	373	1.3	20,531	19,446	66.3	45,557	47,746	163
2005	24,787	27,754	93.8	165	164	0.6	191	356	1.2	20,705	19,093	64.5	45,848	47,366	160
2006	26,256	28,137	94.2	156	155	0.5	190	356	1.2	21,074	19,055	63.8	47,675	47,703	160
2007	26,523	28,141	93.3	146	145	0.5	189	385	1.3	21,962	19,763	65.5	48,817	48,434	160
2008	26,664	27,303	89.6	152	150	0.5	180	343	1.1	23,367	19,415	63.8	50,362	47,211	155
2009	26,068	26,836	87.3	147	147	0.5	177	338	1.1	23,020	19,870	64.7	49,412	47,191	154
2010	26,412	26,390	85.2	145	150	0.5	168	318	1.0	22,456	19,075	61.6	49,180	45,932	148
2011[a]	26,292	25,545	81.9	138	139	0.4	153	295	0.9	22,775	18,384	58.9	49,358	44,363	142
2012[b]	25,286	25,066	79.8	132	132	0.4	152	293	0.9	23,300	18,722	59.6	48,871	44,214	141

[a]Preliminary.

[b]Forecast.

ERS = Economic Research Service.

Notes: Carcass weight equivalent or dressed weight. Beginning in 1977, pork production was no longer reported as "pork, excluding lard." This series has been revised to reflect pork production in prior years on a dressed weight basis that is comparable with the method used to report beef, veal, and lamb and mutton. Edible offals are excluded. Shipments to the U.S. territories are included in domestic consumption.

SOURCE: "Table 7-71. Meats and Lard: Production and Consumption, United States, 2003–2012," in *Agricultural Statistics 2012*, U.S. Department of Agriculture, National Agricultural Statistics Service, 2012, http://www.nass.usda.gov/Publications/Ag_Statistics/2012/chapter07.pdf (accessed March 20, 2013)

The plight of farm animals became a major issue with animal rights activists and welfarists. During the 1980s and early 1990s several groups dedicated to livestock concerns formed organizations such as the Farm Animal Reform Movement, the Humane Farming Association, Farm Sanctuary, and the United Poultry Concerns (UPC). Devoted to the rights or welfare of farm animals, these organizations publicize abuses that occur in the agricultural industry and work to gain new legislation to protect farm animals.

As of May 2013, some of the primary goals included:

- Banning the slaughter of horses for food

- Drafting legislation for poultry that enables them to be covered under the Humane Methods of Slaughter Act

- Outlawing the keeping of veal calves and pregnant and nursing hogs in small crates to prevent them from moving

- Outlawing the keeping of chickens in so-called battery cages (small, stacked wire cages that hold several laying hens)

- Publicizing the abuse and mishandling of animals at factory farms and slaughterhouses

ANIMAL PRODUCTS

Animal products are used in many ways by modern society. People consume and wear them and buy items every day that contain animal-derived components. Animals killed for meat must be processed immediately. This means that meat animals must arrive alive at the slaughterhouse. They cannot be humanely euthanized with drugs as pets are when put to sleep because humans will be consuming them. Those parts that are not readily edible by humans are rendered into other marketable products. Bones, hooves, beaks, feet, feathers, fat, and inedible organs and tissues are recycled at one of several hundred rendering plants in the United States. The fat is processed for industrial use, and the other by-products are ground into a powder or boiled to make gelatin. Tallow (rendered fat) is used to make soap, candles, and lubricants.

According to the National Renderers Association in "U.S. Production, Consumption, and Export of Rendered Products for 2004–2009" (January 11, 2011, http://nation alrenderers.org/assets/4d2db43ddabe9d5d71000042/us _production_consumption_and_export_of_rendered_prod ucts_for_20042009.pdf), just over 18 billion pounds (8.2 billion kg) of animal by-products were produced by the rendering industry in 2009. Of this amount, roughly half was fats and greases, and the other half was ground-up bones, feathers, and other by-products.

Rendered by-products are sold to a variety of industries and become ingredients in lubricants, paints, varnishes, waxes, soaps, candles, cement, pharmaceuticals, pet food, toothpaste, and cosmetics (such as lipstick and shampoo). Gelatin is an ingredient in many food products, including some types of ice cream, yogurt, candy, and marshmallows. Before the 1990s a primary use of rendered by-products was as a protein supplement (or food source) for livestock. In 1997 the U.S. Food and Drug Administration (FDA) outlawed the use of most mammal-based protein in feed that is intended for cattle. This is to prevent the spread of disease, particularly mad cow disease. Rendering plants also process whole carcasses of farm animals that die of illness or injury and other dead animals, including euthanized pets.

ROUTINE FARMING PRACTICES

Historically, farm animals have not been covered by animal welfare legislation. As a result, some practices relating to the treatment of farm animals are considered standard by farmers but may be thought of as cruel or inhumane by animal activists and other people. Such practices include culling, castration, dehorning, branding, and various forms of physical alteration. Culling means the rejection of inferior or undesirable animals. Because it costs money to feed and care for livestock, unwanted farm animals are usually killed. This is particularly true in the hen-breeding business. Male chicks of laying breeds will never lay eggs and are not suitable meat chickens. As a result, millions of them are routinely killed each year when they are only one day old.

Another ancient farming practice is animal castration (removal of the male sex organs). Humans have used castration to control the reproduction of farm animals for centuries. This is particularly true in cattle and hog farming. Only the males with the most desirable characteristics are allowed to remain intact for breeding purposes. This is believed to be beneficial for herd management because castration reduces aggressive behavior and physical confrontations between males that might damage their meat. In addition, sexually mature males release hormones that can affect the taste of meat.

The vast majority of cattle are dehorned to make them easier to handle and to prevent them from accidentally or intentionally injuring each other. In grown cattle the fully developed horns are cut off, but a more common practice is to treat the emerging horn buds of baby calves with a caustic salve to prevent horns from developing. Branding and other forms of identification, such as ear notching, are used to distinguish ownership. Cattle and swine have their tails clipped to prevent them from chewing on each other's tails and to improve cleanliness and reduce disease. Chicken beaks are trimmed to reduce injuries that might result from the animals pecking at each other.

Castration, dehorning, branding, ear notching, tail clipping (also called "docking"), and beak trimming are widely conducted in the United States without the use of anesthetics or pain medication. These procedures are regarded as practical and necessary livestock husbandry practices by many farm animal producers and considered inhumane by many animal welfarists. Welfarists have worked with little success to achieve legislation outlawing the practices. In "Timeline of Major Farm Animal Protection Advancements" (May 3, 2013, http://www.humanesociety.org/issues/confinement_farm/timelines/timeline_farm_animal_protection.html), the HSUS lists some of the major state legislative changes that have occurred since 2002 pertaining to livestock welfare. The agency notes that cattle tail docking was outlawed in California in 2009 and in Rhode Island in 2012.

FACTORY FARMING
What Is a Farm?

The farming of livestock has changed dramatically over the past century. Many people think of a farm in a rural setting, in which a barn, several outbuildings, and fields are run by one farming family. In reality, some farms are massive industrial facilities that are owned and operated by large corporations. These are called factory farms. Even though they make up a small percentage of U.S. farms, they handle a large percentage of the animals that are killed for food in the United States.

In *2007 Census of Agriculture*, the USDA defines a farm as an establishment that produces or sells $1,000 or more of agricultural products during a year. According to the 2007 census, 2.2 million farms operated in the United States, just over half of which produced livestock.

Consolidation of Agricultural Businesses

The USDA reports in *2007 Census of Agriculture* that 1.9 million farms were owned and operated by individuals and families in 2007. About 96,000 farms were owned by corporations, but many small farms owned by individuals and families actually operate under contract to corporations. The farmers sometimes sign away ownership of their animals and are paid to raise them to a contracted age or weight. The animals are then turned over to the companies for finishing or slaughtering.

How Factory Farms Work

The most visible symbol of factory farming is the animal feeding operation (AFO). The U.S. Environmental Protection Agency (EPA) notes in "Animal Feeding Operations" (March 13, 2013, http://www.epa.gov/oecaagct/anafoidx.html#About%20Animal%20Feeding%20Operations) that AFOs are enterprises that "congregate animals, feed, manure and urine, dead animals, and production operations on a small land area. Feed is brought to the animals rather than the animals grazing or otherwise seeking feed in pastures, fields, or on rangeland." In other words, an AFO is a highly concentrated confinement area

with no pasture or grazing land. The EPA estimates there were approximately 450,000 AFOs in the United States in 2013.

AFOs allow animals to be housed, fed, medicated, and processed with the utmost efficiency. Every aspect of animal life and behavior is controlled to ensure that productivity and profits are maximized. The animals are kept in the smallest space possible and fed the cheapest food that will quickly and effectively fatten them up. Breeding facilities ensure a constant supply of replacements.

Modern technology is employed whenever it is economically feasible. Females are artificially inseminated rather than mated. Pregnancies are spaced close together to increase production. Mothers and offspring are separated quickly to keep the process moving. Antibiotics, hormones, and growth-enhancing drugs are administered to ensure rapid growth and to prevent deadly diseases. Slaughterhouses are run like assembly lines with an emphasis on speed and meat quantity.

The overwhelming advantage of the factory farming system to society is economic: satisfaction of the demand for meat at acceptable prices. Factory farming provides the United States with a continuous and relatively inexpensive meat supply. However, animal rights activists blame the factory farming system for many animal abuses. They believe the industry's emphasis on profits, efficiency, and productivity has contributed greatly to inhumane treatment and sloppy slaughtering of farm animals.

CATTLE

Cattle are bovines that descend from ancient animals called aurochs. They eat vegetation and have complex four-compartment stomachs called rumens. In nature, cattle swallow their food whole. Later, the partially digested food, or cud, is regurgitated into their mouths for them to chew. "Chewing the cud" is a well-known cattle trait. The natural life span for cattle is 20 to 25 years.

There are many different breeds of cattle. Some are specially bred for meat (such as Angus and Hereford), whereas others are bred to produce milk (such as Jerseys). Adult female cattle are called cows. They produce milk for their newborn calves for months. People learned long ago to take calves away from their mothers and collect the milk for human consumption. Young female cows that have not yet given birth are called heifers. Uncastrated adult male cattle are called bulls. They are used only for breeding purposes. Male cattle castrated before they reach sexual maturity are called steers. They are a major source of beef in the United States.

There were nearly 98 million cattle on U.S. farms as of July 1, 2012. (See Figure 4.3.) The inventory was down considerably from the early 1980s, when it topped 120 million head.

FIGURE 4.3

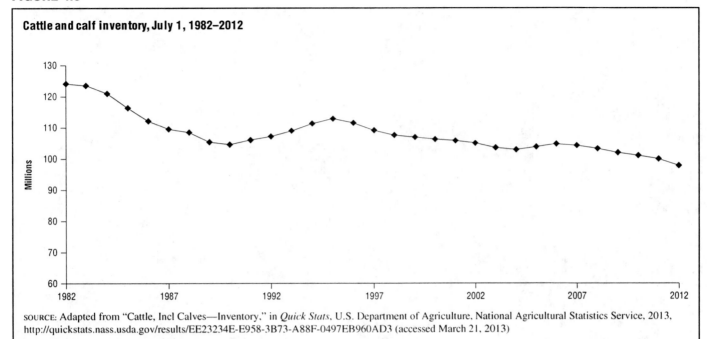

Cattle and calf inventory, July 1, 1982–2012

SOURCE: Adapted from "Cattle, Incl Calves—Inventory," in *Quick Stats*, U.S. Department of Agriculture, National Agricultural Statistics Service, 2013, http://quickstats.nass.usda.gov/results/EE23234E-E958-3B73-A88F-0497EB960AD3 (accessed March 21, 2013)

Beef Cattle

HISTORY. At the beginning of the 20th century, the U.S. cattle industry was concentrated in the western states. Cattle were herded by cowboys to markets in large cities with railroad hubs. Cattle were shipped by rail to massive stockyards and slaughtering or processing centers in places such as Chicago, Illinois, and Kansas City, Missouri. As refrigeration and electricity spread throughout the country, slaughterhouses were able to move away from the big cities and into rural areas.

During the 1950s large meat companies began setting up feedlots for cattle, first in the Great Plains and later farther west. (See Figure 4.4.) Before that time cattle mostly ate grass, with some corn and other grains added to fatten them. They were slaughtered when they reached marketable size, about three to four years of age. U.S. farmers began producing a surplus of corn during the mid-1950s, and it became a primary feed for beef cattle. Cattle fed a diet rich in corn got fatter much faster and could be slaughtered much earlier than grass-fed cattle. Corn-fed beef had a rich fatty taste with a marbled texture and was more tender than grass-fed beef. It was also much cheaper. Heavy marketing by grocery stores led to huge demand for corn-fed beef.

CURRENT CONDITIONS. As shown in Figure 4.5, there were 729,000 beef cattle operations in the United States at yearend 2012. This number was down dramatically from 1986, when there were about 1 million of these operations. Table 4.3 provides a breakdown by size of the beef cattle operations at yearend 2012. The 581,000 operations with less than 50 cattle each accounted for 80% of all operations but held only 27.7% of all cattle.

Less than 1% (i.e., 5,600) of the cattle operations had more than 500 cattle each, but accounted for 16.7% of the total inventory.

Most beef cattle are slaughtered about the age of 14 to 16 months. Calves spend the first six to eight months of their lives with their mothers, drinking milk and grazing on grass at farms and ranches throughout the country. This is called the cow-calf stage of the business. Following weaning, most calves are moved to large crowded feedlots (outdoor grassless enclosures) to be "finished" for slaughter. During finishing the cattle receive virtually no exercise to prevent muscle buildup and fat loss. The animals are given various drugs to help them digest the rich corn diet and fend off disease from the crowded and often dirty conditions.

Ranchers use the feedlot system because it is much cheaper for them than finishing the cattle at a ranch. The price of beef is so low that the profit margins on cattle are slim. Ranchers and farmers must cut costs wherever they can. Many ranchers sell their calves to corporations and companies that operate feedlots. Others retain ownership and pay rent to the feedlot during the finishing process.

Table 4.2 shows beef production and consumption data between 2003 and 2012. The number of pounds of beef produced in 2012 was 25.3 billion pounds (11.5 billion kg). This number had changed little from values for previous years. The estimated per capita consumption of beef in 2012 was 79.8 pounds (36.2 kg). This value is down considerably from 2004 when it was at 94.6 pounds (42.9 kg).

FIGURE 4.4

Cattle at a feedlot. (© Thoma/Shutterstock.com.)

FIGURE 4.5

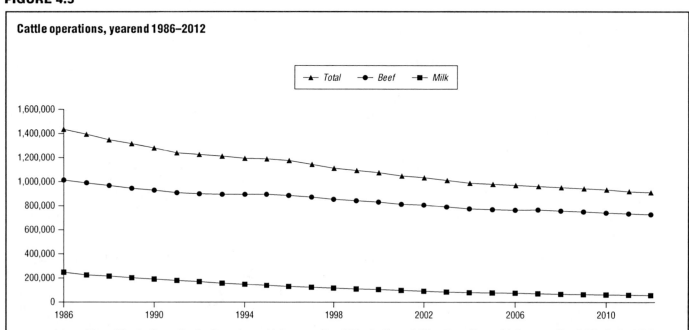

Cattle operations, yearend 1986–2012

Legend: ▲ Total ● Beef ■ Milk

SOURCE: Adapted from "Cattle, Cows, Beef—Operations with Inventory," and "Cattle, Cows, Milk—Operations with Inventory," and "Cattle, Incl Calves—Operations with Inventory," in *Quick Stats*, U.S. Department of Agriculture, National Agricultural Statistics Service, 2013, http://quickstats.nass.usda.gov/results/B5C6EEB1-99CD-3385-9CC9-C879149E7ECF (accessed March 21, 2013)

Dairy Cattle

Dairy cattle are a valuable commodity because they produce milk that can be consumed as a drink or used to make other dairy products. The USDA's Economic Research Service (ERS) notes in "Milk: Supply and Utilization of All Dairy Products" (September 11, 2012, http://www.ers.usda.gov/datafiles/Dairy_Data/milksandu _1_.xls) that the average per capita consumption of all dairy products in the United States in 2011 was 604 pounds (274 kg). Dairy products include fluid milk, yogurt, cheese, cottage cheese, frozen dairy products, and evaporated, condensed, and dry milk.

In "Milk Cows and Production by State and Region" (April 30, 2013, http://www.ers.usda.gov/datafiles/Dairy _Data/milkcowsandprod_1_.xls), the ERS indicates that there were approximately 9.2 million dairy cows in the United States in 2012. As shown in Figure 4.5, there were about 58,000 domestic dairy cow operations in 2012. This number is down considerably from 1986 when there were more than 200,000 dairy operations. However, annual per cow milk production has increased dramatically over the decades from about 4,000 pounds (1,814.4 kg) in 1924 to nearly 22,000 pounds (9,979 kg) in 2012. (See Figure 4.6.) The combination of factory farming, high-tech breeding, and modern medicine has resulted in a dramatic increase in the production of milk per cow over time. Table 4.4 provides a breakdown by size of the dairy cow operations for 2010 and 2011. In general, large numbers of operations had small cow inventories while a relatively small number of operations held large inventories. For example, in 2011 only 800 out of 60,000 total operations had 2,000 head or more each. Nevertheless, these operations accounted for roughly a third (32.5%) of the total milk cow inventory and more than a third (34.6%) of total dairy production.

Even though the public might assume that dairy cattle spend leisurely days in rolling fields of grass and are only occasionally milked, the reality is that dairy cows are regarded as milk-producing machines. Most dairy cows live in small indoor stalls or are confined to large dirt pens called dry lots. To produce milk, the cows must have calves. Modern farmers keep dairy cows pregnant almost continuously, often through artificial insemination. They take the calves away from their mothers as soon as possible after birth to prevent the calves from drinking the valuable milk. Male calves and any cows that cease to produce milk are slaughtered for beef.

TABLE 4.3

Beef cattle operations and percentage of inventory, yearend 2012

Operation size in head	Number of operations	Percent of inventory
1–49	581,000	27.7
50–99	79,000	17.2
100–499	63,400	38.4
500+	5,600	16.7
Total	**729,000**	**100**

SOURCE: Adapted from "U.S. Beef Cow Operations & Inventory," in *Charts and Maps: Beef Cows: Operations and Inventory by Size Group, U.S.*, U.S. Department of Agriculture, National Agricultural Statistics Service, February 19, 2013, http://www.nass.usda.gov/Charts_and_Maps/Cattle/bcow_ops.asp (accessed March 20, 2013)

FIGURE 4.6

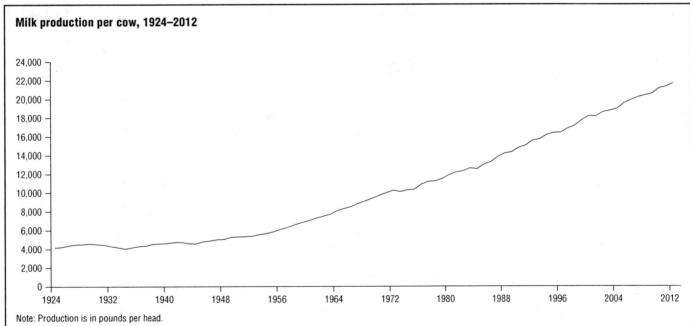

Milk production per cow, 1924–2012

Note: Production is in pounds per head.

SOURCE: "Milk-Production, Measured in Lb/Head," in *Quick Stats*, U.S. Department of Agriculture, National Agricultural Statistics Service, 2013, http://quickstats.nass.usda.gov/ (accessed March 20, 2013)

TABLE 4.4

Milk cow operations and percentage of inventory and production, 2010–11

[By size group]

Head	Operations		Percent of inventory		Percent of production*	
	2010	**2011**	**2010**	**2011**	**2010**	**2011**
	Number	Number	Percent	Percent	Percent	Percent
1–29	20,000	19,400	1.7	1.6	1.1	1.0
30–49	10,800	10,100	4.7	4.3	3.5	3.2
50–99	15,800	14,800	12.2	11.2	10.6	9.4
100–199	8,600	8,300	12.3	11.9	11.3	10.9
200–499	3,950	4,000	12.5	12.5	12.6	12.6
500–999	1,670	1,650	12.4	12.3	12.7	12.6
1,000–1,999	920	950	13.3	13.7	15.5	15.7
2,000+	760	800	30.9	32.5	32.7	34.6
Total	**62,500**	**60,000**	**100.0**	**100.0**	**100.0**	**100.0**

Note: An operation is any place having one or more head of milk cows on hand on December 31.
*Percents reflect average distributions of various probablity surveys conducted during the year.
NASS = National Agricultural Statistics Service.

SOURCE: "Table 8-2. Milk Cows: Number of Operations, Percent of Inventory and Percent of Milk Production by Size Group, United States, 2010–2011," in *Agricultural Statistics 2012*, U.S. Department of Agriculture, National Agricultural Statistics Service, 2012, http://www.nass.usda.gov/Publications/Ag_Statistics/2012/chapter08.pdf (accessed March 20, 2013)

Common health problems in dairy cows include mastitis (an udder infection) and lameness due to back and leg problems.

Many dairy cattle are given antibiotics and other drugs regularly. One of the most controversial drugs is called bovine growth hormone (bGH). Animal welfarists complain that bGH enlarges cows' udders to such a degree that the cows suffer from spine and back problems and have difficulty keeping their udders from dragging in dirt and manure. In "IDFA Position on Bovine Somatotropin (bST or bGH)" (2013, http://www.idfa.org/key-issues/category/labeling--standards/rbst/), the International Dairy Foods Association states that bGH has been used in U.S. dairy herds since 1993. The association reports that the milk has been deemed safe for human consumption "by the Food and Drug Administration..., the World Health Organization, the American Medical Association, the National Institutes of Health, the American Diabetic Association and regulatory agencies in 50 countries." The use of bGH, which is also called bovine somatotropin, is banned in Europe and Canada because of its effects on cow health, including reproductive and foot problems.

Another criticism of the factory farming of dairy cattle is that the cows spend long periods standing on hard surfaces. This includes concrete floors, metal gratings, and dirt-packed dry lots. Welfarists contend this contributes to lameness problems in dairy cattle. Lameness is a major reason for cows to be culled (killed) during the raising process.

Veal

Veal is meat from young calves that are raised in a way that produces very tender, light-colored flesh. This meat is highly prized for its pale color and delicate flavor. According to the American Veal Association in "Producing a Special Product" (March 2001, http://www.veal farm.com/CMDocs/VealFarm/Producing-a-special-product.pdf), veal farmers purchase unwanted calves from the dairy industry (mostly male Holstein calves) and raise them to the desired weight. The Cattlemen's Beef Board and the National Cattlemen's Beef Association explain in "Veal Production" (2013, http://www.vealfoodservice.com/production.aspx) that most veal calves are fed only milk or a milk supplement and are typically three weeks to six months old when they are slaughtered.

THE CONTROVERSY. Veal production is harshly criticized by both animal rights supporters and welfarists. They view the early separation of calves from their mothers as inhumane. In addition, they have waged a highly public battle against the use of narrow stalls or boxes for raising veal calves. The purpose of the housing is to separate the calves and to limit their movement so they will not build muscle. Critics also accuse producers of feeding the calves diets that are extremely low in iron to prevent the flesh from darkening. This results in anemic calves that suffer from health problems and stress brought on by their living conditions. The British government requires that calves be fed a diet containing sufficient iron and fiber and has banned the use of veal crates that do not allow a calf to turn around.

The use of highly restrictive veal stalls in the United States is being phased out by legislative decree in some states and through voluntary actions by the nation's veal industry. In "Farming/Food Production: Related Statutes" (2013, http://www.animallaw.info/statutes/topic statutes/sttoffp.htm), the Michigan State University (MSU)

College of Law indicates that Arizona, Colorado, Maine, Michigan, and Rhode Island have all passed bans that were in effect by 2013. These laws do not prohibit the use of veal crates but rather the use of veal crates that are highly restrictive. For example, MSU notes that Maine's law prohibits veal calves from being confined "the majority of a day in a manner that prevents the animal from lying down, standing up and fully extending the animal's limbs, and turning around freely." In November 2008 a legislative initiative called Proposition 2 was passed by California voters that outlaws the caging of farm animals in such a manner that the animals cannot stand, turn around, lie down, or fully extend their limbs. This law goes into effect in 2015 and will prohibit the use of very restrictive veal crates in California.

The American Veal Association (AVA; http://www .americanveal.com/) notes that in 2007 its members pledged to eliminate crate confinement in lieu of group housing by 2017. The organization still defends the practicality of using individual stalls to raise veal calves noting the practice helps prevent interaction among the calves and reduce possible disease transmission. In "Frequently Asked Questions" (http://www.vealfarm.com/faq1.aspx), the AVA claims "the stalls are of adequate size to allow the calves to stand, stretch, lie down, and groom themselves." Nevertheless, the association indicates in "Housing" (http://www.vealfarm.com/housing.aspx) that as of 2013 approximately 30% of U.S. veal farmers had already transitioned to group housing for veal calves.

CONSUMPTION OF VEAL. Table 4.2 shows annual U.S. production and consumption data for veal between 2003 and 2012. An estimated 132 million pounds (59.9 million kg) of veal were produced in 2012, down from 202 million pounds (91.6 million kg) produced in 2003. Americans consumed only 0.4 of a pound (0.2 kg) of veal per person in 2012, down from 0.7 of a pound (0.3 kg) per person in 2003.

Cattle Slaughter

Cattle killed at federally inspected slaughterhouses are required by law to be killed humanely. In most plants the preferred method begins with the use of a stun gun. Cattle are directed single-file through chutes that lead to the stunner. As each animal passes by, the stunner shoots a stun bolt into the animal's forehead to render it unconscious. The animal is rendered unconscious, rather than killed at this step, so that its heart will continue to operate and help pump out blood during the next step.

The animal is then hoisted up by one rear leg to hang from a bleed rail. At that time, its throat is cut so that all of its blood can drain out. The throat-cutting and subsequent blood loss is what kills the animal. Federal law requires that no animal fall into the blood of other slaughtered animals. This is why bloodletting is performed while the animal is suspended in the air. Following bloodletting, the animal's carcass moves down the line to a number of processing stations where the tail and hocks are cut off, the belly is cut open, and the hide is removed.

SPECIALLY DESIGNED METHODS. Temple Grandin (1947–) of Colorado State University is a renowned expert on cattle handling and slaughter. She maintains a comprehensive website (http://www.grandin.com) that provides information on this subject. Grandin designed the systems that are in use at most U.S. slaughterhouses and has written many guidance documents for the AMI. She became more well known to the general public in 2010, when her life story was featured in the HBO film *Temple Grandin.*

Grandin suffers from autism and says it allows her to see the world "in pictures," which is how animals are believed to see it. She has published many books and articles on the proper design of livestock chute systems. For example, chutes must be curved to trick the animals into thinking they are going back to where they came. The chutes must have high walls to keep the animals from seeing what is going on around them. Each animal should only see the rear end of the animal in front of it as it walks toward the stunner.

Grandin's recommendations are designed to keep cattle moving efficiently and peacefully. This has both economic and welfare benefits. Cattle that balk (refuse to move ahead or try to go back down a chute) hold up production. Also, animals that panic are believed to release stress chemicals that taint their meat. Therefore, it is in the best interest of producers that their cattle remain calm in the slaughterhouse. Maintaining quiet and calm also leads to less stress for the animals, which is of importance to animal welfarists.

Grandin says that she is often asked if animals entering the slaughterhouse know they are about to die. She believes the animals do not suspect their fate, because if they did, they would balk and panic. She reports that cattle will calmly walk into restraining devices covered with the blood of other cattle, as long as the previous cattle were also calm. However, cattle will refuse to approach a location in which a stressed animal has been killed. Grandin believes that animals that become agitated for several minutes release fear pheromones that other animals can smell.

In "Animal Welfare Audits for Cattle, Pigs, and Chickens That Use the HACCP Principles of Critical Control Points" (September 2011, http://www.grandin .com/welfare.audit.using.haccp.html), Grandin discusses an audit procedure with which cattle, hog, and chicken slaughterhouses can be graded on how well they meet AMI guidelines. The audit procedure centers on five main performance categories that can be graded numerically:

- Stunning proficiency (the percentage of animals that are stunned correctly on the first try)

- Insensibility on the bleed rail (the percentage of cattle that are not still breathing, not moving their eyes or blinking, not making sounds, or not trying to lift themselves up)

- Electric prod usage (the percentage of animals that are not prodded to keep them moving)

- Slipping and falling (the percentage of animals that do not slip and fall while they are being moved through the plant)

- Vocalization (the percentage of animals that do not moo, bellow, or make some other noise during handling and stunning)

In addition, the auditor assesses how the plant handles nonambulatory animals (downers), the condition of flooring and pens, truck unloading and handling procedures, the presence of drinking water in the pens, problems with overcrowding, and the general health condition of the cattle at the plant.

A facility automatically fails an audit if its handlers engage in any of the following "acts of abuse":

- Dragging sensible nonambulatory animals.

- Poking the animal in sensitive areas such as the eyes, ears, nose, or rectum with an electric prod or other object.

- Deliberately driving animals over the top of other animals.

- Slamming gates on animals.

- Beating animals or breaking tails.

Grandin reports in "Survey of Stunning and Handling in Federally Inspected Beef, Veal, Pork, and Sheep Slaughter Plants" (January 7, 1997, http://www.grandin.com/survey/usdarpt.html), an audit she did for the USDA in 1996 of 10 federally inspected slaughterhouses in various states, that only three of the plants were able to stun at least 95% of the cattle with a single shot. She also describes problems with poor equipment maintenance, lack of management supervision, excessive use of electric prods, transport of downed animals with forklifts, and other such practices.

Grandin notes in "Corporations Can Be Agents of Great Improvements in Animal Welfare and Food Safety and the Need for Minimum Decent Standards" (April 4, 2001, http://www.grandin.com/welfare/corporation.agents.html) that in 1999 she was hired by McDonald's Corporation to audit the company's beef and pork suppliers for their compliance with the standards. She states that

compliance greatly improved after McDonald's fired a supplier that failed the audit. For example, 90% of the plants audited after that firing were able to stun at least 95% of the cattle with a single shot. In addition, the use of electric prods was reduced or eliminated, and most abusive behavior by employees stopped.

Between 2001 and 2011 Grandin oversaw audits that were conducted for restaurants at hundreds of beef and pork plants. As of May 2013, the most recent audit findings were reported by Grandin in "2011 Restaurant Animal Welfare and Humane Slaughter Audits in Federally Inspected Beef and Pork Slaughter Plants in the U.S." (2011, http://www.grandin.com/survey/2011.restaurant.audits.html).

In 2011, 34 beef plants and 22 pork plants in the United States and Canada were audited on behalf of two major restaurant companies unnamed in the report. Grandin reports that 33 of the beef plants received passing scores on all audit criteria. The other beef plant received a "not acceptable" score for rendering 92% (as opposed to 99% to 100%) of the cattle insensible with a single shot from the captive bolt device. All of the plants rendered 100% of their cattle insensible before reaching the bleed rail. In regards to the pork plants that were audited, Grandin notes that 12 of them used group carbon dioxide stunning and the other 10 plants used electric stunning. Twenty plants total received passing scores on all audit criteria. One plant using electric stunning was faulted for failing to render all of the pigs insensible before they were hanged on the bleed rail.

Grandin notes that better stunning technology and equipment maintenance have led to continuous improvements in the audits she has conducted over the years. She warns plants that they must have zero tolerance for hoisting, skinning, or cutting any animal showing any obvious signs of sensibility or even partial return to sensibility after stunning. In the 2011 audit results, Grandin reports that many plants have begun videotaping operations for review via third-party auditors. She notes that "video auditing has resulted in big improvements, and it solves the problem of people 'acting good' when they know they are being watched." However, she cautions that "to be effective, video cameras need to be watched by auditors outside the plant."

RITUAL SLAUGHTER. The Humane Methods of Slaughter Act has exceptions for ritual slaughter—that is, slaughter conducted according to religious dictates. Ritual slaughter is practiced by some orthodox Jews and Muslims. Their teachings require that animals killed for food be moving and healthy when they are killed by having their throats slit. This was originally intended to ensure that sick animals were not eaten by humans. Meat from animals that are killed in this manner is said to be kosher in Jewish tradition and halal in Muslim tradition.

Regarding ritual slaughter, the Humane Methods of Slaughter Act does require "simultaneous and instantaneous" cutting of the throat arteries "with a sharp instrument" to render the animal insensible (unconscious).

Animal welfarists complain that strict interpretation of the directives for ritual slaughter means that cattle are not stunned before being bled out. They may be jerked up to the bleed rail by a hind leg while still fully conscious. The jerking action can break the leg and tear apart joints, causing severe pain. Their thrashing makes it more difficult for the cutter to cleanly cut their throats, which prolongs the entire process.

There are upright restraining devices that hold animals more humanely while their throats are being cut. The AMI strongly recommends the use of these devices, both for the welfare of the animals and for the safety of the plant workers. Grandin and Gary C. Smith report in "Animal Welfare and Humane Slaughter" (November 2004, http://www.grandin.com/references/humane.slaughter.html) that throat cutting must be done precisely with a long razor-sharp knife to induce "near-immediate collapse." Otherwise, the animal can remain conscious for more than a minute. Animals that struggle against their restraints or become agitated stay conscious the longest.

Singer states in *Animal Liberation* that critics of ritual slaughter are often accused of being racist or anti-Semitic. He points out that parts of ritually killed animals wind up on supermarket shelves and are purchased by people who may not be aware of how the animal was killed. This is because Jewish law requires the removal of the lymph nodes and sciatic nerve from cattle. Singer explains this is difficult to do efficiently on the hindquarters of cattle, so often only the front portion is sold as kosher and the back portion is usually processed and sold in commercial markets.

POULTRY

Poultry are domesticated birds that are cultivated for their eggs or meat. This includes chickens, turkeys, geese, and ducks. Chickens are by far the most common type of poultry raised in the United States, primarily for their meat. As shown in Table 4.1, 8.6 billion chickens, 250.2 million turkeys, and 24.2 million ducks were slaughtered in 2012. The economic value of poultry products—broilers (meat chickens), other chickens, turkeys, and eggs—was about $35 billion in 2011. (See Figure 4.7.)

Chickens

Chickens were originally domesticated from wild Asian jungle fowl. In natural conditions chickens tend to live in small groups composed of one male chicken (called a rooster or cock) and a dozen or more female chickens (called hens). Chickens are known for their hierarchy, or "pecking order." Each member of the group has a particular rank that determines its place in society. The average natural life span of a chicken is six to 10 years, although they can live as long as 25 years.

FIGURE 4.7

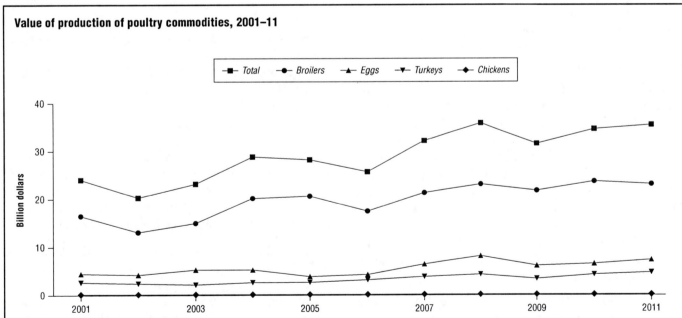

Value of production of poultry commodities, 2001–11

SOURCE: "Value of Production: Broilers, Eggs, Turkeys, Chickens, and Total, United States, 2001–2011," in *Charts and Maps: Poultry: Production and Value of Production by Year, U.S.*, U.S. Department of Agriculture, National Agricultural Statistics Service, April 2012, http://www.nass.usda.gov/Charts_and_Maps/Poultry/valprdbetc.asp (accessed March 20, 2013)

Chickens are omnivores, meaning that they will feed on both vegetable and animal substances. They spend a good part of their day foraging and pecking at the ground for food. They also like to perch, flap their wings, and take dust baths. Hens prefer to lay eggs in a private nest. Young hens above the age of five months produce 200 to 300 eggs per year. Unless the hen has recently mated with a rooster, however, the egg is infertile and does not develop into a chick. In the wild the hen would leave infertile eggs to rot or be eaten by predators.

CHICKEN BECOMES BIG BUSINESS. Before the 1920s chicken meat was not common in the American diet. Female chickens were valued on the farm for egg production. Besides being sometimes used for cockfighting, male chickens were not considered valuable. They were relatively scrawny and aggressive. This began to change during the 1920s, when enterprising farmers started cultivating chickens for meat. Scientific advances led to chicken breeds that were much meatier and grew faster. The use of vitamins, antibiotics, and growth hormones allowed the mass production of chickens to become a thriving business. During the 1950s producers began using large AFOs. This became the preferred method for raising chickens.

CHICKEN WELFARE CONCERNS. Chickens raised in crowded conditions are prone to aggression. They peck and claw at each other, which can cause feather loss and injury. Injured chickens may be pecked to death and even eaten by other chickens. As a result, it is a common practice in the factory farming of chickens to debeak a certain percentage of chickens by removing part of the upper and/or lower beak. Toe clipping involves cutting off parts of the chicken claw. Producers explain these practices are for the good of the chickens because it spares them from becoming injured. They claim the chickens do not experience any pain because beaks are similar to human fingernails.

United Poultry Concerns (UPC) is a nonprofit group that advocates for the humane treatment of domestic poultry. The UPC claims in "Debeaking Birds Has Got to Stop" (*Poultry Press*, vol. 17, no. 3, winter 2007) that scientific studies show that chicken beaks contain nerves and pain receptors. Thus, debeaked chickens suffer pain, as noted by one experiment, which found that newborn chicks "were said to 'vocalize' in response to an increase in 'energy density' indicating they were feeling 'discomfort.'" The UPC notes that some types of debeaking techniques do not work properly the first time, so newborn chicks must go through the process a second time.

Animal welfarists say debeaking and toe clipping would not be necessary if chickens were raised in more natural environments. They believe it is the stress of living in cramped cages in buildings housing tens of thousands of other chickens that drives chickens to demonstrate aggressive behavior. Welfarists maintain that producers accommodate these brutal systems by mutilating the chickens instead of changing the way in which chickens are raised.

Chicken producers defend these practices as necessary. The National Chicken Council (NCC) is an industry organization for companies that produce, process, and market chickens. In *Animal Welfare Guidelines and Audit Checklist for Broilers* (April 16, 2010, http://www.nationalchickencouncil.org/wp-content/uploads/2012/01/NCC-Animal-Welfare-Guidelines-2010-Revision-BROILERS.pdf), the NCC states that "today's chicken has been purposefully selected to thrive under modern management. We believe current good management practices that avoid destructive behavior, prevent disease, and promote good health and production are consistent with the generally accepted criteria of humane treatment."

BROILERS. Chicken meat is extremely popular in the United States. As shown in Table 4.5, the annual consumption was 31.1 billion pounds (14.1 billion kg) or 100 pounds (45.4 kg) per capita in 2011. Figure 4.1 shows that annual broiler production has actually exceeded beef production and hog production (in pounds produced) since early in the first decade of the 21st century. Billions of broilers are raised and slaughtered each year to keep up with the demand for chicken meat.

Table 4.6 lists the top 20 broiler-producing states for 2010 and 2011. Broiler production is heavily concentrated in the South and central Atlantic states. The major broiler-producing states in 2011 were Georgia (1.4 billion), Arkansas (1 billion), and Alabama (1 billion).

Broiler-type chicks are bred to gain weight fast. They start their lives at hatcheries. Day-old chicks are typically moved into chicken houses that may be hundreds of feet long and contain tens of thousands of chickens. These buildings are windowless and usually have dim lighting, because this is considered more calming. In modern chicken houses food and water are dispensed by machine. Chicks are vaccinated against common poultry diseases. Broilers are routinely given antibiotics and other drugs to overcome disease and speed up growth. However, as noted by the FDA in "Food Labeling: Meat and Poultry Labeling Terms" (April 12, 2011, http://www.fsis.usda.gov/factsheets/Meat_&_Poultry_Labeling_Terms/index.asp), federal law prohibits the use of hormones in poultry.

The NCC specifies in *Animal Welfare Guidelines and Audit Checklist for Broilers* that bird density should not exceed 8.5 pounds per square foot (3.9 kg per 929 square cm) of living space. Because a typical broiler weighs 4 to 5 pounds (1.8 to 2.3 kg) at slaughter weight, two birds of this size would have approximately 1 square foot (929 square cm) of space under this system. The NCC also recommends that broilers not be debeaked.

TABLE 4.5

Chicken supply, distribution, and consumption, 2002–11

[Per capita, ready-to-cook basis]

	Production						Consumption	
Year	Commercial broilers	Other chickens	Total[a]	Commercial storage at beginning of year	Exports	Commercial storage at end of year	Total[a, b]	Per capita
	Million pounds	Million pounds	Million pounds	Million pounds	Million pounds	Million pounds	Million pounds	Pounds
2002	31,895	547	32,441	720	4,940	768	27,468	95
2003	32,399	502	32,901	768	5,015	600	28,069	97
2004	33,699	504	34,203	600	4,940	705	29,129	99
2005	34,986	516	35,502	705	5,015	913	29,997	101
2006	35,120	504	35,624	913	4,997	738	30,484	102
2007	35,772	498	36,270	738	5,365	721	30,280	100
2008	36,511	559	37,070	721	6,072	748	30,036	99
2009	35,131	500	35,631	748	7,110	618	28,948	94
2010	36,516	503	37,019	618	5,925	777	30,128	97
2011[c]	36,991	522	37,513	777	5,925	704	31,128	100

[a]Totals may not add due to rounding.
[b]Shipments to territories now included in total consumption.
[c]Preliminary.
ERS = Economic Research Service.

SOURCE: "Table 8-46. Chickens: Supply, Distribution, and per Capita Consumption, Ready-to-Cook Basis, United States, 2002–2011," in *Agricultural Statistics 2012*, U.S. Department of Agriculture, National Agricultural Statistics Service, 2012, http://www.nass.usda.gov/Publications/Ag_Statistics/2012/chapter08.pdf (accessed March 20, 2013)

TABLE 4.6

Broiler production and value, by selected states, 2010–11

	2010			2011		
State	Number produced	Pounds produced	Value of production	Number produced	Pounds produced	Value of production
	Thousands	1,000 pounds	1,000 dollars	Thousands	1,000 pounds	1,000 dollars
AL	1,033,400	5,787,000	2,789,334	1,021,100	5,718,200	2,664,681
AR	1,043,500	5,937,500	2,861,875	1,027,300	5,855,600	2,728,710
DE	234,200	1,625,300	783,395	217,800	1524,600	710,464
FL	51,700	314,300	151,493	61,800	383,200	178,571
GA	1,313,500	6,882,700	3,317,461	1,375,200	7,426,100	3,460,563
KY	309,800	1,672,900	806,338	310,000	1,705,000	794,530
MD	300,500	1,433,400	690,899	311,100	1,555,500	724,863
MN	42,100	231,100	111,390	41,600	235,000	109,510
MS	807,800	4,766,000	2,297,212	784,000	4,625,600	2,155,530
MO[a]	—	—	—	285,200	1,369,000	637,954
NC	766,500	5,419,200	2,612,054	786,900	5,587,000	2,603,542
OH	60,000	376,800	181,618	59,600	375,500	174,983
OK	225,000	1,503,000	724,446	214,700	1,524,400	710,370
PA	149,300	839,100	404,446	155,600	871,400	406,072
SC	241,000	1,556,900	750,426	223,400	1,496,800	697,509
TN	193,100	986,700	475,589	190,300	989,600	461,154
TX	653,300	3,645,400	1,757,083	630,500	3,593,900	1,674,757
VA	250,400	1,292,100	622,792	243,800	1,292,100	602,119
WV	87,600	346,000	166,772	85,400	341,600	159,186
WI	46,500	197,600	95,243	46,500	200,000	93,200
Other[b] states	814,400	4,339,600	2,091,687	535,800	3,032,200	1,413,006
Total	**8,623,600**	**49,152,600**	**23,691,553**	**8,607,600**	**49 702,300**	**23,161,274**

Notes: Annual estimates cover the period December 1 previous year through November 30. Broiler production including other domestic meat-type strains. Excludes states producing less than 500,000 broilers.
[a]Including in "other states" in 2010.
[b]CA, IN, IA, LA, MI, NE, NY, OR, & WA combined to avoid disclosing individual operations.
NASS = National Agricultural Statistics Service.

SOURCE: "Table 8-48. Broilers: Production and Value, by State and Total, 2010–2011," in *Agricultural Statistics 2012*, U.S. Department of Agriculture, National Agricultural Statistics Service, 2012, http://www.nass.usda.gov/Publications/Ag_Statistics/2012/chapter08.pdf (accessed March 20, 2013)

LAYING HENS. Laying hens, or "layers," are chickens that are specifically bred for their egg-laying abilities, rather than for meat production. According to the NASS in *Agricultural Statistics 2012* (March 2013, http://www.nass.usda.gov/Publications/Ag_Statistics/2012/chapter08.pdf), there were 338.5 million layers on U.S. farms in

TABLE 4.7

Egg supply, distribution, and consumption, 2002–11

[Per capita.]

Year	Total egg production	Storage at beginning of the year[a]	Imports[b]	Exports[b]	Eggs used for hatching	Consumption		
						Storage at end of the year[b]	Total[c]	Per capita
	Million dozen	Million dozen	Million dozen	Million dozen	Million dozen	Million dozen	Million dozen	Number
2002	7,270	10	15	174	961	10	6,150	256
2003	7,299	10	13	146	959	14	6,204	256
2004	7,450	14	13	168	988	15	6,306	258
2005	7,538	15	9	203	997	16	6,345	257
2006	7,650	16	9	202	992	13	6,468	260
2007	7,587	13	14	250	1,016	11	6,335	252
2008	7,501	11	14	206	996	17	6,307	248
2009	7,546	17	11	242	955	18	6,358	248
2010	7,622	18	12	258	983	19	6,391	247
2011[d]	7,627	19	24	282	963	20	6,405	246

[a]Calendar years.
[b]Shell eggs and the approximate shell-egg equivalent of egg product.
[c]Shipments to territories now included in total consumption.
[d]Preliminary.
ERS = Economic Research Service.

SOURCE: "Table 8-57. Eggs: Supply, Distribution, and per Capita Consumption, United States, 2002–2011," in *Agricultural Statistics 2012*, U.S. Department of Agriculture, National Agricultural Statistics Service, 2012, http://www.nass.usda.gov/Publications/Ag_Statistics/2012/chapter08.pdf (accessed March 20, 2013)

2011. The three states with the largest inventories were Iowa (52.6 million), Ohio (28.4 million), and Pennsylvania (25.2 million). In 2011 the NASS notes that another 101.9 million pullets (young female chickens not yet of laying age) were also being raised throughout the United States. As shown in Table 4.7, laying hens produced 7.6 billion dozen eggs in 2011. Per capita annual consumption was 246 eggs. The meat of laying hens is generally considered tough and stringy; thus, laying hens have little market value once they are spent (i.e., quit laying eggs because of age). When spent hens are slaughtered, their meat is typically sold for use in compost or animal feed, including pet foods.

In "Progress for Egg-Laying Hens" (April 26, 2013, http://www.humanesociety.org/issues/confinement_farm/timelines/eggs_timeline.html), the HSUS calls laying hens "arguably the most abused animals in agribusiness." Animal protection groups are highly critical of three common practices in the factory farming of laying hens: killing male chicks, forced molting, and use of battery cages.

Laying-hen chicks are sorted by gender when they are one day old. Only the females are kept. The males are killed because they have not been bred for meat production and will not grow up to be meaty enough for human consumption. According to animal rights groups, millions of culled male chicks are thrown into garbage bags, where they suffocate. The poultry industry does not generally discuss its methods of culling male chicks, but it is widely believed that methods including suffocation and maceration (instantaneous death in a high-speed grinder) are commonly used.

Under natural conditions hens can lay eggs for more than a decade, but the egg-laying production of hens in

factory farms ceases dramatically after the first year. One method that producers use to rejuvenate laying in poorly producing hens is forced molting, in which all food is withheld from the hens for either a set number of days (usually five to 14), or until the hens lose a particular amount of weight. This forced fast mimics the conditions that wild chickens experience during the fall or winter, when food is not as plentiful. Lower food intake causes a hen to molt (lose her feathers). Also, her reproductive system temporarily ceases producing eggs. When food is fully restored, the hen is much more productive at making eggs than she was before.

Animal welfarists are extremely critical of forced molting, saying that because all food is withheld from the hens, it is much more brutal than natural molting. They equate the practice to forced starvation and note that food deprivation for the purpose of forced molting is banned in Europe.

The United Egg Producers (UEP), an industry group that represents the interests of many of the nation's egg producers, explains in *United Egg Producers Animal Husbandry Guidelines for U.S. Egg Laying Flocks* (2010, http://www.uepcertified.com/pdf/2010-uep-animal-welfare-guidelines.pdf) that approximately 95% of all commercial laying hens in the United States are confined to plain-wire cages called battery cages. Animal welfarists complain the cages are so small that the birds cannot spread their wings or engage in nesting, perching, and other natural behaviors. Battery cages have been banned in the European Union since 2012. Many animal welfare organizations urge consumers to buy eggs only from cage-free chickens. However, the HSUS notes in "Cage-Free

vs. Battery-Cage Eggs" (September 1, 2009, http://www
.humanesociety.org/issues/confinement_farm/facts/cage-
free_vs_battery-cage.html) that even cage-free chickens
may suffer from welfare problems, including overcrowding within buildings, lack of access to the outdoors,
debeaking, and/or forced molting.

Proposition 2, which was passed by California voters
in November 2008, will profoundly affect the way in
which chickens are caged in that state beginning in 2015.
The new law bans the caging of farm animals in such a
manner that the animals cannot stand, turn around, lie
down, or fully extend their limbs. In *Agricultural Statistics
2012* the NASS notes that California had the fifth-largest
layer inventory of any state in 2011 with 19.8 million
layers.

In "The Economics of Regulations on Hen Housing
in California" (*Journal of Agricultural and Applied
Economics*, vol. 42, no. 3, August 2010), Daniel A. Sumner et al. of the Agricultural Issues Center of the University of California, Davis, estimate that Proposition 2
will increase the production costs for California egg
farmers by $0.20 per dozen. It is not anticipated to raise
the retail price of eggs in the state, because out-of-state
producers are expected to increase their supply to
California. However, Sumner et al. indicate that the
future does not bode well for the state's egg farmers.
The researchers note that the "the main result of the
new regulations will be a drastic reduction in the number
of eggs produced in California."

The Congressional Research Service (CRS) is the
investigative arm of the U.S. Congress. In *Table Egg
Production and Hen Welfare: Agreement and Legislative
Proposals* (January 11, 2013, http://www.nationalaglaw
center.org/assets/crs/R42534.pdf), Joel L. Greene and
Tadlock Cowan of the CRS note that Michigan passed a
law in 2009 that will phase out battery cages by 2019. In
addition, in 2010 Ohio legislators "agreed to place a
moratorium on the construction of new conventional
cages as part of an agreement to stop a ballot initiative."
Greene and Cowan note that in July 2011 the HSUS and
the UEP entered into an agreement to work together to
achieve passage of federal legislation regarding the
welfare of layers hens. According to Greene and Cowan,
the farm animal industry was "stunned" by the
announcement, because the UEP and HSUS "have been
adversaries for many years." The two organizations seek
a federal law that would be phased in over 18 years and
require that layer cages meet minimum size requirements
and provide an "enriched" environment, e.g., through
inclusion of perches or nesting boxes. In addition, the
law would forbid the withholding of food or water to
induce forced molting, regulate ammonia levels in egg-
laying houses, and govern methods of euthanasia. In
exchange for UEP cooperation the HSUS reportedly

agreed to cease its efforts in Oregon and Washington to
obtain state laws outlawing battery cages. As of May
2013 no federal legislation had been passed regarding
layer production. In "Progress for Egg-Laying Hens,"
the HSUS lists dozens of national retailers and food
service providers that have pledged to switch some or
all of their egg purchases to cage-free eggs.

CHICKEN SLAUGHTER. Chickens selected for slaughter are gathered by their feet by handlers, who carry them
upside down to put into crates. At the slaughterhouse the
chickens are shackled upside down by their feet to a
conveyor belt. The Humane Methods of Slaughter Act
does not apply to poultry, which means that chickens do
not have to be stunned unconscious before having their
throats slit. Some plants do, however, use a stunning
method based on the availability of electricity.

Each live chicken that is shackled to the conveyor
belt has its head dunked into a water bath containing salt.
An electric current is passed through the shackles to
knock the chicken unconscious. Then the birds pass by
an automated cutting blade that slits their throat. After the
blood is drained (which takes about 90 seconds), the birds
are dipped into scalding water baths to loosen their feathers before moving on to cutting stations.

Turkeys

Turkeys are one of the few domesticated animals
native to North America. Present-day turkeys, however,
have little resemblance to their wild ancestors. Modern
turkeys are bred to gain weight quickly, particularly in
the breast. Turkeys are raised much the same way that
broiler chickens are raised. At about six weeks of age, the
baby birds are moved into growing houses in which they
spend the remainder of their lives. Conditions there are
crowded, as they are for chickens, and can lead to
feather-pecking and cannibalism. Turkeys are slaughtered similarly to chickens at about three to six months
of age. Figure 4.8 shows that the U.S. turkey inventory
grew steadily from 1972 to the 1990s, peaking at roughly
300 million turkeys per year during the mid-1990s.
Production fell to about 250 million turkeys by 2005
and remained near that value in 2012. The annual turkey
consumption was 16.1 pounds (7.3 kg) per capita in
2011. (See Table 4.8.) Just over 5 billion pounds (2.3 billion kg) of turkey were consumed in 2011.

Ducks and Geese

Domestic ducks and geese are raised for their meat,
eggs, and feathers. Most ducks are raised indoors, similarly to chickens, and are fed fortified corn and soybeans.
Geese are raised in covered enclosures for the first six
weeks of their lives and then allowed to forage for grass
in fields. The USDA explains in "Poultry Preparation:
Duck and Goose from Farm to Table" (May 13, 2011,

FIGURE 4.8

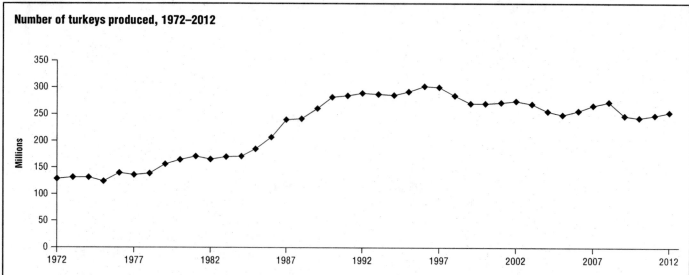

Number of turkeys produced, 1972–2012

SOURCE: Adapted from "U.S. Turkeys Raised, 1961–2011," in *Charts and Maps: Turkeys: Inventory by Year, U.S.*, U.S. Department of Agriculture, National Agricultural Statistics Service, April 2012, http://www.nass.usda.gov/Charts_and_Maps/Poultry/tkyprd.asp (accessed March 20, 2013)

TABLE 4.8

Turkey supply, distribution, and consumption, 2002–11

[Per capita, ready-to-cook basis]

Year	Production	Commercial storage at beginning of year	Exports	Commercial storage at end of year	Consumption Total[a, b]	Per capita
	Million pounds	Million pounds	Million pounds	Million pounds	Million pounds	Pounds
2002	5,638	241	439	333	5,108	17.7
2003	5,576	333	484	354	5,074	17.4
2004	5,383	354	442	288	5,010	17.1
2005	5,432	288	570	206	4,954	16.7
2006	5,607	206	547	218	5,064	16.9
2007	5,873	218	547	261	5,300	17.5
2008	6,165	261	676	396	5,367	17.6
2009	5,589	396	534	262	5,210	17.0
2010	5,570	262	582	192	5,083	16.4
2011[c]	5,715	192	703	211	5,014	16.1

[a]Totals may not add due to rounding.
[b]Shipments to territories now included in consumption.
[c]Preliminary.
ERS = Economic Research Service.

SOURCE: "Table 8-51. Turkeys: Supply, Distribution, and per Capita Consumption, Ready-to-Cook Basis, United States, 2002–2011," in *Agricultural Statistics 2012*, U.S. Department of Agriculture, National Agricultural Statistics Service, 2012, http://www.nass.usda.gov/Publications/Ag_Statistics/2012/chapter08.pdf (accessed March 20, 2013)

http://www.fsis.usda.gov/Fact_Sheets/Duck_&_Goose_from_Farm_to_Table/index.asp) that "very few drugs have been approved for ducks and geese, so antibiotics are not routinely given and are not useful for feed efficiency." As noted earlier, federal law prohibits the use of hormones in poultry production. Ducks and geese are slaughtered with electrocution baths followed by throat slitting.

Duck and geese products are mostly sold in specialty markets. The tongues and feet of the animals are considered a delicacy in parts of Asia (particularly Hong Kong) and are also sold in Asian-American markets. High-value products from ducks and geese include down feathers, smoked meat products, liver pâté (paste), and foie gras (pronounced *fwah grah*, meaning "fat liver" in French).

FOIE GRAS CONTROVERSY. Foie gras is obtained by force-feeding male ducks and geese a rich mixture containing corn, fat, salt, and water over a short amount of time. This regimen causes the birds' livers to become fatty and hugely swollen, six to 10 times their normal size.

The feeding process, called gavage, is usually started two to four weeks before slaughter. It is accomplished using an electronic pump that forces food through a 12- to 16-inch (30.5- to 40.6-centimeter) tube that is placed down a bird's throat. The birds are force-fed several times a day and held in cramped cages or pens so that they cannot move. This prevents them from losing weight during the fattening process.

Animal welfarists are highly critical of gavage. The HSUS states that the birds suffer pain from swollen abdomens and lesions in their throats. It also says that necropsies (postmortem examinations) conducted on birds subjected to gavage show severe liver, heart, and esophagus disorders.

Foie gras is a gourmet delicacy that is expensive, selling for up to $50 per pound. It is available at upscale restaurants and specialty stores. Most foie gras comes from France. As of May 2013, only one commercial producer of foie gras operated in the United States— Hudson Valley Foie Gras of Ferndale, New York, which processed duck livers. The producer defends the use of the gavage process, saying that it does not gag the birds because they do not chew their food anyway.

In 2004 the California governor Arnold Schwarzenegger (1947–) signed a bill into law that banned, beginning July 1, 2012, the force feeding of ducks and geese to produce foie gras and banned the sale of the product in California. In 2006 the Chicago City Council passed an ordinance banning the sale of foie gras within the city limits; this ordinance, however, was repealed in 2008. According to the article "MEPs Put Foie Gras Controversy Back on the Table" (October 18, 2012, http://fin channel.com), as of late 2012 the production of foie gras (but not the sale or possession of) was banned in 22 European Union countries.

HOGS AND PIGS

Hogs and pigs are domesticated swine. A pig is a young swine that is not yet sexually mature. A young female hog is called a gilt. A female adult hog is called a sow. The generic term *hog* is generally used to refer to all hogs. Hogs are curious and intelligent animals, supposedly smarter than dogs. They have sensitive noses, which they use to root around the ground for their food and explore their surroundings. Pregnant sows like to build nests of grass. Under natural conditions sows give birth to (or farrow) a litter of piglets twice per year. Each litter averages eight piglets that suckle for about three months. The normal life expectancy of a hog is 12 to 15 years.

Modern Hog Industry

As of September 1, 2012, the total U.S. hog inventory was nearly 68 million. (See Figure 4.9.) This value was up considerably from the late 1980s when the inventory totaled about 58 million. As shown in Figure 4.10, there were 68,300 hog operations in the United States at yearend 2012. This number was down dramatically from the mid-1960s, when more than 1 million operations were reported. Hog production has become increasingly concentrated with fewer operations containing more hogs. Even though there were 48,700 operations that had from one to 99 hogs in 2012, they accounted for only 0.8% of the total U.S. hog inventory. (See Figure 4.11.) The majority (61.9%) of the hog inventory was located at operations with 5,000 or more hogs. Thus, most hogs raised in the United States are concentrated on a few massive AFOs. These facilities not only finish the hogs,

FIGURE 4.9

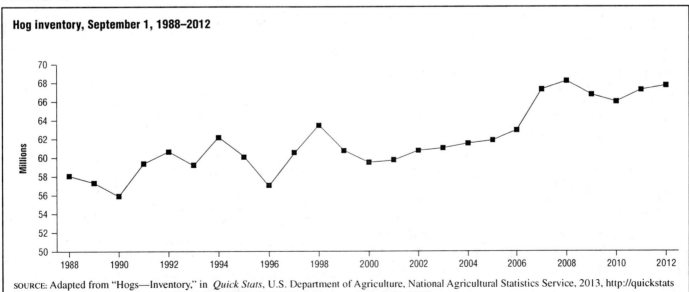

Hog inventory, September 1, 1988–2012

SOURCE: Adapted from "Hogs—Inventory," in *Quick Stats*, U.S. Department of Agriculture, National Agricultural Statistics Service, 2013, http://quickstats .nass.usda.gov/results/FB79C424-71FD-306E-952F-FD0C7CCD3034 (accessed March 21, 2013)

FIGURE 4.10

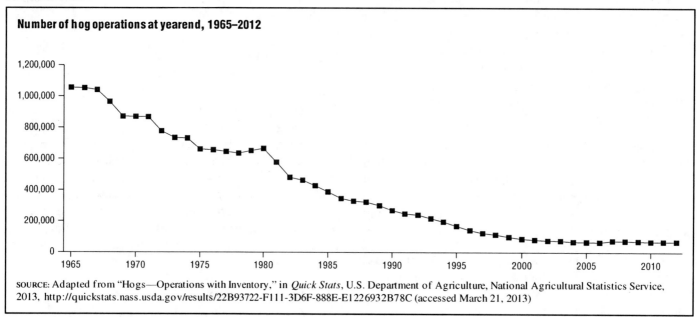

Number of hog operations at yearend, 1965–2012

SOURCE: Adapted from "Hogs—Operations with Inventory," in *Quick Stats*, U.S. Department of Agriculture, National Agricultural Statistics Service, 2013, http://quickstats.nass.usda.gov/results/22B93722-F111-3D6F-888E-E1226932B78C (accessed March 21, 2013)

FIGURE 4.11

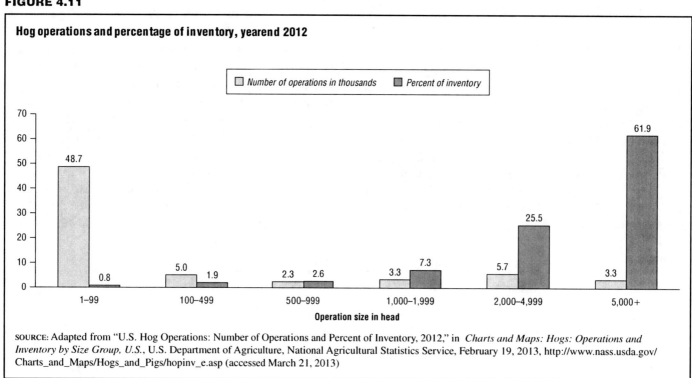

Hog operations and percentage of inventory, yearend 2012

SOURCE: Adapted from "U.S. Hog Operations: Number of Operations and Percent of Inventory, 2012," in *Charts and Maps: Hogs: Operations and Inventory by Size Group, U.S.*, U.S. Department of Agriculture, National Agricultural Statistics Service, February 19, 2013, http://www.nass.usda.gov/Charts_and_Maps/Hogs_and_Pigs/hopinv_e.asp (accessed March 21, 2013)

as is done in the cattle industry, but also raise them. Major pork producers operate farrowing complexes, nurseries, and growing-feeding units.

As shown in Table 4.1, 113.2 million hogs were slaughtered for commercial purposes in 2012. Total production in 2012 was 23.3 billion pounds (10.6 billion kg), while per capita consumption was 59.6 pounds (27 kg). (See Table 4.2.) The consumption value was down from 66.9 pounds (30.3 kg) in 2003. The economic

value of hog production in 2011 was estimated at about $20 billion. (See Figure 4.2.)

Hog-Raising Practices

Confinement buildings for hogs can be hundreds of feet long and contain thousands of hogs. They typically feature concrete or slatted floors—concrete floors can be easily cleaned, and slatted floors allow manure and urine to fall into pits. Hogs are kept on short tethers or confined in cages and pens to prevent them from getting exercise, which might build muscle instead of fat and toughen the meat. Crowded conditions can lead to aggressive behavior among the hogs, including tail chewing, biting, and fighting. Tail docking and teeth clipping are commonly practiced to help prevent injuries from these behaviors. Antibiotics, hormones, and other drugs are routinely administered to speed growth and prevent deadly diseases.

GESTATION CRATES. Breeding sows are often kept in individual stalls or confined with tethers until they are ready to farrow. Gestation crates, as they are called, are typically about 7 feet (2.1 meters) long and 2 feet (0.6 meters) wide—just wide enough for the sow to lie down but not to turn around. The sow eats, urinates, and defecates where she stands. When she is ready to give birth, the sow may be moved to a farrowing pen in which she and her piglets will be kept tightly confined. As shown in Figure 4.12, more than 11.6 million sows were farrowed in 2012.

The USDA's National Animal Health Monitoring System conducts a national swine survey every six years. As of May 2013, the most recent published report was *Swine 2006* (http://www.aphis.usda.gov/animal_health/nahms/swine/index.shtml#swine2006) which was published in October 2007. (Data collection for the upcoming *Swine 2012* was conducted through site visits and questionnaires that began in July 2012.)

In "Info Sheet: Sow and Gilt Management in Swine 2000 and Swine 2006" (January 2009, http://www.aphis.usda.gov/animal_health/nahms/swine/downloads/swine2006/Swine2006_is_sowgilt.pdf), an excerpt report based on *Swine 2006*, the USDA notes that 67.7% of sows on U.S. farms were farrowed in total confinement facilities in 2006. Industry officials defend the use of gestation crates, saying that the crates are necessary to keep aggressive sows from fighting with each other over food. Fighting can cause injuries that lead to miscarried fetuses. Pork producers believe caged sows receive beneficial individual attention to their health and nutrition needs. The National Pork Producers Council indicates in "Sow Housing" (2013, http://www.nppc.org/issues/animal-health-safety/sow-housing/) that it supports gestation crates as a means to minimize aggression between sows and protect them from environmental extremes and exposure to hazards.

As of 2013 the European Union had phased out use of gestation crates. In "Timeline of Major Farm Animal Protection Advancements" the HSUS notes that as of May 2013 legislation banning the use of gestation crates had been passed in Arizona, California, Florida, Maine, Michigan, Ohio, Oregon, and Rhode Island. According to the National Pork Producers Council, Colorado pig farmers began a voluntary phase-out of gestation stalls in 2008. In addition, the HSUS notes that dozens of national chain stores and restaurants have pledged to phase out the use of gestation crates among their pork suppliers.

OTHER PRACTICES. Generally, week-old pigs are subjected to teeth clipping, tail docking, and ear notching. The males are castrated at this time. These procedures are done without anesthesia. Once the piglets reach approximately 55 pounds (25 kg), they are moved to indoor finishing pens. Piglets are raised to slaughter weight, typically 250 pounds (113 kg), at about four to six months of age. Spent breeding sows are usually slaughtered at two to three years of age.

Animal welfarists are critical of hog-raising practices in the United States. They consider the intense confinement too stressful for intelligent and social animals such

FIGURE 4.12

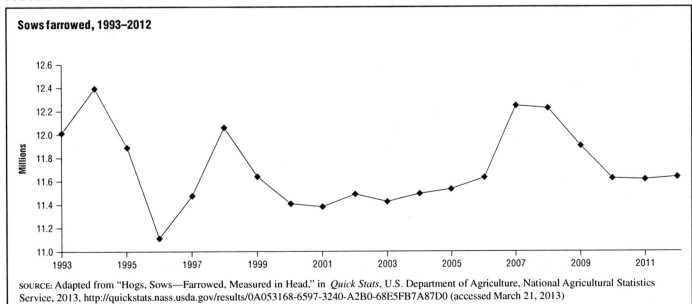

Sows farrowed, 1993–2012

SOURCE: Adapted from "Hogs, Sows—Farrowed, Measured in Head," in *Quick Stats*, U.S. Department of Agriculture, National Agricultural Statistics Service, 2013, http://quickstats.nass.usda.gov/results/0A053168-6597-3240-A2B0-68E5FB7A87D0 (accessed March 21, 2013)

as hogs. They also condemn early weaning as cruel to sows and piglets. Factory-farmed hogs not only suffer from excessive crowding, stress, and boredom but also experience serious breathing disorders because of high concentrations of ammonia from their waste materials. Critics also note that hogs experience feet and leg deformities from standing on floors made of improper materials.

Hog Slaughter

Hogs are generally killed via electrocution or by stunning followed by bleeding out. Electrocution is accomplished by stunning the hog with a wand with sufficient shock to stop its heart. This is called cardiac arrest stunning and is the technique most large-scale hog slaughter plants use. Hogs can also be given an electrical shock to the head or exposed to carbon dioxide inside a chamber to render them unconscious. Next, the animals are hoisted up by their back feet and bled via a small incision in the chest. Fully electrocuted hogs are also bled out in this manner. The dead hogs are then lowered into vats of scalding water to remove hair. The meat can then be processed.

According to Grandin's instructions for electrical stunning, a hog stunned with sufficient amperage in the correct location will feel no pain. Insufficient amperage and an improper current path will cause the animal pain. Grandin recommends that head-stunned hogs be bled out within 30 seconds of being stunned to prevent them from regaining consciousness.

SHEEP AND LAMBS

Sheep, like cattle, are cud-chewing animals. Lambs are immature sheep, typically less than one year old. There are dozens of sheep breeds. Most have been propagated to produce good-tasting meat and/or long strong hair (fleece).

The latter is shaved off (shorn) and used to make wool. The animals can be shorn repeatedly throughout their lifetime; they do not have to be killed to harvest the fleece. Sheep are also raised for milk and cheese production.

As shown in Figure 4.13, about 5.3 million sheep and lambs were kept on U.S. farms as of January 1, 2013. This value was down considerably from the mid-1980s, when more than 11 million head were reported. There were nearly 80,000 sheep operations with inventory at yearend 2012. (See Figure 4.14.) The NASS notes that the total value of the nation's sheep and lambs was $946.2 million as of January 1, 2013. (See Table 4.9.) As shown in Table 4.1, nearly 2.2 million sheep and lambs were slaughtered for commercial purposes in 2012. Sheep and lambs are covered by the Humane Methods of Slaughter Act. Lamb and mutton (sheep meat) consumption is very low in the United States. The USDA estimates that the annual consumption was 0.9 pounds (0.4 kg) per capita in 2012. (See Table 4.2.) Approximately 338 million pounds (153.3 million kg) of lamb and mutton were consumed in 2009. As shown in Figure 4.15, the number of U.S. head shorn declined dramatically from about 11 million head in 1985 to roughly 4 million head in 2012.

HORSES

APHIS reports in "USDA's Role in Equine Health Monitoring" (June 1996, http://www.aphis.usda.gov/animal _health/nahms/equine/downloads/equine98/eqrole.pdf) that approximately 20 million horses lived on U.S. farms in 1900. This number declined significantly over the next century. In *2007 Census of Agriculture*, the USDA notes that there were just over 4 million horses living in the United States in 2007. The country's total horse inventory could be much higher, because exact inventories are not known for

FIGURE 4.13

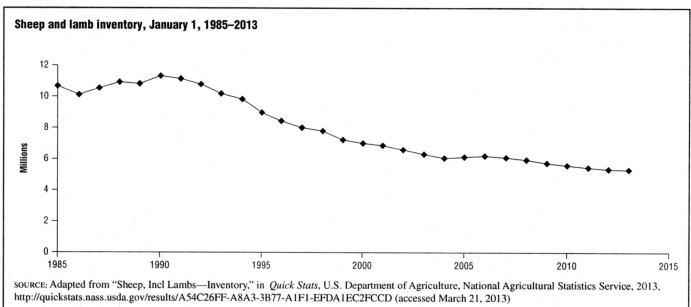

Sheep and lamb inventory, January 1, 1985–2013

SOURCE: Adapted from "Sheep, Incl Lambs—Inventory," in *Quick Stats*, U.S. Department of Agriculture, National Agricultural Statistics Service, 2013, http://quickstats.nass.usda.gov/results/A54C26FF-A8A3-3B77-A1F1-EFDA1EC2FCCD (accessed March 21, 2013)

FIGURE 4.14

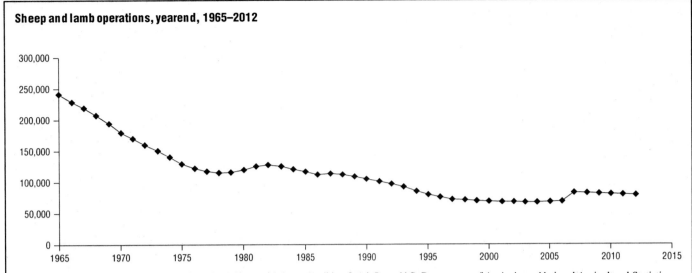

Sheep and lamb operations, yearend, 1965–2012

SOURCE: Adapted from "Sheep, Incl Lambs—Operations with Inventory." in *Quick Stats*, U.S. Department of Agriculture, National Agricultural Statistics Service, 2013, http://quickstats.nass.usda.gov/results/F0D370C2-C8E8-30A4-BDD0-CB6A1235EDD1 (accessed March 21, 2013)

TABLE 4.9

Value of sheep and lamb inventory, January 1, 2004–13

[In dollars]

Year	Value
2004	720,443,000
2005	798,209,000
2006	872,351,000
2007	818,491,000
2008	823,424,000
2009	765,194,000
2010	761,115,000
2011	931,008,000
2012	1,185,075,000
2013	946,194,000

SOURCE: Adapted from "Sheep, Incl Lambs—Inventory, Measured In $." in *Quick Stats*, U.S. Department of Agriculture, National Agricultural Statistics Service, 2013, http://quickstats.nass.usda.gov/results/54478111-7B02-3A01-8438-067CC8994AAB (accessed March 21, 2013)

horses that are kept for racing, breeding, showing, and pleasure purposes.

Horsemeat Controversy

Banning the slaughter of horses for food is the goal of many animal welfare groups. Even though horses are not specifically cultivated in the United States for human consumption, there is a growing overseas market for this meat, primarily in Europe and Asia. Horsemeat is increasingly popular in these regions because of the scare concerning mad cow disease.

Horses that are destined for slaughter are typically sold at auction terminals and transported in trailers to horse slaughter plants in Mexico or Canada. Before 2007 there were three horse slaughter plants in the United States: two in Texas and one in Illinois. The Homes for

Horses Coalition notes in "Facts and FAQs about Horse Slaughter" (2013, http://www.homesforhorses.org/faq .php) that Texas and Illinois passed laws in 2007 that closed down the horse slaughter plants. Figure 4.16 shows the number of horses slaughtered in the United States from 1990 through 2007. In 2006, the last full year in which domestic horse slaughterhouses operated, nearly 105,000 horses were slaughtered. Horses slaughtered in the United States were covered by the Humane Methods of Slaughter Act. They had to be rendered unconscious before being hoisted onto the bleed rail and cut open. Like cattle, horses were stunned by a shot in the head with a bolt gun. The cessation of the domestic industry led to an increase in the number of horses exported for slaughter in foreign countries. As shown in Figure 4.17, U.S. exports of horses intended for slaughter increased from 78,061 in 2007 to 137,984 in 2010.

In "USDA May Approve Horse Slaughtering" (February 28, 2013, http://www.nytimes.com/2013/03/01/busi ness/usda-may-approve-horse-slaughter-plant.html), Stephanie Strom notes that between 2007 and 2010 the U.S. Congress passed appropriation bills including riders (tacked-on amendments) that prohibited the USDA from spending money on inspection services for horse meat. However, Strom indicates that in 2011 "Congress quietly removed" the rider from a spending act that it passed, and a meat company then sued the USDA for the agency's failure to restart its horse slaughter inspection service. The company—Valley Meat Company—has applied to the USDA to begin operating a horse slaughter plant in Roswell, New Mexico, and that application is expected to be approved. Strom notes that the company has been supported by thousands of cattle ranchers who say they need the facility "to humanely dispose" of

FIGURE 4.15

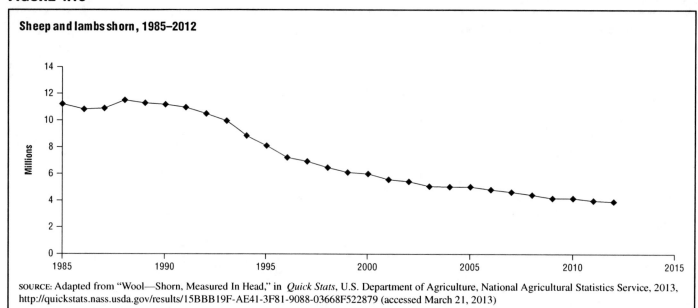

Sheep and lambs shorn, 1985–2012

SOURCE: Adapted from "Wool—Shorn, Measured In Head," in *Quick Stats*, U.S. Department of Agriculture, National Agricultural Statistics Service, 2013, http://quickstats.nass.usda.gov/results/15BBB19F-AE41-3F81-9088-03668F522879 (accessed March 21, 2013)

horses that are no longer needed due to advanced age or other inability to work. In "Lawyer: Inspectors Clear Roswell Horse Slaughterhouse" (April 23, 2013, http://www.currentargus.com/carlsbad-news/ci_23088492/lawyer-inspectors-clear-roswell-horse-slaughterhouse), Jeri Clausing of the Associated Press indicates that the slaughterhouse owners have received death threats and threats of violence against their children and the business.

Some animal welfare groups seek federal legislation that will ban domestic horse slaughtering nationwide. They also advocate humane euthanasia for horses that are severely ill or injured and promote horse rescue and adoption programs. However, horse advocates are not universal in their opposition to domestic slaughterhouses for the animals. In "Rethinking Horse Slaughterhouses" (*Wall Street Journal*, January 5, 2011), Stephanie Simon describes a coalition of animal welfare groups, horse owners, and ranchers who want to reinstate horse slaughterhouses in the United States. The movement is driven by both economic and welfare concerns. Simon notes that "hiring a veterinarian to euthanize and dispose of a horse can cost hundreds of dollars." As a result, unwanted horses are sold for as little as $10 to $20 each and shipped long distances to Mexican slaughterhouses. Welfarists complain that the horses "often suffer greatly on the journey." Simon notes that some horse advocates and animal welfare groups believe unwanted horses would be better off being slaughtered in the United States at facilities that are bound by humane handling regulations.

As noted earlier, some animal protection groups favor a federal ban on exporting horses for slaughter. However, some welfarists fear that if a total slaughter ban is implemented, then horse owners may abandon unwanted animals. In fact, media stories published since the 2007 slaughter ban report increasing numbers of tame horses being turned loose onto public lands, presumably because the owners can no longer afford to feed or care for them. Simon notes that other alternatives advocated by animal welfarists include "providing free hay to economically strapped owners; opening low-cost clinics to geld horses to reduce breeding; even requiring anyone buying a horse to pay an up-front fee to cover euthanasia by a veterinarian when needed."

EXPOSING AGRICULTURE INDUSTRY PROBLEMS

One of the goals of animal protection groups is to expose and publicize alleged animal mishandling and abuse in the agricultural industry. To accomplish this goal, these groups sometimes conduct undercover operations, such as by sending activists who are equipped with hidden cameras to work at agricultural facilities and document alleged abuses. Numerous such videos have been released to the public either through social media channels or via news outlets.

In general, the meat industry strongly condemns the commission of undercover operations at its facilities and questions the validity of the information that is gathered. In "Animal Well-Being Important to America's Egg Producers" (November 21, 2011, http://animalagalliance.org/current/home.cfm?Section=CareImportantToEgg Produce&Category=Press_Releases#), the Animal Agriculture Alliance (AAA), an industry organization for animal agriculture, complains about an undercover video released in November 2011 that was taken at "one of the country's largest egg farms." The video was taken by an activist for Mercy for Animals, an animal rights

FIGURE 4.16

Horses slaughtered, 1990–2007

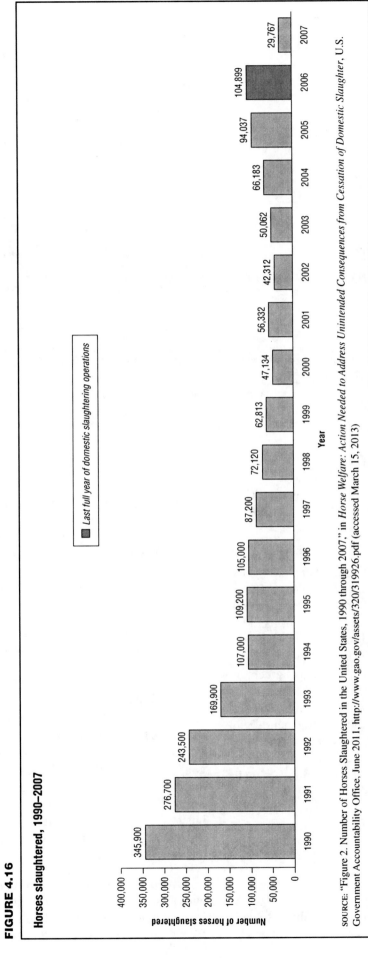

SOURCE: "Figure 2. Number of Horses Slaughtered in the United States, 1990 through 2007," in *Horse Welfare: Action Needed to Address Unintended Consequences from Cessation of Domestic Slaughter*, U.S. Government Accountability Office, June 2011, http://www.gao.gov/assets/320/319926.pdf (accessed March 15, 2013)

FIGURE 4.17

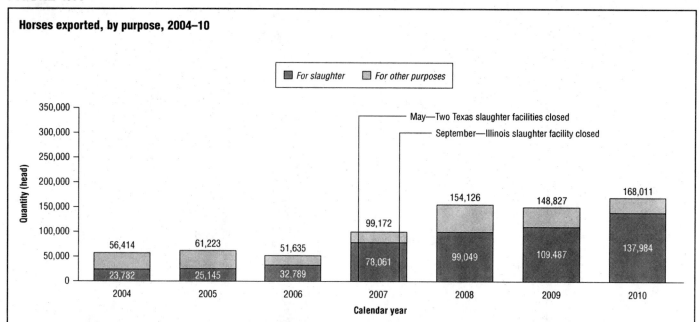

Horses exported, by purpose, 2004–10

Note: U.S. exports of horses intended for slaughter are unofficial estimates because official U.S. export trade data do not specify the quantity or value of horses exported for slaughter. Thus, while official U.S. trade data can be used to determine total U.S. live horse exports (the sum of horses exported for slaughter or other purposes, such as breeding and showing), an estimate of horses intended for slaughter can only be determined using Canadian and Mexican official trade statistics.

SOURCE: "Figure 3. U.S. Exports of Horses Intended for Slaughter and Other Purposes, 2004 through 2010," in *Horse Welfare: Action Needed to Address Unintended Consequences from Cessation of Domestic Slaughter*, U.S. Government Accountability Office, June 2011, http://www.gao.gov/assets/320/319926.pdf (accessed March 15, 2013).

organization. The AAA states "while all abuse or mistreatment is condemned, it is imperative that activists in such positions be held accountable as well for failing to follow a company's policy to immediately report any mistreatment to the appropriate authorities."

The AAA points out that the egg producer targeted in the video was not a member of the UEP and notes that this "is unlikely to be a coincidence." The AAA refers to the agreement mentioned earlier that the UEP forged with the HSUS in 2011 and indicates "the agreement included a conditional moratorium on so-called 'undercover investigations' of UEP members." The HSUS (http://www.human esociety.org/news/press_releases/2011/07/egg_agreement .html) makes no mention of such a moratorium in its publications about the agreement with the UEP. However, in "The HSUS-United Egg Producer Agreement: Two Reactions" (July 12, 2011, http://www.abolitionistapp roach.com/the-hsus-united-egg-producer-agreement-two-reactions/#.UYPU0ijD_IV), Gary L. Francione, a well-known animal rights activist, asserts that as part of the agreement the HSUS agreed "not to conduct undercover investigations at large egg farms unless it was aware of especially egregious practices."

Ag Gag Laws

In 2012 Iowa passed a law (IA Code § 717A.3A) forbidding "agricultural production facility fraud." Under the new law a person commits a crime if he or she:

- Obtains access to an agricultural production facility under false pretenses.

- Makes a false statement or representation as part of an application or agreement to be employed at an agricultural production facility, if the person knows the statement to be false, and makes the statement with an intent to commit an act not authorized by the owner of the agricultural production facility, knowing that the act is not authorized.

Critics call the Iowa law an "ag gag law," because they insist the intent of the law is to prevent activists from publicizing abusive behavior that is captured on video at animal production facilities. In "Taping of Farm Cruelty Is Becoming the Crime" (April 7, 2013, http://www.nytimes .com/2013/04/07/us/taping-of-farm-cruelty-is-becoming-the-crime.html?pagewanted=all&_r=0), Richard A. Oppel Jr. notes that in 2012 Utah and Missouri also passed "ag gag" laws and in early 2013 dozens of states were considering following suit. According to Oppel, the laws have been driven by farmers and ranchers who claim "their businesses have suffered financially from unfair videos that are less about protecting animals than persuading consumers to stop eating meat."

Advocates for undercover investigations at animal enterprises point out that such videos have exposed criminal behavior and protected public health. In 2008 video footage taken covertly at a slaughterhouse operated by

Hallmark Meat Packing Company in Chino, California, resulted in the largest meat recall in U.S. history. Numerous other videos have resulted in criminal prosecutions of workers and/or client backlash. For example, in "'Ag Gag': More States Move to Ban Hidden Cameras on Farms" (March 15, 2013, http://abcnews.go.com/Blotter/states-move-ban-hidden-cameras-farms/story?id=187381 08#.UYPpiSjD_IW), Cindy Galli and Randy Kreider note that the 2010 undercover video taken by a Mercy for Animals activist showed "unsanitary conditions and repeated acts of cruelty on chickens." According to Galli and Kreider after the video was aired on television by ABC News the egg producer lost major clients, including McDonald's and Target.

FISH

Fish farming, or aquaculture, has been around for at least a millennium. Historians believe the Chinese practiced aquaculture in AD 900 to raise fish for their emperor's dinner table. China is still a leading producer of farmed fish. Commercial aquaculture is also a big business in the United States. According to the USDA in *2007 Census of Agriculture*, 6,409 fish farms were operating in the United States in 2007 that sold products worth more than $1.4 billion. Nearly all the rainbow trout and catfish consumed in the United States come from farm operations. Besides freshwater fish, saltwater fish are also raised in farm environments.

Fish farming is accomplished in one of two ways. Producers use netted enclosures in near-offshore ocean waters or they build separate enclosures inland. The second method is considered more environmentally friendly because the farmed fish and their waste are separated from fish living in natural waters. In-ocean farms occasionally lose fish to the surrounding waters, and environmentalists fear that these fish may spread diseases to their wild counterparts. In-ocean farms can also only be used for saltwater species, not freshwater. Fish farms typically keep as many fish as possible in the smallest amount of space possible. These confined operations can cause health problems, particularly sea lice infestation, in the farmed fish.

Several animal welfare groups oppose aquaculture, claiming that farmed fish are subjected to severe overcrowding in water pens that are contaminated with large amounts of fecal matter. In addition, there is controversy over the production of genetically engineered fish. One example goes by the trade name AquaAdvantage and is a modified Atlantic Salmon. In "Panel Leans in Favor of Engineered Salmon" (*New York Times*, September 21, 2010), Andrew Pollack reports the salmon "contain an extra growth hormone gene that allows them to grow to marketable size about twice as fast as conventional fish." In December 2012 the FDA (http://www.fda.gov/Animal Veterinary/NewsEvents/CVMUpdates/ucm339270.htm)

issued a draft Environmental Assessment and a preliminary Finding of No Significant Impact indicating the agency's initial approval of AquaAdvantage Salmon. The FDA established a public comment period, and as of May 2013 a final decision on FDA approval had not been made.

OTHER FARM ANIMALS

Inventory data for various other farm animals were collected by the USDA in *2007 Census of Agriculture*. In 2007 the nation included 3.1 million goats, which are raised for their meat, hair, and milk; and 2.9 million bee colonies, which are farmed for honey production.

Another farm animal of particular interest is the bison (or American buffalo). The bison was driven to the brink of extinction during the 1800s because of overhunting of wild herds. Only a few hundred wild and farmed bison survived. In *2007 Census of Agriculture*, the USDA estimates that 4,499 farms had an inventory of 198,234 bison in 2007. Bison meat is being heavily marketed by the American business executive Ted Turner (1938–). In 2001 Turner opened a chain of restaurants called Ted's Montana Grills (http://www.tedsmontana grill.com/) that feature bison meat. The bison is considered an "exotic" animal under federal law. Its slaughter for commercial human consumption is governed by the Code of Federal Regulations (CFR) Title 9, Part 352 (http://www.access.gpo.gov/nara/cfr/waisidx_10/9cfr352 _10.html), which requires the animal to be rendered unconscious before bloodletting in conventional (nonreligious) slaughterhouse procedures.

WELFARE-FRIENDLY FARMING?

The most strict animal rights activists are opposed to the farming of animals to produce products for human consumption and use. They often embrace a vegan lifestyle, in which no animal products are consumed or used. Others are vegetarians. Vegetarians do not eat meat, but they may consume secondary products, such as milk or eggs. For example, lacto-vegetarians eat dairy products, whereas ovo-vegetarians eat eggs. Lacto-ovo vegetarians eat both.

Vegans and vegetarians make up a small minority of the U.S. population. Table 4.10 shows the results of polls conducted on the subject by the Gallup Organization. In July 2012, 5% of those who were asked considered themselves vegetarians. This percentage was down from 6% reported in Gallup surveys conducted in 1999 and 2001. As shown in Table 4.11 a slightly higher proportion of females (7%) than males (4%) identified themselves as vegetarians in July 2012. Respondents over the age of 50 were slightly more likely than younger people to be vegetarian. Although the results by educational status were mixed, there were distinctions based on

TABLE 4.10

Percentage of Americans considering themselves vegetarians, 1999, 2001, and 2012

IN TERMS OF YOUR EATING PREFERENCES, DO YOU CONSIDER YOURSELF TO BE A VEGETARIAN, OR NOT?

[Among national adults]

	Yes	No
	%	%
Jul 9–12, 2012	5	94
Jul 19–22, 2001	6	94
Sep 23–26, 1999	6	94

SOURCE: Frank Newport, "In terms of your eating preferences, do you consider yourself to be a vegetarian, or not?" in *In U.S., 5% Consider Themselves Vegetarians*, The Gallup Organization, July 26, 2012, http://www.gallup.com/poll/156215/Consider-Themselves-Vegetarians.aspx (accessed March 15, 2013). Copyright © 2012 Gallup, Inc. All rights reserved. The content is used with permission; however, Gallup retains all rights of republication.

TABLE 4.11

Percentage of Americans considering themselves vegetarians, by demographic group, July 2012

IN TERMS OF YOUR EATING PREFERENCES, DO YOU CONSIDER YOURSELF TO BE A VEGETARIAN, OR NOT?

	Yes	No
	%	%
Male	4	96
Female	7	93
18 to 29	5	95
30 to 49	4	96
50 to 64	7	93
65+	7	93
High school or less	6	94
Some college	6	94
College graduate only	3	97
Postgraduate	5	95
Conservative	5	95
Moderate	5	95
Liberal	7	93
Married	3	97
Not married	8	92

SOURCE: Frank Newport, "In terms of your eating preferences, do you consider yourself to be a vegetarian, or not?" in *In U.S., 5% Consider Themselves Vegetarians*, The Gallup Organization, July 26, 2012, http://www.gallup.com/poll/156215/Consider-Themselves-Vegetarians.aspx (accessed March 15, 2013). Copyright © 2012 Gallup, Inc. All rights reserved. The content is used with permission; however, Gallup retains all rights of republication.

political view and marital status. As shown in Table 4.11, liberals were slightly more likely than moderates or conservatives to be vegetarian. In addition, more unmarried people (8%) than married people (3%) considered themselves vegetarian. It should be noted that not all vegetarians embrace their chosen diet for animal rights reasons; many have health, environmental, and/or religious reasons instead of or besides ethical ones. In "In U.S., 5% Consider Themselves Vegetarians," (July 26, 2012, http://www.gallup.com/poll/156215/Consider-Themselves-Vegetarians.aspx), Frank Newport of Gallup reports that in July 2012, only 2% of poll participants considered themselves to be vegan.

There is also growing demand in the United States that more humane methods be employed for animals that are raised and slaughtered for meat and other products. Food suppliers are beginning to make changes that represent significant reforms in animal welfare and slaughter. Some of these changes have no doubt been driven by pressure from vocal animal rights groups. For example, People for the Ethical Treatment of Animals (PETA) has been conducting aggressive publicity and picketing campaigns against major fast-food chains in the United States, and many fast-food chains are implementing more welfare-friendly policies.

Some farmers have initiated reforms on their own. For example, some smaller hog farms are allowing their sows to farrow in straw-filled huts or barns instead of in gestation crates. Welfare-friendly farming is considered part of a larger movement called organic farming. Organic farming of crops involves no use of pesticides or herbicides. This produces a more natural product that many consumers consider healthier and more environmentally friendly. In "Organic Market Overview" (June 19, 2012, http://www.ers.usda.gov/topics/natural-resources-environment/organic-agriculture/organic-market-overview.aspx), the USDA's ERS reports booming consumer demand for organically produced goods. The agency notes that in 2008 organic dairy accounted for 16% of the U.S. organic food sales. Organic meat, fish, and poultry accounted for 3% of the total.

Farmers are not allowed to label their products as organic unless they meet specific requirements that have been established by the U.S. government in the National Organic Program. The organic standards govern living conditions, access to the outdoors, feed rations, and health care practices. No growth hormones or genetic engineering are allowed, and the animals are not fed animal by-products. There are also restrictions on manure management and slaughter procedures. The farmers must provide documentation to the USDA demonstrating that they are following these standards to use the organic label.

Some animal protection groups have implemented their own programs to define and certify welfare-friendly farming operations. In 2000 the American Humane Association (AHA) established the American Humane Certified Program (formerly called the Free Farmed Program). Producers that want to be certified by the AHA must meet specific standards for food and water management, living conditions, and transport, handling, and slaughter techniques. Humane Farm Animal Care (HFAC) is an independent nonprofit organization that administers the

Certified Humane Raised and Handled Program. The HFAC program is funded by various animal welfare organizations, including the HSUS and the American Society for the Prevention of Cruelty to Animals. Products are labeled "Certified humane" if the producers meet specific criteria for animal care that are enforced through an inspection and verification process.

It has also become common for livestock farmers to market products labeled "all natural," "cage free," "grass fed," "pasture raised," "free range," or "free roaming." Critics suggest that these labels are marketing ploys and are not clearly defined or verified by regulatory agencies or animal welfare groups. For example, the label "cage free" has no legally enforceable meaning.

In the fact sheet "Food Labeling: Meat and Poultry Labeling Terms" (April 12, 2011, http://www.fsis.usda .gov/Fact_Sheets/Meat_&_Poultry_Labeling_Terms/index .asp), the USDA states that "a product containing no artificial ingredient or added color and is only minimally processed (a process that does not fundamentally alter the raw product) may be labeled natural. The label must explain the use of the term natural (such as—no added colorings or artificial ingredients; minimally processed)." However, the label can be applied to meat from animals that received antibiotics and other drugs to promote growth. Producers that market free-range or free-roaming chickens are required by the USDA to provide their chickens access to the outside. However, there is no verification process in place to prove this claim. Critics point out that the requirement is satisfied at some chicken houses by including a small door that leads out into a small caged area open to the environment.

The USDA definitions of *free range*, *pasture fed*, and *free roaming* for nonpoultry animals indicate that the animals must be allowed to eat grass and live outdoors for at least part of their lives. Animal welfare groups claim the USDA rarely performs inspections to verify such claims but relies on the statements of livestock producers.

HUMAN HEALTH ISSUES

Because humans consume so many animal products, there is a correlation between the health of farm animals and human health. Even people who do not have moral or philosophical problems with the treatment or consumption of livestock are concerned about some factory farming methods.

Use of Antibiotics

One of the biggest concerns is the routine administration of low doses of antibiotics to farm animals to prevent them from developing diseases and to cure any that might already have diseases. This is called nontherapeutic, subtherapeutic, or preventive antibiotic use. Many people fear that it could lead to the development of antibiotic-resistant diseases in animals and humans. Scientists already know that some bacteria are able to adjust to and tolerate low dosages of weaker antibiotics. Once they achieve this resistance, stronger types of antibiotics are needed to kill them.

In April 2011 researchers at the nonprofit Translational Genomics Research Institute and Northern Arizona University published a study suggesting widespread prevalence of antibiotic-resistant *Staphylococcus aureus* bacteria in the U.S. meat and poultry supply. According to Andrew E. Waters et al., in "Multidrug-Resistant *Staphylococcus aureus* in U.S. Meat and Poultry" (*Clinical and Infectious Diseases*, vol. 52, no. 10, April 15, 2011), the bacteria were found in nearly half of the 136 meat products tested. The products were purchased at retail stores at various locations throughout the country. Nearly all (96%) of the bacterial strains were resistant to at least one antibiotic; more than half (52%) were resistant to multiple antibiotics. Waters et al. note that antibiotics are "routinely administered in feed and water for extended periods to healthy animals" in the United States.

Animal-to-Human Disease Transmission

Another concern related to animal welfare is the fear that U.S. farm animals could transmit diseases to humans, either through live contact or from the consumption of tainted meat products.

Diseases that can be transmitted from animals to humans are called zoonoses. Zoonoses that are associated with farm animals include:

- Anthrax (an infectious disease caused by spore-forming bacterium)

- Avian influenza (sometimes called "bird flu")

- Bovine tuberculosis (a respiratory disease)

- Brucellosis (a flulike illness transmitted by bacteria)

- Leptospirosis (a bacterial disease that can cause a variety of symptoms in humans)

- Orf (a viral skin disease)

- Ringworm (a fungal skin disease)

- Streptococcus suis (a meningitis-like disease mostly associated with pigs)

Of major concern is a group of diseases called transmissible spongiform encephalopathies (TSEs). One TSE is called bovine spongiform encephalopathy (BSE), commonly known as mad cow disease. BSE devastated farm animal populations in England during the 1980s and 1990s. Millions of animals were killed because they either had the disease or as a precaution against the disease. Since 1990 the USDA has conducted a BSE surveillance program on U.S. cattle.

The Centers for Disease Control and Prevention reports in "BSE (Bovine Spongiform Encephalopathy, or Mad Cow Disease)" (February 21, 2013, http://www.cdc.gov/ncidod/dvrd/bse/) that between 1993 and 2012, 23 BSE cases had been reported in North America; only four cases were in the United States—in 2003, 2004, 2006, and 2012.

FUR FARMING

Fur farming is a unique agricultural enterprise for two reasons. First, most of the animals involved are wild instead of domesticated. Second, the animals are raised and killed for their pelts only. The most popular fur animal is mink. According to FurKills.org, in "The Truth about Fur Farming" (2013, http://furkills.org/furfarming.shtml), it takes about 60 female or 35 male mink pelts to produce one fur coat.

Mink are wild animals that are kept in cages on fur farms. They typically breed in the early spring and give birth to litters in the late spring. An average litter contains four or five kits (babies) that are weaned after six to eight weeks. The kits are vaccinated against common diseases. During the late summer and early fall the mink naturally molt (lose their summer fur) and regrow a thick winter coat. The mink are killed in late autumn or early winter. Some are retained for breeding purposes.

In *Mink* (July 6, 2012, http://www.furcommission.com/documents/2012/10/2011-mink-production-in-the-us.pdf/?9338be), the USDA reports that in 2011 there were 268 operational mink farms in the United States that produced a total of 3.1 million pelts, up 9% from 2010. Wisconsin (1.1 million pelts) and Utah (698,960 pelts) were the two largest producing states. The total economic value of pelt production in 2011 was $292 million, up 25% from 2010. According to the USDA, the average price per pelt obtained by mink farmers in 2011 was $94.30, up 15% from $81.90 in 2010.

Animal rights activists and welfarists are extremely critical of the fur industry because they indicate the animals are kept in miserable conditions and in small cages. The HSUS explains that overbreeding by farmers to produce desirable coat colors leads to serious and painful deformities in the animals. The farming and slaughter of fur animals are not regulated by the USDA. The most common killing techniques are gassing, electrocution, and breaking the animals' necks. Fur farming has been banned in many European countries.

Animal welfarists and rights activists have conducted antifur campaigns since the 1960s. PETA's "I'd rather go naked than wear fur" campaign was begun in the 1990s and has featured celebrities such as Pamela Anderson (1967–) and Kim Basinger (1953–) posing nude. PETA activists also regularly disrupt fashion shows featuring fur-clad models and protest outside stores selling fur. In spite of these campaigns, fur sales have continued to rise. Industry analysts indicate that fur demand is driven by weather and economy rather than by animal issues. Foreign demand, particularly in China, is also a key factor.

A Gallup poll conducted in May 2012 found that 60% of those asked said the buying and wearing of clothing made of animal fur is morally acceptable. (See Table 4.12.) In contrast, 35% said it is morally wrong. This breakdown has changed little since the question was asked in 2001.

U.S. mink farmers defend their animal husbandry and slaughtering procedures as humane. They argue that mink in the wild rarely live longer than one year and insist that the mink are handled carefully, both for their welfare and to protect their valuable coats from damage. Producers also insist that the mink are killed quickly and humanely using veterinary-approved methods.

CHAPTER 5
RESEARCH ANIMALS

Research animals are animals that humans use solely in scientific research; in medical and veterinary investigations and training; in the testing of drugs, cosmetics, and other consumer products; and in educational programs. It is not known how many animals are used annually in research, testing, and medical and veterinary training programs in the United States, but the number is certainly in the millions. The Animal Welfare Act only requires certain species to be counted; it excludes birds and specific breeds of mice and rats. Mice in particular are believed to make up the vast majority of the animals used. In *Some We Love, Some We Hate, Some We Eat* (2010), Hal Herzog of Western Carolina University presents estimates of the number of mice that are used in U.S. laboratories, ranging from 17 million to "well over 100 million." Millions more research animals may be kept as classroom pets or teaching aids to educate children in schools.

Living animals that are used as specimens to test drugs and products, practice medical and surgical procedures, and investigate diseases and bodily systems are called laboratory animals. Laboratory animals often die from these procedures or are euthanized by researchers after they are no longer needed. The plight of laboratory animals has been a major issue for animal rights advocates since the 1970s.

People who support the use of animals in research are passionate in their belief that the benefits to people far outweigh the consequences to animals. They point out the important medical and veterinary advances that have resulted. On the contrary, animal rights activists uniformly condemn this use. The most extreme activists have broken into laboratories, released animals, and physically harassed the researchers involved. Animal welfarists work to minimize the pain these animals experience during testing and to improve their living conditions.

The Gallup Organization includes a question about laboratory animals in the morality poll it conducts each year. In 2012, 55% of respondents said "medical testing on animals" is morally acceptable, whereas 38% said it is morally wrong. (See Table 5.1.) Another 4% said the morality depends on the situation, and 1% said it is not a moral issue. The remaining 2% had no opinion on the matter. In general, the moral acceptability of medical testing on animals has fallen since 2001, when 65% of respondents said it is morally acceptable and 26% said it is morally wrong.

Many people react emotionally to the thought of animals in distress. Scientists and researchers—those who work with the animals directly—use clinical terms to describe their work. They refer to laboratory animals as animal models and speak of them as specimens. Antivivisection groups gain support for their views by publicizing the gruesome details of experiments. Photographs of restrained animals with bolts inserted into their skulls or sores on their bodies can disturb the public, regardless of how scientifically justified the experiments may be.

HISTORY

Vivisection on animals and humans dates back to at least the ancient Greeks and Romans. By the Middle Ages moral and religious concerns prohibited most vivisection on humans. There was little debate about the morality of using animals for these purposes. The 17th-century French philosopher René Descartes (1596–1650) and his followers believed that animals were unthinking and unfeeling machines. In the next century the British philosopher and political scientist Jeremy Bentham (1748–1832) summarized his very different thoughts on the subject in *An Introduction to the Principles of Morals and Legislation* (1789): "The question is not, Can they reason? nor, Can they talk? but, Can they suffer?" (See Figure 5.1.)

TABLE 5.1

Public opinion on the morality of medical testing on animals, 2001–12

	Morally acceptable	Morally wrong	Depends on situation (vol.)	Not a moral issue (vol.)	No opinion
2012 May 3–6	55	38	4	1	2
2011 May 5–8	55	38	4	*	3
2010 May 3–6	59	34	4	1	2
2009 May 7–10	57	36	5	*	2
2008 May 8–11	56	38	3	*	3
2007 May 10–13	59	37	3	*	1
2006 May 8–11	61	32	5	*	2
2005 May 2–5	66	30	2	*	2
2004 May 2–4	62	32	4	*	2
2003 May 5–7	63	33	3	*	1
2002 May 6–9	63	30	3	1	3
2001 May 10–14	65	26	5	1	3

Vol. = volunteer.
*Less than 0.5%.

SOURCE: Jeff Jones and Lydia Saad, "18. Next, I'm going to read you a list of issues. Regardless of whether or not you think it should be legal, for each one, please tell me whether you personally believe that in general it is morally acceptable or morally wrong. How about—D. Medical testing on animals?" in *Gallup Poll Social Series: Values and Beliefs—Final Topline*, The Gallup Organization, May 2012, http://www.gallup.com/file/poll/154748/Moral_acceptabilty_120522 .pdf (accessed March 15, 2013). Copyright © 2012 Gallup, Inc. All rights reserved. The content is used with permission; however, Gallup retains all rights of republication.

FIGURE 5.1

Jeremy Bentham. (© *Georgios Kollidas/Shutterstock.com.*)

Throughout the 18th and 19th centuries philosophers debated the moral issues that were involved in animal vivisection. According to historians, the poor and working-class people of the time opposed animal vivisection because they associated it with the dissection of human corpses. The unclaimed bodies of poor people and criminals were often turned over to medical colleges for dissection. There were also well-publicized cases of grave robbing and body snatching to supply researchers with human corpses. These events horrified the common people and made them suspicious of scientists and doctors who were engaged in medical research.

The modern antivivisection movement began during the 19th century. In *Animals' Rights Considered in Relation to Social Progress* (1894), the British humanitarian Henry S. Salt (1851–1939) wrote that "the practice of vivisection is revolting to the human conscience, even among the ordinary members of a not over-sensitive society." The century witnessed organized efforts from animal welfare organizations to achieve legislation against animal cruelty in the United Kingdom and the United States. The Cruelty to Animals Act was passed in the United Kingdom in 1849 and amended in 1876 to restrict the use of animals in research. In 1875 the Society for the Protection of Animals Liable to Vivisection was founded by Frances Power Cobbe (1822–1904). It was later called the Victorian Street Society. In 1898 Cobbe founded the British Union for the Abolition of Vivisection, an organization that is still active.

Vivisection was also fought by welfarists in the United States. In 1871 Harvard University founded one of the first vivisection laboratories in the country, despite opposition from the Massachusetts Society for the Prevention of Cruelty to Animals. Various antivivisection groups were founded, including the American Anti-Vivisection Society in 1883 and the New England Anti-Vivisection Society in 1895. The new antivivisection groups tried, unsuccessfully, to outlaw the practice of vivisection. Regardless, legislation was passed during the 1890s that outlawed repetition of painful animal experiments for the purpose of teaching or demonstrating well-known and accepted facts.

First Half of the 20th Century

In December 1903 the American writer Mark Twain (1835–1910) published the short story "A Dog's Tale" in *Harper's Magazine*. The story was written to protest cruelty to animals and their use in research. It is told from the viewpoint of a dog that lives with the family of a scientist. The dog saves the family's baby from a nursery fire but later sees her own puppy blinded and killed during an experiment that was performed by the scientist to impress his friends. Even though some critics condemned the work as overly sentimental, animal welfarists of the time were pleased that it brought public attention to the issue of animal experimentation.

In 1906 Congress passed the Pure Food and Drug Act (PFDA). The original act did not require any type of testing to ensure that a product was safe or effective. This would change after some tragic events occurred. According to Susan E. Wilson-Sanders of the University of Arizona, in "Mrs. Brown's Sad Story: A History of the Food, Drug, and Cosmetic Act" (September 26, 2011, http://www.uac.arizona.edu/VSC443/Alternmethod/Fda pap03.htm), many Americans were injured, sickened, or even killed by unsafe potions, "snake oils," and patent medicines that were sold by entrepreneurs during the early decades of the 20th century. Some of these products contained incredibly toxic substances, such as dinitrophenol, a compound used to make explosives.

During the 1920s and 1930s hair dyes containing an aniline compound called paraphenylenediamine became popular. Even though it was well known that aniline compounds were harmful to the eyes, a cosmetics company still chose to introduce a brand of mascara called Lash-Lure that contained these chemicals. Doctors reported thousands of eye injuries that were caused by the product, and even a few deaths after patients suffered serious infections. Many states banned the use of aniline dyes in personal-care products.

Wilson-Sanders mentions several other popular cosmetic products of the time that caused injury, such as Anti-Mole, Berry's Freckle Ointment, Bleachodent (a teeth whitener), Dr. Dennis's Compound, Koremlu cream, and Dewsberry Hair Tonic. These products contained high concentrations of acids or other toxic chemicals. Whisker dyes marketed to men contained dangerous levels of silver or lead acetate. A popular depilatory (hair removal cream) contained rat poison.

According to Wilson-Sanders, doctors lobbied Congress throughout the 1930s to crack down on dangerous

drugs and personal products that were sold to Americans, but they were opposed by powerful marketing groups. In 1937 nearly 100 people (mostly children) died after drinking a product called Elixir of Sulfanilamide that contained sulfa antibiotics dissolved in diethylene glycol (antifreeze). The public was outraged and pressured Congress to strengthen the original PFDA and include cosmetics. The Food, Drug, and Cosmetic Act (FDCA) was passed in 1938. It contained a requirement for animal testing.

Wilson-Sanders notes that the first tests were conducted on rats and could last less than one month. The testing requirements were gradually amended to include different species and to last for longer periods. By 1957 drug testing had to be performed on rats or dogs for up to six months. By the 1980s testing was required to last 12 to 18 months. Testing on pregnant animals was instituted during the 1960s following the thalidomide tragedy. Thalidomide is a drug that was widely prescribed in Canada and Europe during the late 1950s to treat nausea in pregnant women. More than 10,000 babies with birth defects resulted. The drug had been extensively tested on animals, but it had not been tested on pregnant animals. New guidelines for testing the effects of drugs on animal reproduction and fetus development were incorporated into the FDCA.

Second Half of the 20th Century

Historians note that the antivivisection movement subsided with the advent of World War I (1914–1918) and did not resurge until the 1960s. One of the driving forces behind the movement's rebirth was the story of Pepper, a Dalmatian who disappeared from her family's backyard in Pennsylvania in July 1965. The family tracked the dog to an animal dealer in New York, but he refused to return the dog. The family enlisted the help of the Animal Welfare Institute, the Pennsylvania State Police, and Representative Joseph Resnick (1924–1969; D-NY), but they were too late. Pepper had been sold to a hospital in New York City that conducted an experiment on her and euthanized her.

The story was widely publicized and led to public outrage. Bills were introduced in the U.S. House of Representatives and the U.S. Senate that called for animal dealers and laboratories to be licensed and inspected by the U.S. Department of Agriculture (USDA) and be required to meet certain humane standards of care. The bills were opposed by strong lobbying groups and were in danger of failing until a story ran in the February 4, 1966, issue of *Life* magazine.

"Concentration Camps for Dogs" was the story of a police raid on a dog dealer's facility in Maryland. The story included horrific photographs of abused dogs that were kept in filthy cages until they could be sold to research laboratories. According to the article, the dogs were to be sold at auction for $0.30 per pound. Letters flooded politicians' offices and editorials appeared in major newspapers around the country calling for federal legislation.

A few months later Congress passed the Laboratory Animal Welfare Act of 1966. It called for the licensing of animal dealers and the regulation of laboratory animals. The original act applied to cats, dogs, guinea pigs, hamsters, primates, and rabbits. In 1970 the act was renamed the Animal Welfare Act (AWA) and amended to cover several other warm-blooded animals. A year later the USDA decided to exclude birds, mice, and rats from coverage under the act, arguing that the department did not have the staff needed to regulate the huge numbers of such animals involved. It also noted that most of these small animals were used at research institutions that had other oversight protections in place to regulate their use.

The publication of *Animal Liberation: A New Ethics for Our Treatment of Animals* (1975) by the Australian philosopher Peter Singer (1946–) brought more coverage to the use of animals in scientific research. The book includes disturbing photographs and descriptions of animals being subjected to all sorts of painful procedures for questionable purposes. Singer argues that the pain and suffering inflicted on the animals is too high a moral price to pay for scientific research.

In 1976 the animal activist Henry Spira (1927–1998) led a campaign protesting the American Museum of Natural History's research on the effects of castration and mutilation on cats' sexual behavior. The campaign was hailed as a success by activists after the museum halted the research a year later. Spira then turned his attention to the testing of cosmetics on animals and formed a coalition of animal welfare and antivivisection groups to educate the public about the subject. In full-page advertisements in major newspapers, Spira accused major cosmetics companies of being cruel to animals. Public response was immediate. Several companies, including Revlon and Avon, announced their intention to cease animal testing and find new alternatives. In 1981 the Cosmetics, Toiletries, and Fragrance Association funded the founding of the Center for Alternatives to Animal Testing (CAAT) at Johns Hopkins University. By the end of the 1980s Revlon and Avon had ceased animal testing.

In 1985 Congress amended the AWA to require that researchers minimize animal pain and distress whenever possible through the use of anesthesia, analgesics (painkillers), and humane euthanasia. New requirements were added regarding the physical and psychological well-being of dogs and primates used in research work. Throughout the 1980s and 1990s animal welfare groups petitioned and sued the USDA to add birds, mice, and rats to the animals covered under the AWA but were unsuccessful. In 1990 AWA coverage was extended to horses and other farm animals.

Scientists engaged in animal research watched with concern as animal welfare and antivivisection groups launched aggressive publicity campaigns against them. In 1979 the National Association for Biomedical Research was founded. In "About NABR" (2013, http://www.nabr.org/About_NABR.aspx), the organization states that it "works to protect the ability of biomedical researchers to use animals in ethical and responsible research that will one day benefit the health of people and animals." In 1981 the Foundation for Biomedical Research and the Michigan Society for Medical Research (MISMR) were founded with similar goals. These organizations work to counter claims by animal rights activists that animal research and testing are cruel practices with little to no scientific value.

PEOPLE FOR THE ETHICAL TREATMENT OF ANIMALS AND THE SILVER SPRING MONKEY CASE. In 1981 a little-known organization called People for the Ethical Treatment of Animals (PETA) gained national prominence through an exposé on paralysis experiments that were being conducted on monkeys at the Institute of Behavioral Research in Silver Spring, Maryland. The research was funded by the National Institutes of Health (NIH) and led by the psychologist Edward Taub (1931–). It involved depriving monkeys of sensory input into their spinal cords to give them denervated arms, or arms in which the nerves were not active. The monkeys gnawed and licked their arms, producing wounds. Taub hired Alex Pacheco (1958–) to work as a laboratory assistant. He was not aware that Pacheco had cofounded PETA the year before. Pacheco secretly photographed the monkeys, then reported the lab to authorities. A subsequent raid led to the filing of animal cruelty charges against Taub.

The incident came to be known as the Silver Spring Monkey Case. Even though the charges against Taub were eventually dropped, the publicity made PETA famous. The monkeys were confiscated, and Congress forced the NIH to cease the research. This was viewed as a major triumph by people involved in antivivisection and the growing animal rights movement.

ANIMAL ENTERPRISE PROTECTION ACT. During the late 1970s and 1980s animal research institutions and animal industries experienced an increasing number of violent acts that were committed by animal rights extremists. Activists broke into laboratories and fur farms to "liberate" animals and damage buildings and equipment. Some of these activists claimed to be part of the Animal Liberation Front (ALF), an emerging movement that embraced radical and illegal actions on behalf of animals. The rise of the ALF is described in the 1993 report *Report to Congress on the Extent and Effects of Domestic and International Terrorism on Animal Enterprises* (http://www.naiaonline.org/articles/article/report-to-congress-on-the-extent-and-effects-of-domestic-and-internati) by the U.S. Department of Justice. The report notes that even though PETA disavowed taking part in violent activities, the group publicized them on its website and praised the activists for their actions on behalf of animals.

Rising concern among research scientists and animal industries about animal activist violence led to the passage of the Animal Enterprise Protection Act (AEPA) of 1992. It prohibits "causing physical disruption to the functioning of an animal enterprise." Three types of animal enterprises are defined:

- Commercial or academic enterprises that use animals to produce food or fiber or for agriculture, research, or testing

- Zoos, aquariums, circuses, rodeos, and other legal sporting events

- Fairs and similar events that are designed to advance agricultural arts and sciences

Offenses that can be charged under the AEPA include using the mail to cause physical disruption at animal enterprises and stealing, damaging, or causing the loss of property used by animal enterprises. Property includes animals and records.

In 2006 the AEPA was amended and strengthened through the Animal Enterprise Terrorism Act (AETA). According to Brent J. McIntosh (May 23, 2006, http://www.justice.gov/olp/pdf/animal_enterprise_terrorism_act _brent_mcintosh_testimony.pdf), the former U.S. deputy assistant attorney general, the AETA broadens the definition of "animal enterprise" and allows perpetrators to be prosecuted for acts that are committed against individuals (e.g., the employees of animal enterprises), rather than just against facilities or companies. The constitutionality of the AETA has been challenged by civil liberties groups, including the Center for Constitutional Rights (CCR). In "Blum v. Holder" (2013, http://www.ccrjustice .org/ourcases/Blum), the CCR notes that in 2011 it filed a federal lawsuit—*Blum v. Holder*—challenging the AETA "as an unconstitutional infringement on free speech." The organization took the case on behalf of five plaintiffs the CCR describes as "longtime animal rights activists whose advocacy work has been chilled due to fear of being prosecuted as a terrorist under the AETA." The case was dismissed in March 2013 after a judge found the plaintiffs "did not have standing to bring the case." The CCR indicates it appealed the ruling. As of May 2013, no additional information on the appeal was available.

HUNTINGDON LIFE SCIENCES BECOMES A TARGET. During the 1990s, PETA continued to use infiltration to secretly obtain photographs and videotapes, which were then publicized to make the public aware of the realities of animal research. In 1996 and 1997 the group conducted an eight-month undercover investigation at a Huntingdon Life Sciences (HLS) facility in New Jersey. HLS

is a major target of antivivisection groups because it is one of the largest contract companies that conducts animal research. A PETA member began working at the HLS facility and secretly collected documents, photographs, and videotapes that PETA used to file a formal complaint against HLS with the USDA. PETA also released some of the material to the media.

HLS countersued PETA, claiming that the materials were obtained by illegal means and that PETA had violated the Economic Espionage Act and the AEPA. In December 1997 a mutual settlement was reached in which PETA agreed to turn over all records taken from HLS and cease trying to infiltrate HLS property for five years, and HLS agreed to drop its lawsuit against PETA.

In 1999 Stop Huntingdon Animal Cruelty (SHAC), a new animal rights group, began using radical and violent means against the HLS headquarters in the United Kingdom. Cars were firebombed and company executives were assaulted outside their homes. Several activists were arrested and jailed for violent crimes. SHAC then shifted its focus to target companies that provided HLS with services, funding, and equipment. Activists picketed and flooded the companies with threatening messages. Employees were harassed, assaulted, and had their homes vandalized. The intimidation tactics worked, and many companies severed their business ties with HLS. According to Alan Cowell, in "Scene Shifts in Fight against British Testing Lab" (NYTimes.com, January 22, 2002), the company's stock dropped in value from $3 per share in 1993 to $0.06 a share in 2002, even though the company was making a modest profit.

In 2002 HLS moved its stock market listing to the United States. Cowell reports that HLS was taken over "on paper" by Life Sciences Research, a company that was set up by HLS and incorporated in Maryland. This arrangement allowed HLS to take advantage of U.S. privacy laws that protect the identity of certain investors. An American arm of SHAC known as SHAC USA was formed to lead an intimidation campaign against HLS and companies that do business with it. In 2004 SHAC USA and seven individuals associated with it were indicted in New Jersey under federal charges for violating the AEPA, stalking, and conspiracy to commit terrorism. In 2006 the organization and six of the individuals were found guilty. They were sentenced to various prison terms. SHAC USA officially ceased to exist; however, animal activists developed a new website (http://www .shac7.com) that as of May 2013 continued to publicize the case and accuse HLS of abusing animals.

HLS became a private company in 2009. In the press release "Continued Full AAALAC Accreditation for HLS PRC Facility" (March 22, 2013, http://www.huntingdon .com/News/2013-03-22/Continued-Full-AAALAC-Accredi tation-for-HLS-PRC-facility/#.UYTaNSjD_IU), the company states that it is "very proud of our animal welfare and care standards" and notes that its Princeton Research Centre in East Millstone, New Jersey, is accredited by the Association for Assessment and Accreditation of Laboratory Animal Care (AAALAC). The AAALAC is an independent nonprofit organization founded in 1965 by scientists and veterinarians engaged in animal research. The AAALAC notes in "Benefits of AAALAC International Accreditation" (2011, http://www.aaalac.org/accreditation/benefits.cfm) that accreditation "demonstrates a willingness to go above and beyond the minimums required by law. It tells the public that the institution is committed to the responsible care and use of animals in science."

OTHER ACTIVIST VIOLENCE. During the first decade of the 21st century, research facilities and individual researchers were targeted in Iowa and California, respectively. In 2004 vandals damaged some research laboratories and offices at the University of Iowa and released mice, pigeons, and rats that were being used for animal research. Two animal activists suspected in the crime were later arrested, but released because of lack of evidence. The article "Animal Activists Attacking Scientists' Homes" (Associated Press, July 7, 2008) describes a rash of incidents that were waged against researchers at California universities. These incidents included harassment (e.g., loud chanting and setting off firecrackers outside homes), vandalism of private homes and vehicles, threatening phone calls and e-mails, and even firebombings. In August 2008 a firebomb ignited the front door of the home of the biologist David Feldheim of the University of California, Santa Cruz (UCSC). Feldheim and his family escaped through a second-story window. A second firebomb detonated only minutes later, damaging a car that was owned by another UCSC scientist.

Will Potter notes in "New Grand Jury Subpoenas Related to UC-Santa Cruz Investigation" (May 15, 2012, http://www.greenisthenewred.com/blog/grand-jury-uc-santa-cruz-california/6104/) that in May 2012 a grand jury investigation of the incidents was ongoing and two individuals had been subpoenaed as witnesses. As of May 2013, no arrests had been made in the 2008 firebombings. Mainstream antivivisection and welfarist groups condemn any violent or threatening tactics that are used by radical animal rights activists and instead wage public relations and political campaigns against the use of research animals.

PETA VIDEOS. In September 2010 PETA made national headlines when it released a video that showed apparent animal abuse and neglect at a rural North Carolina facility. In "Professional Laboratory and Research Services Undercover Investigation" (2013, http://www.peta.org/features/professional-laboratory-and-research-services.aspx), PETA reports that the facility tested animal products, such as flea and tick preventatives, for major pharmaceutical companies. An undercover PETA operative worked at the facility for nine months and documented many instances of what PETA calls "shocking" mistreatment and neglect, including workers shouting and cursing at the animals, squirting animals with bleach, dragging animals by their ears and throwing them, allowing animals to live in excrement, and not treating sores and other health conditions. PETA reports that in September 2010, shortly after the organization made its findings public, the facility relinquished all of its animals to shelters and rescue organizations and closed down.

In April 2013 PETA released an undercover video that it says shows "cruel medical training exercises" being conducted on cats at Washington University in St. Louis, Missouri (WUSL). In "Shocking Video Exposes Cat Intubation Cruelty" (2013, https://secure.peta.org/site/Advocacy?cmd=display&page=UserAction&id=4757), PETA notes that the school has students conduct intubation procedures on cats in order to learn how to intubate human infants. Intubation is the insertion of tubing through the mouth and down the windpipe, most often done to facilitate breathing in a patient that is injured or ill. According to PETA, there was no reason to teach this potentially painful procedure using cats, and that almost all other medical schools used infant simulators instead. Furthermore, PETA complained that the cats at WUSL were not being properly anesthetized before the procedures and were being intubated so often they risked injury. Sam Levin indicates in "Bob Barker Writes to Washington University: I'll Pay You $75,000 to Stop Abusing Cats" (RiverfrontTimes.com, April 25, 2013) that the television personality Bob Barker (1923–), an advocate for animal welfare causes, offered to donate $75,000 to the university for the purchase of infant simulators. According to Levin, the college "has repeatedly defended its practice," argues that the cats "feel no pain" from the practice sessions, and insists that all of the cats "do ultimately get adopted."

FEDERAL LEGISLATION AND OVERSIGHT

Facilities that use certain species of live laboratory animals for research and testing purposes must abide by laws and policies governing their use. Even though there are a few state laws that also apply, most of the applicable legislation and oversight is provided by federal agencies. Table 5.2 lists the acronyms, laws, and regulations that are related to the federal oversight of laboratory animal usage.

Animal Welfare Act

AWA regulations are enforced by the Animal Care unit of the USDA's Animal and Plant Health Inspection Service (APHIS). The regulations govern the housing and

TABLE 5.2

Acronyms and common terms associated with laboratory animal oversight

AAALAC	Association for Assessment and Accreditation of Laboratory Animal Care International. Independent organization that accredits animal care and use programs.
AALAS	American Association for Laboratory Animal Science. Organization of laboratory animal technicians, veterinarians, and other professionals that serves society through education and the advancement of responsible laboratory animal care and use.
ACLAM	American College of Laboratory Animal Medicine. Organization that establishes standards for board certification in the veterinary medical specialty of laboratory animal medicine. Board certified veterinarians are known as ACLAM diplomats.
AHRQ	Agency for Healthcare Research and Quality. Agency of the Public Health Service.
APHIS	Animal and Plant Health Inspection Service. Component of the USDA that administers the Animal Welfare Act. Within APHIS, Animal Care (AC) is the agency that is responsible for ensuring compliance with the Animal Welfare Regulations.
AVMA	American Veterinary Medical Association. Professional organization of veterinarians.
AWA	Animal Welfare Act. Federal law regulating the use, sale, and handling of animals.
AWIC	Animal Welfare Information Center. Part of the United States Department of Agriculture's National Agricultural Library, AWIC provides information and publications on many aspects of animal welfare and alternatives to the use of animals.
Animal Welfare Regulations	USDA regulations that implement the Animal Welfare Act.
CDC	Centers for Disease Control and Prevention. Agency of the Public Health Service.
FDA	Food and Drug Administration. Agency of the Public Health Service.
FOIA	Freedom of Information Act. Statute allowing the public access to certain information on file in federal agencies.
Guide	Guide for the Care and Use of Laboratory Animals. Manual of standards for animal care and use developed under the auspices of the Institute for Laboratory Animal Research.
Health Research Extension Act of 1985	Federal law that mandates the PHS Policy.
HRSA	Health Resources and Services Administration. Agency of the Public Health Service.
IACUC	Institutional Animal Care and Use Committee. Committee charged with oversight of institutional animal care and use program.
IHS	Indian Health Service. Agency of the Public Health Service.
ILAR	Institute for Laboratory Animal Research. Component of the National Research Council, National Academy of Sciences, responsible for developing and disseminating information on humane care and appropriate use of animals.
IRAC	Interagency Research Animal Committee. Author of U.S. Principles and the focal point for coordinating federal policies involving all animal species needed for biomedical research and testing, especially their care, use, and conservation.
NIH	National Institutes of Health. Agency of the Public Health Service.
OLAW	Office of Laboratory Animal Welfare. NIH office with responsibility for implementation of the PHS Policy.
OPRR	Office for Protection from Research Risks. The OPRR Division of Animal Welfare was renamed the Office of Laboratory Animal Welfare in March, 2000.
PHS	Public Health Service. Component of the Department of Health and Human Services that includes eight different agencies.
PHS Policy	PHS Policy on Humane Care and Use of Laboratory Animals. Document that implements the Health Research Extension Act of 1985, and governs activities involving animals conducted or supported by PHS agencies.
Principles	United States Government Principles for the Utilization and Care of Vertebrate Animals Used in Testing, Research, and Training. Nine principles that provide a foundation for humane care and use of animals in the United States.
SAMHSA	Substance Abuse and Mental Health Services Administration. Agency of the Public Health Service.
USDA	United States Department of Agriculture. Federal agency responsible for implementation and enforcement of the Animal Welfare Act.

SOURCE: *Acronym Glossary and Additional Resources*, National Institutes of Health, Office of Laboratory Animal Welfare, December 1, 2011, http://grants1.nih.gov/grants/olaw/tutorial/glossary.htm (accessed March 26, 2013)

care of the animals and include licensing, registration, veterinary, and record-keeping requirements. Covered facilities must register with the USDA.

As of May 2013, the AWA covered cats, dogs, guinea pigs, hamsters, marine mammals, primates, rabbits, and "other warm-blooded animals." It did not apply to cold-blooded animals, birds, or certain species of mice or rats, which were excluded from the definition of *animal* under the law. Nor does it cover farm animals that are used for food or fiber.

Under the AWA each research facility must have an attending veterinarian who is required to provide adequate veterinary care to the facility's animals. The law defines adequate veterinary care as "what is currently the accepted professional practice or treatment for that particular circumstance or condition." Each research facility must have an institutional officer who is responsible for legally committing the facility to meet AWA requirements. This officer or the chief executive officer of the facility must appoint an institutional animal care and use committee (IACUC) to assess the research facility's animal program, buildings, and procedures. The IACUC must include at least three members (a chairperson, a veterinarian, and a person not affiliated with the institute) to represent "general community interests." IACUC members have to be qualified based on their experience and expertise.

The IACUC is responsible for reviewing the research facility's animal use program and inspecting the facilities in which animals are housed and studied. These evaluations must be done at least once every six months. Written reports are required and must be made available to APHIS and to any federal agencies that provide funding to the facility. The IACUC is also responsible for investigating any complaints that are lodged against the research facility regarding the care and use of the animals. This includes complaints from the general public. The IACUC has the power to approve or disapprove proposed animal care and use activities and to ask for modifications in these activities. It can also suspend particular animal activities if it believes they are not being conducted in accordance with its wishes.

Under the AWA proposed animal activities must meet certain criteria. Some of the major requirements include:

- Procedures must "avoid or minimize discomfort, distress, and pain to the animals."

- Researchers must consider alternative procedures that will not cause more than momentary or slight pain and provide reasons in cases where alternatives cannot be used.

- Researchers must provide written assurance that the activities "do not unnecessarily duplicate previous experiments."

Any procedures that may cause more than momentary or slight pain or distress require that pain-relieving drugs be administered, "unless withholding such drugs is scientifically justified." Animals cannot be administered paralyzing drugs unless they are also given anesthesia. Animals that experience severe or chronic pain or distress that cannot be relieved are required to be painlessly euthanized as soon as possible, unless researchers seek and receive an exemption from the IACUC.

RESEARCH FACILITIES AND ANNUAL REPORTS. According to APHIS, in fiscal year (FY) 2012 there were 1,240 registered research facilities in the United States. (See Table 5.3.) This number has decreased since FY 2003, when 1,396 research facilities were registered with the USDA. The facilities are mostly colleges and universities, pharmaceutical companies, hospitals, and biotechnology laboratories. Table 5.4 lists the number of registered research facilities by state for FY 2012. The states with the largest numbers were California (153), New York (88), and Texas (88).

All research facilities are required to comply with AWA regulations and standards. Federal facilities are not

TABLE 5.3

Number of facilities submitting an "Annual Report of Research Facility," fiscal years 2003–12

Fiscal year	Number of facilities
2003	1,396
2004	1,353
2005	1,337
2006	1,313
2007	1,312
2008	1,305
2009	1,321
2010	1,306
2011	1,290
2012	1,240

SOURCE: Adapted from "Annual Report Information," in *Animal Care Information System Search Tool: Advanced Search: Annual Report Search*, U.S. Department of Agriculture, Animal and Plant Health Inspection Service, 2013, http://acissearch.aphis.usda.gov/LPASearch/faces/Warning.jspx (accessed March 22, 2013)

TABLE 5.4

Number of facilities submitting an "Annual Report of Research Facility," by state, fiscal year 2012

State	Number of facilities
Alabama	11
Alaska	3
Arizona	14
Arkansas	12
California	153
Colorado	23
Connecticut	15
Delaware	3
District of Columbia	9
Florida	33
Georgia	23
Hawaii	3
Idaho	9
Illinois	42
Indiana	25
Iowa	23
Kansas	16
Kentucky	6
Louisiana	14
Maine	12
Maryland	42
Massachusetts	81
Michigan	34
Minnesota	30
Mississippi	8
Missouri	31
Montana	5
Nebraska	11
Nevada	4
New Hampshire	2
New Jersey	31
New Mexico	9
New York	88
North Carolina	33
North Dakota	2
Ohio	47
Oklahoma	14
Oregon	10
Pennsylvania	59
Puerto Rico	2
Rhode Island	8
South Carolina	16
South Dakota	5
Tennessee	19
Texas	88
Utah	11
Vermont	6
Virginia	27
Washington	26
West Virginia	6
Wisconsin	33
Wyoming	3
Total	**1,240**

SOURCE: Adapted from "Annual Report Information," in *Animal Care Information System Search Tool: Advanced Search: Annual Report Search*, U.S. Department of Agriculture, Animal and Plant Health Inspection Service, 2013, http://acissearch.aphis.usda.gov/LPASearch/faces/Warning.jspx (accessed March 22, 2013)

required to register with the USDA and are not subject to USDA inspections, though they are required to comply with USDA standards for animal care that are established under the AWA and must submit annual reports to the USDA regarding their use of regulated laboratory animals. The AWA requires that nonfederal research facilities receive at least one inspection per year to determine compliance with the law.

Research facilities covered under the AWA are required to file an Annual Report of Research Facility (ARRF) with APHIS. ARRFs dating back to 2009 are available through the Animal Care Information System (ACIS) Search Tool (http://acissearch.aphis.usda.gov/LPASearch/faces/Warning.jspx); some older reports are available at "Annual Report of Research Facility (APHIS Form 7023)" (http://www.aphis.usda.gov/animal_welfare/efoia/7023.shtml). ARRFs must show the number and species of animals used in research, testing, and experimentation and indicate whether pain-relieving drugs were administered. If the drugs were not administered for procedures that caused pain or distress, the report must explain why their use would have interfered with the research or experiment.

Health Research Extension Act

In 1985 the Health Research Extension Act (HREA) was passed. This act requires that facilities conducting animal research, training, and testing activities that receive funding from the Public Health Service (PHS) follow an animal welfare policy called the Public Health Service Policy on the Humane Care and Use of Laboratory Animals (PHSP). The PHS includes government agencies such as the Centers for Disease Control and Prevention, the U.S. Food and Drug Administration (FDA), and the NIH. The NIH is the main public source of funding for biomedical research in the United States.

The animal research facilities that fall under the HREA must follow the recommendations given in the National Academy of Sciences' *Guide for the Care and Use of Laboratory Animals*. As of May 2013, the most recent edition was the eighth edition (http://grants.nih.gov/grants/olaw/Guide-for-the-Care-and-Use-of-Laboratory-Animals.pdf), which was published in 2011. The guide covers housing, cleanliness, husbandry, veterinary care, and use of measures to alleviate pain and distress. The standards are similar to those found in the AWA, but the HREA applies to all vertebrates, including birds, mice, and rats.

The HREA requires facilities to file annual reports that describe their animal care and use programs and how they comply with the AWA and the PHSP. The PHSP is administered by the NIH Office for Protection from Research Risks. Research facilities that receive funding from the NIH must have at least five people on their IACUC. The NIH also reviews planned animal studies to ensure that animal models are appropriate and that no more animals than necessary are used.

Food, Drug, and Cosmetic Act

Another major piece of federal legislation that affects laboratory animals is the Food, Drug, and Cosmetic Act (FDCA) of 1938, which has been amended several times. The FDCA defines drugs as:

- Articles intended for use in the diagnosis, cure, mitigation, treatment, or prevention of disease in man or other animals; and

- Articles (other than food) intended to affect the structure or any function of the body of man or other animals

Drugs must receive FDA approval before they can be sold in the United States. Even though the FDA does not specify the tests that must be done, the agency does not allow human testing to occur if animal safety testing is considered inadequate or incomplete.

Cosmetics are defined as articles other than soap that are applied to the human body for "cleansing, beautifying, promoting attractiveness, or altering the appearance." Soaps are specifically excluded from the regulatory definition of cosmetics, so they do not fall under the FDCA.

Cosmetic products and their ingredients (except for color additives) are not subject to premarket FDA approval. However, it is illegal to distribute cosmetics that contain substances that could harm consumers under normal use. Thus, even though animal testing is not required by the law, it is recommended by the FDA to ensure product safety. Cosmetic products that are not adequately tested for safety must have a warning statement on their front label reading "WARNING—The safety of this product has not been determined."

Some consumer products are considered to be both a drug and a cosmetic under the law, such as dandruff shampoos, fluoride-containing toothpastes, combination antiperspirants/deodorants, and makeup products or moisturizers that contain sunscreens. These products are subject to provisions of the laws that apply to both drugs and cosmetics.

Chimpanzee Health Improvement, Maintenance, and Protection Act

In 2000 the Chimpanzee Health Improvement, Maintenance, and Protection (CHIMP) Act was passed, calling for the creation of a national sanctuary system for chimpanzees no longer needed in research programs that are conducted or supported by federal agencies. Most chimpanzees involved in federal research programs have been or are used in hepatitis, human immunodeficiency virus (HIV), and acquired immunodeficiency syndrome (AIDS) research. In 2002 the NIH awarded a contract to Chimp Haven Inc. to establish and operate a sanctuary under the CHIMP Act in Shreveport, Louisiana. The facility was dedicated in 2004. In "Meet the Chimps" (2013, http://www.chimphaven.org/meet-the-chimps/), the organization reports that it is home to more than 120 chimpanzees, including former pets, chimps used in the entertainment industry, and research subjects. The sanctuary notes that "many of the chimpanzees have been infected with HIV and Hepatitis. Chimp Haven is the only facility in the nation able to provide care for chimpanzees with infectious diseases." As of May 2013, Chimp Haven was the only sanctuary in the national chimpanzee sanctuary system. It was supported by federal funding and private donations.

Tadlock Cowan of the Congressional Research Service notes in *The Animal Welfare Act: Background and Selected Legislation* (September 27, 2012, http://www .nationalaglawcenter.org/assets/crs/RS22493.pdf) that during the 1980s the NIH enthusiastically bred chimps captured from the wild, because it assumed they "would be ideal laboratory models for AIDS." However, this assumption proved disappointing, and the NIH eventually ceased its chimp breeding program. Cowan indicates that the NIH originally considered euthanizing its "surplus" chimps, but instead decided to rehome them in sanctuaries. As of September 2012, the federal government had retired 152 chimps to Chimp Haven. Approximately 500 additional chimps had been placed in private sanctuaries. The latter chimps had been used for military, air, and space research. Cowan points out that "the United States is the only developed country that continues large-scale confinement of chimpanzees in federal laboratories. The European Union, Japan, and New Zealand have banned or strictly limited their use."

In January 2013 a panel that was convened to consider the NIH's use of chimpanzees in research published its final report. In *Council of Councils Working Group on the Use of Chimpanzees in NIH-Supported Research: Report* (http://dpcpsi.nih.gov/council/pdf/FNL_Report _WG_Chimpanzees.pdf), the panel states that "in light of evidence suggesting that research involving chimpanzees has rarely accelerated new discoveries or the advancement of human health for infectious diseases, with a few notable exceptions such as the hepatitis viruses, the NIH should emphasize the development and refinement of other approaches, especially alternative animal models (e.g., genetically altered mice), for research on new, emerging, and reemerging diseases." The panel recommends that "the majority of NIH-owned chimpanzees" be retired to the federal sanctuary system and that about 50 chimps be kept for future research purposes. According to the panel, the NIH owned or financially supported 670 chimps as of October 23, 2012. This included 561 chimps at research facilities and 109 retired chimps at Chimp Haven. In addition, the NIH supported research projects involving 91 chimps at the Southwest National Primate Research Center in San Antonio, Texas. The panel notes that in September 2012, 110 of the NIH-owned chimps were "designated as permanently ineligible for biomedical

research" and were slated to be retired to Chimp Haven before the end of 2013. According to Chimp Haven, 50 of the newly retired chimps arrived at the sanctuary in January 2013.

Other Federal Legislation

The Federal Hazardous Substances Labeling Act was passed in 1960. The Consumer Product Safety Commission administers the law as it applies to household products. This law affects animals because household products (such as cleaners) that contain hazardous chemicals must warn consumers about their potential hazards. A hazardous substance is defined as one that is toxic, corrosive, flammable, or combustible; that is extremely irritating or sensitizing; or that generates pressure through heat, decomposition, or other means. Toxicity tests are required to determine these conditions. Other laws governing chemicals that must be tested for toxicity include the Federal Insecticide, Fungicide, and Rodenticide Act of 1947 and the Toxic Substances Control Act of 1976. Both of these laws are administered by the U.S. Environmental Protection Agency. Animals are commonly used to test the products that are regulated by all of these laws.

LABORATORY ANIMALS AND THEIR USES

Determining the number of animals that are used for research in the United States is extremely difficult because birds, cold-blooded animals, and some species of mice and rats are not regulated by the AWA and do not have to be counted. However, it is widely agreed that mice and rats make up a huge majority of research animals.

As noted earlier, data on AWA-regulated animals at USDA-registered research facilities can be accessed using the ACIS Search Tool. Table 5.5 shows that 937,580 live animals were used by these facilities in FY 2012. California used the most regulated animals (101,184), followed by Massachusetts (67,299) and Ohio (64,467). Table 5.5 and Figure 5.2 provide a breakdown of the research animals used by species. Guinea pigs accounted for the largest number (22%, or 203,384), followed by rabbits (20%, or 184,924). As shown in Table 5.6, the total number of covered animals used at registered research facilities was just under 1 million in FY 2008. It rose to 1.1 million in FY 2010 and then declined. Guinea pigs and rabbits were the most-used species between FYs 2008 and 2012.

Biomedical Research

The vast majority of research animals are used in biomedical research. Biomedicine is a medical discipline that is based on principles of the natural sciences, particularly biology and biochemistry.

TABLE 5.5

Number of animals used in research, by species and state, fiscal year 2012

	Dogs	Cats	Guinea pigs	Hamsters	Rabbits	Non-human primates	Sheep	Pigs	Other farm animals	All other covered species	Total
Alabama	1,156	157	203	42	770	223	49	777	497	1,077	4,951
Alaska	0	0	0	42	0	0	0	0	0	419	461
Arizona	335	90	60	107	180	34	40	495	33	3,977	5,351
Arkansas	343	113	166	1	1,085	110	0	865	297	13	2,993
California	2,920	1,246	13,180	4,317	31,867	4,193	2,208	4,513	11,798	24,942	101,184
Colorado	697	366	2,466	1,020	449	0	607	579	228	1,664	8,076
Connecticut	388	0	187	981	733	272	28	463	0	787	3,839
Delaware	0	0	10	0	8,702	0	26	10	408	28	9,184
District of Columbia	12	7	272	490	154	229	53	677	0	1,800	3,694
Florida	1,135	517	283	360	454	495	215	1,518	228	2,550	7,755
Georgia	2,567	663	1,309	10,220	3,161	2,873	105	1,097	568	6,699	29,262
Hawaii	51	13	0	0	8	0	0	101	0	6	179
Idaho	119	46	36	0	49	0	72	2	83	167	574
Illinois	3,538	1,110	2,124	2,088	2,725	619	595	1,548	631	5,460	20,438
Indiana	1,129	530	119	974	803	119	194	759	106	3,619	8,352
Iowa	1,119	564	1,487	18,513	2,754	23	605	1,312	713	4,122	31,212
Kansas	1,687	675	1,219	92	188	199	64	362	312	1,283	6,081
Kentucky	302	98	31	174	143	107	31	422	27	391	1,726
Louisiana	447	103	7	72	476	2,869	0	38	225	881	5,118
Maine	52	376	0	0	123	0	4	15	102	473	1,145
Maryland	934	6	12,893	4,051	3,244	7,757	330	1,943	256	23,048	54,462
Massachusetts	1,319	57	20,845	6,255	16,649	5,968	492	6,950	1,056	7,708	67,299
Michigan	4,887	439	17,830	1,185	6,332	3,673	791	2,468	421	4,492	42,518
Minnesota	4,087	3,495	28,058	498	8,929	203	1,262	3,259	1,446	3,333	54,570
Mississippi	150	20	301	16	511	63	25	219	8	53	1,366
Missouri	2,768	1,862	7,896	26,604	4,688	164	138	1,821	114	1,130	47,185
Montana	0	0	38	271	32	4	31	0	55	115	546
Nebraska	116	103	17	341	32	37	10	75	280	2,292	3,303
Nevada	465	26	61	0	30	0	30	96	356	1,582	2,646
New Hampshire	2	0	0	902	1	6	0	96	0	659	1,666
New Jersey	4,140	330	13,965	11,274	8,964	4,884	21	792	0	503	44,873
New Mexico	58	40	0	43	118	0	0	0	0	72	331
New York	3,569	1,778	11,224	28,396	7,021	1,929	319	1,293	490	7,340	63,359
North Carolina	2,139	1,074	9,366	920	2,619	1,718	197	1,842	4,507	1,976	26,358
North Dakota	94	139	1	3	0	0	165	27	201	107	737
Ohio	6,169	2,178	31,057	1,946	14,049	1,990	194	3,025	263	3,596	64,467
Oklahoma	597	88	622	8	101	95	0	24	55	499	2,089
Oregon	648	241	595	25	277	3,354	445	440	1,366	1,551	8,942
Pennsylvania	3,393	1,707	3,319	953	21,066	1,716	665	3,530	1,498	2,674	40,521
Puerto Rico	0	0	0	70	23	4,135	0	26	0	30	4,284
Rhode Island	0	0	0	348	652	40	47	91	0	169	1,347
South Carolina	305	241	310	72	240	144	4	323	73	2,473	4,185
South Dakota	26	13	6	24	5	5	57	0	157	7	300
Tennessee	425	106	136	570	221	103	19	1,670	118	1,330	4,698
Texas	1,734	402	12,003	3,586	15,298	3,492	561	3,370	5,405	10,866	56,717
Utah	781	515	1,995	2,397	1,566	1	394	193	192	1,053	9,087
Vermont	9	9	176	0	4	0	1,572	34	5	195	2,004
Virginia	234	54	136	339	480	101	86	4,175	271	1,833	7,709
Washington	884	429	3,809	96	1,080	2,079	11	1,779	358	15,185	25,710
West Virginia	40	56	9	8	112	0	73	0	0	10	308
Wisconsin	5,521	334	3,553	3,650	15,749	7,350	210	777	398	4,565	42,107
Wyoming	42	30	4	2	7	0	69	0	35	122	311
Total	63,533	22,446	203,384	134,346	184,924	63,376	13,114	55,891	35,640	160,926	937,580

SOURCE: Adapted from "Annual Report Information," in *Animal Care Information System Search Tool: Advanced Search: Annual Report Search*, U.S. Department of Agriculture, Animal and Plant Health Inspection Service, 2013, http://acissearch.aphis.usda.gov/LPASearch/faces/Warning.jspx (accessed March 22, 2013)

The NIH maintains the database Report Expenditures and Results (http://projectreporter.nih.gov/reporter.cfm), which describes biomedical research projects that have received funding from federal agencies dating back to 1972. The database can be searched to find information about federally funded research projects at universities, hospitals, and other research institutions. Information supplied about each project includes the name of the principal investigator, the name and address of the research institution, the starting and ending dates of the project, the federal agency providing funding, and a description of the project.

DRUG TESTING. According to the FDA, in "The Beginnings: Laboratory and Animal Studies" (August 12, 2011, http://www.fda.gov/Drugs/ResourcesForYou/Consumers/ucm143475.htm), drug companies typically test new drugs on at least two different animal species to see if they are affected differently. Animal testing is performed to determine specific characteristics, such as:

- How much of the drug is absorbed into the blood-stream
- Any toxic side effects
- Appropriate dosage levels
- How the drug is metabolized (broken down) by the body
- How quickly the drug is excreted from the body

The results from animal tests tell researchers if and how new drugs should then be tested on humans.

FIGURE 5.2

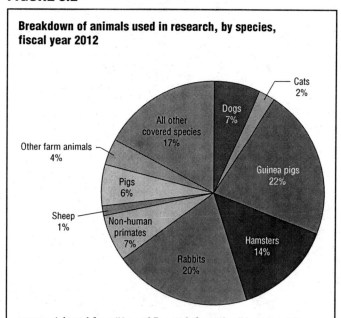

Breakdown of animals used in research, by species, fiscal year 2012

- Cats 2%
- Dogs 7%
- All other covered species 17%
- Other farm animals 4%
- Guinea pigs 22%
- Pigs 6%
- Sheep 1%
- Non-human primates 7%
- Hamsters 14%
- Rabbits 20%

SOURCE: Adapted from "Annual Report Information," in *Animal Care Information System Search Tool: Advanced Search: Annual Report Search*, U.S. Department of Agriculture, Animal and Plant Health Inspection Service, 2013, http://acissearch.aphis.usda.gov/LPASearch/faces/Warning.jspx (accessed March 22, 2013)

Product Testing

Millions of research animals are used to test products that are intended for industrial and consumer markets in the United States. Product safety testing exposes animals to chemicals to determine factors such as eye and skin irritancy. Common product safety tests that are conducted on animals include:

- Acute toxicity tests to determine the immediate effects of chemical exposure. The LD-50 test is an example. In this test animals are exposed to chemicals through ingestion, inhalation, or skin contact to determine the concentration necessary to kill 50% of the test group within a specific period.
- Skin and eye irritancy tests to determine the effects on skin and eyes of chemical exposure. One animal-based example is the Draize eye test. Rabbits are commonly used because they cannot blink and wash out the chemicals.
- Chronic and subchronic toxicity tests to determine the effects of long-term chemical exposure.
- Genetic toxicity tests to determine the effects of chemical exposure on reproductive organs.
- Birth defects tests to determine the effects of chemical exposure on offspring.
- Cancer potential tests to determine the potential of chemical exposures for causing cancer.

CONSUMER PRODUCTS. Some companies selling consumer products, such as cosmetics and household cleaners, advertise that they do not conduct animal testing on their products or that their products are "cruelty-free." However, CAAT notes in "FAQs (Frequently Asked Questions)" (2013, http://altweb.jhsph.edu/resources/faqs.html) that such claims are not regulated by the federal government and "can mean different things to different companies." For example, CAAT states that even if a company making such a claim does not conduct animal testing it might buy supplies from other companies that do,

TABLE 5.6

Number of animals used in research, by species, fiscal years 2008–12

Fiscal year	Dogs	Cats	Guinea pigs	Hamsters	Rabbits	Sheep	Pigs	Other farm animals	Marine mammals	Non-human primates	All other covered species	Total
2008	70,305	20,305	227,629	153,607	234,808	14,286	58,763	30,371	0	71,256	118,468	999,798
2009	67,337	20,160	203,098	150,051	222,167	13,551	57,966	29,620	0	70,444	145,378	979,772
2010	64,930	21,578	213,029	145,895	210,172	13,271	53,260	38,008	126	71,317	303,107	1,134,693
2011	60,115	21,648	137,306	142,368	176,243	13,032	57,860	37,674	*	64,966	154,350	865,562
2012	63,533	22,446	203,384	134,346	184,924	13,114	55,891	35,640	*	63,376	160,926	937,580

*Included in "All other covered species."

SOURCE: Adapted from "Annual Report Information," in *Animal Care Information System Search Tool: Advanced Search: Annual Report Search*, U.S. Department of Agriculture, Animal and Plant Health Inspection Service, 2013, http://acissearch.aphis.usda.gov/LPASearch/faces/Warning.jspx (accessed March 22, 2013)

or that such a claim might only mean that the finished product was not tested on animals after a certain date.

CAAT points out that the vast majority of cosmetic ingredients that are used by the industry have been tested on animals at some point in time, or are known to be safe based on decades of use. It notes that smaller cosmetics companies tend to produce final products that are made from purchased ingredients, rather than from ingredients that are developed in-house. Larger companies that develop new ingredients for cosmetics must use animal testing or viable alternatives to prove that the ingredients are safe for consumer use.

The National Anti-Vivisection Society maintains the website "Cruelty-Free Product Search" (http://www.navs.org/page.aspx?pid=431), at which consumers can search for information about companies that produce personal care (e.g., bath products, deodorants, and antiperspirants), household (e.g., bathroom and kitchen cleaners and furniture polishes), pet care, and cosmetic products and find out whether these companies do or do not test their products on animals. Other animal organizations, such as PETA, maintain similar types of lists. Some provide a seal that compliant companies can use to mark their products for easy identification by shoppers.

The European Union (EU) states in the press release "Full EU Ban on Animal Testing for Cosmetics Enters into Force" (http://europa.eu/rapid/press-release_IP-13-210_en.htm) that a complete ban on the marketing of cosmetic products that have been tested on animals went into effect on March 11, 2013. Products that had been tested on animals could no longer be marketed within the EU's member nations after this date. This followed a 2004 ban on the testing of cosmetics on animals, and a more limited 2009 marketing ban that had permitted testing for "the most complex human health effects," such as carcinogenity (the ability or tendency to cause cancer) and reproductive toxicity. The EU notes that "full replacement of animal testing by alternative methods" had not yet been achieved by March 2013, but that the EU and the cosmetics industry continued to fund research into nonanimal-based testing methods.

Dissection

Dead animals used for dissection in schools are believed to make up a small portion of all research animals. The HSUS explains in "Questions and Answers about Dissection" (September 28, 2009, http://www.humanesociety.org/issues/dissection/qa/questions_answers.html) that millions of animals—mostly frogs, pig fetuses, and cats—are dissected by U.S. schoolchildren each year. Dissection has been considered a staple of biology classes since the 1960s, when the National Science Foundation urged schools to implement a more hands-on science curriculum.

The first legal challenge against school dissection lodged by a student occurred in California in 1987. A high school student sued her school for not allowing her to perform an alternative to dissection. California and Florida became the first states to allow students to opt out of dissection during the mid- to late 1980s. Other states have since followed suit with choice-in-dissection laws or policies.

By the early 21st century many students were expressing ethical and moral concerns about the practice of dissection in the classroom. In response, some school districts began offering students alternatives, such as computer models. The National Science Teachers Association defends dissection as a valuable learning tool for children, but urges teachers to be flexible in offering alternatives.

Surgical/Medical Training and Behavior Research

It is estimated that the use of laboratory animals for surgical/medical training and behavior research makes up only a small part of the number of research animals that are used every year. However, this category is one that is particularly criticized by antivivisection groups. In the past, surgeons training to operate on humans and animals almost always practiced on live animals. Many of these surgeries were terminal surgeries, meaning that the animals were not allowed to regain consciousness. The animals were euthanized while they were under the effects of anesthesia.

Many veterinary schools are limiting the number of terminal surgeries that are required of their students. Some veterinary schools conduct dissection labs. According to the Physicians Committee for Responsible Medicine, many schools now use animal cadavers that are donated by people whose pets or livestock have died of natural causes or have been humanely euthanized because of illness or injury.

SOURCES OF RESEARCH ANIMALS

Research animals are obtained by laboratories from animal breeders and brokers who are licensed by the USDA. These licenses fall into two types:

- Class A—breeders who sell animals that they have bred and raised on their own premises and who buy animals only to replenish their breeding stock

- Class B—breeders, dealers, brokers, and operators of auction sales that purchase and/or resell live or dead animals, often obtained from city or county animal shelters

Breeders who sell fewer than 25 dogs and/or cats per year that are born and raised on their own premises, for research, teaching, or testing purposes, are exempt.

A May 2013 search of APHIS records using the ACIS Search Tool revealed that 4,424 breeders and 1,360 dealers had registered with the agency. However, only 2,244 breeders and 795 dealers were active as of May 2013. It should be noted that not all breeders and dealers sell animals to research laboratories. Some sell animals to pet stores and other animal enterprises.

Laboratory animal suppliers advertise their animals in the *Lab Animal Buyer's Guide* (http://guide.labanimal.com/guide/index.html/). As of May 2013, the guide listed 437 companies that provide products and services. Animals available included birds, cats, cattle, chickens, dogs, ducks, ferrets, fish, frogs, goats, newts, nonhuman primates (excluding chimpanzees), opossums, rabbits, salamanders, sheep, swine, toads, woodchucks, exotic animals, invertebrates, and a wide assortment of rodents.

Purpose-Bred Animals

The vast majority of laboratory research animals are purpose-bred, meaning that they are born and raised under controlled conditions and may be genetically manipulated. Purpose-breeding of laboratory animals is becoming more and more common as researchers demand animals with particular genetic makeups. For example, researchers investigating narcolepsy use dogs that are bred to be born with the condition. Charles River Laboratories in Wilmington, Massachusetts, is a leading breeder and supplier of purpose-bred animals.

Random-Source Animals

Laboratory research animals can also be purchased from random sources. For example, cats and dogs obtained from animal shelters are considered random-source animals. Researchers acquire these animals from dealers with USDA Class B licenses or directly from shelters. Class B dealers can acquire random-source cats and dogs for resale, but only from the following sources:

- Other USDA licensed dealers

- State-, county-, or city-owned and operated animal pounds or shelters

- Humane groups and contract pounds that are organized as legal entities under the laws of their state

- People who have bred and raised the animals on their own premises

Class B dealers are prohibited from obtaining cats and dogs from private individuals who did not breed and raise the animals on their own premises.

The rules that Class B dealers must follow when acquiring animals are primarily intended to prevent them from selling pets to research facilities. For example, Class B dealers must hold live cats and dogs for specific periods before reselling them, and the dealers have to

TABLE 5.7

Holding periods required for dogs and cats held by USDA-licensed "B" dealers

IF the source is	AND the dog/cat's age is	THEN the holding period is
a private pound, contract pound or shelter	any age	10 full days, not including the day of acquisition and the time in transit
a state, city, or county operated pound or shelter	any age	5 full days, not including the day of acquisition and the time in transit
a private individual who bred and raised the dog/cat on his/her premises	< or = 120 days	24 hours, not including the time in transit
a private individual who bred and raised the dog/cat on his/her premises	>120 days	5 full days, not including the day of acquisition and the time in transit
another USDA licensed dealer or exhibitor who has already held the dog/cat for the required holding period	any age	24 hours, not including the time in transit
another USDA licensed dealer or exhibitor who has not held the dog/cat for the required holding period	any age	5 full days, not including the day of acquisition and the time in transit

SOURCE: Adapted from "Random Source Dog and Cat Dealer Inspection," in *Animal Care Inspection Guide*, U.S. Department of Agriculture, Animal and Plant Health Inspection Service, September 2010, http://www.aphis.usda.gov/animal_welfare/downloads/Consolidated_Inspection_Guide/AC%20Consolidated%20Inspection%20Guide%20-%20Complete.pdf (accessed March 23, 2013)

keep records, including physical information about each animal (age, color, sex, species, and breed) and the names and addresses of the seller and buyer of each animal. (See Table 5.7.) This gives pet owners a chance to track down lost pets that were sold to Class B dealers by animal shelters. Random-source dealers are listed in the *Lab Animal Buyer's Guide*. Some animal protection groups also maintain lists of Class B dealers that they believe sell random-source cats and dogs to laboratories.

Random-source animals are used in research where genetic diversity is important. According to the MISMR, in "The Use of Pound Animals in Biomedical Research" (2013, http://www.mismr.org/educational/pound.html), random-source animals are primarily used in biomedical research on arthritis, blindness, birth defects, cancer, cardiovascular diseases, diabetes, hearing loss, lung disorders, and orthopedics. Cats are the subject of choice for research that focuses on the central nervous system, strokes, and disorders of the brain, eyes, and ears. Dogs are frequently used for research into heart and kidney disease. The MISMR notes in "About Michigan Society for Medical Research (MISMR)" (2013, http://www.mismr.org/about/) that use of these animals in research benefits not only human medicine but also veterinary medicine.

In "Use of Pound Animals in Biomedical Research," the MISMR explains that random-source cats and dogs are far less expensive than those that are purpose-bred. It also claims that less than 2% of the 10 million animals that reside in shelters each year are used for medical research. The organization claims that if these animals were not used for research they would be euthanized in the shelters anyway because of the pet overpopulation problem.

Animal welfare organizations, however, disagree, claiming that neither municipal animal shelters nor Class B dealers all follow the regulations. They may fail to keep animals for the assigned period or do not keep detailed records of the animals they sell. Despite industry regulations, lost family pets may become the subjects of experiments when they are not held for the entire waiting period. In addition, there has been much controversy over Class B dealers, some of whom have been known to steal pets from homes and yards. Welfarists and animal rights activists often criticize the NIH for funding research projects that use pound/shelter cats and dogs. The NIH leaves source decisions to individual research institutions. Although some people are pushing for legislation to outlaw the use of pound/shelter animals in medical research, the MISMR argues that this would drive up the cost of research and the costs to local communities that must house and euthanize unwanted animals. Those involved in the animal welfare and rights movement respond with evidence that more and more animal shelters are adopting a "no-kill" policy—meaning they will euthanize only in cases of severe illness or temperament problems but not because of overpopulation—so shelter animals will not necessarily be euthanized and may instead be adopted.

The HSUS reports in "The Humane Society of the United States Applauds the Minnesota Legislature and Governor Dayton for Protecting Pets" (May 4, 2012, http://www.humanesociety.org/news/press_releases/2012/05/minnesota_ends_pound_seizure_050412.html) that some states allow, or even require, publicly funded animal pounds and shelters to turn over their animals to research facilities upon request. According to the HSUS, as of August 2012, 10 states specifically allowed pound seizure, and one state (Oklahoma) required it unless prohibited by local ordinance. Seventeen states had banned pound seizure, most recently Minnesota in 2012. The remaining states did not specifically address pound seizure in their laws.

CLASS B DEALER BUSTED BY THE USDA. In August 2003 federal authorities raided Martin Creek Kennels in Williford, Arkansas, and confiscated more than 100 dogs and one cat. The facility had a USDA Class B license to purchase and resell animals. The raid resulted from an undercover videotape that was obtained by the animal protection group Last Chance for Animals (LCA). The videotape documented many cases of abuse and neglect at the facility and several incidences of dogs being shot to death and thrown into mass graves. Brenda Shoss reports in "Pet Theft Thugs: They're Real. They're Nearby" (March 24, 2005, http://www.kinshipcircle.org/columns_articles/0052.html) that the kennel had purchased stolen pets from bunchers (people who steal pets, pick up strays, and take in dogs and cats that are given away for free and sell them to Class B dealers). The kennel bought stolen pets for $5 to $30 per animal and sold them using falsified paperwork to research laboratories for $150 to $700 per dog and $50 to $200 per cat.

Shoss notes that the kennel had been in business for 16 years, and during that time it sold thousands of animals to research laboratories. In February 2005 C. C. Baird, the owner of the kennel, and his family were fined $262,700 by the USDA and had their Class A and B licenses revoked permanently, as part of a plea agreement in a civil case. The LCA reports in "'Dealing Dogs'—The Sentencing" (2013, http://lcanimal.org/index.php/campaigns/class-b-dealers-and-pet-theft/dealing-dogs-class-b-dealer-cc-baird-investigation/the-sentencing) that C. C. Baird and his wife, Patsy Baird, also faced federal criminal charges, which in another plea agreement resulted in additional fines and property forfeitures of over $1 million and several years of probation. In 2006 HBO produced the documentary *Dealing Dogs*, which used footage from the Last Chance for Animals videotape.

Because of cases such as this, those in the animal rights and welfare community, as well as veterinarians, frequently warn against placing "free to good home" advertisements, fearing that the animals offered will end up in the hands of bunchers or Class B dealers.

In *Animal Welfare: USDA's Oversight of Dealers of Random Source Dogs and Cats Would Benefit from Additional Management Information and Analysis* (September 2010, http://www.gao.gov/new.items/d10945.pdf), the U.S. Government Accountability Office (GAO) reports that as of July 2010 only nine Class B dealers were licensed by APHIS to sell random-source cats and dogs to research facilities. By contrast, more than 100 dealers were operating during the early 1990s. Between November 2007 and November 2008 Class B dealers sold 3,139 animals to research facilities. The GAO finds that APHIS inspections had revealed "numerous" violations at Class B dealer facilities, "such as the condition of animal housing and inadequate veterinary care." As of July 2010, the GAO reports that "several dealers were under further APHIS investigation due to repeated violations." In addition, the GAO notes that APHIS was insufficient in its "traceback" procedures, which ensure that random-source cats and dogs originally came to the dealers from legitimate sources. The GAO complains that APHIS "cannot systematically detect problems with tracebacks and take all available steps to ensure random source dealers obtain dogs and cats from legitimate sources."

REDUCTION, REFINEMENT, AND REPLACEMENT

In 1959 William M. S. Russell (1925–2006) and Rex L. Burch (1926–1996) published *Principles of Humane Experimental Technique*, which advocates three principles for the animal research industry: reduction, refinement, and replacement. The first principle calls for reducing the number of animals used in research and the number of procedures that require the use of whole animals. Refinement involves refining practices to reduce animal suffering and distress and encourage animal well-being. Replacement involves replacing animal testing with alternative methods and replacing higher animal species with lower species. Russell and Burch called these three principles "the three R's for the removal of inhumanity" in the scientific community.

The book was largely ignored until the 1980s, when public protest against the use of animals in laboratory testing became more widespread. Scientists and animal welfare organizations then embraced the three Rs as scientifically reasonable and humane goals for the industry. The three Rs, however, are guiding principles, not legal requirements.

Search for Alternatives to Animal Tests

In 1993 the National Institutes of Health Revitalization Act was passed, requiring the formation of an agency to oversee validation of alternatives to toxicological animal testing. The result was the Interagency Coordinating Committee for the Validation of Alternative Methods (ICCVAM) and the National Toxicology Program Interagency Center for the Evaluation of Alternative Toxicological Methods (NICEATM).

The ICCVAM is responsible for establishing validation criteria and for encouraging government agencies that regulate toxicity testing to accept validated methods. Table 5.8 lists the federal government agencies that are associated with the ICCVAM. The NICEATM facilitates information sharing among all the parties involved. Table 5.9 lists the major duties of the ICCVAM and the NICEATM. The first duty is to evaluate the scientific validity of new or revised testing methods and strategies. Table 5.10 shows the test methods and approaches that had been evaluated by the ICCVAM as of March 2012. Some of the tests, such as the isolated chicken eye test, rely on parts from dead animals. In "Isolated Chicken Eye (ICE) Test Method" (January 19, 2011, http://iccvam.niehs.nih.gov/meetings/Implement-2011/Ocular-present/8-Allen.pdf), David Allen notes that "although chickens are required as a source of eyes, only chickens humanely killed for food or other non-laboratory purposes are used as eye donors (i.e., no live animals are used in this assay)." In addition, the ICE test is much quicker (one day to complete) than the

TABLE 5.8

Member agencies of the Interagency Coordinating Committee on the Validation of Alternative Methods (ICCVAM)

[Member agencies are indicated in boldface]

- **Consumer Product Safety Commission**
- **Department of Agriculture**
- **Department of Defense**
- **Department of Energy**
- Department of Health and Human Services
  Centers for Disease Control and Prevention
  - **Agency for Toxic Substances and Disease Registry**
  - **National Institute for Occupational Safety and Health**
  Food and Drug Administration
  National Institutes of Health
  - **National Cancer Institute**
  - **National Institute of Environmental Health Services**
  - **National Library of Medicine**
- **Department of the Interior**
- Department of Labor
  Occupational Safety and Health Administration
- **Department of Transportation**
- **Environmental Protection Agency**

ICCVAM = Interagency Coordinating Committee on the Validation of Alternative Methods.

SOURCE: "ICCVAM Member Agencies," in *NICEATM and ICCVAM: Advancing Public Health and Animal Welfare*, U.S. Department of Health and Human Services, National Toxicology Program, March 6, 2012, http://iccvam.niehs.nih.gov/docs/about_docs/NICEATM-GenInfo-2012-508.pdf (accessed March 23, 2013)

TABLE 5.9

Major duties of the National Toxicology Program Interagency Center for the Evaluation of Alternative Toxicological Methods (NICEATM) and the Interagency Coordinating Committee on the Validation of Alternative Methods (ICCVAM)

What is NICEATM?

NICEATM provides scientific and operational support for ICCVAM. NICEATM works closely with ICCVAM to:
- Carry out test method evaluations
- Sponsor test method validation studies
- Organize workshops and peer reviews
- Communicate with ICCVAM stakeholders

What are the major duties of NICEATM and ICCVAM?

- Evaluate the scientific validity of new, revised, and alternative safety testing methods and testing strategies
- Provide recommendations on test method usefulness and limitations to U.S. Federal agencies
- Provide guidance on test method development and scientific validation
- Develop standardized protocols for new and revised test methods
- Identify reference substances for test method validation studies
- Develop performance standards for new test methods
- Collaborate with other national and international validation and test guideline organizations
- Communicate findings to regulatory agencies, the scientific community, and other stakeholders

Notes: NICEATM = National Toxicology Program Interagency Center for the Evaluation of Alternative Toxicological Methods. ICCVAM = Interagency Coordinating Committee on the Validation of Alternative Methods.

SOURCE: "What Are the Major Duties of NICEATM and ICCVAM?" in *NICEATM and ICCVAM: Advancing Public Health and Animal Welfare*, U.S. Department of Health and Human Services, National Toxicology Program, March 6, 2012, http://iccvam.niehs.nih.gov/docs/about_docs/NICEATM-GenInfo-2012-508.pdf (accessed March 23, 2013)

TABLE 5.10

Alternative test methods and approaches evaluated by the Interagency Coordinating Committee on the Validation of Alternative Methods (ICCVAM)

Test methods and approaches evaluated by ICCVAM include:

- Ocular toxicity
  - Bovine corneal opacity and permeability test
  - Cytosensor microphysiometer test
  - Isolated chicken eye test
  - Use of anesthetics, analgesics, humane endpoints
- Acute oral toxicity
  - Up and down procedure
  - *In vitro* methods to set starting doses
- Skin corrosivity and irritation
  - Corrositex®
  - EpiSkin™
  - EpiDerm™
  - SkinEthic™
  - Rat skin transcutaneous electrical resistance assay
- Skin sensitization
  - Local lymph node assay (LLNA)
  - Reduced LLNA
  - Non radioisotopic LLNA protocols
  - Using the LLNA for mixtures and potency assessments
- Endocrine disruption
  - *In vitro* estrogen receptor assays
  - *In vitro* androgen receptor assays
- Pyrogenicity
  - *In vitro* pyrogen tests

Note: ICCVAM = Interagency Coordinating Committee on the Validation of Alternative Methods.

SOURCE: "Test Methods and Approaches Evaluated by ICCVAM Include," in *NICEATM and ICCVAM: Advancing Public Health and Animal Welfare*, U.S. Department of Health and Human Services, National Toxicology Program, March 6, 2012, http://iccvam.niehs.nih.gov/docs/about_docs/NICEATM-GenInfo-2012-508.pdf (accessed March 23, 2013)

traditional test using live rabbits, which takes 21 days to complete. Several of the tests listed in Table 5.10 are conducted in vitro (conducted in a test tube or other controlled environment rather than within a living organism) and rely on synthetically produced human skin, rather than live animal skin.

As shown in Figure 5.3 and Figure 5.4, each test method is thoroughly tested and independently peer-reviewed (reviewed by other qualified scientists not directly involved in creating the test) to determine its acceptability. Upon approval, the ICCVAM transmits is final recommendations regarding each test method to federal agencies and international organizations, such as the United Nations, so that they can make informed decisions about whether or not to accept and begin using the method.

Pain and Distress

One of the goals of refinement is to relieve animal pain and distress. APHIS tracks the occurrence of pain and distress in regulated animals based on data provided by registered facilities in their ARRFs. For FYs 2008 through 2010 the agency has summarized pain and distress data for all covered facilities. (As of May 2013, the data for subsequent years were available only on a facility-by-facility basis from the APHIS database using the ACIS Search Tool.) In FY 2008, 76,387 covered animals reportedly experienced pain during testing or research and were not given drugs to relieve the pain. (See Table 5.11.) This represented approximately 7.6% of the total 999,798 animals used that year. Guinea pigs (31,673) and dogs (28,731) were the animals most often subjected to painful procedures without drug relief. In FY 2009, 76,441 animals out of 979,772 (or 7.8%) were categorized as experiencing pain with no drug relief. (See Table 5.12.) Hamsters (32,503) and Guinea pigs (30,775) accounted for the largest numbers by species. As shown in Table 5.13, in FY 2010, 97,123 out of 1.1 million regulated animals (or 8.6%) suffered pain but were not administered pain-relieving drugs. Again, hamsters (48,015) and guinea pigs (33,652) were the most common subjects.

Animal welfare groups express doubts about the validity of APHIS pain and distress numbers, saying that these numbers are greatly underreported by research institutions. In 1998 the HSUS launched the Pain and Distress Campaign to focus attention on issues that are involved in assessing and relieving pain in laboratory animals. In "Questions and Answers about Pain and Distress in Research Animals" (April 20, 2011, http://www.humanesociety.org/issues/pain_distress/qa/questions_answers.html), the HSUS notes that the goal of the initiative is to eliminate pain and distress in research animals by 2020. By contrast, animal rights advocates seek an end to all animal testing.

DISAPPOINTING MOUSE RESULTS

In January 2013 animal researchers were stunned to learn that a detailed study had found mice to be unsuitable for researching certain diseases in humans. In "Genomic Responses in Mouse Models Poorly Mimic Human Inflammatory Diseases" (*Proceedings of the National Academy of Sciences*, January 7, 2013), Junhee Seok et al. report the results of a systematic study that showed that mice used as research animals poorly mimic human inflammatory diseases. In "Of Mice, Men, and Medicine" (February 19, 2013, http://directorsblog.nih.gov/of-mice-men-and-medicine/), Francis Collins (1950–), the director of the NIH, publicly states his disappointment at hearing the news: "The humble laboratory mouse has taught us a phenomenal amount about embryonic development, disease, and evolution. And, for decades, the pharmaceutical industry has relied on these critters to test the safety and efficacy of new drug candidates. If it works in mice, so we thought, it should work in humans. But when it comes to molecules designed to target a sepsis-like condition, 150 drugs that successfully treated this condition in mice later failed in human clinical trials—a heartbreaking loss of decades

FIGURE 5.3

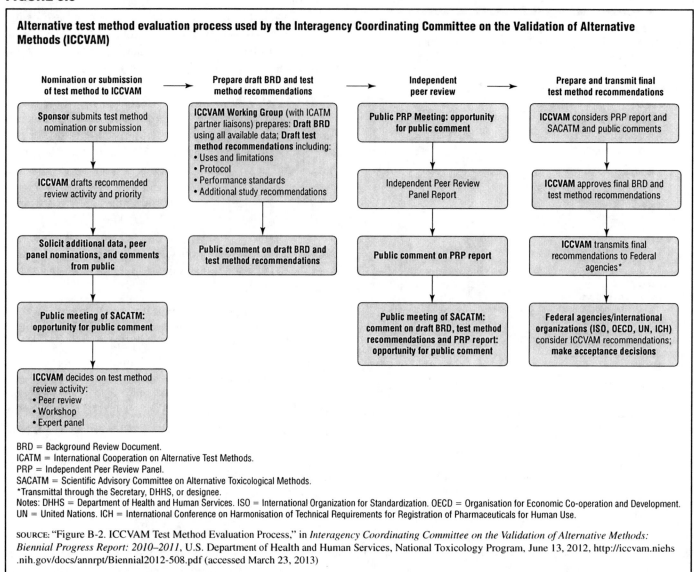

Alternative test method evaluation process used by the Interagency Coordinating Committee on the Validation of Alternative Methods (ICCVAM)

BRD = Background Review Document.
ICATM = International Cooperation on Alternative Test Methods.
PRP = Independent Peer Review Panel.
SACATM = Scientific Advisory Committee on Alternative Toxicological Methods.
*Transmittal through the Secretary, DHHS, or designee.
Notes: DHHS = Department of Health and Human Services. ISO = International Organization for Standardization. OECD = Organisation for Economic Co-operation and Development.
UN = United Nations. ICH = International Conference on Harmonisation of Technical Requirements for Registration of Pharmaceuticals for Human Use.

SOURCE: "Figure B-2. ICCVAM Test Method Evaluation Process," in *Interagency Coordinating Committee on the Validation of Alternative Methods: Biennial Progress Report: 2010–2011*, U.S. Department of Health and Human Services, National Toxicology Program, June 13, 2012, http://iccvam.niehs .nih.gov/docs/annrpt/Biennial2012-508.pdf (accessed March 23, 2013)

of research and billions of dollars." Many animal rights and welfare groups immediately seized on the failure of the mouse model as justification for eliminating animal experimentation and relying instead on nonanimal-based alternatives.

GENETIC ENGINEERING

Genetic engineering is the scientific manipulation of genetic material. Animals have been the subject of genetic engineering research and experiments for several decades. Transgenic animals are animals that carry a foreign gene that has been deliberately inserted through genetic engineering. They are widely used in biomedical research and pharmaceutical development. "Knocking out" a normal gene and replacing it with a nonfunctional version gives scientists insight into what the normal gene does. Transgenic animals have also been genetically engineered to be especially good test subjects for various types of research. For example, DuPont describes in "Testing Methods

Using OncoMouse Transgenic Models of Cancer" (2008, http://dupont.t2h.yet2.com/t2h/page/techpak?id=26128) "OncoMouse" transgenic mice that are especially susceptible to cancer and are therefore useful to scientists studying that disease.

Raising transgenic animals for the cultivation of pharmaceutical products is known as pharming. Most of the animals used for pharming are farm animals. For example, scientists have pharmed transgenic sheep and goats that produce foreign proteins in their milk. Production of these proteins could have enormous medical and industrial benefits for humans. As of May 2013, pharmed substances were still in the development stage and had not yet been commercialized.

In xenotransplantation, organs from animals are transplanted into humans. The term *xeno* comes from the Greek word *xenos*, meaning "foreign" or "strange." Recipients of xenotransplanted organs often reject these organs. That is, their bodies' immune systems consider the xenotransplanted organs to be dangerous foreign material and attack them. Research continues on the genetic

engineering of pigs so that they can grow organs that will not be rejected by human bodies. Scientists believe that harvesting organs from transgenic pigs could one day solve the human organ shortage that at present exists, saving millions of human lives. Some people consider this to be medical progress, whereas others see it as another injustice that is perpetrated against animals for the sake of humans, noting that there would not be an organ shortage if more people were willing to become organ donors.

Cloning is a form of genetic manipulation in which a later-born genetic twin can be produced. In July 1996 the first mammal cloned from adult cells was born, a product of research at the Roslin Institute in Edinburgh, Scotland. Dolly was cloned from an udder cell that was taken from a six-year-old sheep. She was a fairly healthy clone and produced six lambs of her own. Before she was euthanized by lethal injection in February 2003 Dolly had been suffering from lung cancer and arthritis. A necropsy (postmortem examination) of Dolly revealed that, other than her cancer and arthritis, she was anatomically like other sheep. (See Figure 5.5.) Between 1996 and 2013 more than a dozen other animal species were cloned for the first time, including cats, cattle, deer, and dogs. Not all the clones survived, and some were born with compromised immunity and genetic disorders. Cloning is still new technology, and the success rate is low.

A Gallup poll conducted in May 2012 found that 34% of respondents said the cloning of animals is morally acceptable. (See Table 5.14.) Another 60% of respondents said animal cloning is morally wrong. These values have changed little since the question was first asked in 2001.

FIGURE 5.4

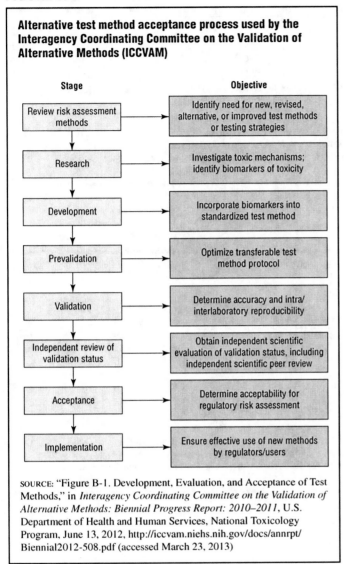

Alternative test method acceptance process used by the Interagency Coordinating Committee on the Validation of Alternative Methods (ICCVAM)

SOURCE: "Figure B-1. Development, Evaluation, and Acceptance of Test Methods," in *Interagency Coordinating Committee on the Validation of Alternative Methods: Biennial Progress Report: 2010–2011*, U.S. Department of Health and Human Services, National Toxicology Program, June 13, 2012, http://iccvam.niehs.nih.gov/docs/annrpt/Biennial2012-508.pdf (accessed March 23, 2013)

TABLE 5.11

Animals at USDA-registered research facilities, by use category, fiscal year 2008

Use category	Dogs	Cats	Guinea pigs	Hamsters	Rabbits	Sheep	Pigs	Other farm animals	Non-human primates	All other covered species	Total
Animal not yet used	8,748	8,734	11,036	2,342	19,508	1,705	3,975	8,144	55,343	37,930	157,465
Used: no pain, no drugs	126,222	41,939	80,905	10,568	123,398	4,391	10,469	18,880	42,808	74,429	534,009
Used: with pain, with drugs	72,676	26,912	41,029	9,155	104,429	9,806	47,210	11,313	27,411	39,461	389,402
Used: with pain, no drugs	28,731	1,454	31,673	582	6,981	89	1,084	178	1,037	4,578	76,387
Total used	**227,629**	**70,305**	**153,607**	**20,305**	**234,808**	**14,286**	**58,763**	**30,371**	**71,256**	**118,468**	**999,798**
Total not yet used and used	**236,377**	**79,039**	**164,643**	**22,647**	**254,316**	**15,991**	**62,738**	**38,515**	**126,599**	**156,398**	**773,013**

Note: USDA = United States Department of Agriculture.

SOURCE: Adapted from "Pain Type: Total," "Pain Type: With Pain, with Drugs," "Pain Type: With Pain, No Drugs," "Pain Type: No Pain, No Drugs," and "Pain Type: Animal Not Yet Used," in *Annual Report Animal Usage by Fiscal Year, Fiscal Year 2008*, U.S. Department of Agriculture, Animal and Plant Health Inspection Service, February 10, 2011, http://www.aphis.usda.gov/animal_welfare/efoia/downloads/2008_Animals_Used_In_Research.pdf (accessed March 22, 2013)

TABLE 5.12

Animals at USDA-registered research facilities, by use category, fiscal year 2009

Use category	Dogs	Cats	Guinea pigs	Hamsters	Rabbits	Sheep	Pigs	Other farm animals	Nonhuman primates	All other covered species	Total
Animal not yet used	8,525	1,680	9,211	8,916	18,894	1,117	4,078	8,214	53,941	36,858	151,434
Used: no pain, no drugs	40,397	11,850	107,067	76,568	128,020	4,683	14,146	22,295	41,975	101,477	548,478
Used: with pain, with drugs	26,158	8,130	65,256	40,980	88,538	8,811	43,215	7,093	26,758	39,914	354,853
Used: with pain, no drugs	782	180	30,775	32,503	5,609	57	605	232	1,711	3,987	76,441
Total used	**67,337**	**20,160**	**203,098**	**150,051**	**222,167**	**13,551**	**57,966**	**29,620**	**70,444**	**145,378**	**979,772**
Total not yet used and used	**75,862**	**21,840**	**212,309**	**158,967**	**241,061**	**14,668**	**62,044**	**37,834**	**124,385**	**182,236**	**1,131,206**

Note: USDA = United States Department of Agriculture.

SOURCE: Adapted from "Pain Type: Total," "Pain Type: With Pain, with Drugs," "Pain Type: With Pain, No Drugs," "Pain Type: No Pain, No Drugs," and "Pain Type: Animal Not Yet Used," in *Annual Report Animal Usage by Fiscal Year, Fiscal Year 2009*, U.S. Department of Agriculture, Animal and Plant Health Inspection Service, February 10, 2011, http://www.aphis.usda.gov/animal_welfare/efoia/downloads/2009_Animals_Used_In_Research.pdf (accessed March 22, 2013)

TABLE 5.13

Animals at USDA-registered research facilities, by use category, fiscal year 2010

Use category	Dogs	Cats	Guinea pigs	Hamsters	Rabbits	Sheep	Pigs	Other farm animals	Marine mammals	Nonhuman primates	All other covered species	Total
Animal not yet used	9,368	2,136	8,489	11,416	17,219	2,027	7,634	8,064	0	54,435	29,221	150,009
Used: no pain, no drugs	39,523	12,830	115,488	63,676	122,873	4,983	11,579	24,937	116	40,509	261,287	697,801
Used: with pain, with drugs	24,710	8,595	63,889	34,204	81,303	8,223	40,911	12,884	10	29,413	35,627	339,769
Used: with pain, no drugs	697	153	33,652	48,015	5,996	65	770	187	0	1,395	6,193	97,123
Total used	**64,930**	**21,578**	**213,029**	**145,895**	**210,172**	**13,271**	**53,260**	**38,008**	**126**	**71,317**	**303,107**	**1,134,693**
Total not yet used and used	**74,298**	**23,714**	**221,518**	**157,311**	**227,391**	**15,298**	**60,894**	**46,072**	**126**	**125,752**	**332,328**	**1,284,702**

Note: USDA = United States Department of Agriculture.

SOURCE: Adapted from "Pain Type: Total," "Pain Type: With Pain, with Drugs," "Pain Type: With Pain, No Drugs," "Pain Type: No Pain, No Drugs," and "Pain Type: Animal Not Yet Used," in *Annual Report Animal Usage by Fiscal Year, Fiscal Year 2010*, U.S. Department of Agriculture, Animal and Plant Health Inspection Service, July 27, 2011, http://www.aphis.usda.gov/animal_welfare/efoia/downloads/2010_Animals_Used_In_Research.pdf (accessed March 22, 2013)

FIGURE 5.5

Dolly, the first cloned mammal. *(© PPL Therapeutics/BWP Media/Getty Images.)*

TABLE 5.14

Public opinion on the morality of cloning animals, 2001–12

	Morally acceptable	Morally wrong	Depends on situation (vol.)	Not a moral issue (vol.)	No opinion
2012 May 3–6	34	60	2	1	4
2011 May 5–8	32	62	2	1	3
2010 May 3–6	31	63	1	1	4
2009 May 7–10	34	63	1	1	2
2008 May 8–11	33	61	2	1	3
2007 May 10–13	36	59	2	1	3
2006 May 8–11	29	65	2	1	3
2005 May 2–5	35	61	1	*	3
2004 May 2–4	32	64	1	1	2
2003 May 5–7	29	68	1	*	2
2002 May 6–9	29	66	3	1	1
2001 May 10–14	31	63	2	1	3

Vol. = volunteer.
*Less than 0.5%.

SOURCE: Jeff Jones and Lydia Saad, "18. Next, I'm going to read you a list of issues. Regardless of whether or not you think it should be legal, for each one, please tell me whether you personally believe that in general it is morally acceptable or morally wrong. How about—I. Cloning animals?" in *Gallup Poll Social Series: Values and Beliefs—Final Topline*, The Gallup Organization, May 2012, http://www.gallup.com/file/poll/154748/Moral_acceptabilty_120522.pdf (accessed March 15, 2013). Copyright © 2012 Gallup, Inc. All rights reserved. The content is used with permission; however, Gallup retains all rights of republication.

CHAPTER 6
ANIMALS IN SPORTS

Merriam-Webster's Collegiate Dictionary (2003) defines a sport as recreation that includes physical activity. Most people think of a sport as an athletic competition that demonstrates skills such as physical strength, stamina, agility, and speed. Humans recognized centuries ago that many animals possess such skills naturally and could be used in sporting events.

In the United States the major sports that animals are involved in are horse racing, rodeos, greyhound racing, sled dog racing, and organized animal fighting. Except for animal fighting, all these are considered to be legitimate sports.

The legitimate sports probably began as friendly competitions between people wanting to show off their animals, but the most popular evolved into businesses in which large amounts of money are involved. Horse racing and greyhound racing are intertwined with the legalized gambling industry. Rodeos and sled dog races largely depend on sponsors. Sponsors are companies that provide financial backing in exchange for being allowed to advertise during an event—for example, by placing advertisements around an arena, in programs, or on uniforms or vehicles. Even animal fighting has become a business of sorts, with profits driven almost entirely by illegal gambling.

In all these sports, skilled animals can be quite profitable for the people who own, train, and manage them. Some animals involved in the sports industry are well cared for during their athletic "careers"; others are horribly abused. Sports animals that are less skilled, injured, past their prime, or unwilling or unable to compete anymore have different prospects. Some retire and live comfortably, whereas others are sold to the slaughterhouse or are killed.

The fate and well-being of sports animals lie in the hands of humans. To some animal rights activists this is the root of the problem. They believe that animals should not be used by people for any purpose at all, including sports. Animal welfarists focus their attention on uncovering, publicizing, and outlawing practices in animal sports that they consider harmful to the animals. Animal participation is defended by insiders and fans who feel their right to enjoy a recreational activity is being threatened by overzealous activists who do not understand the nature of these sports. The Gallup Organization conducts an annual poll on animal-related issues. As of May 2013, the most recent poll to ask about animal involvement in sports was conducted in May 2008. In *Post-Derby Tragedy, 38% Support Banning Animal Racing* (May 15, 2008, http://www.gallup.com/poll/107293/PostDerby-Tragedy-38-Support-Banning-Animal-Racing.aspx), Frank Newport of the Gallup Organization indicates that more than one-third (38%) of the people asked supported banning sports involving competition between animals (including horse racing and dog racing). In contrast, 59% of the respondents were opposed to such a ban.

MAJOR ANIMAL SPORTS CONTROVERSIES

Animal sports enthusiasts argue that the animals are doing what they do naturally. Horses and greyhounds love to run, cocks naturally fight with each other in the barnyard, wild dogs fight over who will lead the pack, and unbroken livestock naturally try to buck off a rider. People who are involved in legitimate animal sports contend that the animals are well cared for because their welfare is crucial to the success of the sport and the people involved. In other words, they say it makes no sense for the owner or manager of a sports animal to mistreat that animal and perhaps lose money as a result. They also insist that safeguards are in place to ensure that animals are not mistreated during a sporting event and receive proper medical care if they are injured.

Critics counter by explaining that animal sports are not sports at all, but performances forced out of animals that have no choice in the matter. They believe sports animals are not behaving naturally but are doing things that they are either trained to do or have been bred over many generations to do. Because so much money is involved in animal sports, animal welfare and rights advocates indicate that greed and financial advancement are the main motivators behind animal sports. General problems with animal sports revolve around four main issues:

- Overbreeding of the animals
- Mistreatment during training, performances, and the off-season
- Lack of veterinary care
- Ways in which unwanted sports animals are destroyed

HORSE SPORTS

Horses are the most versatile sporting animal. Besides racing and rodeos, horses participate on a large scale in many other types of sports, shows, and competitions. (See Table 6.1.) None of these events, however, is performed by horses alone. All of them include humans, who ride the horses, run alongside them, or are pulled behind in carts.

Thoroughbred Racing

Thoroughbred horse racing is the king of animal sports in the United States. It is a multibillion-dollar industry that involves people who breed, manage, train, own, and ride the horses, and the people who own and manage the racetracks. Indirectly, the industry provides income to feed and equipment suppliers, veterinarians, and other support personnel. The industry is also a source of income for those state governments that allow gambling at racetracks and/or off-track betting locations.

THE RACES. The Jockey Club reports in "Number of Races" (2013, http://www.jockeyclub.com/factbook.asp?section=6) that there were 45,086 Thoroughbred horse races in the United States in 2012. That number is down dramatically from 1989, when 74,071 races were held. In "Analysis of Races by State or Province—2012" (2013, http://www.jockeyclub.com/factbook/races_pass.asp?whatyr=2012), the Jockey Club notes that the states with the largest number of races in 2012 were Pennsylvania (4,459), California (4,064), and West Virginia (4,063). Thoroughbred racing is financially supported by gambling. In betting terminology the "purse" is the amount won by the owners of the winning horses. According to the Jockey Club, in "Gross Purses" (2013, http://www.jockeyclub.com/factbook.asp?section=7), the U.S. purse increased from around $700 million per year during the late 1980s to $1.1 billion in 2012.

The three most prestigious Thoroughbred races in the United States are the Kentucky Derby at the Churchill Downs track in Kentucky, the Preakness Stakes at Pimlico in Maryland, and the Belmont Stakes at Belmont Park in New York. The races are held over a five-week period between May and June of each year. A horse that wins all three races in one year is said to have won the "Triple Crown." As of May 2013, only 11 horses had captured the Triple Crown—the most recent was by a horse named Affirmed in 1978.

WELFARE OF RACING HORSES. The racehorse industry prides itself on the enormous investments it has made

TABLE 6.1

Horse sports other than racing and rodeos

Category	Description	Organizations
Cattle events	Cutting or herd work: Rider on horseback selects a single calf from a herd in the arena, guides it into the center of the arena, and then using fast starts and turns, prevents it from escaping back to the herd. Reining: Rider maneuvers horse through various moves, including figure-eight patterns, 360 degree spins, and sliding stops. Cow work: Rider maneuvers horse to control the movements of a running steer, including herding it back and forth along a fence and circling around an arena. Team penning or sorting: Team of 2 or 3 riders on horseback must cut specifically marked cattle from a herd and herd them to designated areas.	National Reined Cow Horse Association, National Reining Horse Association, National Cutting Horse Association, United States Team Penning Association
Dressage	Rider moves horse through a series of carefully choreographed movements and patterns.	United States Dressage Federation
Endurance	Long-distance trail riding conducted over natural terrain.	American Endurance Ride Conference
Eventing or combined training	A three-in-one competition including dressage, cross-country jumping, and show jumping.	Fédération Equestre Internationale
Foxhunting	A sport in which riders and dogs hunt foxes in the countryside.	American Masters of Foxhound Association
Hunter-jumper	Equestrian event in which horses and riders jump over obstacles.	National Hunter and Jumper Association
Polo	Two teams of players riding thoroughbred horses play a game similar to hockey using a small ball and mallets.	United States Polo Association
Polocrosse	Combination of polo and lacrosse in which riders use racquets instead of mallets.	American Polocrosse Association
Ride and tie	Long-distance race in which two people and one horse form a racing team. During a race the people alternate riding the horse and running.	Ride and Tie Association
Steeple chase	Equestrian event in which horses and riders jump over fences.	National Steeplechase Association
Vaulting	Sport in which a rider uses gymnastic moves to vault onto and dismount from moving horse.	American Vaulting Association

SOURCE: Created by Kim Masters Evans for Gale, 2011

in horse health issues. Millions of dollars have been spent on researching the injuries and illnesses that affect racehorses. The Grayson-Jockey Club Research Foundation is the leading private source of funding for research into horse health issues. The foundation, which dates back to 1940, is operated by the Jockey Club and accepts donations from private individuals, Thoroughbred clubs, racetracks, and other organizations. The foundation indicates in "Where the Dollars Go" (2013, http://www.grayson-jockeyclub.org/default.asp?section=2&area=dollars&menu=2) that as of early 2013 it had funded 299 research projects at 40 universities, spending nearly $20 million total. In "Grayson-Jockey Club Research Foundation Research Results" (August 2012, http://www.grayson-jockeyclub.org/resources/brochure%20for%20web.pdf), the foundation summarizes some of the achievements it has obtained, including the development of vaccines, deoxyribonucleic acid findings, and factors affecting various horse illnesses and injuries.

Most animal welfare groups are opposed to horse racing and contend that racehorses are treated as investments rather than as living beings. Specifically, they make the following claims regarding the sport:

- Thoroughbred racehorses have been inbred to the point that their bodies are too heavy for their slender, fragile legs.
- Broodmares are forced to come into season too often and at unnatural times to lengthen the potential training season for their offspring.
- Racehorses are drugged when they have injuries or illnesses so that they can still compete.
- Track surfaces are too hard.
- The racing season is too long.
- Horses are run too young, risking damage to bones that are not fully mature.
- The industry is regulated by state governments that have a vested interest in making the industry profitable, not in safeguarding animal welfare.
- Racehorses suffer injuries and deaths during training and races.

Between 2006 and 2008 there was a series of on-track "breakdowns" by championship Thoroughbreds. Barbaro won the Kentucky Derby in early May 2006 and then shattered a right leg while running the Preakness Stakes two weeks later. After suffering a series of complications from the injury, the horse was euthanized eight months later. Pine Island dislocated an ankle while competing in the November 2006 Breeders' Cup Distaff and was euthanized. Fleet Indian suffered a serious leg injury during the same race and was retired from racing. In May 2008 Eight Belles had to be euthanized on the racetrack after breaking both front ankles during the Kentucky Derby.

Tragedies at the nation's top racing events attract widespread attention; however, deaths among racehorses at all levels are not uncommon. According to the article "Study Shows 5,000 Racehorse Deaths since '03" (Associated Press, June 14, 2008), approximately 5,000 Thoroughbred racehorses died between 2003 and 2008. Most of the horses were euthanized after suffering serious injuries on the racetrack. The article notes that "countless other deaths went unreported because of lax record keeping." The article "Racehorse Deaths by State in 2007" (Associated Press, June 14, 2008) provides a breakdown by state of the more than 1,000 known Thoroughbred racehorse deaths that occurred in 2007. No data are provided for Arkansas, Michigan, and Nebraska because these states reportedly do not compile such information.

The article "Race Horse Deaths down Slightly in U.S." (United Press International, December 15, 2010) quotes statistics from the Jockey Club indicating that 1,510 Thoroughbreds died on U.S. horse racetracks between November 1, 2008, and October 31, 2010. As shown in Table 6.2, there were 278 racehorse fatalities in California alone between July 1, 2011, and June 30, 2012. Racehorses sustained the most fatal injuries during training and racing.

In 2012 the *New York Times* published a series of articles about the horse racing industry under the heading "Breakdown: Death and Disarray at Racetracks" (http://www.nytimes.com/interactive/2012/04/30/us/breakdown-horses-series.html). The exposé presents data from 2009 to 2011 on horse fatalities and jockey injuries and explores the role of horse doping, casino gambling, and state regulations in the rising number of problems at U.S. racetracks.

In "Mangled Horses, Maimed Jockeys" (NYTimes.com, March 24, 2012), Walt Bogdanich et al. note that "a computer analysis of data from more than 150,000 races, along with injury reports, drug test results and interviews, shows an industry still mired in a culture of drugs and lax regulation and a fatal breakdown rate that remains far worse than in most of the world." Among the claims for the period 2009 to 2011 are:

- 3,600 racehorses died during racing or training at state-regulated tracks
- 6,600 racehorses "broke down or showed signs of injury"
- 3,800 instances of trainers caught "illegally drugging" racehorses

Bogdanich et al. indicate that the doping statistic "vastly understates the problem because only a small percentage

TABLE 6.2

Racehorse fatalities in California, fiscal year 2011–12

Track	Racing[a]			Training[b]			Other[c]	Total
	Dirt	Synthetic	Turf	Dirt	Synthetic	Turf		
Cal Expo (harness)							7	7
Cal Expo (state fair)								
Del Mar		2	4	6			1	13
Fairplex (Pomona)	2						1	3
Ferndale	2							2
Fresno	1						1	2
Golden Gate Fields		15	1		22		11	49
Hollywood Park		8	5	2	21		8	44
Los Alamitos	37			8			21	66
Pleasanton	1			9			9	19
San Luis Rey Downs				1				1
Santa Anita	12		5	40		2	12	71
Santa Rosa	1							1
Total	**56**	**25**	**15**	**60**	**49**	**2**	**71**	**278**

[a]Racing includes any fatality associated with racing.
[b]Training includes any fatality associated with training.
[c]Other includes any non-exercise related fatality. The most common cause of death in the Other group is gastro-intestinal diseases, such as colic, colitis, and enteritis, followed by respiratory disease, primarily pneumonia and pleuropneumonia, and neurological diseases, including West Nile Virus and equine protozoal myeloencephalitis (EPM).

SOURCE: "Fatalities at CHRB Facilities by Track and Surface: July 1, 2011–June 30, 2012," in *42nd Annual Report of the California Horse Racing Board: A Summary of Fiscal Year 2011–12 Revenue and Calendar Year 2012 Racing in California*, California Horse Racing Board, 2012, http://www.chrb.ca.gov/ annual_reports/ 2012_annual_report.pdf (accessed March 25, 2013)

of horses are actually tested." In addition, horse fatality and drug data were not available from all states.

Although the public is familiar with high-profile races, such as the Kentucky Derby, the majority of Thoroughbred races held around the country each year are low-level races called claiming races during which each horse is up for sale (i.e., up for claim). According to Bogdenich et al., horses in claiming races between 2009 and 2011 had a 22% higher rate of breakdowns or injuries than horses in higher-level races. Many claiming races take place at racinos, which are racetracks that include casino-type gambling, such as slot machines. Bogdenich et al. note that "faced with a steep loss of customers, racetracks have increasingly added casino gambling to their operations, resulting in higher purses but also providing an incentive for trainers to race unfit horses."

Horse breakdowns are particularly troubling incidents. Bogdenich et al. quote Rick Arthur, the horse medical director for the California Horse Racing Board, who said, "In humans you never see someone snap their leg off running in the Olympics. But you see it in horse racing." According to Bogdenich et al., industry insiders debate the various causes for horse breakdowns, "but the discussion inevitably comes back to drugs." Some drugs used in racehorses are for pain relief. Critics assert that sore and injured horses are given drugs to mask pain so they will still race. This makes the horses more prone to breakdowns and serious injuries. Bogdenich et al. claim that research on California racehorses that broke down shows that "as many as 90 percent" of the horses had preexisting injuries.

Numerous other performance-enhancing drugs are believed to be used on racehorses, including steroids and stimulants and obscure substances, such as cobra venom. The article "Godolphin Scandal Raises Debate on Steroid Use" (SI.com, May 2, 2013) notes that steroid use is banned in the United States only on race day. In other words, steroids can be used during training. The article indicates that the United States allows the use of the anti-inflammatory drug phenylbutazone during races, even though most other nations ban its use. According to Bogdenich et al., England forbids horses from racing "on any drugs" and has breakdown rates that are half of those found in the United States.

The slaughter of racehorses is another controversial topic. Ray Paulick reports in "Death of a Derby Winner: Slaughterhouse Likely Fate for Ferdinand" (*Blood-Horse Magazine*, July 25, 2003) that Ferdinand, the winner of the 1986 Kentucky Derby, was possibly slaughtered for meat in Japan. Demand for horsemeat has skyrocketed in parts of Asia and Europe because of the scare concerning mad cow disease. As described in Chapter 4, horses that are intended for human consumption cannot be injected with drugs, either as painkillers or as a humane method of euthanization. As such, horses sold for horsemeat are given no painkillers in transit, and when they reach the slaughterhouse, they are knocked unconscious and their throats are cut (in the same way that cattle are slaughtered). By contrast, horses sold to rendering plants can be given drugs for pain in transit and can be euthanized by lethal injection.

Animal welfare groups allege that many injured racehorses are not humanely euthanized but are shipped off to slaughter without being given painkillers. As of May 2013, no horsemeat slaughterhouses had operated in the United States since 2007. Welfarists complain that racehorses shipped to Canada or Mexico to be slaughtered travel for many hours in cramped carriers with no food or water. As noted in Chapter 4, a horse slaughterhouse under construction in Roswell, New Mexico, was expected to be operational by the end of 2013.

RETIRED RACING HORSE ADOPTION. There are several organizations around the country that rescue retired racehorses and either adopt them out or provide lifetime sanctuary and care for them. The two largest are the Thoroughbred Retirement Foundation and the New Vocations Racehorse Adoption Program. The New Vocations Racehorse Adoption Program (2013, http://www.ho rseadoption.com/about/) notes that most of the horses it takes in "are injured and thin, suffering the normal occupational hazards of racing." Because these horses lack "a useful skill to offer," many of them would likely have wound up at livestock auctions and ultimately slaughterhouses if they had not been rescued.

Rodeos

The word *rodeo* comes from the Spanish word *rodear*, meaning "to surround." Originally, a rodeo was a roundup of cattle that happened once or twice per year. Open-range grazing was common in western North America during the 1800s, and cowboys were hired to round up the cattle and herd them to market. Following these cattle drives, as they were called, the cowboys would often congregate and hold informal contests to show off their skills at riding and roping.

THE RODEO BUSINESS. Rodeos now take place all over North America, even in big cities. They are seen by their fans as wholesome family entertainment that glorifies the rugged and hardworking cowboys of the Old West.

Animal welfare groups estimate that several thousand rodeos take place each year. Professional rodeo stars travel from event to event and compete for millions of dollars in prize money. Most big-money rodeos in the United States are sponsored by the Professional Rodeo and Cowboy Association (PRCA). Besides professional rodeos, the organization also sponsors amateur rodeo events for children and youth.

The animals that are used in rodeos include horses, bulls, steers (male cattle that have been castrated before reaching sexual maturity), and calves. Typical rodeo events include bareback bull riding, saddle bronc riding (in which a bucking horse, or bronco, is ridden), bareback horse riding, steer wrestling, calf and steer roping, and barrel racing (in which riders guide their horses around barrels that are positioned around an arena).

WELFARE OF RODEO ANIMALS. The PRCA defends the treatment of the animals that are used in the rodeos it sponsors, claiming that it has an extensive animal welfare program that governs the care and handling of rodeo animals and requires that a veterinarian be on-site during a rodeo. Animal welfare organizations are opposed to rodeos. They argue that rodeos are not representative of Old West ranching ways but are businesses that use animals as pieces of athletic equipment. They say that most injured rodeo animals are not humanely euthanized but are sent to slaughterhouses without receiving veterinary attention or painkillers. They also point out that the rodeo animals of the 21st century are not naturally wild and unbroken as they might have been when rodeos first started during the 1800s but are relatively tame animals that must be physically provoked into displaying wild behavior, for example, with use of tight straps, spurs, caustic salves, or even cattle prods. The PRCA denies that rodeo animals are provoked using painful methods and notes that even though spurs are used in some events, the organization requires the spur points to be dull so they will not hurt the animals.

Gait Competitions

Some horses are bred and trained to walk with an exaggerated gait in which they lift their front legs high in the air. Walking horses, particularly Tennessee Walking Horses, are breeds that are associated with this gait. These horses compete in shows in which they demonstrate their high-stepping skills to earn prizes for their owners and trainers. Animal protection groups complain that many of the training methods that are used to elicit high stepping are abusive, for example, repeated use of heavy chains or other weights around the legs trains horses to use a lot of force to lift their legs to walk. Once the weights are removed, the same amount of force lifts the legs high in the air. Some unscrupulous owners and trainers use a process called soring on their horses to achieve an exaggerated gait. Soring is achieved by applying a caustic or irritating chemical substance to a horse's legs or hoofs, by putting objects between a horse's hoof and shoe, or by cutting a horse's hoof too short to expose sensitive underlying tissue. Sored horses lift their legs high because of the pain. Continued use of soring techniques can lead to permanent scarring.

The Horse Protection Act (HPA) prohibits sored horses from competing in horse shows. The U.S. Department of Agriculture's (USDA) Animal and Plant Health Inspection Service (APHIS) explains in the fact sheet "The Horse Protection Act" (September 2009, http://www.aphis.usda.gov/publications/animal_welfare/content/printable_version/faq_rev_horsep.pdf) that the act was originally passed in 1970 after soring became a widespread practice during the 1960s. Under the HPA, specially trained individuals called designated qualified persons (DQPs) act on behalf of the USDA to inspect horses before shows, sales, and auctions. Sored horses are disqualified from competing, being sold, or being auctioned off. Owners and trainers accused of soring can face criminal or civil charges and can be disqualified from participating in future shows, sales, and auctions. The USDA relies heavily on DQP inspectors, because it lacks the funds to have its own veterinarians perform more than just a few inspections at the dozens of horse shows that take place annually.

In 2010 the USDA's Office of Inspector General (OIG) released a scathing report that criticized both the DQP program and the walking horse industry. In *Animal and Plant Health Inspection Service Administration of the Horse Protection Program and the Slaughter Horse Transport Program* (September 2010, http://www.usda.gov/oig/webdocs/33601-02-KC.pdf), the OIG concludes: "We found that APHIS' program for inspecting horses for soring is not adequate to ensure that these animals are not being abused." In particular, the OIG finds that DQPs "do not always inspect horses to effectively enforce the law and regulations, and in some cases where they do find violations, they deliberately issue tickets to friends or family members of responsible individuals so that the responsible person could avoid receiving a penalty for violating the Horse Protection Act." The OIG notes that DQPs are often horse exhibiters themselves, and thus are reluctant to rigorously enforce the rules against their colleagues.

The OIG finds that DQPs tended to enforce the rules much more strongly when they were being overseen by APHIS employees. Between 2005 and 2008 APHIS observers conducted spot inspections at 6% of the horse shows held. In spite of this small sample, nearly half (49%) of all DQP-issued violations came from those specific horse shows. In addition, the OIG faulted the industry itself, noting that "the environment for enforcing the Horse Protection Act is hostile. Many in the horse show industry do not regard the abuse of horses as a serious problem, and resent USDA performing inspections. The practice of soring has been ingrained as an acceptable practice in the industry for decades. APHIS records showed that there was an environment at horse shows, sales, and other horse-related events in which APHIS employees were subjected to intimidation and attempts to prevent them from inspecting horses."

Animal advocates have long complained that the HPA is poorly enforced. In 2011 the Tennessee Walking Horse trainer Barney Davis and three of his associates were prosecuted for soring. Todd South reports in "Trainer Says Horse Soring Widespread" (TimesFree Press.com, February 28, 2012) that "for the first time in 20 years the crime has been prosecuted in the United States." Davis was sentenced to a year in prison and fined $4,000. His three codefendants received probation and fines. At his sentencing hearing, Davis told the judge that soring was widespread in the industry, noting, "Every walking horse that enters into a show is sored." South indicates that Marty Irby, the president of the Tennessee Walking Horse Breeder's and Exhibitor's Association, insisted that "horse abuse should not be tolerated" and stated the organization supports "rigorous but fair enforcement" of the HPA.

In 2012 an undercover video taken by a Humane Society of the United States (HSUS) operative showed Jackie McConnell, a prominent Tennessee Walking Horse trainer, beating show horses with sticks and placing caustic agents on their ankles in clear violation of the HPA. Some of the sored horses writhed on the ground in agony, unable to stand up. The video, which was shown on television in May 2012 by ABC News (http://abcnews.go.com/Blotter/tennessee-walking-horses-abused/story?id=16360835#.UYZZqyjD_IW), resulted in federal charges against McConnell and his stable hands. McConnell pleaded guilty and in September 2012 was put on probation and fined $75,000. In "Tennessee Walking Horse Trainer Jackie McConnell Gets Probation, $75,000 Fine" (Tennessean.com, September 19, 2012), Bobby Allyn notes that the sentence was more lenient than expected and resulted from a plea agreement deal that the judge considered "unusual." According to Allyn, McConnell's two stable hands were put on probation, but not fined, for their actions in the case.

In April 2013 Larry Joe Wheelon, another Tennessee Walking Horse trainer, was arrested on a federal warrant alleging that he had sored horses. Iva Butler reports in "Wheelon Eviction Sought: Horse Soring Suspect Makes Court Appearance" (TheDailyTimes.com, May 1, 2013) that Wheelon was arrested following a raid on his rented horse barn by the OIG. According to Butler, an OIG affidavit indicated that 19 of 27 horses at the barn "were found to be sore by a USDA veterinarian." In addition, authorities reportedly confiscated containers of caustic chemicals from the property. As of May 2013, Wheelon's case had not been heard in court.

Table 6.3 lists the horse shows at which HPA inspections were conducted during 2012. Table 6.4 provides the full names of many of the horse industry organizations listed in Table 6.3. As shown in Table 6.3, 9,962 inspections resulted in 582 violations during 2012. Most of the violations involved soring that was deemed unilateral (affecting one front leg) or bilateral (affecting both front legs). Scar rule violations are triggered by certain leg scars, which can indicate past soring. In addition, there are rules regulating the use of chains or other devices and horse shoeing.

TABLE 6.3

Horse event inspections conducted for the Horse Protection Program, 2012

Date	Event	HIO	Inspections	Violations	Type of violations
3/29–30/2012	Mississippi Charity Horse Show; Jackson, MS	SHOW	394	13	3 Bilateral 8 Unilateral 1 Scar rule 1 Action device
4/7/2012	MSU Spring Horse Show; Morehead, KY	KWHA	104	11	1 Bilateral 3 Unilateral 5 Scar rule 2 Shoeing/action
4/12–14/2012	National Trainers Horse Show; White Pine, TN	SHOW	293	15	1 Bilateral 7 Unilateral 7 Scar rule
4/13–14/2012	South Carolina Ladies Aux Horse Show; Clemson, SC	PRIDE	71	13	1 Bilateral 4 Unilateral 5 Scar rule 2 Shoeing/action 1 Non HPA
4/20–21/2012	Urohea Spring Horse Show, White Pine, TN	KWHA	72	4	2 Bilateral 1 Unilateral 1 Scar rule
4/20/2012	Bedford 4H Horse Show; Shelbyville, TN	SHOW	166	3	1 Scar rule 1 Bad image 1 Shoeing/action
4/21/2012	Reeltown Lions Horse Show; Reeltown, AL	PRIDE	88	10	5 Unilateral 1 Scar rule 4 Shoeing/action
4/26–28/2012	Gulf Coast Charity Horse Show; Panama City, FL	SHOW	210	14	5 Unilateral 8 Scar rule 1 Shoeing/action
4/27/2012	Cumberland Classic Horse Show; Harriman, TN	NWHA	158	0	0
4/28/2012	So. Central Ruritan Horse Show; Chuckey, TN	KWHA	133	9	2 Bilateral 6 Unilateral 1 Scar rule
4/29/2012	WHOA Versatility Horse Show; Murfreesboro, TN	WHOA	85	0	0
5/18/2012	7th Annual Petersburg Lions Horse Show, Petersburg, TN	SHOW	112	3	2 Unilateral 1 Low chain
5/18–19/2012	Smokey MT Classic Horse Show; Harriman, TN	KWHA	63	2	2 Unilateral
5/19/2012	Celina Walking Horse Show; Celina, TN	PRIDE	65	7	3 Unilateral 1 Scar rule 2 Shoeing/action 1 Unruly
5/19/2012	Twin Cities Classic Horse Show; Smith Station, AL	PRIDE	111	6	3 Unilateral 1 Scar rule 1 Unacceptable
5/24–25/2012	Spring Fun Horse Show; Shelbyville, TN	SHOW	422	18	13 Unilateral 3 Scar rule 2 Unacceptable
5/25/2012	Burlington Horse Show; Burlington, KY	N/A	65	2	2 Low chains
5/26/2012	Brodhead Lions Club Horse Show; Brodhead, KY	KWHA	100	9	1 Bilateral 1 Unilateral 5 Scar rule 2 High band
5/26/2012	Mississippi State Racking & Walking Horse Show; Booneville, MS	KWHA	66	7	1 Bilateral 6 Scar rule
6/1/2012	Columbia Spring Jubilee Horse Show; Columbia, TN	SHOW	146	8	4 Unilateral 4 Scar rule
6/2/2012	Ohio-KY WHRA Horse Show; Greenup, KY	KWHA	174	3	2 Scar rule 1 Low chain
6/2/2012	38th Annual Pikeville Spring Horse Show, Pikeville, TN	PRIDE	155	5	2 Unilateral 3 Scar rule
6/8/2012	Lawrenceburg Lions Club Horse Show; Lawrenceburg, TN	PRIDE	185	17	1 Bilateral 1 Unilateral 11 Scar rule 3 Shoeing/action 1 Unacceptable
6/8–9/2012	Carter County Shrine Horse Show; Olive Hill, KY	KWHA	60	5	2 Unilateral 4 Foreign substance 1 Low chain
6/9/2012	6th Annual Cumberland County Open Horse Show; Crossville, TN	PRIDE	111	9	2 Unilateral 5 Scar rule 1 Open lesion 1 Shoeing/action

TABLE 6.3

Horse event inspections conducted for the Horse Protection Program, 2012 [CONTINUED]

Date	Event	HIO	Inspections	Violations	Type of violations
6/15–16/2012	East Tennessee Classic; White Pine, TN	PRIDE	77	12	1 Bilateral 2 Unilateral 8 Scar rule 1 High band
6/15–16/2012	Hawha Spring Classic Horse Show; Mt. Vernon, MO	HAWHA	91	14	3 Bilateral 3 Unilateral 5 Scar rule 3 Long chain
6/15/2012	36th Annual Shelbyville Mid Summer Classic; Decatur, AL	KWHA	51	7	6 Scar rule 1 Bilateral
6/16/2012	Walking Horse Association of Alabama Summer Classic; Arab, AL	PRIDE	79	10	8 Scar rule 1 Heavy chains 1 Lame horse
6/22/2012	1st Annual Sam Gibbons Memorial Horse Show; Athens, GA	PRIDE	13	3	1 Bilateral 1 Unilateral 1 Scar rule
6/22/2012	Guntown Lions Club Horse Show; Guntown, MS	SHOW	30	6	1 Bilateral 3 Scar rule 1 Foreign substance 1 High band
6/22/2012	Ohio Classic Horse Show; Wilmington, OH	NWHA	55	0	0
6/23/2012	Billy M. Cary Memorial Horse Show; Huntingdon, TN	SHOW	19	0	0
6/23/2012	GWHEA Summer Classic Horse Show; Buckhead, GA	PRIDE	1	1	1 Scar rule/foreign substance
6/30/2012	Gilbert McCarley Memorial Walking Horse Show; Tuscaloosa, AL	PRIDE	22	0	0
7/2–4/2012	Owingsville Lions Club Horse Show; Owingsville, KY	PRIDE	121	4	1 Scar rule/band 3 Scar rule
7/5/2012	Tony Rice Center Horse Show; Shelbyville, TN	SHOW	81	5	2 Bilateral 3 Unilateral
7/6/2012	Warren County Lions Club Horse Show; McMinnville, TN	SHOW	77	4	1 Bilateral 2 Unilateral 1 Scar rule
7/7/2012	Midwest Walking Horse Show; Buffalo, MO	HAWHA	25	1	1 Scar rule
7/7/2012	Adair County Fair Horse Show; Columbia, KY	PRIDE	60	0	0
7/13/2012	SSHBEA Mid Season Horse Show; Lewisburg, TN	PRIDE	74	0	0
7/13–15/2012	Pacific NW Jamboree; Elma, WA	WIWHA	379	1	1 Scar rule
7/13/2012	Billy Masters Walking Horse Show; Irvine, KY	PRIDE	18	2	1 Scar rule 1 Foreign substance
7/14/2012	MSHSA 24th Annual Charity Walking Horse Show; Oakfield, TN	SHOW	134	11	1 Bilateral 4 Unilateral 5 Scar rule
7/20–21/2012	55th Annual Tollesboro Lions Club Horse Show; Tollesboro, KY	KWHA	88	1	1 Scar rule
7/21/2012	Parkers Crossroads Horse Show; Wildersville, TN	SHOW	50	10	1 Bilateral 4 Unilateral 5 Scar rule
7/26/2012	Dickson Saddle & Bridle Horse Show; Dickson, TN	SHOW	79	10	4 Bilateral 5 Unilateral 1 Non HPA
7/27/2012	Marshal County Horseman's Assoc; Lewisburg, TN	SHOW	173	13	7 Unilateral 6 Scar rule
7/28/2012	Pulaski Red Carpet Horse Show; Pulaski, TN	SHOW	117	6	1 Bilateral 4 Unilateral 1 Scar rule
7/28/2012	Shelbyville Open Horse Show; Shelbyville, TN	N/A	0	0	0
7/31–8/2/2012	Missouri State Society Horse Show; Sedalia, MO	HAWHA	54	10	3 Bilateral 2 Unilateral 3 Scar rule 2 Foreign sub
8/2/2012	31st Annual Fayetteville Blue Ribbon Horse Show; Fayetteville, TN	SHOW	34	7	3 Unilateral 4 Scar rule
8/3/2012	Belfast Lions Club 52nd Horse Show; Belfast, TN	SHOW	97	10	2 Bilateral 4 Unilateral 3 Scar rule 1 Shoeing/action
8/3/2012	Russell County Jaycees Fair Horse Show; Estill, KY	PRIDE	42	4	2 Scar rule 2 Heel/toe
8/4/2012	Wartrace Horse Show; Wartrace, TN	SHOW	115	18	1 Bilateral 4 Unilateral 11 Scar rule 1 Uni/scar/FS 1 Uni/scar

TABLE 6.3

Horse event inspections conducted for the Horse Protection Program, 2012 [CONTINUED]

Date	Event	HIO	Inspections	Violations	Type of violations
8/4/2012	Carter County Shrine Club Horse Show; Olive Hill, KY	PRIDE	72	2	2 Scar rule
8/11/2012	Jefferson County Trail Riders Club Horse Show; Grubville, MO	N/A	15	0	0
8/11/2012	Trail Ridge Saddle Club Fun Show; Stoutland, MO	N/A	6	0	0
8/16–18/2012	Illinois State Fair; Springfield, IL	N/A	222	5	2 Bilateral 1 Unilateral 2 Scar rule
8/18/2012	BPWHA Horse Show; Hodgenville, KY	IWHA	79	0	0
8/23–9/1/2012	74th Annual Tennessee Walking Horse Celebration Horse Show; Shelbyville, TN	SHOW	1,849	166	25 Bilateral 49 Unilateral 67 Scar rule 11 Foreign substance 12 Shoeing 2 Heavy chains
9/8/2012	American Classic Horse Show; Quentin (Lebanon), PA	WHOA	124	0	0
9/28–29/2012	CBWHA 2012 Fall Classic; Cedar Rapids, IA	HAWHA	42	3	1 Bilateral 2 Unilateral
10/5–6/2012	NWHA National Championships; Wilmington, OH	NWHA	192	0	0
10/5–6/2012	28th Annual SSHBEA Fall World Championships; Shelbyville, TN	PRIDE	212	1	1 Open lesion
10/12–13/2012	North Carolina State Fair; Raleigh, NC	PRIDE	291	12	1 Bilateral 2 Unilateral 9 Scar rule
10/21/2012	Plantation Walking Horses of Maryland Horse Show; Bel Air, MD	N/A	128	0	0
11/3–4/2012	Western States Celebration Horse Show; Indio, CA	SHOW	80	1	1 Unilateral
11/8-9-10/2012	Tunica Fall Classic Horse Show; Tunica, MS	SHOW	508	19	5 Bilateral 10 Unilateral 2 Scar rule 1 Heavy chains 1 Bad image
11/17/2012	Walking for Angels Horse Show Shelbyville, TN	SHOW	277	10	1 Bilateral 9 Unilateral
Total events = 100 (includes 78 shows)			**9,962**	**582**	

Notes: HPA = Horse Protection Act. KY-WHRA = Western Harley Racing Association. GWHEA = Georgia Walking Horse Exhibitors Association. MSHSA = Montana State Horse Show Association. FS = flexor surface. BPWHA = Bluegrass Pleasure & Walking Horse Association.

SOURCE: Adapted from "USDA Horse Program Activity Report 2012 (as of January 3, 2013)," in *Animal Welfare*, U.S. Department of Agriculture, Animal and Plant Health Inspection Service, January 3, 2013, http://www.aphis.usda.gov/animal_welfare/downloads/hp/usda_hp_activity_report_2012.pdf (accessed March 25, 2013)

TABLE 6.4

Horse Industry Organization (HIO) list maintained by the Animal and Plant Health Inspection Service (APHIS) Horse Protection Program

Organization short name	Organization long name	Location
FOSH	Friends of Sound Horses	Ellicottville, NY
HAWHA	Heart of America Walking Horse Association	Bolivar, MO
IWHA	International Walking Horse Association	Indianapolis, IN
KWHA	Kentucky Walking Horse Association	McKinney, KY
KY-HIO	Kentucky Horse Association-HIO	Frankfort, KY
MFTHBA	Missouri Fox Trotting Horse Breed Association Inc.	Ava, MO
NWHA	National Walking Horse Association	Lexington, KY
N/A	Non-Affiliated	Riverdale, MD
OHA	Oklahoma Horse Association	Muskogee, OK
PRIDE	Professional Regulation and Inspection for Dedicated Equestrians	Mount Vernon, KY
SHOW	Sound Horse Honest Judging Objective Inspections Winning Fairly	Shelbyville, TN
SSHBEA	Spotted Saddle Horse Breeders and Exhibitors Association	Shelbyville, TN
WHOA	Walking Horse Owners' Association	Murfreesboro, TN
WIWHA	Western International Walking Horse Association	Sherwood, OR

SOURCE: Adapted from *USDA Horse Protection Program: HIO Contact Information*, U.S. Department of Agriculture, Animal and Plant Health Inspection Service, 2013, http://acissearch.aphis.usda.gov/HPA/faces/pdf.jspx?rt=7&sd=&ed=&hio=ALL (accessed March 25, 2013), and *USDA Horse Protection Program: Certified Horse Industry Organizations (HIO) Reference List, updated May 2011*, U.S. Department of Agriculture, Animal and Plant Health Inspection Service, May 2011, http://www.aphis.usda.gov/animal_welfare/hp/downloads/hio/HIOLIST_2011.pdf (accessed March 25, 2013)

Dog Sports

Dogs participate on a large scale in three sports: greyhound racing, sled dog racing, and organized fighting. These sports differ widely in their legitimacy. Sled dog racing evolved as a sport to show off the skills of hardy dogs that have been pulling sleds in snowbound regions for centuries. By contrast, greyhound racing began as a competition between fast and graceful dogs but evolved into a gambling pastime. Organized dogfighting is illegal in every state. Its roots lie in the blood sports that were enjoyed by the ancient Romans at the Coliseum.

There are also a variety of new amateur sporting events that are emerging for dogs. Agility-based competitions, such as catching Frisbees and traversing obstacles, are growing in popularity. One of the newest dog sports is called fly ball. This is a relay event in which teams of dogs compete against each other to jump over hurdles and race to retrieve a ball. In 2000 the International Federation of Cynological Sports (IFCS) was formed in Europe to unite organizations holding dog sports in various countries around the world. (Cynology is the scientific study of canines.) The IFCS is working to bring dog sports, such as those involving agility, to the Olympic Games.

Greyhound Racing

According to the National Greyhound Association (NGA), in "Race Tracks" (http://ngagreyhounds.com/directory/race-tracks), as of May 2013 there were 23 greyhound racetracks operating in the following states: Alabama (2), Arizona (2), Arkansas (1), Florida (11), Iowa (2), Texas (3), and West Virginia (2). Greyhound racing was most prevalent in Florida. The Florida Department of Business and Professional Regulation's Division of Pari-mutuel Wagering reports in *Division of Pari-mutuel Wagering 81st Annual Report Fiscal Year 2011–2012* (March 2013, http://www.myfloridalicense.com/dbpr/pmw/documents/AnnualReport2011-2012–81st–revised2013-03-29.pdf) that $265 million was wagered at the state's greyhound tracks in fiscal year (FY) 2012. This value was down considerably from the nearly $600 million that was wagered in FY 2003.

According to *Greyhound Network News* (October 1, 2011, http://www.greyhoundnetworknews.org/Racetrack_List_October%201%202011.pdf), 38 greyhound racetracks have closed since 1991. Live greyhound racing has been banned in 10 states: Idaho, Maine, Massachusetts, Nevada, New Hampshire, North Carolina, Pennsylvania, Vermont, Virginia, and Washington.

Three major organizations manage greyhound racing in the United States: the NGA, the American Greyhound Track Operators Association (AGTOA), and the American Greyhound Council (AGC; a joint effort of the NGA and the AGTOA). The NGA represents greyhound owners and is the official registry for racing greyhounds. All greyhounds that race on U.S. tracks must first be registered with the NGA. The AGTOA represents greyhound track operators. The AGC manages the industry's animal welfare programs, including farm inspections and adoptions.

WELFARE OF RACING GREYHOUNDS. The HSUS and other animal welfare organizations are strongly opposed to greyhound racing for the following reasons:

- It is not governed by the Animal Welfare Act (AWA) under APHIS as are other commercial animal enterprises, such as zoos and circuses.

- The industry severely overbreeds greyhounds in the hopes of producing winners, leading to the destruction of thousands of puppies each year.

- A racing greyhound's career is typically over at the age of four, well below its average life span of 12 years, meaning that thousands of adult dogs are also destroyed each year when they are no longer useful.

The AGC states that it has adopted standard guidelines for the care of greyhounds and the maintenance of kennel facilities. All the nation's greyhound breeding farms and kennels are subject to unannounced inspections to verify that they are complying with the industry's animal welfare guidelines. Violators can be expelled from the sport.

In "Adoption Programs" (2013, http://www.agcouncil.com/node/5), the AGC claims that greyhound racetracks contribute more than $2 million each year to local greyhound adoption programs and that more than 90% of all registered greyhounds are retired to farms for breeding purposes or adopted out as pets. However, animal welfare groups claim that thousands of adult greyhounds are destroyed each year by the racing industry. For example, the Greyhound Protection League (2013, http://www.greyhounds.org/gpl/contents/common.html) estimates that more than 1 million unwanted racing greyhounds have been culled (killed) by the industry since the 1930s.

MASS KILLING AND NEGLECT CASES. David M. Halbfinger reports in "Dismal End for Race Dogs, Alabama Authorities Say" (NYTimes.com, May 23, 2002) that in May 2002 Robert L. Rhodes was arrested and charged with felony animal cruelty after the remains of more than 2,000 greyhounds were found on his property in Baldwin County, Alabama. The man, who worked as a security guard at the Pensacola Greyhound Track in Florida, claimed that the track paid him $10 apiece to shoot the dogs and dispose of their carcasses on his 18-acre (7.3-hectare) farm. He admitted to performing the service for 40 years at the request of race dog owners. Authorities report that necropsies (postmortem examinations) indicate some of the dogs were not killed instantly and therefore suffered before they died. It is a felony in Alabama to torture an animal. Racetrack officials denied involvement in the case and fired Rhodes along with several other security guards and a kennel operator.

Alabama authorities eventually charged four greyhound owners and trainers under the state's animal cruelty law based on statements from Rhodes and Clarence Ray Patterson, a kennel owner at the Pensacola Greyhound Track. At an April 2004 hearing, the Baldwin County sheriff testified that Rhodes, who died in 2003, had admitted to killing between 2,000 and 3,000 greyhounds that were too sick or old to race. Florida investigators testified that Florida kennel owners and trainers paid Rhodes to shoot unwanted greyhounds because it was cheaper than having the animals humanely euthanized by a veterinarian. However, in 2005 the defendants' lawyers succeeded in having the case dropped after arguing that insufficient evidence existed and that the deceased Rhodes could not be cross-examined.

The article "Investigation Continues into Florida Greyhound Deaths" (Associated Press, November 5, 2010) reports that in October 2010, 37 dead greyhounds were found in a kennel at the Ebro Greyhound Park in Washington County, Florida. The dogs had apparently starved to death. Five barely alive dogs were also discovered; some had duct tape wrapped around their necks, reportedly so tight "the dogs could barely breathe." The dogs' trainer, Ronald Williams, was arrested and charged with animal cruelty. In October 2011 he was sentenced to five years in prison.

A DYING INDUSTRY? A. G. Sulzberger notes in "Greyhound Races Face Extinction at the Hands of Casinos They Fostered" (NYTimes.com, March 8, 2012) that the nation's greyhound racetracks face ever-declining interest from consumers. Some survived the mass closures that characterized the industry during the first decade of the 21st century by convincing state legislators to allow them to add slot machines and poker tables at the facilities. The casino-type operations proved profitable, whereas the tracks continued to lose money. According to Sulzberger, many of the tracks gained approval for the casino operations by agreeing to subsidize the racing with casino profits. As a result, some tracks continue to run races even though those races lose millions of dollars each year. Frustrated track owners have begun lobbying their legislatures for permission to cut back on racing events or even close the tracks and keep the lucrative casino operations open. Sulzberger indicates that it remains to be seen if this business strategy will be favored by state legislators; however, he notes that "the effort has intensified the concern that the end may be near for a century-old pastime."

Sled Dog Racing

The sport of sled dog racing is small but extremely popular throughout Alaska, Canada, and parts of northern Europe. In North America the sport traces its origins to Native Americans, who for centuries have used hardy dogs bred for cold weather to pull their sleds. Typical draft animals, such as horses and oxen, were unsuitable for this purpose because of their weight and food requirements.

IDITAROD. The most famous sled dog race is the Iditarod Trail Sled Dog Race (commonly called the Iditarod). It is held in Alaska in early March of each year and includes dozens of teams that compete for thousands of dollars in prize money. In general, the race covers roughly 1,150 miles (1,850 kilometers; from Anchorage to Nome, Alaska) and is completed in anywhere from eight to 16 days. The speed record (set in 2002) is eight days, 22 hours, and 46 minutes. The Iditarod indicates in "2013 Prize Money by Finish Position" (2013, http://d3r6t1k4mqz5i.cloudfront.net/wp-content/uploads/2011/12/PURSE-BY-POSITION-2013.pdf?d0edd7) that $600,000 in prize money was awarded to the top-30 winning racers for the 2013 Iditarod.

Mushers (human sled drivers) drive dog teams that typically include 15 dogs, one of which is the leader. The dogs wear booties on their paws to help protect against cuts and abrasions. The Iditarod includes about 24 checkpoints along the way. Each team is required to take three breaks during the race: one 24-hour break and two eight-hour breaks. Mushers leave dogs that are sick, tired, or injured at one of the checkpoints for transport back to the starting point. According to race officials, each checkpoint has a veterinarian available. Hazards of the race include weather conditions, wildlife, and unpredictable terrain.

The Iditarod received little media attention outside of Alaska until 1985, when Libby Riddles (1956–) became the first woman to win the race. Another woman, Susan Butcher (1954–2006), won the Iditarod four times between 1986 and 1990. The resulting publicity not only boosted the profile of the race but also brought more scrutiny and criticism from animal welfare organizations.

During the 2013 Iditarod a dog named Dorado died. According to the Iditarod, in the press release "Results of the Iditarod Trail Committee's Investigation into the Death of Dorado and Potential Mitigation Measures" (March 30, 2013, http://d3r6t1k4mqz5i.cloudfront.net/), preliminary results indicate the dog died of asphyxiation from heavy snow. The dog had been dropped off at a checkpoint and was under the care of race officials when the death occurred.

WELFARE OF SLED DOGS. The animal welfare group Sled Dog Action Coalition (SDAC; 2013, http://www

.helpsleddogs.org/) opposes the Iditarod, citing the following problems:

- The race experiences dog deaths and injuries almost every year.

- At least 142 sled dogs are known to have died during the race since its inception in 1973. Dogs have died from heart and other organ failures due to overexertion, pneumonia, and injuries, including being strangled in towlines (the ropes that stretch from the dogs' harnesses to the sled) and rammed by sleds.

- At least three mushers have been disqualified from races for beating or kicking dogs or forcing dogs to run through dangerously deep slush. Two of the dogs in these cases died.

- Race dogs have suffered heat stress, dehydration, diarrhea, pulled tendons, and cut paws because of their participation in the Iditarod.

- Sled dog breeders kill puppies that are unable or unwilling to become good racers.

The SDAC also notes that most sled dogs are confined to short tethers in large dog yards when they are not racing. Tethering as a means of primary confinement is not permitted by the USDA for its licensed dog breeders and is opposed by the HSUS. In "How You Can Help" (2013, http://www.helpsleddogs.org/help.htm), the SDAC calls for opponents of the Iditarod to boycott the race sponsors, to discourage the race from being promoted in schools, and to write letters to celebrities who support the race.

Iditarod mushers and supporters acknowledge that the race is grueling and can be dangerous, but they believe that sufficient rules and safeguards are in place to protect the dogs from injury and abuse. Many people involved in the sport believe that the dangers and wildness of the race enhance its allure.

ANIMAL FIGHTING

Cockfighting

A cock is the adult male of the domestic fowl (*Gallus gallus*), also known as a rooster. Cocks participate in only one organized sport: cockfighting. Cockfighting is considered to be a blood sport because the roosters that participate are frequently killed or mutilated during the fight. Cockfighting is performed by cocks that are outfitted with sharp spikes called gaffs on their legs. Two cocks are thrown into a pit together, where they fight to the death. Cockfighting was banned by most states during the 1800s. As of May 2013, it was illegal in all states. States differ in their treatment of cockfight spectators and those caught in possession of birds for fighting.

Pet-abuse.com (http://www.pet-abuse.com/pages/cruelty_database.php) tracks and logs media reports about acts of animal abuse, including the use of animals in fighting. It notes that in 2012 there were six reports involving cockfighting. Authorities reportedly seized more than 200 birds, some of them dead, while investigating these cases.

Because cockfighting is legal in Mexico and in many Asian countries, there is a commercial breeding industry in the United States. However, the AWA prohibits the exporting of fighting gamecocks to foreign countries.

Dogfighting

Dogfighting is widely considered to be a horrific form of animal abuse. In the United States dogfighting is an illegal, multimillion-dollar gambling industry that is often associated with gangs, auto theft, arms smuggling, money laundering, and drug trafficking. Dogs most often used in dogfighting are pit bulls, which are not considered a specific breed but are rather a mix of breeds, the most predominant being the American Staffordshire terrier. Pit bulls are not necessarily aggressive by nature, but because they are extremely loyal to their owners and have powerful, muscular bodies and strong jaws, they can be bred and trained to exhibit aggressive behavior toward other dogs. Fights typically go on for hours, sometimes to the death. Generally, a fight goes on until a dog gives up or an owner concedes defeat. Dogs that survive the fights frequently die hours or days later from shock, blood loss, or infections.

Fighting dogs are judged on their gameness, which is determined by a dog's willingness and eagerness to fight and its reluctance to yield or back down during the fight. Selective breeding and grueling, cruel training methods are used to enhance gameness. Fighting dogs are usually drugged with steroids and other stimulants to enhance their aggression.

Fighting dogs are often trained on treadmills or devices called catmills. A catmill holds an animal, such as a cat, rabbit, or small dog, just out of reach of the training dog while it runs. Police report that these bait animals are often pets stolen from local neighborhoods and are usually killed during the training. Mild-tempered pit bulls that show no fighting inclinations are also used as bait dogs.

Dogfighting is a felony in all 50 states. (See Table 6.5.) Possession of a dog for fighting and even being a spectator at a dogfight are felonies in some states. As noted earlier, Pet-abuse.com (http://www.pet-abuse.com/pages/cruelty_database.php) tracks media reports about animal abuse incidents. This includes incidents involving dogfighting. It notes that in 2012 there were 18 reports involving dogfighting.

Animal welfare groups want to strengthen state laws that deal with dogfighting. They also ask major newspapers not to accept advertisements selling dogs that use descriptive words such as *game dog* or *game bred*,

TABLE 6.5

State dog fighting laws ranked by the Humane Society of the United States as to seriousness of penalty, January 2013

State	Dogfighting	Spectator at a dogfight	Possession of dogs for fighting	Rank
3 Felony				
New Jersey	Crime of the 3rd degree 3–5 years $3,000–$5,000	Crime of the 3rd degree 3–5 years Max $15,000	Crime of the 3rd degree 3–5 years Max $15,000	1
Louisiana	Felony 1–10 years $1,000–$25,000	Felony 1–10 years $1,000–$25,000	Felony 1–10 years $1,000–$25,000	2
Alabama	Class C felony 1–10 years Max $5,000	Class C felony 1–10 years Max $5,000	Class C felony 1–10 years Max $5,000	3
Illinois	Class 4 felony 1–3 years Max $25,000	Class 4 felony 1–3 years Max $25,000	Class 4 felony 1–3 years Max $25,000	4
Colorado	Class 5 felony 1–3 years Max $1,000	Class 5 felony 1–3 years Max $1,000	Class 5 felony 1–3 years Max $1,000	5
Mississippi	Felony 1–3 years $1,000–$5,000	Felony Max 1 year $500–$5,000	Felony 1–3 years $1,000–$5,000	6
Arizona	Class 5 felony 9 months–2 years Max $150,000	Class 6 felony 6 months–1½ years Max $150,000	Class 5 felony 9 months–2 years Max $150,000	7
Ohio	4th degree felony 6–18 months $5,000	4th degree felony 6–18 months $5,000	4th degree felony 6–18 months $5,000	8
North Carolina	Class H felony 4–8 months–5–10 months	Class H felony 4–8 months–5–10 months	Class H felony 4–8 months–5–10 months	9
Hawaii	Class B felony Max 10 years Max $25,000	Felony Max 5 years Max $10,000	Class B felony Max 10 years Max $25,000	10
Pennsylvania	3rd degree felony Max 7 years Max $15,000	3rd degree felony Max 7 years Max $15,000	3rd degree felony Max 7 years Max $15,000	11
New Hampshire	Class B felony Max 7 years Max $4,000	Class B felony Max 7 years Max $4,000	Class B felony Max 7 years Max $4,000	12
Oregon	Class C felony Max 5 years Max $125,000	Class C felony Max 5 years Max $125,000	Class C felony Max 5 years Max $125,000	13
District of Columbia	Felony Max 5 years Max $25,000	Felony Max 5 years Max $25,000	Felony Max 5 years Max $25,000	14
Nebraska	Class IV felony Max 5 years Max $10,000	Class IV felony Max 5 years Max $10,000	Class IV felony Max 5 years Max $10,000	15
Washington	Class C felony Max 5 years Max $10,000	Class C felony Max 5 years Max $10,000	Class C Felony Max 5 years Max $10,000	16
Connecticut	Felony Max 5 years Max $5,000	Felony Max 5 years Max $5,000	Felony Max 5 years Max $5,000	17
Florida	3rd degree felony Max 5 years Max $5,000	3rd degree felony Max 5 years Max $5,000	3rd degree felony Max 5 years Max $5,000	18
Vermont	Felony Max 5 years Max $5,000	Felony Max 5 years Max $5,000	Felony Max 5 years Max $5,000	19
Virginia	Class 6 felony Max 5 years Max $2,500	Class 6 felony Max 5 years Max $2,500	Class 6 felony Max 5 years Max $2,500	20
Massachusetts	Felony equivalent Max 5 years (state prison) or Max 1 year (house of correction) Max $1,000	Felony equivalent Max 5 years (state prison) or Max 2.5 years (house of correction) Max $1,000	Felony equivalent Max 5 years (state prison) or Max 1 year (house of correction) Max $1,000	21
Delaware	Class E felony Max 5 years Discretionary fine	Class F felony Max 3 years Discretionary fine	Class E felony Max 5 years Discretionary fine	22

because these terms imply that the dog is intended for fighting. The HSUS asks people to notify it whenever such advertisements appear in their local newspapers. HSUS activists monitor websites and magazines that are devoted to game dogs and alert police when they believe a dogfight is going to take place.

TABLE 6.5

State	Dogfighting	Spectator at a dogfight	Possession of dogs for fighting	Rank
Michigan	Felony Max 4 years $5,000–$50,000 500–100 hours community service	Felony Max 4 years $1,000–$5,000 250–500 hours community service	Felony Max 4 years $5,000–$50,000 500–100 hours community service	23
Rhode Island	Felony Max 2 years Max $1,000	Felony Max 2 years Max $1,500	Felony Max 2 years Max $1,000	24
New Mexico	4th degree felony 18 months Max $5,000	4th degree felony 18 months Max $5,000	4th degree felony 18 months Max $5,000	25
2 Felony				
Oklahoma	Felony 1–10 years $2,000–$25,000	Misdemeanor Max 1 year Max $500	Felony 1–10 years $2,000–$25,000	26
Georgia	Felony 1–5 years Min $5,000	Misdemeanor Max 1 year Max $1,000	Felony 1–5 years Min $5,000	27
Kansas	Level 10 nonperson felony 1–5 years Max $100,000	Class B nonperson misdemeanor Max 6 months Max $1,000	Level 10 nonperson felony 1–5 years Max $100,000	28
Minnesota	Felony Min 1 year 1 day	Misdemeanor Max 90 days Max $1,000	Felony Min 1 year 1 day	29
Tennessee	Class E felony 1–6 years Max $3,000	Class C misdemeanor Max of 30 days Max $50	Class E felony 1–6 years Max $3,000	30
Kentucky	Class D felony 1–5 years $1,000–$10,000	Misdemeanor	Class D felony 1–5 years $1,000–$10,000	31
Indiana	Class D felony 6 months–3 years Max $10,000	Class A misdemeanor Max 1 year Max $5,000	Class D felony 6 months–3 years Max $10,000	32
Missouri	Class D felony Max 10 years	Class A misdemeanor Min 6 months	Class D felony Max 10 years	33
Arkansas	Class D felony Max 6 years Max $10,000	Class A misdemeanor Max 1 year Max $1,000	Class D felony Max 6 years Max $10,000	34
Idaho	Felony Max 5 years Max $50,000	Misdemeanor Max 6 months $100–$5,000	Felony Max 5 years Max $50,000	35
Utah	3rd degree felony Max 5 years Max $25,000	Class B misdemeanor Max 6 months Max $1,000	3rd degree felony Max 5 years Max $25,000	36
Alaska	Class C felony Max 5 years Max $50,000	Violation No jail time Max $500	Class C felony Max 5 years Max $50,000	37
Iowa	Class D felony Max 5 years $750–$7,500	Aggravated misdemeanor Max 2 years	Class D felony Max 5 years $750–$7,500	38
Maine	Class C crime Court must impose a fine of $500 max, in addition to: Max 5 years Max $5,000	$500–$5,000 Class D crime Max 1 year Max $2,000	Class C crime Court must impose a fine of $500 max, in addition to: Max 5 years Max $5,000	39
North Dakota	Class C felony Max 5 years Max $5,000	Class A misdemeanor Max 1 year Max $2,000	Class C felony Max 5 years Max $5,000	40
South Carolina	Felony Max 5 years Max $5,000	Misdemeanor Max 6 months Max $500	Felony Max 5 years Max $5,000	41
Wisconsin	Class I felony Max 3 years, 6 months Max $10,000	Class A misdemeanor Max 9 months Max $10,000	Class I felony Max 3 years, 6 months Max $10,000	42
Maryland	Felony Max 3 years Max $5,000	Misdemeanor Max 1 year Max $2,500	Felony Max 3 years Max $5,000	43
California	Felony 16 months or 2 or 3 years Max $50,000	Misdemeanor Max 6 months Max $1,000	Felony 16 months or 2 or 3 years Max $50,000	44

In 2007 dogfighting became national news after the Atlanta Falcons quarterback Michael Vick (1980–) was arrested for running a dogfighting operation on property he owned in Virginia. Investigators alleged that Vick and his coconspirators killed poorly performing fighting dogs by electrocuting, hanging, drowning, or beating

TABLE 6.5

State dog fighting laws ranked by the Humane Society of the United States as to seriousness of penalty, January 2013 [CONTINUED]

State	Dogfighting	Spectator at a dogfight	Possession of dogs for fighting	Rank
South Dakota	Class 6 Felony Max 2 years Max $4,000	Class 1 misdemeanor Max 1 year Max $2,000	Class 6 felony Max 2 years Max $4,000	45
Wyoming	Felony Max 2 years Max $5,000	Misdemeanor Max 6 months Max $750	Felony Max 2 years Max $5,000	46
1 Felony				
West Virginia	Felony 1–5 years $1,000–$5,000	Misdemeanor Max 1 year $100–$1,000	Misdemeanor Max 6 months $300–$2,000	47
Nevada	Category D felony 1–4 years Max $5,000	Misdemeanor Max 6 months Max $1,000	Gross misdemeanor Max 1 year Max $2,000	48
Texas	State jail felony 180 days–2 years	Class A misdemeanor Max 1 year Max $4,000	Class A misdemeanor Max 1 year Max $4,000	49
New York	Felony Max 4 years Max $25,000	Misdemeanor Max 1 year Max $1,000	Misdemeanor Max 1 year Max $15,000	50
1 Legal				
Montana	Felony 1–5 years Max $5,000	Legal	Felony 1–5 years Max $5,000	51

SOURCE: "Ranking of State Dogfighting Laws," in *State Animal Protection Laws*, Humane Society of the United States, January 2013, http://www.humanesociety.org/assets/pdfs/animal_fighting/dogfighting_statelaws.pdf (accessed March 25, 2013).

them to death. In December 2007 Vick was sentenced to 23 months in prison for his role in the operation and for lying to authorities about his involvement. Vick lost his multimillion-dollar contract with the Atlanta Falcons and millions of dollars more in endorsement deals. He was released from prison in March 2009.

In "What Happened to Michael Vick's Dogs" (SI.com, December 23, 2008), Jim Gorant gives a detailed account on the fate of the surviving dogs that were rescued from Vick's dogfighting compound. Gorant reports that 51 dogs were originally rescued. Four died or were euthanized in shelters after being seized. Initially, some animal welfare groups—including the HSUS and People for the Ethical Treatment of Animals—called for all the dogs to be euthanized. Their reasoning was that the money and time required to rehabilitate the fighting dogs would be better spent on much more adoptable dogs already languishing in shelters. However, there was widespread public interest in the welfare of the surviving dogs. As a result, they were handed over to well-respected rescue groups and individuals who are experienced in rehabilitating former fighting dogs. Twenty-two of the dogs went to the Best Friends Animal Sanctuary in Utah. Another 10 went to the group Bay Area Doglovers Responsible about Pitbulls in California. The remaining 15 dogs went to permanent homes or foster homes around the country.

As of May 2013, Vick was a quarterback for the Philadelphia Eagles, a job he acquired in late 2009 after being released from prison. Vick has teamed with the HSUS to engage in anti-dogfighting speeches to youth, particularly those in urban neighborhoods. According to the HSUS, in "Michael Vick and End Dogfighting" (March 30, 2012, http://www.humanesociety.org/issues/dogfighting/qa/vick_faq.html), Vick has expressed remorse for his dogfighting past. The HSUS acknowledges that its decision to team with Vick has been criticized by some animal protection groups, but notes, "We realized the potential that Vick has to reach at-risk youth and pull them out of the quicksand of animal fighting."

Federal Legislation against Animal Fighting

One of the outcomes of the Vick case was intense public notice and concern about dogfighting. In May 2007 President George W. Bush (1946–) signed the Animal Fighting Prohibition Enforcement Act, which made it a felony to violate the animal fighting provisions of the AWA or to possess dogfighting or cockfighting implements. The new law also provides additional resources for federal investigation and enforcement related to animal fighting. The AWA prohibits the selling, purchasing, or transporting across state lines or in international commerce of an animal that is intended for fighting.

CHAPTER 7
ENTERTAINMENT ANIMALS

Entertainment animals are those that perform or are displayed publicly to amuse people. These animals appear in circuses, carnivals, animal shows and exhibits, amusement and wildlife theme parks, aquariums, zoos, museums, fairs, motion pictures, and television programs. Even though these venues are diverse, they all have one thing in common: They use animals for human purposes. Many of these purposes are purely recreational. Others combine recreation with educational goals, such as teaching the public about the conservation and preservation of endangered species. In either case, the animals are a source of income for their owners.

Entertainment animals include both wild and domesticated types. Wild exotic animals such as elephants, lions, and tigers are the most popular. They are objects of curiosity because people do not encounter them in their daily life. The word *exotic* means "foreign" or "not native" but also suggests an air of mystery and danger that is alluring to people, who will often pay to see exotic animals living in cages. By contrast, domestic animals must do something to make money, because most people will not pay to see ordinary cats and dogs lying around. They might, however, pay to see them jump through fiery hoops or walk on their hind legs pushing baby carriages. They will pay even more to see wild animals do such things.

Animal rights groups believe wild animals should live in the wild, unaffected by human interference, and not be forced to do things that do not come naturally to them. Animal welfarists fear that exotic animals are not housed, trained, and cared for in a humane manner, particularly at circuses, carnivals, and roadside zoos and parks. The animals at these venues may be treated poorly and live in deplorable conditions without access to veterinary care. Performing animals must be trained to be entertainers, and trainers may use cruel and abusive methods.

Animal rights advocates feel that even nonperforming captive wild animals live unnatural existences. They are either removed from their natural habitats or born into captivity. Some people argue that this is beneficial for the animals and the perpetuation of their species. Animals in the wild face many dangers, including natural predators, starvation, hunters, and poachers. Their natural habitats in many parts of the world are shrinking as human development takes up more and more space.

Some exotic animals live longer in captivity than they would in the wild, and some species might die out completely if humans do not capture specimens of them to preserve. Large zoos often do this kind of work, and they may also take in exotic animals that have been surrendered by or rescued from smaller, less capable zoos and parks. However, even these large zoos are in the entertainment business, earning money by displaying captive animals to the public. Does the end justify the means? This is one of the fundamental questions in the debate over animals in entertainment.

HISTORY

The movie and television industry became a major media outlet for animal entertainment during the latter part of the 20th century. Circuses and other traditional shows that featured live wild animal acts faded in popularity as they competed with new venues, such as theme parks and aquariums with exotic animals. In 1964 the first SeaWorld marine park opened in San Diego, California. The San Diego Zoo's Wild Animal Park was established in 1969. Busch Gardens of Florida began during the late 1950s as a beer-tasting factory open to the public. Over the following two decades the company added elaborate bird and animal acts and amusement park rides to create a theme park. During the late 1990s SeaWorld and Walt Disney World both added massive animal theme parks to their existing attractions.

Exotic animal acts evolved during the 20th century to allow greater human-animal interaction. These shows are often marketed as a chance for people to get closer to nature and to help protect endangered species. For example, tourists pay to swim with captive dolphins at beach resorts.

U.S. LEGISLATION AND REGULATION

Performing animals in the United States had little legal protection until 1970, when the Animal Welfare Act (AWA) was amended to include animals exhibited to the public. Regulation and enforcement of the act is handled by the Animal and Plant Health Inspection Service (APHIS) of the U.S. Department of Agriculture (USDA). Animal exhibitors that show animals for compensation and either obtain or dispose of animals in commercial transactions must be licensed. (See Table 7.1.) Table 7.2 lists the licensing fees for exhibitors. The fees increase with increasing numbers of animals. Exhibitors that do not receive compensation and do not buy, sell, or transport animals only need to register.

As shown in Table 7.3, registration is required for various kinds of animal exhibitions, including circuses, zoos, and wildlife parks. Table 7.4 lists the types of exhibition activities that are exempt from regulation under the AWA. The list includes horse and dog races, rodeos, and various agriculturally based events, such as county fairs. In addition, animal preserves or sanctuaries that do not exhibit or use their animals for promotional purposes or sell animals are exempt. Exhibitors showing only coldblooded animals, such as fish and reptiles, are also exempt from AWA regulation.

In "Legislative History of the Animal Welfare Act" (September 2007, http://www.nal.usda.gov/awic/pubs/AWA2007/intro.shtml), the USDA indicates that the original AWA that passed in 1966 covered only a few species: cats, dogs, guinea pigs, hamsters, nonhuman primates, and rabbits. A 1970 amendment to the law added coverage for all warm-blooded animals. However, the secretary of agriculture "administratively excluded rats, mice, and birds from the definition of animal in the accompanying regulations." Following legal challenges from animal welfare and rights groups, in 2000 the USDA

TABLE 7.1

Animal exhibitors, as defined by the Animal Welfare Act

Under the AWA, an "exhibitor" is defined as an individual or business that:
• Allows the public to view animals for compensation;
• Trains, handles, or owns animals used in film or television;
• Uses photographs of live animals in promotional materials such as fliers and other advertisements;
• Operates a travelling, roadside, or stationary zoo;
• Performs with animals such as in a circus or other type of show; or
• Uses animals in educational presentations.

SOURCE: Adapted from "Regulated Animal Exhibitors," in *Animal Welfare Act Guidelines for County and State Fairs*, U.S. Department of Agriculture, Animal and Plant Health Inspection Service, February 2012, http://www.aphis.usda.gov/publications/animal_welfare/content/printable_version/fs_fairex.pdf (accessed March 25, 2013)

TABLE 7.2

License fees for exhibitors needing Class "C" licenses

Number of animals	Initial license fee	Annual or changed class of license fee
1 to 5	$30	$40
6 to 25	75	85
26 to 50	175	185
51 to 500	225	235
501 and up	300	310

SOURCE: "Table 2. Exhibitors—Class 'C' License," in *Code of Federal Regulations, Title 9—Animals and Animal Products*, U.S. Government Printing Office, January 1, 2012, http://www.gpo.gov/fdsys/pkg/CFR-2012-title9-vol1/pdf/CFR-2012-title9-vol1-chapI.pdf (accessed March 25, 2013)

TABLE 7.3

Types of animal exhibitions licensed as Class C under the Animal Welfare Act

• Circuses
• Zoos
• Petting farms/zoos
• Animal acts
• Wildlife parks
• Marine mammal parks
• Sanctuaries that exhibit or use animals for promotional purposes, including fundraising, or sell animals
• Photo shoots
• Animal rides

SOURCE: Adapted from "Regulated Animal Exhibitors," in *Animal Welfare Act Guidelines for County and State Fairs*, U.S. Department of Agriculture, Animal and Plant Health Inspection Service, February 2012, http://www.aphis.usda.gov/publications/animal_welfare/content/printable_version/fs_fairex.pdf (accessed March 25, 2013), and "Regulated Animal Exhibitors," in *Animal Exhibitors*, U.S. Department of Agriculture, Animal and Plant Health Inspection Service, February 2012, http://www.aphis.usda.gov/publications/animal_welfare/content/printable_version/fs_anexhit.pdf (accessed March 25, 2013)

TABLE 7.4

Examples of animal exhibitors exempted from federal regulation under the Animal Welfare Act

• Agricultural events including farm animals only
• State and county fairs
• Livestock shows
• Purebred dog and cat shows
• Dog races
• Horse races
• Rodeos
• Animal preserves or sanctuaries maintaining exotic or wild animals if they do not exhibit or use the animals for promotional purposes, including fundraising, or sell animals
• Exhibitors showing only coldblooded animals, such as fish and reptiles

SOURCE: Adapted from "Exempted Animal Exhibitors," in *Animal Exhibitors*, U.S. Department of Agriculture, Animal and Plant Health Inspection Service, February 2012, http://www.aphis.usda.gov/publications/animal_welfare/content/printable_version/fs_anexhit.pdf (accessed March 25, 2013)

agreed to cover these animals as well. Before new regulations were implemented, however, the Farm Security and Rural Investment Act of 2002 was passed. APHIS explains in the fact sheet "Questions and Answers: Rats, Mice, and Birds to Be Included in the Animal Welfare Act" (August 2011, http://www.aphis .usda.gov/publications/animal_welfare/2011/FS_QArmb.pdf) that this law specified that birds, mice of the genus *Mus*, and rats of the genus *Rattus* would be regulated under the AWA, except for those animals that are bred for research purposes. APHIS states that in 2004 it publicized its intention to begin regulating the animals under the AWA and took public comments regarding the decision. However, as of May 2013 an official proposal had not been issued. The agency indicates that few mice and rats are bred for nonresearch purposes; thus, the new regulation will mainly impact birds. APHIS estimates that at least 5 million birds will fall under AWA coverage, based on estimates that as many as 75,000 bird breeding facilities were operating in the United States. It was unknown how many birds were used in animal exhibits.

In the fact sheet "Animal Exhibitors" (February 2012, http://www.aphis.usda.gov/publications/animal_welfare/content/printable_version/fs_anexhit.pdf), APHIS explains that under the AWA licensed exhibitors must provide "adequate care and treatment in the areas of housing, handling, transportation, sanitation, nutrition, water, general husbandry, veterinary care, and protection from extreme weather and temperatures." The exhibitors are required to keep records detailing the veterinary care that the animals receive and "minimize harmful risks to animals and the public" during public exhibitions. In addition, the AWA limits the amounts of time that animals can be exhibited and governs the conditions under which they are exhibited. For example, APHIS notes that "exhibitors must not physically abuse animals while training or working them or use tranquilizing drugs to facilitate public handling of the animals." In addition, the animals must be protected from "rough handling during public contact sessions." Exhibitors that violate standards are subject to warnings and civil actions such as license suspensions or fines.

As explained in Chapter 5, APHIS maintains a database of AWA records that is accessible through the Animal Care Information System (ACIS) Search Tool (http://acissearch.aphis.usda.gov/LPASearch/faces/Warning.jspx). As of May 2013, the database included records for 3,857 licensees and registrants identified as exhibitors. However, only 2,788 of the exhibitors were active at that time. California had the largest number of active animal exhibitors (299), followed by Florida (260), Texas (212), New York (133), and Illinois (118). Together, these five states accounted for more than one-third of all active exhibitors.

Criticisms of the AWA and APHIS

The AWA regulations are criticized by animal welfarists as being minimal standards that provide little protection and are poorly enforced. In addition, penalties for violating the AWA are civil, not criminal. Entertainment animals are often protected by state and local anticruelty laws, but the Humane Society of the United States (HSUS) claims that some states exempt USDA-licensed animal acts (particularly circuses) from meeting anticruelty standards. However, some local governments do forbid or tightly regulate animal acts.

CIRCUSES

Circuses have used performing animals, mostly bears, elephants, horses, lions, monkeys, and tigers, for centuries. Animal rights and welfare groups are critical of circuses that feature animals. They say the animals are treated poorly and spend long hours in small cages or chained to the ground. In "Circus Myths: The True Cruelty under the Big Top" (September 25, 2009, http://www.humanesociety.org/issues/circuses_entertainment/facts/circus_myths.html), the HSUS makes the following claims against circuses:

- Many circus animals are not owned by the circuses but are leased from exotic animal dealers under seasonal contracts.

- Circuses do not provide proper veterinary care for the animals they own or lease.

- Circus animals spend too much time in transport in trucks and railcars that are not air conditioned or heated.

- Traveling circus animals are often deprived of food and water for long periods.

- Circus training methods include beatings and food deprivation.

Major animal welfare and rights groups, such as the HSUS, People for the Ethical Treatment of Animals (PETA), and Born Free USA, advocate animal-free circuses. Born Free USA lists in "Exotic Animal Incidents, Facility Type: Circus" (2013, http://www.bornfreeusa.org/database/exo_incidents.php?facility=C) 108 animal incidents (attacks, escapes, accidents, and alleged abuse cases) that are associated with circuses.

ZOOS

In 1874 the first American zoo opened to the public in Philadelphia, Pennsylvania. It featured animals from around the world, as well as elaborate gardens, architecture, and art. Early zoos kept wild animals in cages, but during the mid-1800s the German exhibitor Carl Hagenbeck (1844–1913) advocated the use of natural settings for zoo animals. In 1907 he opened a zoo near Hamburg,

Germany, in which the animals were exhibited on artificial islands that resembled their natural habitats. He felt this approach was better for both the animals and the spectators. Even though few other zookeepers adopted his ideas at the time, they were one of the hallmarks of a top zoo by the end of the 20th century.

Accredited Zoos

Originally founded in 1924 as the American Association of Zoological Parks and Aquariums, the Association of Zoos and Aquariums (AZA) is a nonprofit organization that works to advance conservation, education, science, and recreation at zoos and aquariums. The AZA explains in "AZA 5-Year Strategic Plan" (2013, http://www.aza .org/StrategicPlan/) that it "provides its members the services, high standards and best practices needed to be leaders and innovators in animal care, wildlife conservation and science, conservation education, the guest experience, and community engagement." Zoos and aquariums that meet the AZA's professional standards can be accredited by the organization. As of May 2013, there were 222 AZA-accredited zoos and aquariums, located mostly in North America. According to the AZA, these facilities attract approximately 175 million visitors each year. The AZA also works to ensure the long-term breeding and conservation of a variety of species.

The zoos that are accredited by the AZA in the United States are generally well respected by the public and even by many animal welfarists. The latter acknowledge that large zoos educate the public about wildlife and help conserve, preserve, and restore endangered species. However, this does not spare accredited zoos from some criticisms. The chief criticism relates to the disposal practices for their unwanted animals.

Unwanted Animals

In "Cruel and Usual: How Some of America's Best Zoos Get Rid of Their Old, Infirm, and Unwanted Animals" (USNews.com, July 28, 2002), Michael Satchell examines the animal disposal practices of some of the major zoos in the United States. Satchell tracked down a dozen birds, primates, and other exotic animals that had left the prestigious Rosamond Gifford Zoo in Syracuse, New York, for a menagerie in Texas. He found the animals living in filthy cages alongside an interstate highway amid trash and weeds. The menagerie had gone out of business.

The AZA explains in "AZA Acquisition-Disposition Policy" (2009, http://www.aza.org/ad-policy/) that it requires accredited institutions to acquire animals from and dispose of animals to other AZA institutions or to non-AZA members with "the expertise, records management practices, financial stability, facilities, and resources required to properly care for and maintain the animals."

Satchell claims this procedure is often violated by AZA zoos that "loan" or "donate" unwanted animals to unaccredited roadside zoos and animal parks. These facilities are frequently substandard and provide poor care. Satchell quotes Richard Farinato of the HSUS as saying that the practice of "dumping animals is the big, respectable zoos' dirty little secret."

Satchell bases his accusations on a review of database records from the International Species Information System (http://isis.org/Pages/default.aspx), which is used by major zoos to track animal transfers, and from interviews with government, zoo, and animal rights personnel. Satchell concludes that large zoos in Alabama, Arizona, California, Colorado, the District of Columbia, Georgia, Hawaii, Missouri, New York, and Tennessee have transferred unwanted animals to substandard facilities and to dealers with alleged links to the exotic animal trade.

Unaccredited Zoos

According to the AZA, in "What Is Accreditation?" (2013, http://www.aza.org/what-is-accreditation/), it accredits less than 10% of U.S. animal exhibits. As such, there are thousands of unaccredited small roadside zoos, petting zoos, animal parks, and similar exhibits that display animals to the public. The HSUS suggests that these small zoos often barely meet minimal federal standards for animal care. Most of these facilities include exotic animals, such as lions and tigers. Many are run by entrepreneurs with little experience in the proper care of exotic animals and with limited financial resources. Some call themselves animal preserves and achieve a tax-exempt status so that they can solicit donations for their so-called conservation work.

All licensed animal exhibits are subject to USDA inspection, but animal welfare groups claim that poorly run facilities often receive bad inspection reports for years and are still not closed down. A case in point is ZooCats Inc. (also known as Zoo Dynamics) in Kaufman, Texas. On September 24, 2008, APHIS issued an administrative order (http://www.da.usda.gov/oaljdecisions/ 080924_AWA_03-0035DO.pdf) forbidding ZooCats from exhibiting exotic animals and permanently revoking its license. The order cited ZooCats and its owner, Marcus Cook, for several AWA violations that occurred between 2002 and 2007. According to court records, ZooCats was registered with the USDA as a nonprofit corporation but had exhibited exotic and wild animals for profit at the Six Flags over Texas amusement park and at other venues around the country, including shopping malls and fairs. These exhibits often included baby tigers that children were allowed to pet and feed without proper supervision. APHIS cited many deficiencies over several years found by APHIS inspectors involving the handling, housing, feeding, and veterinary care provided for the tigers and for the company's other exotic animals, including prairie dogs, lions, and a bear. Some of the tigers were malnourished and had untreated injuries and illnesses. Jonathan Betz reports in "Controversial Exhibitor Owner of Seized Tigers, Lion" (March 24, 2009, http://www.wfaa.com/archive/64747682.html) that in March 2009 the USDA seized two tigers and a lion from ZooCats and sent them to the In-Sync Exotics Wildlife Rescue and Educational Center in Texas. The animals reportedly had numerous health problems, including malnourishment and wounds.

This was not the end of Cook's exotic animal operations, however. He appealed the decision against him. Numerous administrative motions and orders were filed in the case over the following years. In "Navy Pier Shuts Down Royal White Tigers" (ChicagoTribune.com, January 25, 2012), John Kass indicates that in January 2012 he found Cook operating a popular white tiger exhibit at the Navy Pier, a family entertainment complex in Chicago, Illinois. According to Kass, the complex had paid $27,000 to Cook for the show and failed to investigate the exhibitor's past. Kass notes that "all Navy Pier had to do was put Cook's name into Google. But apparently no one did, and now nobody wants to own up to the white tiger idea." Kass indicates that the Navy Pier canceled the show after he informed them of the USDA order revoking Cook's license. He reports that "Cook denied the USDA's claims" and that Cook called one USDA official "an animal rights activist with a political agenda aimed at eliminating all traveling zoos, exhibitors and other such entertainments from the American landscape." Kass himself adds, "I'm still trying to figure out who's really at fault here, if anyone. And I feel bad about the tigers leaving and the kids who won't get a chance to see them."

In February 2012 Cook and a co-respondent were fined $7,500 as a civil penalty under the AWA. A search of the APHIS database using the ACIS Search Tool reveals that on February 17, 2012, the USDA revoked ZooCats' AWA certificate (74-C-0426).

THE FIGHT OVER CIRCUS AND ZOO ELEPHANTS

The keeping of elephants in captivity by circuses and zoos is a highly controversial issue for animal welfare and rights groups. Elephants are difficult to keep in confinement because of their immense size. Welfarists claim that many circus elephants are mistreated, malnourished, and sick with tuberculosis. A common tool for training elephants is called an ankus or bullhook, which is a long rod with a sharp hook on the end. Critics charge that elephant trainers beat the animals with the rod and poke the hook into tender areas of the elephant's hide, such as behind its ears. In 2002 the animal rights group In

Defense of Animals (IDA) sponsored speaking engagements around the country for a former circus animal trainer, who described how elephants were beaten with bullhooks. He claimed that brutal training methods are routinely used at the Clyde Beatty–Cole Brothers Circus and the Ringling Brothers and Barnum and Bailey Circus (commonly called the Ringling Brothers). The IDA also obtained video footage of what it says are abusive training methods being used on circus elephants.

Circuses and zoos insist that keeping elephants in captivity is a conservation measure that will help ensure the survival of the species for the future. For example, the Ringling Brothers defends its elephant training and breeding programs. The circus operates an animal retirement facility and the Center for Elephant Conservation (CEC) in Florida. The CEC explains in "About the CEC" (2013, http://www.elephantcenter.com/About_The_Cec.aspx) that it was founded in 1995 to conserve, study, and breed Asian elephants. The CEC is a $5-million, 200-acre (81-hectare) facility that is dedicated to preserving the species. The center is not open to the public but admits researchers, conservationists, and academics by arrangement. As of May 2013, the CEC had experienced 25 elephant births.

Animal rights groups contend that breeding elephants to work in the circus or to display at zoos is not really conservation. They believe that wild animals should live undisturbed in their natural environments and that resources should be focused on protecting and expanding natural habitats. They oppose the use of captivity as a conservation tool.

The Ringling Brothers

The Ringling Brothers is owned by Feld Entertainment. The company has long been criticized by animal welfare groups for its handling and use of Asian elephants. In 2000 Ringling Brothers and Feld Entertainment were sued by a group of plaintiffs including the Performing Animal Welfare Society (PAWS), the American Society for the Prevention of Cruelty to Animals (ASPCA), the Animal Welfare Institute, the Animal Protection Institute (API), the Fund for Animals, and Tom Rider, a former Ringling Brothers elephant handler.

The suit claimed that the Ringling Brothers had violated the "taking" provision under the Endangered Species Act. The act's definition of taking includes harming, harassing, and/or wounding. Specifically, the circus was accused of physically abusing its elephants with bullhooks, chaining the elephants for up to 20 hours at a time, and forcibly separating elephant mothers from their babies at an early age. In 2001 PAWS dropped out of the lawsuit due to separate litigation that was brought against it by Feld Entertainment. Feld Entertainment staunchly denied the allegations against it and countersued the remaining plaintiffs in 2007, claiming malicious prosecution and abuse of process on their part.

In 2009, after many years of delays, the original lawsuit, *ASPCA et al. v. Feld Entertainment, Inc.*), was heard in federal court. The court found Rider's testimony unconvincing, in part because he had received at least $190,000 from the animal groups involved. The court ruled that Rider and the API did not have legal standing in the case. In October 2011 an appeals court upheld the ruling.

Feld Entertainment's own lawsuit against its accusers continued. In the press release "ASPCA Pays $9.3 Million in Landmark Ringling Bros. and Barnum & Bailey Circus Settlement" (December 28, 2012, http://www.feld entertainment.com/Press/PressRelease.aspx?id=62237), Feld Entertainment announces that it reached a legal settlement with the ASPCA. The ASPCA agreed to pay Feld Entertainment $9.3 million to settle Feld Entertainment's claims. The press release indicates that Feld Entertainment continued to pursue legal proceedings against the other parties to the original 2000 lawsuit against it. Kenneth Feld, the company's chief executive officer, is quoted as saying: "These defendants attempted to destroy our family-owned business with a hired plaintiff who made statements that the court did not believe. Animal activists have been attacking our family, our company, and our employees for decades because they oppose animals in circuses."

While these lawsuits were ongoing, in late 2011 *Mother Jones* magazine published an exposé about its own year-long investigation into elephant treatment by Feld Entertainment. In "The Cruelest Show on Earth" (November–December 2011, http://www.motherjones.com/environment/2011/10/ringling-bros-elephant-abuse), Deborah Nelson claims that "Ringling elephants spend most of their long lives either in chains or on trains, under constant threat of the bullhook, or ankus—the menacing tool used to control elephants. They are lame from balancing their 8,000-pound frames on tiny tubs and from being confined in cramped spaces, sometimes for days at a time. They are afflicted with tuberculosis and herpes, potentially deadly diseases rare in the wild and linked to captivity."

In November 2011 Feld Entertainment was assessed a $270,000 civil penalty under the AWA. The USDA notes in the press release "USDA and Feld Entertainment, Inc., Reach Settlement Agreement" (November 28, 2011, http://www.usda.gov/wps/portal/usda/usdamediafb?contentid=2011/11/0494.xml&printable=true) that the penalty was for "alleged violations of the Animal Welfare Act (AWA) dating from June 2007 to August 2011" and was the largest civil penalty ever assessed against an animal exhibitor under the AWA. The company denied any wrongdoing, but agreed to implement new training and handling procedures and to establish an AWA compliance position on its staff.

MOVIES AND TELEVISION

Animals have been performing in movies and on television shows ever since these media were invented. Rin Tin Tin was a famous war dog that starred in silent movies during the 1920s. The story of another dog, Lassie, appeared in book form in 1940, in a movie in 1943, and on television in 1954. The original television show ran for 17 years. Another dog gained fame in the title role of the movie *Benji* in 1974. Popular animal movies of the 1980s included *White Fang* and *Turner and Hooch*.

The orca Keiko became famous because of the 1993 movie *Free Willy*. In the movie Keiko portrayed an orca that was liberated from captivity with the help of a boy. According to the Free Willy-Keiko Foundation, in "Keiko's Story: The Timeline" (2013, http://www.keiko.com/history.html), Keiko was captured as a baby in the wild near Iceland during the late 1970s and was subsequently owned by aquariums and amusement parks in Iceland, Canada, and Mexico. The movie was filmed while Keiko lived at an amusement park in Mexico City. In "Won't Somebody Please Save This Whale?" (*Life*, November 1993), JoBeth McDaniel described the irony of the poor conditions in which Keiko lived at the park. In response, the Free Willy-Keiko Foundation raised millions of dollars to have Keiko moved in 1996 to an aquarium in Oregon. (See Figure 7.1.) There he gained weight and recuperated from various health ailments. In 1998 he was flown to Iceland to live in a bay pen in his native waters. Keiko's handlers tried to teach him skills that he would need in the wild, such as catching live fish on his own. Keiko was released in 2002. However, he did not join an ocean pod of orcas as was hoped. Instead, he took refuge in a calm bay in Norway and remained semidependent on humans for food until his death from pneumonia in 2003. In April 2011 the documentary *Keiko: The Untold Story* was released, providing footage of Keiko after he was released to the wild and describing the difficulties he faced in acclimating to the wild after being in captivity for so many years.

During the 1990s animal stories in the media became so popular that an entire cable television network was devoted to them. Animal Planet was launched in 1996 as a project of Discovery Communications and broadcasts popular shows such as *It's Me or the Dog* and *My Cat from Hell. Animal Precinct* is a reality show that originally aired through 2008 and as of May 2013 was shown in reruns. The show spotlights the work of New York City's Humane Law Enforcement agents. These agents are empowered to respond to cruelty complaints, perform investigations, and arrest people for crimes against animals. They were granted this power in 1866, when the ASPCA established its original charter with the state of New York. *Animal Cops* is a similar series that is based on the work of humane organizations in other cities.

FIGURE 7.1

Keiko, a killer whale, at the Oregon Coast Aquarium, Newport, Oregon, 1998. (© *John Gress/AP Images.*)

The American Humane Association Monitors Animal Welfare

During the filming of the 1939 movie *Jesse James*, a horse was killed when it was forced to jump off a cliff for a scene. Public complaints led to the formation of the film-monitoring unit of the American Humane Association (AHA). The AHA opened an office in Los Angeles, California, in 1940.

In 1980 the AHA was awarded a contract with the Screen Actors Guild (SAG) to monitor the safety and welfare of animals appearing in movies and on television shows filmed in the United States that featured SAG performers. The Producer-Screen Actors Guild Codified Basic Agreement of 1998 includes a provision that producers must notify the AHA before using animals on a set and provide AHA representatives with access to the set while animals are being filmed. This applies to movies, television shows, commercials, and music videos that include SAG performers.

The AHA reviews scripts and works with animal trainers and production staff to ensure that animals are not harmed during filming. The association monitors hundreds of productions each year in the United States. Its contractual authority does not extend beyond the United States; however, producers sometimes invite the AHA to oversee animal filming at foreign locations. The association has no oversight authority on non-SAG productions, such as reality shows and documentaries.

The AHA guidelines are laid out in *American Humane Association Guidelines for the Safe Use of Animals in Filmed Media* (June 2009, http://www.american humane.org/assets/pdfs/animals/pa-film-guidelines.pdf). The guidelines cover what filmmakers and crew should do before and during production to ensure animal safety. In "Movie Review Archives" (2013, http://www.american humanefilmtv.org/movie-review-archives/), the AHA lists its ratings for hundreds of movies based on their adherence to these guidelines. The association also details how particular animal scenes were filmed in dozens of movies by use of deceptive camera angles, body doubles, fake blood, computer graphics, and other tricks.

ANIMAL THEME PARKS

Animal theme parks are large tourist attractions that combine elements of zoos (or aquariums) and amusement parks to entertain the public. The first oceanarium (a large saltwater aquarium) in the United States is thought to be Marine Studios of Florida, later named Marineland. In

FIGURE 7.2

Pamela Franklin and Luke Halpin with the dolphin who plays Flipper in *Flipper's New Adventure*. (© *Metro-Goldwyn-Mayer/Getty Images.*)

1963 came the release of the popular movie *Flipper*, about a dolphin who befriends a young boy. It became a hit television show a year later. (See Figure 7.2.) Public demand for performing dolphins and other sea creatures skyrocketed. In 1964 George Millay (1929–2006) developed a marine life park called SeaWorld in San Diego and in 1965 SeaWorld acquired Shamu, a female orca that was captured from the wild.

Shamu was one of many orcas that were captured during the early 1960s for use in the entertainment industry. According to *Frontline*, in *A Whale of a Business* (November 1997, http://www.pbs.org/wgbh/pages/frontline/shows/whales/), the first captive orca was collected for Marineland of the Pacific in 1961. The animal lived for only one day. She repeatedly smashed herself against the walls of her tank until she died. *Frontline* lists 133 known orcas that were captured between 1961 and 1997, along with their life spans in captivity. Many lived for only a few months, whereas the average life span for an

orca in the wild is 40 to 60 years. *Frontline* estimates that 102 of the 133 captured orcas had died.

The original Shamu survived for six years. In the intervening years SeaWorld has continued to acquire orcas and call at least one of them by the stage name Shamu for performance purposes. Eventually, the company trademarked the name.

During the 1970s and 1980s SeaWorld marine parks opened in Ohio, Florida, and Texas. In 1989 they were purchased by Anheuser-Busch, which already operated Busch Gardens, a popular park in Florida that featured animal shows, bird acts, and amusement park rides. In 2000 the company opened another theme park, also in Florida, named Discovery Cove, where visitors can experience wildlife up close and swim with dolphins and stingrays. The stingers have been removed from the stingrays to make them harmless to people. The park also contains an aviary that includes hundreds of exotic birds that people can hand feed.

Many animal welfare and rights groups are critical of animal resorts. PETA notes in "Deadly Destinations" (2013, http://www.helpinganimals.com/travel_feat_dead lydest.asp) that hundreds of animals have died at these facilities because of improper care. PETA argues that living conditions are not healthy for the animals in captivity and disputes claims by the owner companies of animal parks that they further conservation efforts.

Marine Mammal Concerns

Animal resorts that use trained marine mammals, such as orcas and dolphins, come under harsh criticism from animal rights and welfare groups, because the animals are highly social in the wild and very intelligent.

In February 2010 a trainer at SeaWorld Orlando was killed by an orca named Tilikum following a show. In "SeaWorld Whale Killing Trainer Opens Debate: 'Happy Animals Don't Kill Their Trainers'" (PalmBeachPost .com, February 25, 2010), Curtis Morgan reports that Tilikum had been involved in two previous fatal attacks on humans during the 1990s. Morgan interviews Russ Rector, a former dolphin trainer from another animal theme park, who claims he warned SeaWorld three years before the attack that the theme park "was pushing its show mammals too hard to wow audiences, thereby inviting attacks on trainers." Morgan notes that animal groups believe the performing orcas are stressed by being forced to live in small tanks, when in the wild the animals "roam deep waters in close-knit pods." In March 2011 Tilikum resumed performing shows at SeaWorld. The article "Trainer: Tilikum Past Darker than SeaWorld Said" (CBSNews.com, March 31, 2011) indicates that SeaWorld had implemented new safety measures to better protect trainers from harm.

In September 2012 Tilikum's offspring Nakai suffered a deep wound on his chin during a performance at SeaWorld San Diego. The company said the orca accidentally bumped against the tank wall, but some animal groups insisted that Nakai was injured by fighting with other orcas. In "Injured SeaWorld Killer Whale Healing, Performing" (NBCSanDiego.com, January 30, 2013), Sarah Grieco notes that Nakai resumed performing in December 2012. According to Grieco, PETA staged a protest at SeaWorld after the injury took place and filed a complaint with the USDA alleging that the company was "housing whales together that are incompatible." As of May 2013, the USDA had not commented publicly on PETA's complaint.

In April 2013 SeaWorld issued an initial public offering of stock in the company. Aaron Smith reports in "PETA Takes a Stake in SeaWorld, Demands Whales Be Freed" (CNN.com, April 24, 2013) that PETA purchased 80 shares of SeaWorld stock for just over $2,000. The stock ownership will allow PETA to present information at the company's annual stockholders meetings. According to Smith, PETA also plans to submit shareholder resolutions seeking policy changes, particularly the release of orcas by the company.

DOLPHIN CONTROVERSY. Perhaps no other entertainment animal is more beloved and more controversial than the dolphin. Various species of dolphin are kept in captivity around the world in aquariums, dolphinariums (aquariums that feature only dolphins), and animal resorts. Some venues allow people to swim with the animals or otherwise personally interact with them. Americans' fascination with dolphins can be traced back to the *Flipper* television series of the 1960s. Since that time dolphin shows and interactive exhibits have boomed in popularity. However, as scientists have continued to research dolphins, they have learned that the animals are highly intelligent creatures, which raises troubling questions about the morality of keeping them in captivity, particularly for entertainment purposes.

The work of Diana Reiss (1948–) and Lori Marino, the researchers who provided evidence in 2001 that dolphins could recognize themselves in mirrors, is described in Chapter 2. Both scientists became activists for dolphins following their discovery. For example, both are outspoken critics of the annual dolphin and whale hunt that is conducted in Taiji, Japan, in which hundreds, sometimes thousands, of dolphins are bludgeoned to death each year for their meat. As noted in Chapter 3, some of the dolphins are captured alive and sold to animal resorts and dolphinariums. In fact, the sale of these valuable animals is believed to be the main economic impetus for the hunt. In "Dolphins Are Dying to Amuse Us" (Salon.com, August 7, 2009), Katharine Mieszkowski claims that through the 1980s U.S. aquariums and marine theme parks, including SeaWorld, "imported dolphins captured in Japan in slaughter drives." The practice has not been allowed since the early 1990s, and no wild dolphins have been captured in U.S. waters since 1993. Captive breeding of dolphins has since become the norm in the United States.

The Taiji dolphin hunt was the focus of the award-winning documentary film *The Cove*, which was released in 2009. One of the key figures behind the film was Ric O'Barry (1939–), a former dolphin trainer who was involved in the *Flipper* television show. O'Barry has since become a dolphin activist opposed to keeping dolphins in captivity. Mieszkowski notes that O'Barry felt "somewhat responsible" for his role in creating the "multibillion-dollar industry" that has arisen around captive dolphins. She quotes O'Barry as saying, "It created this desire to swim with them and to kiss them and hold them and hug them and love them to death, and it created all these captures."

Erik Vance notes in "It's Complicated: The Lives of Dolphins & Scientists" (DiscoverMagainze.com,

September 7, 2011) that even though Marino and Reiss are united in their opposition to the Taiji hunt, they have differing views on the morality of keeping dolphins in captivity. Marino is opposed to the practice for any reason, whereas Reiss supports the study of captive dolphins. In fact, as of May 2013, Reiss worked at the National Aquarium (2013, http://www.aqua.org/about) in Baltimore, Maryland, a nonprofit facility whose mission is "to inspire conservation of the world's aquatic treasures." The aquarium operates the Dolphin Discovery exhibit, where paying customers can have an up-close view of view dolphins being fed and trained. For an added fee, people can experience a Dolphin Encounter that the aquarium (2013, http://www.aqua.org/explore/baltimore/immersion-tours/dolphin-encounter) describes as "a hands-on, two-hour-long encounter"; however, participants do not get into the water with the dolphins, but pet them at poolside. Thus, the aquarium financially supports its conservation work by capitalizing on the entertainment value of dolphins. Reiss defends the aquarium's role in educating the public and furthering the conservation of wild dolphins. According to Vance, both Reiss and Marino agree that "releasing dolphins bred in captivity would be signing their death warrant," because the captive animals do not have the skills needed to survive in the wild. Therefore, the key issue is whether dolphins should continue to be bred in captivity and, if so, should they be used to entertain the public to raise funds that could help conserve wild dolphins in their natural habitats. This is a difficult and divisive issue in the animal rights debate.

CHAPTER 8
SERVICE ANIMALS

Service animals are those that work for humans doing particular tasks. These tasks may be as mundane as pulling plows or as sophisticated as finding underwater mines. Throughout history animals have helped humans hunt wildlife, herd livestock, guard people and property, and wage warfare. Animals are also trained for more humanitarian causes, such as rescuing the lost and providing aid and comfort to people with certain physical and psychological needs.

Whatever the task may be, the common factor is that service animals help humans with their needs and desires. Some people see this as a clever use of resources. Many believe it is a mutually beneficial bond, but others see it as a form of slavery. Some animal rights activists believe that humans should not use animals for any purpose. Even though they rarely speak out against uses that the public views as benevolent, they are extremely critical of military uses of animals because the animals are exposed to great danger. This is also true for animals doing some police and rescue jobs.

Welfarists are also concerned that working animals should be trained and treated with care. Animal groups recommend that only positive reinforcement be used when service animals are trained. They also point out that service animals should be carefully screened to ensure that they are a good match with their potential human partners. Finally, they remind people that the needs of service and assistance animals must be considered along with the needs of the people being served. In general, however, welfarists tend to support programs that train service and therapeutic animals because so many of these programs rescue homeless animals from shelters.

HISTORY

The role of service animals in agriculture, hunting, transportation, and warfare changed little over thousands of years. In the United States service animals continued in their traditional roles until the late 1800s. Then the urbanization and innovations of the Industrial Revolution slowly eliminated the need for many of them. Motorized vehicles took over nearly all the work formerly done by horses and beasts of burden in agriculture, transportation, and warfare. Over the next century many people turned to chemicals instead of cats to kill rodents and to electronics instead of dogs to guard their property. Some vital tasks previously performed by working animals have become activities of recreation—for example, hunting and herding with dogs and using horses to pull carriages. The use of animals (particularly dogs) in military and public service, however, continues to grow. In addition, animals serve as aides and provide companionship and therapy to people with specific physical and mental needs.

HUNTING
Falconry

Falconry is a form of hunting that is conducted with the use of trained birds of prey, such as eagles, falcons, hawks, or owls. (See Figure 8.1.) These birds are also called raptors. Falconry has strict licensing requirements because it uses wild birds that are protected species. Animals that are commonly hunted using falconry are pigeons, quail, rabbits, squirrels, and waterfowl. The North American Falconers Association notes in "A Brief History of Falconry in North America" (2013, http://n-a-f-a.com/General_History.htm) that it had nearly 2,000 members as of 2013.

Dogs

Dogs have historically been used in hunting. In the United States dogs are used to hunt upland game birds and waterfowl, such as ducks, partridge, pheasant, pigeons, and quail. Dogs are also used to hunt bears, foxes, mountain lions, raccoons, squirrels, and other prey. The primary dog breeds used in hunting are beagles, griffons, hounds, pointers, retrievers, setters, and spaniels. Dogs that hunt

FIGURE 8.1

Falconry is a form of hunting accomplished using trained birds of prey. (© *Jeff Banke/Shutterstock.com.*)

mostly by scent are called scent hounds, and dogs that hunt mostly by sight are called sight hounds. Hunting dogs perform a variety of tasks, including tracking prey, pointing prey out to the hunter, and retrieving downed prey after it is shot.

One particularly controversial form of hunting that is conducted with the help of dogs and horses is foxhunting. Hunters on horseback pursue foxes across the countryside using packs of hounds. Even though foxhunting was practiced in the United Kingdom for hundreds of years, animal welfare groups had been trying to get it outlawed since the 1940s because they considered it cruel to the foxes. In 2002 Scotland passed a bill outlawing mounted hunting with dogs. After much political maneuvering, a similar bill was passed in England and Wales that went into effect in 2005. The debate over the bill in the United Kingdom was generally divided between social classes, with upper-class landowners opposing it. Foxhunting has traditionally been a pastime of the wealthy in the United Kingdom, including members of the royal family. The

Fox Website (http://www.thefoxwebsite.org/foxhunting/hunthistory.html) notes that in 2013 fox hunting was legal in Australia, Ireland, and North America.

According to the Masters of Foxhounds Association and Foundation in "About Foxhunting" (2013, http://mfha.org/foxhunting.html), there were 165 recognized foxhunting clubs in North America in 2013. This number has reportedly grown over the last decade as foxhunting becomes more popular in the United States.

GUARD DUTY

Guard duty encompasses several tasks that are performed by animals. One is to alert humans to danger. Another is to provide physical protection from danger. Many animals can provide alerts but not protection. For example, canaries were once used in mines to warn miners that dangerous gases were present. Because canaries are sensitive to small dosages of these gases, their deaths gave the miners time to leave dangerous areas before they, too, were overcome. This was not a trained or voluntary response by the canaries. By contrast, dogs can alert people to an approaching predator and defend them against it.

Dogs are still the most popular type of guarding animals. Besides their traditional guard duties, dogs are increasingly used to warn humans about impending natural phenomena, such as earthquakes. For years, researchers have been studying claims that dogs can somehow sense when an earthquake is about to happen. The speculation is that dogs may hear rumbling noises or sense vibrations occurring deep within the earth that precede actual ground movement.

Guarding Territory and People

Dogs are the most popular animal used for guarding territory and people. This job requires large breeds that are strong, protective, and territorial. The breeds most often used for this work are chows, Doberman pinschers, German shepherds, komondors, and rottweilers.

Guard dogs are not the same as watchdogs. Watchdogs bark when a stranger approaches them or their territory. Even small dogs, such as Chihuahuas, make good watchdogs. In contrast, guard dogs are intended to scare away and even attack intruders. Security companies use many guard dogs. They work with handlers and human guards to patrol sites or protect individuals. Other guard dogs work without human accompaniment. They are placed on commercial and industrial properties, such as junkyards, at night.

Animal welfarists are highly critical of the use of unaccompanied guard dogs at commercial and industrial sites. They claim these working dogs are given a minimum amount of food, water, and veterinary care, are kept in isolation in dangerous environments, and are treated cruelly to instill aggressive behavior.

MANUAL LABOR

Manual labor is work that requires physical skill and energy. In the United States mechanized equipment has replaced most of the work done by beasts of burden. Draft horses and mules are still used by a few farmers, particularly those in communities that use traditional farming techniques, such as the Amish. In addition, nearly all developing countries rely heavily on draft animals for agricultural work. (See Figure 8.2.)

In the United States some tasks historically performed by animals have become activities of leisure. For example, entrepreneurs in many large cities offer carriage rides to tourists. Animal welfarists are critical of these ventures, saying that carriage horses are forced to work under hazardous conditions on city streets crowded with traffic and often do not receive proper housing and care.

People for the Ethical Treatment of Animals (PETA) actively advocates against horse-drawn carriages and stagecoaches. The organization (http://www.mediapeta.com/peta/PDF/horse-drawn-carriage-accidents.pdf) maintains a list of nearly 200 accidents and other incidents that have occurred since the mid-1980s involving horse-drawn carriages. In addition, PETA (http://www.peta.org/issues/animals-in-entertainment/horse-drawn-carriages.aspx) notes that horse-drawn carriages have been banned in cities throughout the world, including London and Paris, and in the United States in Biloxi, Mississippi, and several Florida jurisdictions.

LAW ENFORCEMENT

Law enforcement agencies throughout the world use animals (mostly dogs and horses) to help them perform security work. Dogs are, by far, the most common animals used.

Dogs

Many dogs are used by U.S. law enforcement agencies at the local and national levels to perform important tasks. These agencies include police and sheriff's departments, arson investigators, the Federal Bureau of Investigation, the Federal Bureau of Prisons, the U.S. Customs and Border Protection (CBP), the U.S. Department of Agriculture, and the U.S. Drug Enforcement Administration.

FIGURE 8.2

Plowing oxen. (© *rusty426/Shuttertock.com.*)

The dogs are specially trained to work with officers during searches and arrests and to sniff out illegal substances. Dogs have incredibly sensitive noses. Their sense of smell is several thousand times better than that of humans. Dogs can smell tiny quantities of substances and can distinguish particular scents with amazing accuracy. This natural ability has proven to be an extremely useful tool in law enforcement applications.

Many fire departments use dogs as part of their arson investigation teams. Arson dogs are specially trained to sniff for the presence of accelerants, such as gasoline, at sites where arson is suspected. Because of their incredible sense of smell, arson dogs can detect tiny amounts of accelerants lingering on surfaces inside buildings and vehicles or on people's clothes. The dogs indicate a find by either sitting or attempting to gain eye contact with their handlers. Because arsonists often hang around the scene of the crime, arson dogs are discreetly led through the crowds of people who gather to watch fires to sniff for the presence of accelerants on people's clothing or belongings. Any suspicious finds are subjected to detailed laboratory testing.

Federal agencies that guard U.S. borders have used dogs since the 1970s. In 1970 the U.S. Customs Service began using dogs to sniff out narcotics that were being smuggled into the country at major border crossings. The U.S. Immigration and Naturalization Service also used dogs to help intercept illegal aliens and prevent smuggling.

In 2003 these agencies were grouped together into the U.S. Department of Homeland Security. The canine resources of the individual agencies were combined into a new agency called U.S. Customs and Border Protection. Drug-sniffing dogs are also sometimes used in schools. In "Drug-Detecting Police Dog Dies of Nose Cancer from Sniffing out Cocaine" (January 27, 2009, http://www.nydailynews.com/news/world/drug-detecting-police-dog-dies-nose-cancer-sniffing-cocaine-article-1.423585), Lauren Johnston reports that in January 2009 a retired drug-sniffing dog in England died from a rare type of nose cancer. Max was a nine-year-old Springer spaniel. The dog's veterinarian believes that sniffing drugs, particularly cocaine, during his years of service to the police department was a factor in the development of cancer.

Horses

Horses have been used in law enforcement work for centuries. They were the fastest and surest form of transportation for officers for many years. Even after cars became common, many law enforcement agencies continued to use mounted patrols. Mounted units are popular in both rural and metropolitan areas. For example, the United Mounted Peace Officers of Texas (2013,

http://www.tumpot.org/About.html) indicates that in 2013 Texas authorities used 102 mounted units for patrols throughout the state. They are particularly useful in backcountry areas on dirt roads and rugged terrain. Several large U.S. police departments, including the New York Police Department, use mounted patrols for crowd control and to provide greater visibility of officers on the streets.

Mounted units are not without controversy, however. There have been injuries to horses, police, and members of the public. Because mounted units often perform crowd control during protests and demonstrations, the horses and the riders are exposed to people who may be angry and confrontational. There are reports of police horses being pelted with marbles and even garbage. Protesters claim that police have charged their horses into crowds, knocking over and injuring people. Walking for many hours on city streets under stressful conditions is not easy on the horses. A few instances are reported each year of police horses throwing off or kicking their riders.

SEARCH, RESCUE, AND RECOVERY

Search and rescue (SAR) and body recovery work are performed by a variety of public service agencies in conjunction with private organizations. Some SAR units use dogs to help find missing humans, rescue people in danger, and recover bodies after disasters strike. Animals that assist in SAR work are generally considered valuable and noble by modern societies.

One of the most remarkable displays of SAR dogs in action occurred after the September 11, 2001 (9/11), terrorist attacks against the United States. More than 350 dogs scoured the rubble of the World Trade Center in New York City, along with their human trainers, looking for survivors and corpses. These dogs were from all over the United States and from foreign countries. The work was difficult. SAR dogs suffered from paw cuts and burns, dehydration, burning eyes, and psychological stress. Some handlers reported that their dogs became depressed after not finding any live victims and could not eat or sleep normally. Campaigns were begun to collect donated booties and other items needed by the SAR dogs who participated in helping during the 9/11 aftermath, and donations poured in from around the world.

In subsequent years there were reports of sicknesses developing in the human rescuers who were involved in the 9/11 effort. However, Cynthia M. Otto et al. note in "Medical and Behavioral Surveillance of Dogs Deployed to the World Trade Center and the Pentagon from October 2001 to June 2002" (*Journal of the American Veterinary Medical Association*, vol. 225, no. 6, September 15, 2004) that SAR dogs were found to have suffered no lasting side effects from their participation.

HUMANITARIAN MINE DETECTION

Since World War II (1939–1945) trained dogs have been used in military applications to detect land mines on the battlefield. In 1988 the United Nations called on the international community to devote resources to humanitarian demining—that is, detecting and removing land mines left over from many civil and regional conflicts throughout the world. Governments, nongovernmental organizations (NGOs), and commercial enterprises have collaborated to tackle the problem, but millions of land mines are believed remaining in the ground in dozens of countries.

According to the Marshall Legacy Institute (2013, http://marshall-legacy.org/programs-2/k-9-demining/), approximately 900 dogs are used in humanitarian demining operations throughout the world. The dogs' excellent sense of smell is particularly effective for detecting land mines that are made up of nonmetal components. These mines are not detectable using metal-detecting equipment.

During the early 1990s, the Belgian-born product designer Bart Weetjens (1967–) seized on the idea of training rats to detect underground land mines. He began the NGO Anti-persoonsmijnen Ontmijnende Product Ontwikkeling (APOPO; Anti-personnel Mines Demining Product Development). The APOPO collects Gambian giant pouched rats from Africa and trains them to detect land mines while wearing harnesses that are controlled by human handlers.

MEDICAL SERVICE

Animals that provide for the physical and mental well-being of humans are perhaps the most admired of all working animals. They guide, aid, assist, and comfort people with all kinds of physical and mental disabilities, impairments, and problems.

Historically, dogs have been the most widely used animal species to provide medical services to humans. For example, it is believed that dogs have been used to help guide blind people for hundreds of years. Intensive training of dogs for such purposes began during World War I (1914–1918) to aid blind veterans. Since that time many other types of animals have been trained to assist humans with physical and mental problems.

Aiding the Physically Impaired

Some people who are troubled with physical impairments rely on trained animals to improve their quality of life. These animals typically assist humans who are blind or visually impaired, deaf or hearing impaired, or have other physical disabilities.

HELP FOR THE BLIND OR VISUALLY IMPAIRED. As noted earlier, guide dogs have long been trained to assist blind people. Figure 8.3 shows a guide dog at work.

According to the Seeing Eye (2013, http://www.seeingeye.org/aboutUs/default.aspx?M_ID=165), guide dogs for the blind typically work for seven to eight years and are then adopted as pets by their owners or other people.

Guide Dog Users Inc. (GDUI) is an affiliate of the American Council of the Blind. The organization reports increasing problems with aggressive dogs attacking guide dogs while walking on city streets. It wants state laws enacted that will protect blind people and their guide dogs from any harassment or obstruction. The GDUI estimates that it costs up to $60,000 to properly train a guide dog team.

Miniature horses are progressively being used as service animals for blind and visually impaired people. According to the Guide Horse Foundation in "Frequently Asked Miniature Horse Questions" (2013, http://www.guidehorse.org/faq_horses.htm), the most suitable guide horses stand less than 26 inches (66 centimeters) high. The organization notes that guide horses offer several advantages over dogs, including a very long life span. The average miniature horse can live for 25 to 30 years, which is much longer than the average life span of a dog.

HELP FOR THE DEAF OR HEARING IMPAIRED. Hearing animals are specially trained to alert their deaf or hard-of-hearing owners to particular noises, such as a doorbell, knock at the door, oven timer, crying baby, alarm clock, or smoke alarm. When the animals hear these noises, they make physical contact with their owners and lead them to the source of the noise.

HELP FOR OTHER PHYSICAL CONDITIONS. Service animals, primarily dogs and monkeys, do a variety of tasks for people with debilitating conditions, such as epilepsy, lameness, paralysis, or Parkinson's disease. The animals are trained to pick up dropped items, fetch objects (such as a phone), open and close doors, turn light switches on and off, and perform other tasks as needed. Even though dogs were first trained to do these tasks, Capuchin monkeys are becoming increasingly popular. These small primates are friendly, clever, and can live for up to 30 years. Helping Hands (2013, http://www.monkeyhelpers.org/), a nonprofit organization that trains Capuchin monkeys to provide assistance services, notes the animals have "dexterous hands and amazing fine motor skills."

Trained service dogs can pull wheelchairs and assist people who are unsteady on their feet by providing a means of support and balance. Some service dogs are trained to summon help if their human partner needs it.

"Seizure alert dogs" are trained to identify signs—generally undetectable to humans—that their human companion is going to have a seizure. Some dogs have demonstrated an ability to predict when a person is going to have a seizure up to an hour before it happens. No one

FIGURE 8.3

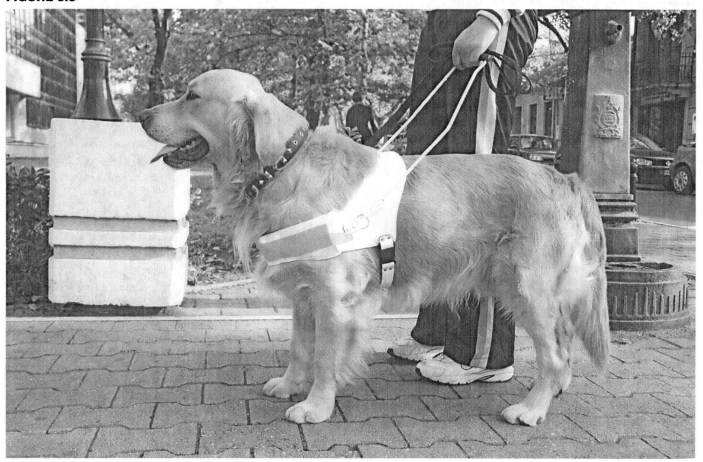

A trained Seeing Eye dog. (© *Boris Djuranovic/Shutterstock.com.*)

knows exactly how these dogs know when a person is going to have a seizure, but some scientists speculate that the dogs may be aware of certain physical or behavioral changes such as dilated pupils or slight changes in skin color or facial expressions that occur. The dog may be trained to remain with the person throughout the seizure, sometimes lying on top of the person to steady him or her and prevent injury, and helping him or her up afterward. In "A New Age for Assistance Dogs" (*Dog Fancy*, vol. 44, no. 6, June 2013), Dina Laverdure describes the plight of a woman who suffers numerous seizures due to a brain injury. Doctors implanted an electrical device under the skin near her collarbone that when activated by a special magnet at the onset of a seizure sends electrical signals to the brain that stop the seizure from occurring. The woman relies on an assistance dog named Brody to sense seizure onset. The magnet is attached to Brody's collar, and he has been specially trained to "snuggle" against the woman to allow the magnet to activate the electrical device. According to Laverdure the dog performs this task dozens of times a year, greatly improving the quality of life enjoyed by the woman who says Brody is her "guardian angel."

NOT WITHOUT CONTROVERSY. One controversial issue associated with assistance dogs is the use of breeding programs to produce them. Many organizations and training schools rescue dogs from pounds and animal shelters. This provides good homes for dogs that might otherwise be euthanized. Animal welfarists are critical of schools that breed their own dogs because there are already so many unwanted dogs in the country.

Mental and Physical Therapy

Another medical service that animals provide is therapeutic rather than utilitarian. Therapy animals provide emotional support or assist in rehabilitation activities. For example, therapy animals can comfort people undergoing psychological counseling. Hippotherapy (therapy involving interacting and sitting or riding on horses) is another popular option. The American Hippotherapy Association (2013, http://www.americanhippotherapyassociation.org/hippotherapy/hippotherapy-as-a-treatment-strategy/) advocates the use of horses in physical, occupational, and language therapy programs.

Many organizations working with abused children use therapy dogs in their programs. Petting and hugging the dogs relaxes the children and allows them to open up to counselors. Similar programs are used to calm children suffering from autism and patients undergoing various types of therapy. Some nursing and retirement homes and other facilities for the elderly or infirm rely on visiting or in-house animals, such as birds, cats, or dogs, to provide comfort and companionship to their human inhabitants. Therapy animals also visit hospitals, orphanages, and similar facilities to cheer people who may be lonely or depressed. Only gentle and social animals with good dispositions are used in this type of work.

Dogs are even used in medical detection, thanks to their extremely keen sense of smell. Dermatologists report stories about patients whose dogs sniffed at moles on their owners' bodies. The moles turned out to be cancerous and were removed. Doctors speculate that dogs may be able to smell some unique scent that is emitted by cancerous skin cells. Dogs have also been tested for their ability to detect by smell the presence of cancerous cells in the urine or breath of cancer patients. Michael McCulloch et al. report in "Diagnostic Accuracy of Canine Scent Detection in Early- and Late-Stage Lung and Breast Cancers" (*Integrative Cancer Therapies*, vol. 5, no. 1, March 2006) that specially trained dogs correctly detected 99% of the samples from lung cancer patients and 88% from breast cancer patients. The dogs made incorrect detections in 1% of lung cancer patients and in 2% of breast cancer patients. It is believed that the dogs are able to detect trace amounts of chemicals not ordinarily present in the breath of healthy people. In "Canine Scent Detection of Human Cancers: A Review of Methods and Accuracy" (*Journal of Veterinary Behavior*, vol. 5, no. 3, May 2010), Emily Moser and Michael McCulloch report the results of a review they conducted of published data regarding the use of dogs to detect cancer. The researchers conclude that "early successes with canine scent detection suggest chemical analysis of exhaled breath may be a valid method for cancer detection." Moser and McCulloch suggest further research to target particular types of tumors and to determine which exhaled compounds may be linked to cancer.

MILITARY SERVICE

Of all the service and assistance animals in use, animals used by the military are the most controversial. To animal welfarists and animal rights activists, the use of animals by the military can be extremely disturbing. These animals are often put into tremendous danger, and many of them die during their service. On the contrary, members of the military say that service animals have saved many human lives in battle. They argue that animal deaths in war are regrettable but permissible if human lives are saved. Animal rights activists and welfarists argue that animals involved in warfare do not know what they are fighting for or against and have poor chances of surviving.

Even though some animal work is classified, it is known that the U.S. military has used beluga whales,

chickens, dogs, dolphins, horses, pigeons, sea lions, and other marine mammals during combat. Besides horses, many of these animals are still used in modern warfare. In "Upgrading the Dogs of War" (August 31, 2012, http://www.bbc.com/future/story/20120829-upgrading-the-dogs-of-war), Sharon Weinberger notes that as of August 2012 an estimated 600 military dogs were deployed with U.S. forces in Afghanistan.

History

According to Nebraska Educational Telecommunications in *Wild Horses: An American Romance* (January 15, 2008, http://netnebraska.org/basic-page/television/wild-horses-waging-war), most of the 6 million horses that served the U.S. military during World War I were killed. The deaths of millions of other horses in military service to other countries severely depleted the world's horse population. World War I was the last war in which horses played a major role in combat. By 1942 all U.S. cavalry units were disbanded or mechanized.

Coincidentally, this was the same year that dogs were first officially inducted into the U.S. Army. A group called Dogs for Defense asked Americans to donate dogs to the army. Dogs were trained for guard and police duty, to pull sleds, to carry packs and messages, to help reconnaissance patrols find hidden enemy soldiers, and to help the medical corps find and rescue wounded soldiers.

Following World War II the surviving dogs were returned to their owners. This was not the case in later wars. Military officials were afraid of a trained military dog attacking someone in civilian life. It became common practice to euthanize unusable and retired war dogs or to leave them behind on the battlefield. Animal welfarists and soldiers were strongly against this policy, particularly after the Vietnam War (1954–1975).

Military historians estimate that war dogs saved thousands of U.S. soldiers from death or injury during the Vietnam War. Approximately 4,000 service dogs guarded troops, alerted them to booby traps, and pulled the wounded to safety. The U.S. War Dog Association (2013, http://www.uswardogs.org/id31.html) lists the names of 230 dogs that it says were killed in action during the war. Most of the service dogs that survived the war were left behind in Vietnam when U.S. troops pulled out. The fate of these dogs is unknown. Many veterans groups, including the Vietnam Dog Handler Association, are lobbying for a national memorial to be built in the District of Columbia to honor the service of war dogs.

In 2000 President Bill Clinton (1946–) signed a law that allows retired military dogs to be adopted rather than euthanized. The new owners have to agree not to hold the government responsible for any injuries or damages that may be caused by the former military dogs. Because of their extensive training, the dogs are expected to be useful in law enforcement and rescue work. In 2005 President George W. Bush (1946–) signed legislation allowing the military to adopt out active-duty military dogs to their handlers under certain circumstances.

Current Uses

Military dogs are trained at the Military Working Dog Center at Lackland Air Force Base in San Antonio, Texas. The most common breeds used are Belgian Malinois (a variety of Belgian shepherd), Dutch shepherds, and German shepherds. The military conducts its own breeding program and purchases suitable dogs from other breeders. Most dogs have a military career of about 10 years and are then retired from the service.

Hundreds of animals were used by the U.S. military during the 2003 invasion of Iraq, including chickens, dogs, dolphins, and pigeons. U.S. forces used two bottle-nosed Atlantic dolphins named Makai and Tacoma to seek out underwater mines along the Iraqi coast. The dolphins were trained to find the mines without detonating them and then alert handlers to their presence. Dogs have also proved particularly useful at helping military personnel find improvised explosive devices (IEDs), which are basically homemade bombs that are often placed beside or buried under roadways used by U.S. troops. IEDs have been responsible for numerous U.S. military deaths and injuries during the war in Afghanistan. According to Weinberger, a U.S. Navy program begun in 2011 specially trains dogs to detect explosive chemicals, such as ammonium nitrate, so that they can alert their handlers in the field to the presence of IEDs.

Frontline reports on the U.S. Navy's historical use of dolphins and other marine mammals in *A Whale of a Business* (November 1997, http://www.pbs.org/wgbh/ pages/frontline/shows/whales/). The navy began its Marine Mammal Program in 1960. Marine mammals were trained to perform tasks such as filming objects underwater, retrieving and delivering equipment, and guarding vessels against enemy divers. They were used during the Vietnam War and later in the Persian Gulf during the 1980s.

Dolphins are trained to detect enemy divers and attach restraining devices to them so they can be apprehended by human handlers. These devices include a line with a buoy that floats to the surface. Sea lions are trained to actually pursue any fleeing divers who go ashore. Mine-hunting dolphins identify and mark underwater mines so that they can be decommissioned or later exploded safely. In 2007 the U.S. Navy announced plans to use dolphins and sea lions to patrol the waters off a naval base near Seattle, Washington. The marine animals are trained to detect and catch potential terrorists attacking from the water.

However, in late 2012 animal groups expressed relief when the U.S. military announced plans to replace many of its marine mammal "soldiers" with robotic devices. In "Robots Replace Costly U.S. Navy Mine-Clearance Dolphins" (November 8, 2012, http://www.bbc.com/future/ story/20121108-final-dive-for-us-navy-dolphins), Weinberger notes that the change is being driven by the high costs associated with mammal use and the advent of advanced robotic technologies. The U.S. Navy plans to make the transition by 2017. At that time its Sea Mammal Program will be largely phased out, and the service will rely on "a new generation of robotic mine hunters." These devices include the Knifefish, a sonar-equipped underwater robot that is still in development. However, Weinberger warns that "the Navy already admits there may still be some specialized missions where sea mammals are needed past 2017."

CHAPTER 9
PETS

Pets are animals that humans keep for pleasure rather than for utility. Their value to humans is mostly emotional. They help to fulfill human desires for affection, companionship, entertainment, and ownership. Historians are not sure when humans first started keeping animals as pets. Keeping an animal for pleasure rather than for food or work was possible only for people who were well off and had the resources to feed extra mouths. For centuries pet ownership was mostly limited to the upper classes of society: royalty, aristocrats, and landowners. The modern age of pet keeping began during the mid-1800s, when a thriving middle class emerged in society. This was the first time that many people had the time and money to keep animals solely for companionship and pleasure. Owning pets eventually became more and more popular.

The American Veterinary Medical Association (AVMA) periodically conducts national surveys on pet ownership. As of May 2013, the most recent results were reported in *U.S. Pet Ownership & Demographics Sourcebook: 2012 Edition* (2013, https://www.avma.org/KB/Resources/Statistics/Pages/Market-research-statistics-US-Pet-Ownership-Demographics-Sourcebook.aspx). The AVMA notes that the 2012 edition is based on data collected from a national survey of more than 50,000 households. In "U.S. Pet Ownership Statistics" (2013, https://www.avma.org/KB/Resources/Statistics/Pages/Market-research-statistics-US-pet-ownership.aspx), the AVMA estimates that in 2012 U.S. pets included 74.1 million cats, 69.9 million dogs, 8.3 million birds, and 4.9 million horses. Various specialty and exotic animals were also kept as pets, notably 57.8 million fish, 12.6 million poultry, 5 million livestock, 3.2 million rabbits, and 2.3 million turtles. Other animals kept as pets included ferrets; rodents, such as hamsters, guinea pigs, and gerbils; snakes and other reptiles; and amphibians, such as frogs.

The American Pet Products Association (APPA) was founded in 1958 and is the nation's leading pet industry trade group. As of May 2013, the APPA (http://www.americanpetproducts.org/member/member_directory.asp) had 1,104 companies that were members of the association. The APPA estimates in "Pet Owners Are Estimated to Spend More Than $55 Billion on Their Pets in 2013" (February 21, 2013, http://media.americanpetproducts.org/press.php?include=144263) that U.S. pet owners spent $53.3 billion in 2012 on pets and pet supplies, equipment, and services. The association anticipates even higher spending—more than $55 billion—in 2013.

Pets have a unique status in modern society. Legally, they are considered to be personal property. This offers them some protection under the law, because damaging someone else's property is a crime. From a psychological standpoint some pets enjoy a higher value and are considered to be members of the family, almost like children. The federal government acknowledged this bond with passage of the Pets Evacuation and Transportation Standards Act of 2006. The act requires that federal, state, and local emergency preparedness officials include pets and service animals (such as seeing-eye dogs) in their plans for evacuating and sheltering people during disasters. The law was spurred by events following Hurricane Katrina along the Gulf Coast in 2005. Many distressed pet owners were forced to leave their animals behind when they were evacuated. Others refused to leave without their pets, putting themselves in great danger.

It surprises many pet owners to learn that some animal rights groups are opposed to the idea of keeping pets. Pet ownership is a thorny issue in the animal rights debate. Some activists believe that any use of any animal for any human purpose is wrong. However, when it comes to pets, many consider this stance too radical. A great number of those who work to improve animal welfare are pet owners. Most animal rights activists and animal welfarists focus their attention on particular pet problems, such as abuse, neglect, and overpopulation. They are particularly critical of breeders and pet stores that sell pets to the public. The keeping of wild animals as pets is condemned by all major organizations working for animal rights and welfare.

Some groups state that people keep pets for the wrong reasons. They argue that some people get pets to compensate for their inability to engage in healthy social contact with other people. Pets may be a crutch or a time-filler to these people. Others rely on pets to build their egos or to make them feel good about themselves in some way. The ability to control another living being can be a powerful motivator. Some people see pets as disposable items to be kept as long as they are useful or fun, and discarded when they are not. Many people think that taking care of a pet is educational for children because it teaches them responsibility and respect for other living creatures. Some people believe keeping a pet has a spiritual basis and that it brings them closer to nature.

The common thread in all these reasons is that they focus on the needs and wants of the pet owner rather than the pet. Some people feel this is only fair, as it is the pet owner who provides food, shelter, and care. Should people be allowed to keep animals as pets as long as they take care of them? There is a movement by some humane organizations to refer to pets as companion animals and to owners as guardians. These terms demonstrate the desire of these groups to elevate pets from property status to wards or dependents.

SHELTERS, POUNDS, AND EUTHANASIA

Despite the popularity of pets, every year millions of them wind up in public and private shelters. The vast majority are cats and dogs. They are either turned in by owners who no longer want them or are picked up as strays. Some are lost pets that are reunited with their owners, but many are homeless animals with no place to go. In "HSUS Pet Overpopulation Estimates" (November 23, 2009, http://www.humanesociety.org/issues/pet_overpopulation/facts/overpopulation_estimates.html), the Humane Society of the United States (HSUS) estimates that U.S. shelters receive 6 million to 8 million cats and dogs each year. Approximately half of these animals are euthanized (killed). The remainder are adopted or reclaimed by owners.

Euthanasia

The word *euthanasia* comes from the Greek term *euthanatos*, which means "easy death." During the 20th century euthanasia of shelter animals was conducted on a massive scale. However, euthanasia rates have been generally declining since the late 20th century. The HSUS reports in *The State of the Animals: 2001* (2001) that the number of euthanized cats and dogs dropped considerably in the United States, from about 13.5 million deaths in 1973 to 4 million to 6 million deaths in 2000, whereas over the same period the total number of cats and dogs nearly doubled.

Animal People is an animal organization that issues the monthly publication *Animal People*. Each year in its July–August edition the newspaper compiles data collected over the three previous years on the number of animals that were killed in shelters in selected representative cities and states around the country. These data are used to estimate national shelter killing rates. Table 9.1 shows data that were collected in 2010, 2011, or 2012. Overall, nearly 3 million shelter animals are estimated to

TABLE 9.1

Estimated number of dogs and cats killed in shelters, by region, 2012

	Animals killed per 1,000 people	Year	1,000s of people	Animals killed
New York City	1.0	2011	8,175	8,151
Springfield, MA	1.9	2011	153	295
Buffalo/Erie County	3.8	2010	919	3,484
NORTHEAST (27%)	**1.3**		**33,823**	**44,185**
NEW JERSEY	**3.8**	**2010**	**8,821**	**33,152**
DELAWARE	**5.4**	**2011**	**907**	**4,929**
Philadelphia	7.0	2010	1,526	10,718
MIDATLANTIC (40%)	**4.3**		**28,169**	**121,127**
Broward County, FL	5.5	2011	1,748	9,672
Wake County, NC	7.3	2012	901	6,560
Palm Beach County	8.3	2011	1,320	11,003
VIRGINIA	**8.9**	**2011**	**8,096**	**72,427**
Atlanta metro area	9.2	2010	5,269	48,372
Jacksonville, FL	9.2	2011	864	7,912
Pasco County, FL	9.7	2011	465	4,500
Alachua County, FL	11.7	2010	247	2,893
Charlotte/Mecklnbrg.	11.8	2012	944	11,144
Tampa/Hillsborough	12.9	2012	1,229	15,876
Pinellas Cty, FL	12.0	2010	917	11,000
Orlando/Orange Cty.	15.3	2011	1,146	17,555
NORTH CAROLINA	**19.9**	**2009**	**9,535**	**190,626**
Clay County, FL	20.2	2010	187	3,778
Oconee County, SC	32.6	2011	74	2,412
SO. ATLANTIC (62%)	**12.8**		**51,923**	**663,067**
Louisville	6.3	2010	1,307	8,265
Russellville (AR)	10.2	2010	60	609
Memphis	18.0	2010	663	11,906
Knoxville	21.5	2011	432	9,287
Kanawha/Charleston	21.3	2010	304	6,474
APPALACHIA	**13.2**		**15,566**	**203,005**
Austin/Travis Cty.	4.6	2010	1,024	4,713
Houston	5.9	2011	3,822	22,500
Houston metro area	9.5	2011	5,946	56,250
San Antonio/Bexar	13.9	2010	1,330	18,545
New Orleans	15.0	2010	344	5,162
Dallas	18.8	2010	1,197	22,521
Fort Worth	22.4	2010	535	12,000
Birmingham	24.2	2010	658	15,907
Tuscaloosa	29.8	2010	195	5,806
El Paso	30.6	2011	800	24,465
Mobile	34.3	2010	195	6,682
Hattiesburg area	46.9	2010	149	6,981
Amarillo	54.5	2011	191	10,411
GULF COAST (31%)	**15.7**		**38,031**	**597,087**
Yavapai County	1.3	2012	154	213
Denver	2.1	2011	2,830	6,054
Reno/Washoe	3.5	2011	426	1,478
UTAH	**10.6**	**2011**	**2,817**	**29,990**
Phoenix/Maricopa	12.7	2010	3,817	48,567
NEVADA	**13.9**	**2010**	**2,701**	**37,745**
Las Vegas/Clark Cty	15.1	2010	1,951	29,652
Tucson	21.9	2011	990	21,720
Navajo Nation	33.3	2010	180	6,000
WEST (88%)	**9.7**		**17,579**	**170,516**

TABLE 9.1

Estimated number of dogs and cats killed in shelters, by region, 2012 [CONTINUED]

	Animals killed per 1,000 people	Year	1,000s of people	Animals killed
Dane County, WI	2.5	2010	488	1,244
MINNESOTA	**5.7**	**2011**	**5,304**	**30,000**
Chicago	6.5	2011	2,696	17,399
MICHIGAN	**9.2**	**2011**	**10,080**	**92,831**
Milwaukee County	6.9	2011	948	6,558
Cleveland	10.3	2011	397	4,100
Indianapolis	11.1	2010	903	10,104
Dayton/Montgomery	11.9	2011	535	6,384
Cincinnati	13.1	2011	802	10,502
Detroit metro area	15.1	2010	1,217	18,364
Fort Wayne/Allen Cty	27.3	2011	355	9,689
MIDWEST (32%)	**8.8**		**67,158**	**587,599**
Whidbey Island	0.8	2011	72	60
San Francisco	1.3	2010	815	1,057
Irvine, CA	1.4	2010	213	300
Seattle	3.1	2010	603	1,893
Orange County, CA	4.5	2010	3,010	13,675
Portland/Multnomah	5.1	2010	2,069	10,477
Los Angeles city	5.1	2010	3,796	22,722
San Diego city/county	6.0	2010	3,095	18,063
CALIFORNIA	**12.1**	**2010**	**37,692**	**455,045**
Kenai borrough, AK	13.2	2011	55	730
Kern/Bakersfield	22.7	2010	824	18,701
Maui	33.4	2011	155	5,174
Fresno	33.4	2011	942	31,500
PACIFIC (98%)	**10.9**		**54,366**	**591,040**
U.S. total (51%)	**9.7**		**308,330**	**2,989,508**

Note: The regional and national totals appearing capitalized and in bold are not tallies of the data used to produce them, but are rather estimates proportionately weighted to reflect demography. The percentage figure in parenthesis is the percentage of the human population encompassed within the shelter service areas from which the totals are derived.

SOURCE: Merritt Clifton, "U.S. Animal Shelter Toll Appears to Drop below Three Million," in *Animal People*, vol. 21, no. 6, July/August 2012, https:// workspaces.acrobat.com/app.html#d=T3qNg*Ol-wI0Uc3ieY7HFg (accessed March 25, 2013)

have been killed annually. The number of shelter animals euthanized per 1,000 Americans was 9.7 animals. The euthanasia rates were highest for the Gulf Coast region (15.7) and Appalachia (13.2) and lowest for the mid-Atlantic (4.3) and Northeast (1.3).

Animal protection groups point to several reasons for regional differences in shelter killing rates. In general, shelters located in the Northeast have the lowest euthanasia rates, whereas shelters in the Southeast have the highest rates. This is attributed to several factors, including the weather, the availability of low-cost spay-neuter programs, and animal control policies. The cold winters in the Northeast lower the fertility rates of cats and dogs and claim the lives of stray animals so that fewer end up in shelters. Animal welfare organizations are much more predominant in the Northeast and provide low-cost spay-neuter programs that help control populations of unwanted animals. Many northeastern municipalities charge pet owners licensing fees with higher amounts for unfixed animals. This is far less common in the South.

Euthanasia Methods

Even though the public assumes that animals euthanized at shelters are killed by lethal injection, this is not always true. The AVMA maintains in *AVMA Guidelines for the Euthanasia of Animals: 2013 Edition* (2013, https://www.avma.org/KB/Policies/Documents/euthanasia.pdf) a list of approved euthanasia methods for various types of animals. Acceptable euthanasia methods for cats and dogs include lethal injection and gassing. The AVMA notes that intravenous injection of barbiturates is the preferred method of euthanasia for horses, cats, dogs, and other small animals. Advantages include rapid and smooth action, minimal physical distress to the animal if the procedure is performed correctly, and relatively low cost compared with other options. The main disadvantages are that each animal must be personally restrained for the procedure, and personnel must be properly trained in giving injections. Also, barbiturates are federally controlled substances that can be purchased only using a U.S. Drug Enforcement Administration registration and order form. Their use is controlled by state law, and there are specific record-keeping requirements that must be met.

Lethal injection is a hands-on procedure in which animals and personnel come into close physical contact. When shelters began practicing humane euthanasia, it was thought that a hands-off approach would be easier for the workers performing euthanasia. Gas chambers were common because the euthanizer could perform the procedure from outside the chamber by opening a valve or flipping a switch.

Many shelters still use gassing to euthanize unwanted animals; however, most animal welfarists condemn gassing as a means of euthanasia and have worked to convince state legislatures to ban the practice. In "Gas Chambers" (2012, http://www.animallawcoalition.com/gas-chambers), the animal organization Animal Law Coalition provides information about gassing bans that have been implemented by states or cities. The organization notes that more than a dozen states have either enacted a ban or mandated nongas euthanasia methods for shelter animals, most recently Pennsylvania in 2012.

Animal shelter workers have an incredibly stressful and emotionally demanding job. Many get into the line of work because they care about animals but become frustrated by the public's seeming lack of concern for the tragic fate of many millions of unwanted pets. Most humane organizations believe the solution to the euthanization problem lies in aggressive sterilization campaigns, better education of pet owners, and successful adoption programs.

Spaying and Neutering

The overpopulation of cats and dogs is a tremendous problem. It is aggravated by the fact that these animals reproduce at high rates. Experts generally agree that massive and sustained birth control methods must be implemented on cat and dog populations to bring the problem under control. Surgical sterilization of female animals is called spaying, or removal of the ovaries, fallopian tubes, and uterus. Male animals are neutered or castrated by having their testicles removed. Pet owners commonly refer to these sterilization procedures as fixing or altering an animal. Increasingly, animal groups use the term *neuter* to refer to sterilization of either males or females.

Some pet owners are resistant to spaying and neutering their pets. Their reasons can include one or more of the following:

- Surgery costs too much or is too painful for the pet.

- Having a litter can be good for the pet and educational for children.

- Fixed animals get fat and lazy.

- Backyard breeding is a fun hobby that brings in extra money.

- Male animals do not need to be fixed because they do not have litters.

- Neutering male dogs robs them of their masculinity and makes them less protective as guard dogs.

- Sterilization is unnatural.

Veterinarians have been promoting spaying and neutering of pets for several decades. According to the animal organization SPAY USA, in "Benefits of Spay/Neuter" (2013, http://www.spayusa.org/benefits.php), sterilization has many behavioral, medical, and social benefits, including:

- Female pets do not go into heat (have fertile cycles) during which scents are emitted that attract male animals. Sterilization eliminates the problems associated with male animals that gather and often fight over females in heat.

- Sterilization usually stops male cats (toms) from marking their territory by spraying strong-smelling urine.

- Sterilization makes pets more likely to stay at home than wander.

- Sterilized females cannot develop ovarian or uterine infections and are less likely to develop mammary cancer.

- Sterilized males usually become less aggressive.

- Sterilization helps reduce the number of stray and unwanted animals in the community. This is advantageous for public health and safety reasons and reduces the enormous cost to taxpayers and private agencies of capturing, impounding, and destroying millions of unwanted animals each year.

Many states and municipalities actively encourage spaying and neutering of pets as a means to reduce overpopulation. Those with licensing programs usually charge pet owners a lower registration fee if their pets are sterilized. A number of states also sell special license plates that benefit spay-neuter programs. In May 2013 Maryland (http://mgaleg.maryland.gov/2013RS/bills/hb/hb0767T.pdf) enacted a law that will establish a Spay/Neuter Fund within the state's Department of Agriculture. The fund will receive monies from a fee charged on dog and cat food sold in Maryland and will be administered by a Spay/Neuter Advisory Board that will "establish a competitive grant program to support the provision of spay/neuter services."

Most animal shelters spay and neuter cats and dogs before adoption or require new owners to do so within a certain period after adoption. In 1998 California passed a law that requires preadoption sterilization of cats and dogs. The Animal Legal and Historical Center at Michigan State University's College of Law (2013, http://www.animallaw.info/articles/armpusspayneuter.htm) notes that as of early 2013, 34 states had laws requiring shelters and other organizations to spay or neuter dogs before adopting them out. In addition, many municipalities have their own spay/neuter laws. The San Francisco Society for the Prevention of Cruelty to Animals was one of the first humane groups in the United States to offer low-cost and early spay-neuter surgery.

Low-cost clinics are often run by humane organizations. They operate under a nonprofit status, which allows them to save on overhead and tax costs. They offer discounted rates either to the general public or to those people who have adopted an animal from their shelter. The rates can be substantially lower than those charged by veterinarians in private practice. Such clinics are not without controversy. Some veterinarians complain that the clinics have an unfair advantage because of their nonprofit status. A few states have passed laws that prohibit veterinarians who are associated with nonprofit groups from operating low-cost spay-neuter clinics. Advocates of the clinics insist that they provide a much-needed service and help reduce animal overpopulation.

No-Kill Shelters

Some animal welfarists and members of the public criticize shelters for using euthanasia at all. They believe every animal that enters a shelter deserves the opportunity to be adopted no matter how long it takes. Critics say this viewpoint is unrealistic. They point out that some animals are too aggressive, injured, or sick to be adopted. There is no practical alternative but to euthanize them. Also, some pet owners rely on shelters rather than on private veterinarians to euthanize their sick and elderly pets.

During the 1990s the concept of no-kill shelters became popular. The name implies that no animals are ever euthanized in these shelters—an idea that appeals to many people. In reality, most no-kill shelters still euthanize animals that are unadoptable because of illness or temperament. Some traditional shelters (or open-admission shelters, as they are called) do not like the use of the term *no-kill*. They feel it can be misleading and accuse some organizations of using the term just to gain financial support and political favor. In addition, welfare organizations argue among themselves about the exact definition of no-kill and which animals are adoptable. Animals turned away from no-kill shelters could be harmed or killed by the people trying to give them away or could wind up at already overburdened open-admission shelters and be euthanized.

The truth is that all shelters (public and private) operate with limited space, personnel, and financial budgets. The people who run them must make life-and-death decisions about the animals that enter the facilities. These decisions are based on moral, political, social, and financial considerations.

Some major animal rights and welfare groups support the use of euthanasia on unwanted pets. Jeneen Interlandi reports in "PETA and Euthanasia" (TheDailyBeast.com, April 27, 2008) that between 1998 and 2008 People for the Ethical Treatment of Animals (PETA) shelters euthanized more than 17,000 animals. That amounts to almost 85% of the animals the organization had taken in. Interlandi quotes a PETA spokesperson as saying, "We would rather offer these animals a painless death than have them tortured, starved or sold for research." PETA supports spay and neuter programs to prevent unwanted animals and ultimately reduce animal suffering. According to Interlandi, the HSUS president Wayne Pacelle has publicly stated his belief that the no-kill idea is "almost unachievable." This pessimism is harshly criticized by other animal advocates.

Restricting Retail Pet Sales

Some jurisdictions have implemented restrictions on the retail sales of pets, such as dogs and cats, to tackle their pet overpopulation problems. Best Friends Animal Society notes in "Jurisdictions with Retail Pet Sale Bans" (http://bestfriends.org/Resources/No-Kill-Resources/Puppy-mill-initiatives/Fighting-Puppy-Mills/Jurisdictions-with-retail-pet-sale-bans/) that as of February 2013, 27 U.S. cities and four Canadian cities had put into place various restrictions on commercial pet sales. For example, in October 2012 the Los Angeles City Council (http://clkrep.lacity.org/onlinedocs/2011/11-0754_rpt_atty_9-20-12.pdf) passed an ordinance that prohibits the sale of "commercially bred dogs, cats and rabbits in pet stores, retail businesses or other commercial establishments." The ban went into effect in December 2012 and will be fully enforceable by June 2013. It does not apply to animals obtained from shelters, humane societies, and properly registered rescue and humane organizations.

PUREBRED DOG INDUSTRY

Many animal welfare groups blame dog overpopulation in part on the purebred dog industry. Purebred dogs are those that have been bred from members of a recognized breed over many generations. This ensures that certain appearance and behavior traits are maintained within a breed. Breeding of this type has been practiced for centuries. It was popularized during the Middle Ages by European monks who earned money by breeding dogs with particular traits for aristocrats and members of royalty. It resulted in breeds that were notable for a specific task, such as hunting wildfowl, or had desirable features in their size, shape, fur, ears, and so forth.

Maintaining desirable qualities in a bloodline requires a careful choice of mating partners. For example, an excellent hunting dog mated with a poor hunting dog will likely produce offspring that are not good hunters, and so the desirable qualities will be lost. Mating together two excellent hunting dogs will greatly increase the likelihood that the offspring will also be great hunters. This makes them much more valuable. Purebred enthusiasts are passionate about protecting certain qualities within a breed, and reputable breeders work to ensure that breed characteristics are maintained and that purebred puppies are placed in good homes. Purebred puppies and dogs can sell for hundreds or even thousands of dollars. Demand for purebred puppies and dogs has resulted in a multibillion-dollar industry that is based on breeding, showing, selling, and registering these dogs. Some common terms used in the purebred dog industry are defined in Table 9.2.

TABLE 9.2

Terminology used in the purebred dog industry

Breed standard	Set of detailed guidelines established to define the particular characteristics of a breed
Conformation points	Specific criteria within the breed standard (e.g., fur color, shape of paws, size, etc.)
Consanguineous	Descended from the same ancestor
Dam	Mother dog
Fault	A characteristic of a purebred dog that doesn't meet a conformation point
Inbreeding	Breeding of immediate relatives (e.g., brother with sister, father with daughter, etc.)
Linebreeding	Breeding of close relatives (e.g., aunt with nephew, grandfather with granddaughter, cousin with cousin, etc.) or of animals with many common ancestors
Outcrossing	Breeding two dogs from different lines
Pedigree	A listing of ancestors; the family tree
Sire	Father dog
True to type	Showing desired breed characteristics. Also desired characteristics are so ingrained that offspring can be certain to have them also.
Type	Overall appearance including characteristics important to the breed standard
Typey	An adjective used to describe a dog that seems to capture the essence of the breed or closely meets the breed standard
Whelped	Born

SOURCE: Created by Kim Masters Evans for Gale, 2011

Registration, Pedigree, and Papers

The American Kennel Club (AKC) was formed in 1884. It is the largest nonprofit organization in the United States that registers purebred dogs. The second-largest registry is maintained by the United Kennel Club (UKC), which was founded in 1898. These are the two most respected purebred registries in the United States. For a fee they provide registration certificates or "papers" showing that dogs are recognized as belonging to a particular breed. These papers provide a written record of a particular dog's ancestry. Each organization is supported by hundreds of local and regional kennel and breed clubs around the country.

The registration papers for purebred dogs are based on information that is supplied by breeders who are members of their respective clubs. Breeders can register litters that are born to registered purebred dogs. The registration papers are then turned over to the puppies' new owners. Each owner chooses a unique name for a registered dog that cannot be repeated. Owners can also request a copy of a pedigree (a family tree) for their registered dogs that goes back several generations.

Purebreds and Genetic Problems

Dogs as a species are prone to genetic diseases. Jonathan Amos states in "Pedigree Dog Health to Be Probed" (BBC.co.uk, January 22, 2004) that "dogs are plagued by the greatest number of documented, naturally occurring genetic disorders of any non-human species." There are approximately 400 inherited disorders that are associated with dogs. As long as the breeding population remains large, the chances of passing along a genetic disorder are small. This is because the dog blueprint is based on around 30,000 genes.

Individual genes determine characteristics of a particular dog, such as hair color. Some genes can also carry the triggers for serious diseases and disorders. Two dogs can carry genes with these dangerous triggers but not suffer from the diseases themselves because the genes are recessive rather than dominant in their genetic makeup. However, if these two dogs mate with each other, there is a good chance that some of their puppies will inherit the problem genes from both parents and develop the disorder. At the very least, most of the puppies will inherit the recessive problem gene and later pass it along to their offspring.

In purebred dogs this inheritance problem is extremely aggravated because closely related dogs are bred with one another. This significantly raises the chances that problem genes will be passed on from parents to offspring.

Amos notes that common genetic diseases within specific breeds include heart disease in boxers, bleeding problems in Dobermans, lymphomas in pointers, hip dysplasia in Labrador retrievers, and eye problems in Irish setters.

In 1966 a group of veterinarians teamed with representatives from the Golden Retriever Club of America and the German Shepherd Club of America to found the Orthopedic Foundation for Animals (OFA). The OFA maintains a database of specific genetic disorders in individual purebred dogs. This information allows conscientious breeders to make informed decisions about which dogs should be mated. The OFA encourages breeders to submit health information for many generations so that trends in inheritance can be deduced. The OFA also issues health ratings for dogs in its database to provide potential consumers with important information. For example, the OFA can certify the condition of hips and elbows in particular dogs. This information can be included with the registration papers that are issued by the AKC. Another certifying organization is the Canine Eye Registration Foundation (CERF). The CERF maintains a database on eye health and can certify that a particular purebred dog's eyes are free of genetic disorders.

Purebred Registries

Neither the AKC nor the UKC guarantees the quality or health of a purebred dog. They simply track ancestry records based on the information they are given by breeders. The AKC and the UKC hold thousands of competitions each year in which registered dogs can compete. Some of these events are called dog shows or conformation shows and are designed to show off dogs that exemplify breed standards. These are basically beauty contests in which the focus is on distinctive features that characterize particular breeds. Other competitions highlight skills in agility, hunting, or obedience.

The AKC and the UKC are recognized as reputable purebred registries in the United States. In addition, some breed clubs maintain well-respected registries—for example, the Australian Shepherd Club of America. However, a number of other registries exist that may operate for dubious purposes. Dog enthusiasts suggest that unscrupulous registries make money by issuing papers indiscriminately for dogs that are not even purebreds or for dogs that are not from recognized breeds. This allows breeders to sell the dogs for high prices to unsuspecting consumers. Many of these unscrupulous registries are believed to have been started by breeders who were kicked out of the AKC or the UKC for rules violations.

Alternative registries often allow crossbreeds to be registered. These are puppies that result from mating two desirable breeds together. Usually, the parents are AKC or UKC registered. However, the puppies cannot be registered by these agencies.

U.S. Department of Agriculture Licenses

All dog breeders meeting certain criteria must be licensed by the Animal and Plant Health Inspection

TABLE 9.3

USDA license fees for dealers, brokers, and operators of auction sales

Over	But not over	Initial license fee	Annual or changed class of license fee
$0	$500	$30	$40
500	2,000	60	70
2,000	10,000	120	130
10,000	25,000	225	235
25,000	50,000	350	360
50,000	100,000	475	485
100,000	—	750	760

SOURCE: "Table 1. Dealers, Brokers, and Operators of an Auction Sale—Class 'A' and 'B' License," in *Code of Federal Regulations, Title 9—Animals and Animal Products*, U.S. Government Printing Office, January 1, 2012, http://www.gpo.gov/fdsys/pkg/CFR-2012-title9-vol1/pdf/CFR-2012-title9-vol1-chapI.pdf (accessed March 25, 2013)

Service (APHIS) of the U.S. Department of Agriculture (USDA). These licenses fall into two types:

• Class A—breeders who sell animals that they have bred and raised on their own premises. People with three or fewer breeding females who sell offspring for pets or exhibition are exempt, as are people who sell animals directly to owners.

• Class B—people who purchase and resell animals, including dealers, brokers, and auction house operators. Retail pet stores selling nondangerous "pet-type" animals are exempt. Class B licensees may also breed the animals they sell.

Annual USDA license fees for Class A and B licenses are listed in Table 9.3.

As noted in Chapter 5, a search of the APHIS database using the ACIS Search Tool (http://acissearch.aphis.usda.gov/LPASearch/faces/Warning.jspx) reveals that as of May 2013, 4,427 breeders and 1,361 dealers had registered with the agency. Only 2,247 breeders and 800 dealers were active as of May 2013. Of these, 1,831 were dog breeders and 283 were dog dealers. The states with the largest numbers of active dog breeders were Missouri (578), Iowa (221), Oklahoma (187), Kansas (156), and Arkansas (127). The vast majority of licensed dog breeders raise puppies for the purebred market. Breeders and brokers sell purebred puppies to pet stores, who in turn sell them to the public. As of May 2013, Missouri had the highest number of active Class B license holders for dog dealers (63).

It should be noted that animal groups believe that thousands of unlicensed breeders also operate in the United States.

Puppy Mills

Puppy mills are facilities that breed puppies in inferior conditions and sell them in commercial markets. The breeding dogs and puppies are not provided adequate veterinary care, food, shelter, and socialization. Animal welfare groups maintain that puppy mills cause suffering of mother dogs and puppies. Female dogs are bred too often and destroyed when they quit producing puppies. The puppies are often transported over long distances in cramped cages and frequently suffer from debilitating conditions and diseases.

In 2008 puppy mills received national attention when the highly popular *Oprah Winfrey Show* (http://www.oprah.com/oprahshow/Investigating-Puppy-Mills) did a feature on them. Lisa Ling, a correspondent for the show, used a hidden camera to film various puppy breeding operations in Pennsylvania. She accompanied Bill Smith, the founder of Main Line Animal Rescue, who often visits the facilities to rescue unwanted males or older females who are going to be killed. Viewers saw breeding dogs and their puppies housed in small wire cages that were stacked on top of each other. Ling and Smith also followed the progress of some of the rescued animals. The show noted that "before they were rescued, many of these dogs spent their entire lives in wire cages and had trouble walking on the ground once they were out. Some had their vocal chords damaged by a pipe in order to keep them from barking. Others were completely filthy, with their coats overgrown and soaked in urine." Smith stated that the dogs were treated "so badly" because they "are considered agricultural products. They're like an ear of corn."

Breeding purebred puppies is big business in the Midwest. It was encouraged by the government following World War II (1939–1945) as a way for rural people to make more income. Many traditional farmers switched from raising pigs to raising puppies when market conditions were favorable. This was particularly true in Missouri.

MISSOURI: "THE PUPPY PIPELINE." As noted earlier, Missouri leads the nation in USDA Class A and B licenses. It is widely agreed that Missouri is the nation's top source for purebred puppies. The state is home to the Hunte Corporation, the world's largest distributor of puppies to pet stores.

In November 2010 Missouri voters narrowly approved the Puppy Mill Cruelty Prevention Act. It would have set specific care and condition standards for large-scale dog breeding operations and limited breeders to 50 breeding dogs. Violations of the law would have been misdemeanors under criminal law. Animal welfarists were thrilled by passage of the new law and then outraged in early March 2011 when the Missouri Senate voted to overturn it. In "Bill to Modify Puppy-Mill Law Goes to Missouri's Governor" (KansasCity.com, April 13, 2011), Jason Noble reports that in April 2011 the Missouri legislature passed a new bill, called the Canine Cruelty Prevention Act, that gutted the Puppy Mill Cruelty Prevention Act. Noble notes that lawmakers believed the original act would put "legitimate" breeders out of business and hurt a "significant industry" in rural Missouri. The new act removed the 50-dog limit and many care and condition restrictions, but increased breeder licensing fees and toughened enforcement standards. Noble reports that animal welfare advocates and some Missouri lawmakers complained that the revised act "undermines the will of the voters." In response to widespread criticism, Jay Nixon (1956–), the governor of Missouri, brokered changes to the new bill to reach a compromise that was acceptable to both sides. The amended Canine Cruelty Prevention Act was signed into law in April 2011. The Missouri Office of Attorney General (MOAG) maintains a listing (http://ago.mo.gov/CanineCruelty/Old%20Law%20vs.%20New%20Law%20SB%20161.pdf) of the major changes between the two laws.

In general, animal welfare groups have been pleased with the new law, mainly because of strict enforcement. The MOAG (http://ago.mo.gov/CanineCruelty/) lists numerous actions that have been brought against breeders since the law was passed, including several breeders who have been shut down permanently.

ANIMAL WELFARE ACT LOOPHOLE. The Animal Welfare Act (AWA) does not cover breeders who sell directly to the public. In "Why You Should Never Buy a Puppy Online" (2013, http://www.aspca.org/fight-animal-cruelty/puppy-mills/puppy-scams-cons.aspx), the American Society for the Prevention of Cruelty to Animals (ASPCA) notes that "the AWA was passed in 1966, prior to the Internet boom, so lawmakers couldn't foresee that commercial breeders would someday have the ability to sell directly to the public via the Internet. This loophole allows many puppy mills to operate without a license and without fear of inspection—meaning they are not accountable to anyone for the way they treat their dogs."

APHIS PERFORMANCE PROBLEMS. Animal groups and other critics have long complained that APHIS does a poor job of enforcing the AWA and penalizing breeders who commit violations. These claims seem to be supported by audits that have been conducted by the USDA's Office of Inspector General (OIG). As of May 2013, the OIG's most recent audit results were published in *Animal and Plant Health Inspection Service Animal Care Program Inspections of Problematic Dealers* (May 2010, http://www.usda.gov/oig/webdocs/33002-4-SF.pdf). The OIG notes that it conducted two similar audits in 1992 and 1995. The first revealed that "APHIS could not ensure the humane care and treatment of animals at all dealer facilities as required by AWA." Following the second audit the OIG concluded that "stronger enforcement actions" are needed for serious or repeat violators because the monetary penalties "were often so low that violators regarded them as a cost of business."

The OIG's 2010 audit findings were also scathing. The agency notes that it conducted the audit due to widespread negative media coverage about commercial dog breeders. The auditors assessed APHIS's Animal Care (AC) enforcement process between fiscal years 2006 and 2008 for dog breeders with a violation history. The latter were defined as licensed dealers who had committed AWA violations within the previous three years. The OIG indicates that the AC inspected 8,289 licensed dealers over the three-year period and found that 5,261 had violated the AWA. A breakdown of the 28,443 violations is provided in Table 9.4.

The OIG finds five "major deficiencies":

- Ineffective enforcement actions—the AC's emphasis on "education and cooperation" rather than on penalizing violators does not achieve dealer compliance. Reinspections that were conducted between fiscal years 2006 and 2008 at the facilities of 4,250 previous violators (out of 5,261 total violators) revealed that 2,416 of them "repeatedly violated" the AWA. More than 860 of the repeat violators continued to violate the same subsections of the law that they had previ-

TABLE 9.4

Violations cited under the Animal Welfare Act at dealer facilities, fiscal years 2006–08

Violation	Count
Housing facilities, general	4,744
Attending veterinarian and adequate veterinary care	3,537
Cleaning, sanitization, housekeeping, and pest control	3,504
Primary enclosures	3,170
Access and inspection of records and property	2,900
Outdoor housing facilities	2,678
Records: dealers and exhibitors	1,601
Time and method of identification	1,260
Sheltered housing facilities	731
Sanitation	651
Indoor housing facilities	576
Feeding	546
Watering	459
Facilities, general	428
Exercise for dogs	254
Facilities, indoor	237
Facilities, outdoor	165
Notification of change of name, address, control	124
Procurement of random source dogs and cats, dealer	82
Environment enhancement to promote psychological selfare	71
Employees	69
Minimum age requirements	69
Requirements and application	68
Compatible grouping	60
Records: operators of auction sales and brokers	55
Handling of animals	52
Others (e.g., health certification, space requirements, care in transit, etc.)	352
Total	**28,443**

SOURCE: "Exhibit C. Violations Cited at Dealer Facilities in FYs 2006–2008," in *Animal and Plant Health Inspection Service Animal Care Program Inspections of Problematic Dealers*, U.S. Department of Agriculture, Office of Inspector General, May 14, 2010, http://www.usda.gov/oig/webdocs/33002-4-SF.pdf (accessed March 25, 2013)

FIGURE 9.1

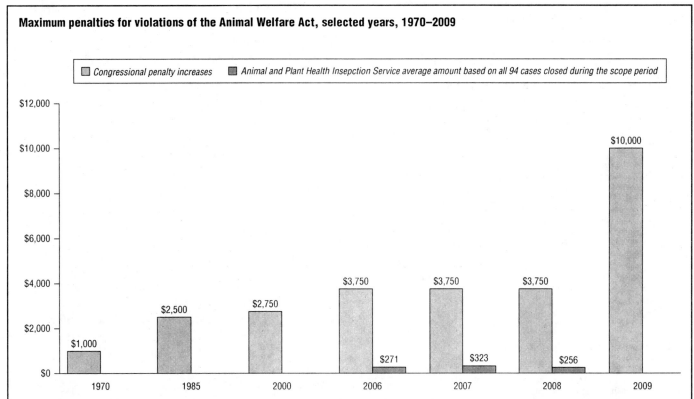

Maximum penalties for violations of the Animal Welfare Act, selected years, 1970–2009

▨ Congressional penalty increases   ▨ Animal and Plant Health Insepction Service average amount based on all 94 cases closed during the scope period

SOURCE: Adapted from "Chart 3. Maximum Penalties Authorized vs. Average Actual Penalties Assessed," in *Animal and Plant Health Inspection Service Animal Care Program Inspections of Problematic Dealers*, U.S. Department of Agriculture, Office of Inspector General, May 14, 2010, http://www.usda .gov/oig/webdocs/33002-4-SF.pdf (accessed March 25, 2013)

ously violated. Some violators also repeatedly "ignored minimum care standards."

• Poor citation and documentation of violations—six of the 19 inspectors "did not correctly report all repeat or direct violations." In addition, some inspectors did not adequately document or photograph evidence of violations. The latter deficiency has been an ongoing problem.

• Minimal penalties that do not deter violators—the OIG notes that since 1970 Congress has steadily increased the monetary penalties that AWA violators face. (See Figure 9.1.) However, the average penalty actually assessed has been extremely low—less than 10% of the maximum allowed. The OIG states that the low penalties do not indicate that the violations cited were "minor or insignificant." In fact, more than half of the violations that occurred between October 2006 and April 2008 were of a "serious" or "grave" nature, meaning that they threatened animal health or directly harmed animals, respectively.

• APHIS inspectors improperly calculate penalties—the AC inspectors "misused" APHIS guidelines in roughly one-third of the cases reviewed. This resulted in low penalties for AWA violations. The OIG states that "AC told us that it assessed lower penalties as an

incentive to encourage violators to pay a stipulated amount rather than exercise their right to a hearing."

• Large-scale breeders selling puppies over the Internet are exempt from the AWA—breeders who sell puppies over the Internet do not have to be inspected by the AC, nor do they have to meet the AC's licensing requirements. The OIG notes that a direct result of this loophole is that "an increasing number of Internet breeders are not monitored for their animals' overall health and humane treatment."

Overall, the OIG complains that the AC took "little or no enforcement actions against" repeat violators, even dealers with serious or grave violations. The OIG report includes horrific photographs of badly wounded and neglected dogs and extremely unsanitary living conditions at some inspected facilities. Four example cases are described in detail to "demonstrate [the AC's] leniency towards violators, the ineffectiveness of its enforcement process, and the harmful effect they had on the animals."

BUYER BEWARE. In response to negative publicity about puppy mills, several states have passed lemon laws to protect consumers who buy puppies at pet stores. Such laws typically enable consumers to be reimbursed by pet stores that sell them puppies that turn out to be in poor

TABLE 9.5

Tips from the Humane Society on picking a responsible dog breeder

- Allows you to visit and willingly shows you all areas where puppies and breeding dogs spend their time. Those areas are clean, spacious, and well-maintained
- Has dogs who appear lively, clean, and healthy, and don't shy away from visitors
- Keeps their breeding dogs as you feel a responsible person would keep their pets: not overpopulated, crowded, dirty, or continually confined to cages
- Keeps their dogs in roomy spaces that meet the needs of their particular breed; for example, most small breeds will be housed in the home, sporting breeds will have plenty of space for exercise, etc. (National breed clubs can provide input on the specific needs of each breed of dog)
- Breeds only one or a few types of dogs and is knowledgeable about the breeds and their special requirements
- Doesn't always have puppies available but may keep a list of interested people for the next available litter or refer people to other responsible breeders or breed clubs
- Meets psychological, as well as physical, needs of their dogs by providing toys, socialization, exercise, and enrichment as befits the specific breed
- Encourages you to spend time with the puppy's parents—at a minimum, the pup's mother—when you visit
- Has a strong relationship with one or more local veterinarians and shows you individual records of veterinary visits for your puppy
- Explains in detail the potential genetic and developmental problems inherent to the breed and provides documentation that the puppy's parents and grandparents have been professionally evaluated in an effort to breed those problems out of their puppies. (This will include testing for genetic diseases for which there are valid testing protocols available)
- Offers guidance for the care and training of your puppy and is available for assistance after you take your puppy home
- Provides references from other families who have previously purchased one of their puppies
- Is often actively involved with local, state, and national clubs that specialize in the specific breed; responsible breeders may also compete with the dogs in conformation events, obedience trials, tracking and agility trials, or other performance events
- Sells puppies only to people he/she has met in person, not to pet stores or to unknown buyers over the Internet
- Encourages multiple visits and wants your entire family to meet the puppy
- Provides you with a written contract and health guarantee and allows plenty of time for you to read it thoroughly
- Doesn't require that you use a specific veterinarian

SOURCE: "A Responsible Breeder," in *How to Find a Responsible Dog Breeder*, Humane Society of the United States, 2012, http://www.humanesociety.org/assets/pdfs/pets/puppy_mills/find_responsible_dog_breeder.pdf (accessed March 25, 2013)

health. The HSUS hopes that such laws will motivate pet stores to pressure breeders to improve the conditions in which puppies are raised. Table 9.5 shows HSUS tips on how consumers can identify a good dog breeder.

Consumers are urged to contact APHIS and ask for copies of federal inspection reports that have been conducted on the breeder and broker of any puppy they purchase. However, backyard breeders, hobby breeders, and commercial breeders selling puppies directly to the public do not have to register with APHIS. Dog enthusiasts encourage consumers to buy only from reputable local breeders and to ask to see the sire and dam of the puppy they are interested in purchasing. A personal visit ensures the consumer that the breeder is operating a clean and well-kept business with healthy, well-adjusted dogs.

ORGANIZATIONS RESPOND. All major animal welfare organizations are opposed to commercial puppy breeding because of the severe pet overpopulation problem. They do not believe that puppies should be commercially bred because millions of unwanted puppies and dogs are euthanized at shelters every year. The HSUS notes in "HSUS Pet Overpopulation Estimates" that approximately 25% of the dogs that wind up in shelters are purebred. Purebred dogs can generally be identified by their coloring, fur, and characteristic appearance.

The AKC does not support random large-scale breeding of dogs for commercial purposes. The organization conducts inspections of breeders who use the AKC registry and of breeders, retail pet shops, and brokers who conduct 25 or more registration transactions per year or breed seven or more litters of puppies per year.

KITTEN MILLS

Although the purebred cat industry in the United States is much smaller than the purebred dog industry, it, too, is troubled by some irresponsible practices by breeders. For example, in January 2012 a woman in Advance, North Carolina, was charged with animal cruelty for operating a kitten mill. According to WGHP News (January 18, 2012, http://daviecounty.myfox8.com/news/news/66631-davie-co-woman-charged-exotic-cat-breeding-operation), the woman was arrested for keeping dozens of cats "in poor conditions and unclean cages." In addition, "many of the cats appeared sickly and dirty." In all, 38 cats were removed from the breeder, who specialized in exotic (wild) and hybrid (i.e., mixtures of wild and domestic breeds) cats.

FERAL CATS

Feral cats are cats that have reverted to a semiwild state because of a lack of human contact and socialization. They avoid humans and often live in large groups called colonies. They may be born into this condition or adjust to it after being a stray, lost, or abandoned for a long time. Feral cats are often confused with strays, but there is a difference. Stray cats generally appear scruffy and unclean because they do not groom themselves. They are accustomed to human care and suffer from stress and hunger without it. Feral cats are adjusted to a wild manner of living. If a natural food source is prevalent, they survive fairly well.

The problem is that they also reproduce well. Many animal welfare groups advocate a trap-neuter-return (TNR) management plan for feral colonies. In these programs feral cats are humanely trapped, vaccinated, sterilized, and returned to their colonies. In most cases volunteers feed the colonies and conduct TNR activities. Kittens and particularly tame adult cats go into adoption programs. In general, it is difficult to turn a truly feral cat into a pet. Where it is possible, it requires a great deal of time and effort. Most welfarists believe their time is better spent sterilizing the cats than trying to tame them.

Alley Cat Allies was founded in 1990 in the District of Columbia to advocate on behalf of feral and stray cats. Many animal control departments try to control feral cat colonies by capturing and euthanizing the cats. According to Alley Cat Allies, in "The Vacuum Effect: Why Catch and Kill Doesn't Work" (2013, http://www.alleycat.org/page.aspx?pid=926), the TNR approach is much more effective and less costly. It prevents the animals from producing kittens, and the adult population gradually decreases.

PET ABUSE AND NEGLECT

Tracking animal abuse cases is difficult because there is no government database of all cases. In 2001 Alison Gianotto began Pet-abuse.com, an online database of abuse cases, after her cat was stolen and set on fire. As of May 2013, the database listed information on 19,265 cases in the United States. Overall, 17,098 of these cases had been categorized as to type of abuse (http://www.pet-abuse.com/pages/cruelty_database/statistics/classifications.php). The largest number of these cases involved neglect or abandonment (32.3%), followed by hoarding (12.4%), shooting (11.3%), fighting (8.7%), and beating (7%). Dogs, cats, and horses are the most common victims noted (http://www.pet-abuse.com/pages/cruelty_database/statistics/animals_by_cruelty_type.php).

Data in the database can be searched by state, date, perpetrator name, type of animal, type of abuse, or sex of perpetrator. Photographs are included for some cases. Each case description includes media and/or law enforcement or court references so that information can be verified. Pet-abuse.com includes data on animal cruelty cases in which there is also documented neglect of a child or elderly person in the household.

Animal Hoarding

Animal hoarding is a form of animal abuse. Animal hoarders collect large numbers of animals and do not provide proper care for them. Most hoarders start out with good intentions by taking in a few strays to care for, but the situation can quickly grow out of control as the animals breed or the person takes in more and more animals. The animals are often kept inside the home and allowed to urinate and defecate there. Hoarders are oblivious to the negative effects of their actions on the animals and even on themselves. They see themselves as animal rescuers. Most will not admit that the severe overcrowding is unsanitary and unhealthy for the animals.

Pet-abuse.com lists 99 hoarding cases for 2012 that involved thousands of animals. In one case alone 700 cats were seized from a cat "sanctuary" in Florida. In another case 71 dogs were found living in a person's home. In all of the cases, investigators reported finding animals in very poor condition due to overcrowding and lack of proper care.

The Hoarding of Animals Research Consortium was founded in 1997 by Gary Patronek to study the hoarding problem and work to increase awareness among mental health and social service workers. The consortium believes that hoarding is a pathological problem. Some psychiatrists suspect that it is a psychological disorder similar to obsessive-compulsive behavior.

In 2001 Illinois became the first state to pass legislation dealing specifically with animal hoarding as a crime separate from animal cruelty or neglect. The Illinois law is considered by some animal activists to be model legislation for other states because it recognizes that hoarding may be a mental health problem and recommends psychiatric treatment for offenders.

The problem of animal hoarding has received much wider attention due to television shows that focus on the issue. One of these shows is *Confessions: Animal Hoarding* (http://animal.discovery.com/tv-shows/confessions-animal-hoarding/), which is broadcast by the Animal Planet television network. Episodes feature in-depth interviews with people who are alleged to be animal hoarders by their families and/or friends. The shows also examine the health and relationship problems that result from hoarding and the denial of these problems that are expressed by the alleged animal hoarders.

EXOTIC PETS

The word *exotic* means "foreign" or "not native," but when the word is used to describe pets, it refers to wild animals that are not normally considered pets. These include bears, lions, primates, tigers, wolves, certain rodents and reptiles, and many other species. Exotic pets appeal to people because they are different and, in some cases, dangerous and threatening to others.

Many people feel they have the right to keep any animal as long as they provide proper care for it. Critics say that exotic animals belong in their natural habitats and not in cages, where they can suffer from abuse, neglect, and boredom. Welfarists believe that even well-treated exotic pets should not be kept in captivity because it violates their wild nature. Law enforcement and animal control officers point out that exotic pets pose a health hazard to people because their temperaments can be unpredictable.

Some people think it is wrong to keep wild animals in captivity, even those born in captivity. Exotic breeders argue that an animal born and raised in a cage does not miss the wild because the animal has never experienced it. Critics do not agree with this argument. They believe captive-born wild animals retain the natural urges and instincts of their species.

Exotic pets are offered for sale in pet stores, on the Internet, at auctions, and in trade publications, such as the *Animal Finder's Guide* (http://www.animalfindersguide.com/). The National Alternative Pet Association (NAPA; http://www.altpet.net/) provides a list of breeders, dealers, and shops that specialize in exotic pets. The association also provides information and Internet links for a variety of clubs and organizations for exotic pet owners. The NAPA complains that people with exotic pets suffer from discrimination and have difficulties finding food, supplies, veterinarians, shelters, and rescue groups for their animals. Zoos are often unwilling to provide needed information and will not take unwanted exotic pets.

Exotic pets are banned or regulated in many states. In "Summary of State Laws Relating to Private Possession of Exotic Animals" (2013, http://www.bornfreeusa.org/b4a2_exotic_animals_summary.php), Born Free USA lists states that completely or partially ban private ownership of bears, big cats, reptiles, wolves, and most nonhuman primates.

The NAPA believes that a few bad incidents involving exotic pets have been blown out of proportion and that exotic pet owners are unfairly blamed for the declining populations of endangered species. The association insists that captive breeding is the only chance for some species. It claims that many public shelters and wildlife rescue groups give preference to zoos and will euthanize exotic animals instead of allowing private individuals to take them.

All major animal rights and welfare groups oppose the keeping of exotic pets, expressing concern about the degradation of natural populations and the care that captive animals receive. Wildlife collectors are blamed for harming sensitive habitats and killing nontarget animals. Animal rights activists and welfarists tend to be opposed to the removal of wild animals from their natural habitats for any purpose. Besides the obvious dangers to the animals, removal can have devastating consequences on the natural habitats of the animals left behind.

Exotic animals kept as pets can suffer from poor nutrition and care at the hands of inexperienced and uninformed owners. The animals may be subjected to painful procedures such as wing clipping, defanging, and declawing. Welfarists believe that only accredited zoos and sanctuaries should care for wild animals that are kept in captivity. This ensures the proper care for the animals and protects the public safety.

Tigers

Various estimates indicate that there are between 5,000 and 10,000 pet tigers in the United States. Wild tigers are an endangered species, and private ownership of them is prohibited by the Endangered Species Act. However, ownership of a captive-born endangered animal is legal in many states.

Accredited zoos have been collecting wild tigers for decades. Many of these tigers were bred in captivity to produce popular zoo babies to bring in crowds. This resulted in an oversupply of adult tigers, many of which wound up in private hands. Pet owners, breeders, circuses, and roadside zoos have interbred different varieties of these animals, resulting in a large population of generic (not purebred) tigers.

Accredited zoos work to preserve endangered tiger species through selective breeding programs. Only purebred tigers with traceable ancestries are used. Generic tigers, or mutts, as they are called, have no value to these programs. Welfarists state that pet tigers are often kept chained or confined in small enclosures and may be beaten into submission.

Nonhuman Primates

The issue of nonhuman primates kept as pets captured national attention in February 2009, when a Connecticut woman was attacked and critically injured by her friend's pet chimpanzee. Stephanie Gallman reports in "Chimp Attack Victim Moved to Cleveland Clinic" (CNN.com, February 19, 2009) that Travis, a 200-pound (91-kilogram) male chimp, was 14 years old. His owner, a 70-year-old woman, reportedly bathed with the chimp and slept in the same bed with him. The chimp had previously been featured in television commercials for various products. Travis was shot and killed by a police officer after the attack. The victim, a 50-year-old woman, suffered severe injuries to her face, including the loss of her eyelids, nose, lips, and sight, and had both hands nearly torn off at the wrists, eventually resulting in the loss of both hands. She received a face transplant in 2011.

The attack spurred calls for tougher laws against the ownership of nonhuman primates as pets. The HSUS and other animal welfare, wildlife, and zoo organizations urged the federal government to pass the Captive Primate Safety Act (CPSA), which would prohibit interstate commerce in primates for the pet trade. However, as of May 2013, neither the CPSA nor similar legislation had been passed at the federal level.

HEALTH AND SAFETY ISSUES
Risks to People from Exotic Pets

The largest health risks to people from pets are zoonoses and animal bites. Zoonoses are diseases that can be passed from animals to humans. Scientists report that there are more than 250 distinct zoonoses that have been documented in medical literature. Zoonoses can occur in domesticated and wild animals. However, zoonoses in livestock, cats, and dogs are well known, heavily researched, and largely controlled through vaccination programs. Diseases that are passed to humans from most other animals, particularly exotic pets, are a different matter. Little is known about them, and they are more difficult to control.

SALMONELLOSIS. Salmonellosis, an infection caused by the bacteria *Salmonella*, can cause abdominal cramps, diarrhea, and fever in patients for several days. Even though it does not generally require hospitalization, it can be quite serious for patients with weak immune systems, children, and the elderly. The infection is caused by eating contaminated food or through direct or indirect contact with amphibians and reptiles, such as frogs, lizards, newts, snakes, and turtles. *Salmonella* occurs naturally in the gastrointestinal tracts of these animals. According to the Centers for Disease Control and Prevention (CDC), in "Diseases from Reptiles" (2013, http://www.cdc.gov/healthypets/animals/reptiles.htm), approximately 70,000 people per year contract salmonellosis from contact with reptiles in the United States.

DOG BITES. Determining the number of dog bites and related injuries that occur in the United States is extremely difficult because there is no nationwide tracking system. In "Dog Bite Prevention" (May 14, 2009, http://www.cdc.gov/HomeandRecreationalSafety/DogBites/biteprevention.html), the CDC indicates that about 4.5 million people experience dog bites each year. Approximately 885,000 of the dog bite victims require medical attention.

Public fears about aggressive dogs have led some jurisdictions around the country to ban particular dog breeds. Some jurisdictions ban breeds outright, whereas others require owners to carry liability insurance or to muzzle their dogs in public. Many animal protection organizations and industry groups, including the AKC and the ASPCA, are opposed to breed-specific legislation. They believe that irresponsible breeders and pet owners should be targeted instead, particularly those who train dogs to be aggressive or refuse to keep their dogs fenced or on leashes. Better enforcement of existing animal control legislation is seen as a more effective measure than breed-specific bans.

IMPORTANT NAMES
AND ADDRESSES

American Anti-Vivisection Society
801 Old York Rd., Ste. 204
Jenkintown, PA 19046-1611
(215) 887-0816
1-800-729-2287
E-mail: aavs@aavs.org
URL: http://www.aavs.org/

American Greyhound Council
PO Box 543
Abilene, KS 67410-0543
(785) 263-4660
E-mail: info@agcouncil.com
URL: http://www.agcouncil.com/

American Humane Association
1400 16th St. NW, Ste. 360
Washington, DC 20036
1-800-227-4645
E-mail: info@americanhumane.org
URL: http://www.americanhumane.org/

American Kennel Club
8051 Arco Corporate Dr., Ste. 100
Raleigh, NC 27617-3390
(919) 233-9767
URL: http://www.akc.org/

American Meat Institute
1150 Connecticut Ave. NW, 12th Floor
Washington, DC 20036
(202) 587-4200
FAX: (202) 587-4300
URL: http://www.meatami.com/

American Pet Products Association
255 Glenville Rd.
Greenwich, CT 06831
(203) 532-0000
1-800-452-1225
FAX: (203) 532-0551
URL: http://www.americanpetproducts.org/

American Rescue Dog Association
PO Box 613
Bristow, VA 20136

E-mail: information@ARDAinc.org
URL: http://www.ardainc.org/

**American Society for the Prevention of
Cruelty to Animals**
424 E. 92nd St.
New York, NY 10128-6804
(212) 876-7700
URL: http://www.aspca.org/

American Veterinary Medical Association
1931 N. Meacham Rd., Ste. 100
Schaumburg, IL 60173-4360
1-800-248-2862
FAX: (847) 925-1329
URL: http://www.avma.org/

Animal Legal Defense Fund
170 E. Cotati Ave.
Cotati, CA 94931
(707) 795-2533
FAX: (707) 795-7280
E-mail: info@aldf.org
URL: http://www.aldf.org/

Animal People
PO Box 960
Clinton, WA 98236
(360) 579-2505
FAX: (360) 579-2575
E-mail: anpeople@whidbey.com
URL: http://www.animalpeoplenews.org/

**Animal and Plant Health Inspection
Service, Animal Care**
U.S. Department of Agriculture
4700 River Rd., Unit 84
Riverdale, MD 20737-1234
(301) 851-3751
FAX: (301) 734-4978
E-mail: ace@aphis.usda.gov
URL: http://www.aphis.usda.gov/

Animal Welfare Institute
900 Pennsylvania Ave. SE
Washington, DC 20003
(202) 337-2332

FAX: (202) 446-2131
E-mail: awi@awionline.org
URL: http://www.awionline.org/

Association of Zoos and Aquariums
8403 Colesville Rd., Ste. 710
Silver Spring, MD 20910-3314
(301) 562-0777
FAX: (301) 562-0888
URL: http://www.aza.org/

Born Free USA
1122 S St.
Sacramento, CA 95811
(916) 447-3085
FAX: (916) 447-3070
E-mail: info@bornfreeusa.org
URL: http://www.bornfreeusa.org/

Bureau of Land Management
1849 C St. NW, Rm. 5665
Washington, DC 20240
(202) 208-3801
FAX: (202) 208-5242
URL: http://www.blm.gov/

**Center for Alternatives to Animal Testing
Bloomberg School of Public Health
Johns Hopkins University**
615 N. Wolfe St., W7032
Baltimore, MD 21205
(410) 614-4990
FAX: (410) 614-2871
E-mail: caat@jhsph.edu
URL: http://caat.jhsph.edu/

**Centers for Disease Control and
Prevention**
1600 Clifton Rd.
Atlanta, GA 30333
1-800-232-4636
E-mail: cdcinfo@cdc.gov
URL: http://www.cdc.gov/

Foundation for Biomedical Research
818 Connecticut Ave. NW, Ste. 900
Washington, DC 20006

(202) 457-0654
FAX: (202) 457-0659
E-mail: info@fbresearch.org
URL: http://www.fbresearch.org/

Fund for Animals
200 W. 57th St.
New York, NY 10019
(202) 452-1100
E-mail: info@fundforanimals.org
URL: http://www.fundforanimals.org/

Greyhound Protection League
PO Box 669
Penn Valley, CA 95946
1-800-446-8637
URL: http://www.greyhounds.org/

Guide Dog Users Inc.
4851 N. Cedar Ave., Apt. 119
Fresno, CA 93726
1-866-799-8436
E-mail: president@gdui.org
URL: http://www.gdui.org/

Humane Society of the United States
2100 L St. NW
Washington, DC 20037
(202) 452-1100
URL: http://www.hsus.org/

In Defense of Animals
3010 Kerner Blvd.
San Rafael, CA 94901
(415) 448-0048
FAX: (415) 454-1031
E-mail: idainfo@idausa.org
URL: http://www.idausa.org/

Jockey Club
40 E. 52nd St.
New York, NY 10022
(212) 371-5970
FAX: (212) 371-6123
URL: http://www.jockeyclub.com/

Michigan Society for Medical Research
PO Box 3237
Ann Arbor, MI 48106-3237
(734) 763-8029
FAX: (734) 930-1568
E-mail: mismr@umich.edu
URL: http://www.mismr.org/

National Agricultural Statistics Service
U.S. Department of Agriculture
1400 Independence Ave. SW
Washington, DC 20250
1-800-727-9540
E-mail: nass@nass.usda.gov
URL: http://www.nass.usda.gov/

National Animal Interest Alliance
PO Box 66579
Portland, OR 97290-6579

(503) 761-8962
URL: http://www.naiaonline.org/

National Association for Biomedical Research
818 Connecticut Ave. NW, Ste. 900
Washington, DC 20006
(202) 857-0540
FAX: (202) 659-1902
URL: http://www.nabr.org/

National Greyhound Association
PO Box 543
Abilene, KS 67410
(785) 263-4660
E-mail: nga@ngagreyhounds.com
URL: http://www.ngagreyhounds.com/

National Institute for Animal Agriculture
13570 Meadowgrass Dr., Ste. 201
Colorado Springs, CO 80921
(719) 538-8843
FAX: (719) 538-8847
E-mail: NIAA@animalagriculture.org
URL: http://www.animalagriculture.org/

National Institutes of Health
9000 Rockville Pike
Bethesda, MD 20892
(301) 496-4000
E-mail: NIHinfo@od.nih.gov
URL: http://www.nih.gov/

National Trappers Association
2815 Washington Ave.
Bedford, IN 47421
(812) 277-9670
1-866-680-8727
FAX: (812) 277-9672
E-mail: ntaheadquarters@nationaltrappers
.com
URL: http://www.nationaltrappers.com/

National Wildlife Federation
11100 Wildlife Center Dr.
Reston, VA 20190
1-800-822-9919
URL: http://www.nwf.org/

New England Anti-Vivisection Society
333 Washington St., Ste. 850
Boston, MA 02108-5100
(617) 523-6020
FAX: (617) 523-7925
E-mail: info@neavs.org
URL: http://www.neavs.org/

People for the Ethical Treatment of Animals
501 Front St.
Norfolk, VA 23510
(757) 622-7382
FAX: (757) 622-0457
URL: http://www.peta.org/

Performing Animal Welfare Society
PO Box 849
Galt, CA 95632
(209) 745-2606
FAX: (209) 745-1809
E-mail: info@pawsweb.org
URL: http://www.pawsweb.org/

Pet-abuse.com
PO Box 5
Southfields, NY 10975
E-mail: info@pet-abuse.com
URL: http://www.pet-abuse.com/

Professional Rodeo Cowboys Association
101 ProRodeo Dr.
Colorado Springs, CO 80919
(719) 593-8840
URL: http://www.prorodeo.com/

Sled Dog Action Coalition
PO Box 562061
Miami, FL 33256
E-mail: SledDogAC@aol.com
URL: http://www.helpsleddogs.org/

Spay/USA
2261 Broadridge Ave.
Stratford, CT 06614
1-800-248-7729
FAX: (516) 883-9641
E-mail: SpayUSA@AnimalLeague.org
URL: http://www.spayusa.org/

United Kennel Club
100 E. Kilgore Rd.
Kalamazoo, MI 49002-5584
(269) 343-9020
FAX: (269) 343-7037
URL: http://www.ukcdogs.com/

United Poultry Concerns
PO Box 150
Machipongo, VA 23405
(757) 678-7875
FAX: (757) 678-5070
E-mail: info@upc-online.org
URL: http://www.upc-online.org/

U.S. Fish and Wildlife Service
U.S. Department of Interior
1849 C St. NW
Washington, DC 20240
1-800-344-WILD
URL: http://www.fws.gov/

U.S. Sportsmen's Alliance
801 Kingsmill Pkwy.
Columbus, OH 43229
(614) 888-4868
FAX: (614) 888-0326
E-mail: info@ussportsmen.org
URL: http://www.ussportsmen.org/

RESOURCES

Several resources useful to this book were published by agencies of the U.S. Department of Agriculture, including the Animal and Plant Health Inspection Service, the Economic Research Service, the National Agricultural Statistics Service, and the Office of Inspector General. Other federal agencies providing information were the Bureau of Land Management, the Centers for Disease Control and Prevention, the National Institutes of Health, the National Marine Fisheries Service, the National Park Service, the U.S. Customs and Border Protection, the U.S. Fish and Wildlife Service, the U.S. Food and Drug Administration, the U.S. Forest Service, the Congressional Research Service, and the U.S. Government Accountability Office, the investigative arm of Congress.

State agencies and educational institutions providing information included the California Horse Racing Board and the Office of the Missouri Attorney General. The Center for Wildlife Law at the University of New Mexico School of Law and the Animal Legal and Historical Center at the Michigan State University were invaluable resources for legal documents.

Information on animal industries and businesses was obtained from associations including the American Greyhound Council, the American Kennel Club, the American Meat Institute, the American Pet Products Association, the American Veal Association, the Association of Zoos and Aquariums, the International Whaling Commission, the Jockey Club, the National Renderers Association, the United Egg Producers, and the U.S. Fur Commission.

The website of the Ringling Brothers and Barnum and Bailey Circus (http://www.ringling.com/) was informative. Temple Grandin's website (http://www.grandin.com/) was particularly useful as a resource on animal husbandry and slaughtering in the modern agriculture industry.

Organizations involved in animal issues that provided helpful statistics and information include the American Veterinary Medical Association, the Foundation for Biomedical Research, the Michigan Society for Medical Research, the National Alternative Pet Association, the National Association for Search and Rescue, the Physicians Committee for Responsible Medicine, the U.S. Sportsmen's Alliance, and the U.S. War Dog Association. The following resources describe a variety of issues that also affect animals: *Ecologist* magazine, Monterey Bay Aquarium, Sierra Club, *Society and Animals: Journal of Human-Animal Studies*, the Union of Concerned Scientists, and *Vegetarian Journal*.

A wealth of information was obtained from groups that are devoted to the causes of animal protection, welfare, and rights. These include Alley Cat Allies, the American Humane Association, the Animal Legal Defense Fund, Animal People, the Animal Welfare Institute, the Best Friends Animal Sanctuary, Born Free USA, Defenders of Wildlife, the Elephant Sanctuary, Fund for Animals, the Greyhound Protection League, the Humane Society of the United States, In Defense of Animals, Last Chance for Animals, Maddie's Fund, the National Anti-Vivisection Society, the New England Anti-Vivisection Society, People for the Ethical Treatment of Animals, Pet-abuse.com, the Sled Dog Action Coalition, and United Poultry Concerns.

Animal rights activists and opponents and scientists studying human-animal interaction have written some important books that were valuable resources for this work. They include *Beast and Man: The Roots of Human Nature* (1978) and *Animals and Why They Matter* (1983) by Mary Midgley; *Animal Liberation: A New Ethics for Our Treatment of Animals* (1975) by Peter Singer; *Animals, Property, and the Law* (1995) by Gary L. Francione; *Putting Humans First: Why We Are Nature's Favorite* (2004) by Tibor R. Machan; *The Animal Rights Debate* (2001) by Carl Cohen and Tom Regan; *The Case for Animal Rights* (1983) by Tom Regan; *Interests and Rights: The Case against Animals* (1980) and *Rights, Killing, and Suffering: Moral*

Vegetarianism and Applied Ethics (1983) by Raymond G. Frey; *The Animals Issue: Moral Theory in Practice* (1992) by Peter Carruthers; *Speciesism* (2004) by Joan Dunayer; *The Animal Rights Crusade: The Growth of a Moral Protest* (1992) by James M. Jasper and Dorothy Nelkin; *Making a Killing: The Political Economy of Animal Rights* (2007) by Bob Torres; and *Some We Love, Some We Hate, Some We Eat* (2010) by Hal Herzog.

Various news organizations and outlets were useful for providing timely stories related to animals, particularly ABC News, BBC News, *Los Angeles Times*, *National Geographic*, *Nature*, *New York Times*, *Scientific American*, and *Sports Illustrated*. The *Frontline* documentary *A Whale of a Business* (November 1997) was very helpful. The Gallup Organization supplied polling results on animal issues.

INDEX

AMI. *See* American Meat Institute

AML. *See* Appropriate management level

Amos, Jonathan, 144

"Analysis of Races by State or Province—2012" (Jockey Club), 106

The Anatomie of Abuses (Stubbes), 6

Anderson, Pamela, 82

Angling
  number of anglers, 48(*f*3.12)
  statistics on, 47–48
  wildlife-related recreation statistics, 44*t*

Anheuser-Busch, 128

Aniline dyes, 85

Animal abuse
  animal welfare law in England, 7
  link to violence against people, 15
  pet abuse, 149

"Animal Activists Attacking Scientists' Homes" (Associated Press), 88

Animal Agriculture Alliance (AAA), 76, 78

Animal and Plant Health Inspection Service (APHIS)
  AWA enforcement, problems with, 146–147
  AWA regulations enforced by, 88–91
  budget for fiscal year 2013, 14(*t*1.9)
  Class B dealers licensed by, 97
  on collisions with wild animals, 35
  contact information, 153
  entertainment animals, regulation of, 122–123
  HIO list maintained by Horse Protection Program, 113(*t*6.4)
  history of, 9–10
  on Horse Protection Act, 109–110
  on horses in U.S., 74
  licenses for dog breeders, 144–145
  major milestones in history of, 12–15
  milestones in history of, 1960s/1970s, 10*t*
  milestones in history of, 1980s, 12*t*
  milestones in history of, 1990s, 13(*t*1.6)
  milestones in history of, first decade of 21st century, 13(*t*1.7)
  milestones in history of, second decade of 21st century, 14(*t*1.8)
  pain/distress of research animals, 99
  on wildlife damage management, 35
  Wildlife Services division, 13
  zoos and, 124–125

Animal and Plant Health Inspection Service Administration of the Horse Protection Program and the Slaughter Horse Transport Program (Office of Inspector General), 110

Animal and Plant Health Inspection Service Animal Care Program Inspections of Problematic Dealers (Office of Inspector General), 146–147

Animal Care Information System (ACIS) Search Tool
  ARRFs available through, 91

for AWA-regulated animals data, 92

dog breeders/dealers in, 145

information on animal exhibitors, 123

for research animal breeders/dealers, 96

Animal cruelty, 6–7
  See also Animal abuse

Animal Crush Video Prohibition Act, 15

Animal Damage Control Act
  APHIS Wildlife Services work under, 13
  requirements of, 10

"Animal Damage Control Act" (USFWS), 10

Animal Damage Control Program, 12

Animal domestication, 1–2

Animal Enterprise Protection Act (AEPA), 86–87

Animal Enterprise Terrorism Act (AETA), 87

Animal exhibitors
  animal exhibitions licensed as Class C under AWA, 122(*t*7.3)
  animal exhibitors, as defined by AWA, 122(*t*7.1)
  animal exhibitors exempted from federal regulation under AWA, 122(*t*7.4)
  legislation/regulation of, 122–123
  license fees for exhibitors needing Class "C" licenses, 122(*t*7.2)

"Animal Exhibitors" (APHIS), 123

Animal feeding operation (AFO)
  for cattle, 59, 61–63
  cattle at feedlot 60*f*(4.4)
  for chickens, 66
  description of, 58
  hog operations, 71–74

"Animal Feeding Operations" (EPA), 58

Animal fighting
  blood sports, history of, 6
  cockfighting, 116
  dogfighting, 116–119
  dogfighting laws, state, ranked by HSUS as to seriousness of penalty, 117*t*–119*t*
  driven by illegal gambling, 105
  federal legislation against, 119
  in Roman Empire, 4

Animal Fighting Prohibition Enforcement Act, 119

Animal hoarding, 149

Animal Law Coalition, 141

Animal Legal and Historical Center
  on early U.S. animal cruelty law, 7
  on spay/neuter laws, 142

Animal Legal Defense Fund (ALDF)
  contact information, 153
  OncoMouse patent, challenge of, 23–24
  work of, 22

Animal Liberation: A New Ethics for Our Treatment of Animals (Singer)
  arguments of, 11
  on ritual slaughter, 65
  on speciesism, 22
  on U.S. factory farms, 55

on use of animals in scientific research, 86

utilitarian logic in, 25

Animal Liberation Front (ALF)
  aim of, 28–29
  methods of, 23
  rise of, 86–87
  work of, 12

Animal Machines: The New Factory Farming Industry (Harrison), 55

Animal People
  contact information, 153
  on euthanasia of animals in shelters, 140–141

Animal People (Animal People), 140–141

Animal Planet (television network), 126, 149

Animal Precinct (television show), 126

Animal products
  human health issues related to, 81–82
  overview of, 57

Animal protection groups
  agriculture industry problems, exposing, 76, 78–79
  hunting, opposition to, 45–46
  missions of, 8

Animal Protection Institute, 125–126

Animal Protection Litigation Section, HSUS, 15

Animal rights
  Animal Welfare Act/amendments, 9*t*
  attitudes toward animals, changing, 7–8
  federal animal-related legislation enacted, 8*t*
  as an issue, 11–12
  state animal anticruelty laws, 16*t*–20*t*
  vegans/vegetarians and, 79–80

Animal rights activists
  Animal Liberation Front, 28–29, 86–87
  animal welfarists and, 28
  antivivisection movement, 84–88
  beliefs of, 22
  circuses, criticism of, 123
  entertainment animals, beliefs about, 121
  exotic pets and, 150
  factory farming and, 58
  farm animals, beliefs about, 53
  fur farming and, 82
  in history of animal rights debate, 22–24
  Huntingdon Life Sciences, campaign against, 87–88
  livestock protection laws and, 57
  on military service animals, 137
  pets, beliefs about, 139–140
  research animals and, 83
  service animals and, 131
  sports animals and, 105, 106
  veal controversy and, 62
  wild animals, beliefs about, 32

ritual slaughter and, 64, 65

Humane Scorecard: The 111th Congress in Review (HSLF), 15

Humane Society International (HSI), 49

Humane Society Legislative Fund (HSLF), 15

Humane Society of the United States (HSUS)

  agenda of, 24

  on animal movement, 12

  on animals in shelters, 140

  on canned hunts, 47

  Certified Humane Raised and Handled Program, 81

  contact information, 154

  dog breeder, tips on picking, 148*t*

  dogfighting and, 117, 119

  dogfighting laws, state, ranked by HSUS as to seriousness of penalty, 117*t*–119*t*

  founding of, 8

  initiative petitions by, 15

  on laying hens, 68–69

  on livestock welfare changes, 58

  Pain and Distress Campaign, 99

  political clout of, 15

  poultry slaughter methods lawsuit, 55

  on research animals for dissection, 95

  on seal trade, 49

  United Egg Producers and, 78

  on use of pound/shelter animals in research, 97

  video of Tennessee Walking Horse trainer, 110

  on welfare of racing greyhounds, 114

"The Humane Society of the United States Applauds the Minnesota Legislature and Governor Dayton for Protecting Pets" (HSUS), 97

Humanitarian mine detection, 135

Humans

  evolution of, 1

  health/safety issues of pets, 150–151

  human-wildlife interaction, animal rights debate and, 32

  interests of humans vs. endangered species, 42–43

  link between animal abuse/violence against people, 15

  pets, reasons for, 139

  protection of human resources from wildlife, 35–37

  rights view and, 26

  utilitarianism and, 25

  welfarism and, 24

  wild animals and, 31

  wildlife control, protection of health/safety, 34–35

Hume, David, 6

Humpback whale, *32f*

Humphrey, Hubert, 8

Hunter-gatherers, 1

Hunting

  conservation movement and, 33

  of deer, 32

  dolphin hunting, 50

  federal laws for conservation of wild animals, 10

  hunters, number of, 44(*f3.5*)

  hunters, number of, total and by animal type, 45(*f3.8*)

  hunters/hunting days, number of, by animal, 45*t*

  hunting days, number of, 45(*f3.6*)

  hunting expenditures, 45(*f3.7*)

  Lacey Act, 8, 33

  on National Wildlife Refuges, 46

  opposition to, 45–46

  public opinion on ban of, 29

  of seals, 49

  service animals for, 131–132, *132f*

  statistics on, 43–44

  trophy hunting/canned hunts, 47

  valuable wildlife, categories of, 31

  as wildlife control/conservation method, 46

  in wildlife management history, 33

  wildlife-related recreation statistics, 44*t*

"Hunting—'The Murderous Business'" (In Defense of Animals), 45–46

Huntingdon Life Sciences (HLS) facility (NJ), 87–88

Hurricane Katrina, 139

I

IACUC (institutional animal care and use committee), 89–90

ICCVAM. *See* Interagency Coordinating Committee on the Validation of Alternative Methods

Iceland, whaling and, 50

IDA. *See* In Defense of Animals

Iditarod Trail Sled Dog Race, 115–116

IEDs (improvised explosive devices), 138

IFCS (International Federation of Cynological Sports), 114

IIHS (Insurance Institute for Highway Safety), 35

Illinois

  animal exhibitors in, 123

  animal hoarding law in, 149

Improved Standards for Laboratory Animals Act, 12

"Improving ESA Implementation" (USFWS), 41

Improvised explosive devices (IEDs), 138

In Defense of Animals (IDA)

  contact information, 154

  elephants in circuses/zoos and, 125

  opposition to hunting, 45–46

"In U.S., 5% Consider Themselves Vegetarians" (Newport), 80

"Info Sheet: Sow and Gilt Management in Swine 2000 and Swine 2006" (USDA), 73

Initiative petitions, 15

"Injured SeaWorld Killer Whale Healing, Performing" (Grieco), 129

In-ocean farms, 79

"Inspection for Food Safety: The Basics" (USDA's Food Safety and Inspection Service), 53

Institute of Behavioral Research, Silver Spring (MD), 86

Institutional animal care and use committee (IACUC), 89–90

Insurance Institute for Highway Safety (IIHS), 35

Interagency Coordinating Committee on the Validation of Alternative Methods (ICCVAM)

  alternative test method acceptance process used by, 101*f*

  alternative test method evaluation process used by, 100*f*

  alternative test methods/approaches evaluated by, 99*t*

  major duties of, 98(*t5.9*)

  member agencies of, 98(*t5.8*)

  search for alternatives to animals tests, 98–99

Interests and Rights: The Case against Animals (Frey), 22, 25

Interlandi, Jeneen, 143

International Dairy Foods Association, 62

International efforts, for protection of endangered animals, 43

International Federation of Cynological Sports (IFCS), 114

International Species Information System, 124

International Whaling Commission (IWC), 50

Internet, sale of puppies over, 146, 147

An Introduction to the Principles of Morals and Legislation (Bentham), 7, 25, 83

"Investigation Continues into Florida Greyhound Deaths" (Associated Press), 115

Investigations. *See* Undercover investigations

Iowa

  "ag gag" law, 78

  targeting of research facility in, 88

Irby, Marty, 110

Islam, 4

"Isolated Chicken Eye (ICE) Test Method" (Allen), 98

Isolated chicken eye test, 98–99

"It's Complicated: The Lives of Dolphins & Scientists" (Vance), 27, 129–130

Ivory, 49–50

IWC (International Whaling Commission), 50

NICEATM/ICCVAM, major duties of, 98(*t5.9*)

number of, 92

overview of, 83

for product testing, 94–95

public opinion on morality of cloning animals, 103*t*

public opinion on morality of medical testing on animals, 84*t*

reduction, refinement, replacement principles, 98–99

sources of, 95–97

for surgical/medical training, behavior research, 95

Research facilities

animal rights activists and, 23, 86–88

animals at USDA-registered research facilities, by use category, fiscal year 2008, 101*t*

animals at USDA-registered research facilities, by use category, fiscal year 2009, 102(*t5.12*)

animals at USDA-registered research facilities, by use category, fiscal year 2010, 102(*t5.13*)

"Annual Report of Research Facility," number of facilities submitting an, 90(*t5.3*)

"Annual Report of Research Facility," number of facilities submitting an, by state, 90(*t5.4*)

AWA regulations/oversight, 88–91

Health Research Extension Act, 91

Resnick, Joseph, 85

Resources

protection of human resources from wildlife, 35–37

resources impacted by wildlife damage, 35*f*

See also Natural resources

"Results of the Iditarod Trail Committee's Investigation into the Death of Dorado and Potential Mitigation Measures" (Iditarod), 115

"Rethinking Horse Slaughterhouses" (Simon), 76

Revised Recovery Plan for the Northern Spotted Owl (Strix occidentalis caurina) (USFWS), 43

Revlon, 86

Rhodes, Robert L., 114–115

Riddles, Libby, 115

Rider, Tom, 125–126

Right, definition of, 21

Rights, 21–22

See also Animal rights debate

Rights, Killing, and Suffering: Moral Vegetarianism and Applied Ethics (Frey), 23

Rights view

philosophy of, 26

practical implications of, 27–29

Rin Tin Tin (dog), 126

"Ringed Seal (*Phoca hispida*)" (NOAA), 41–42

Ringed seals, 41–42

Ringling Brothers and Barnum and Bailey Circus, 125–126

Ritual slaughter, 64–65

"Robots Replace Costly U.S. Navy Mine-Clearance Dolphins" (Weinberger), 138

Rodeo and Cowboy Association, 109

Rodeos, 105, 109

Roman Empire, 4–5

Roosters, 116

Rosamond Gifford Zoo, Syracuse (NY), 124

Roslin Institute, Edinburgh, Scotland, 101

Royal Society for the Prevention of Cruelty to Animals (RSPCA), 7

Russell, William M. S., 98

Ryder, Richard D., 11, 22

S

Sacramento (CA) Bee (newspaper), 36–37

Safari Club International, 46

Safety, wildlife control for protection of, 34–35

SAG (Screen Actors Guild), 127

Salmon, genetically modified, 79

Salmonellosis, 151

Salt, Henry S., 84

San Diego Zoo's Wild Animal Park (CA), 121

SAR (search and rescue), 134

Satchell, Michael, 124

Save Japan Dolphins project, 50

"Scene Shifts in Fight against British Testing Lab" (Cowell), 87

Schwarzenegger, Arnold, 71

Scientific research

Animal Welfare Act and, 8–9

implications of rights view, 27

use of animals in, 8, 23

wild animals used in, 32

See also Research animals

Scotland, 132

Screen Actors Guild (SAG), 127

SDAC (Sled Dog Action Coalition), 115–116, 154

Sea lions, 138

Seals

notable listed species under ESA, 41–42

as wildlife commodity, 49

Search, rescue, and recovery, 134

Search and rescue (SAR), 134

SeaWorld marine parks

opening of first marine park, 121

Orlando, 129

San Diego, 128

use of marine mammals, 11

"SeaWorld Whale Killing Trainer Opens Debate: 'Happy Animals Don't Kill Their Trainers'" (Morgan), 129

Seeing Eye, 135

Seizure alert dogs, 135–136

Sentient property, 28

"Sentient Property: Unleashing Legal Respect for Our Companion Animals" (Matlack), 28

Seok, Junhee, 99

September 11, 2001, terrorist attacks, 134

Service animals

for guard duty, 132–133

history of, 131

humanitarian mine detection, 135

for hunting, 131–132, *132f*

for law enforcement, 133–134

for manual labor, 133, *133f*

for medical service, 135–137, *136f*

for military service, 137–138

overview of, 131

for search, rescue, and recovery, 134

SHAC (Stop Huntingdon Animal Cruelty), 87

SHAC USA, 87

Shamu (orca), 128

Shark Conservation Act, 15

Sharks, 15

Sheep/lambs

domestication of, 2

inventory, 74*f*

inventory, value of, 75*t*

operations, 75*f*

overview of, 74

sheep/lambs shorn, 76*f*

slaughter of, 53

Shelters

dogs/cats killed in shelters, estimated number of, by region, 140*t*–141*t*

euthanasia of animals at, 140–141

no-kill shelters, 142–143

as source of research animals, 96–97

spaying/neutering of animals at, 142

"Shocking Video Exposes Cat Intubation Cruelty" (PETA), 88

Shoss, Brenda, 97

SI.com, 119

Silver Spring Monkey Case, 86

Simon, Stephanie, 76

Singer, Peter

argument of, 11

Great Ape Project, founding of, 26

on ritual slaughter, 65

on speciesism, 22

on U.S. factory farms, 55

on use of animals in scientific research, 86

utilitarian logic of, 25

Skin and eye irritancy tests, 94

Slaughter

at animal feeding operations, 58

animal welfarists and, 24

of beef cattle, 59

milk cow operations/percentage of inventory/production, 62*t*

milk production per cow, 61*f*

poultry commodities, value of production of, 65*f*

public opinion on morality of buying/ wearing clothing made of animal fur, 82*t*

public opinion on morality of cloning animals, 103*t*

public opinion on morality of medical testing on animals, 84*t*

public opinion on morality of various issues, 29*t*

public opinion on morality of various issues, by political affiliation, 30*t*

racehorse fatalities in California, 108*t*

red meat/lard production/consumption, by meat type, 56*t*

resource damage or threats by wildlife, top-20 species involved in occurrences of, 36(*t*3.3)

sheep/lamb inventory, 74*f*

sheep/lamb inventory, value of, 75*t*

sheep/lamb operations, 75*f*

sheep/lambs shorn, 76*f*

slaughter statistics, 54*t*

sows farrowed, 73*f*

turkey supply/distribution/ consumption, 70*t*

turkeys produced, number of, 70*f*

vegetarians, percentage of Americans considering themselves, 80(*t*4.10)

vegetarians, percentage of Americans considering themselves, by demographic group, 80(*t*4.11)

violations cited under AWA at dealer facilities, 146*t*

wild horse/burro herd populations and AML, by state, 37(*t*3.8)

wild horses/burros, adoptions/animals removed, 38*t*

Wildlife and Sport Fish Restoration Program excise taxes, disposition of, 44(*f*3.4)

wildlife damage, resources impacted by, 35*f*

Wildlife Services, top-20 species dispersed by, 36(*t*3.5)

Wildlife Services, top-20 species euthanized or killed by, 37(*t*3.6)

Wildlife Services, top-20 species freed or relocated by, 37(*t*3.7)

Wildlife Services control, fate of wildlife under, 36(*t*3.4)

Wildlife Services funding, by funding source/resource, 34*t*

wildlife watchers, number of, 46*f*

wildlife-related recreation statistics, 44*t*

wildlife-watching days, away-from-home, number of, 47(*f*3.10)

wildlife-watching expenditures, 47(*f*3.11)

"Statutes/Laws" (Animal Legal and Historical Center), 7

Sterilization, 141–142

Steroids, 108, 116

Stone Age, 1

Stop Huntingdon Animal Cruelty (SHAC), 87

Strom, Stephanie, 75–76

Stubbes, Philip, 6

"Study Shows 5,000 Racehorse Deaths since '03" (Associated Press), 107

Stunning
in cattle slaughter, 63
hog slaughter via, 74
in slaughterhouse audit, 64

Suffering, 24, 25

Sulzberger, A. G., 115

"Summary of State Laws Relating to Private Possession of Exotic Animals" (Born Free USA), 150

Sumner, Daniel A., 69

Surgical/medical training, research animals for, 95

"Survey of Stunning and Handling in Federally Inspected Beef, Veal, Pork, and Sheep Slaughter Plants" (Grandin), 64

Swine. *See* Hogs/pigs

Swine 2006 (USDA), 73

Symmetrical reciprocity, 26

T

Table Egg Production and Hen Welfare: Agreement and Legislative Proposals (Greene & Cowan), 69

Taiji, Japan, 27, 50, 129–130

"Taiji Slaughter Season Ends in Blood" (O'Barry), 50

Tail docking, 57, 58, 73

Taming, 2, 31

Taoism, 3

"Taping of Farm Cruelty Is Becoming the Crime" (Oppel), 78

Taub, Edward, 86

Taxes
hunting fees, support of government conservation programs, 46
on hunting/fishing, 43–44
for Sport Fish Restoration Program, 47–48
Wildlife and Sport Fish Restoration Program excise taxes, disposition of, 44(*f*3.4)

Ted's Montana Grills (restaurant chain), 79

Teeth clipping, 73

Television, animals in, 121, 126–127

"Tennessee Walking Horse Trainer Jackie McConnell Gets Probation, $75,000 Fine" (Allyn), 110

Tennessee Walking Horses, 109–110

Testing
alternatives to animal tests, search for, 98–99

of cosmetic products, 91
research animals for drug testing, 93–94
research animals for product testing, 94–95
See also Research animals

"Testing Methods Using OncoMouse Transgenic Models of Cancer" (DuPont), 100

Texas, animal exhibitors in, 123

Thalidomide, 85

"That the Souls of Dumb Animals Are Not Immortal" (Saint Thomas Aquinas), 5

Therapy animals, 136–137

Thomas Aquinas, Saint, 5

Thoroughbred racing
racehorse fatalities in California, 108*t*
races, 106
retired racing horse adoption, 109
welfare of racing horses, 106–109

Thoroughbred Retirement Foundation, 109

Threatened species
definition of, 11, 39
endangered/threatened mammal species of U.S., list of, 40*t*
endangered/threatened species, count of, 39*t*
endangered/threatened species, number of U.S., with critical habitat specified, 41*t*
interests of humans vs., 42–43
notable listed species under ESA, 41–42
polar bears, 41

"Three Wrong Leads in a Search for an Environmental Ethic: Tom Regan on Animal Rights, Inherent Values, and 'Deep Ecology'" (Partridge), 23

Tigers
as commodity, 49
as pets, 150
in unaccredited zoos, 125

Tilikum (orca), 129

Timber wolf, 42*f*

"Timeline of Major Farm Animal Protection Advancements" (HSUS), 58, 73

Tischler, Joyce, 22

TNR (trap-neuter-return) management plan, 148–149

Toe clipping, 66

Torres, Bob, 24

Toxic Substances Control Act, 92

Toxins, in cosmetics, 85

Trade
government monitoring of wildlife trade, 34
sales of wild horses/burros, 37–38
sources of research animals, 95–97
trade prohibitions for listed species under CITES, 43
wild animal commodities, 48–50